FIFTY KEY THINKERS IN INTERNATIONAL RELATIONS

Here in one handy volume is a unique and comprehensive overview of the key thinkers in international relations in the twentieth century. From influential statesmen such as Lenin and Kissinger, to emerging thinkers of hitherto marginalised areas of concern, including feminism, historical sociology and the study of nationalism, the book describes the main elements of each thinker's contribution to the study of international relations. Information, where appropriate, is supplied on the individual thinker's life and career, and signposts to further reading and critical analysis are also provided.

Martin Griffiths is a senior lecturer in the School of Political and International Studies at the Flinders University of South Australia. Previous works include *Realism, Idealism and International Politics* (Routledge, 1992).

FIFTY KEY THINKERS IN INTERNATIONAL RELATIONS

Martin Griffiths

Routledge
Taylor & Francis Group

LONDON AND NEW YORK

First published 1999 by Routledge
2 Park Square, Milton Park, Abingdon, Oxon, OX14 4RN

Simultaneously published in the USA and Canada
by Routledge
270 Madison Ave, New York, NY 10016

Reprinted 2003, 2004, 2005, 2006

Routledge is an imprint of the Taylor & Francis Group

© 1999 Martin Griffiths

Typeset in Times by The Florence Group, Stoodleigh, Devon
Printed and bound in Great Britain by TJ International Ltd, Padstow, Cornwall

British Library Cataloguing in Publication Data
A catalogue record for this book is available from the British Library

Library of Congress Cataloguing in Publication Data
has been applied for

ISBN 0-415-16227-0 (hbk)
ISBN 0-415-16228-9 (pbk)

To the memory of my parents

Richard Tudor (1924–1993)
Lilian Doreen (1926–1996)

CONTENTS

PREFACE   ix

ACKNOWLEDGEMENTS   xi

REALISM   1
Raymond Aron   3
Edward Hallett Carr   7
Robert Gilpin   11
John Herz   16
George Kennan   21
Henry Kissinger   25
Stephen Krasner   31
Hans Morgenthau   36
Susan Strange   41
Kenneth Waltz   46

LIBERALISM   51
Norman Angell   53
Charles Beitz   58
Michael Doyle   63
Francis Fukuyama   68
David Held   75
John Hobson   80
Stanley Hoffmann   85
Richard Rosecrance   89
Woodrow Wilson   95
Alfred Zimmern   100

RADICAL/CRITICAL THEORY   107
John Burton   109
Robert Cox   113
Richard A. Falk   119
André Gunder Frank   124
Johan Galtung   129
Vladimir I. Lenin   134
Andrew Linklater   138

CONTENTS

THEORY OF INTERNATIONAL SOCIETY 145
Hedley Bull 147
Terry Nardin 151
John Vincent 156
Michael Walzer 162
Martin Wight 168

INTERNATIONAL ORGANISATION 175
Karl W. Deutsch 177
Ernst Haas 181
Robert Keohane 185
David Mitrany 191
John Ruggie 194
Alexander Wendt 199

POSTMODERNISM 205
Richard Ashley 207
Robert B. J. Walker 211

GENDER AND INTERNATIONAL RELATIONS 217
Jean Bethke Elshtain 219
Cynthia Enloe 223
J. Ann Tickner 227

HISTORICAL SOCIOLOGY/THEORIES OF THE STATE 233
Anthony Giddens 235
Michael Mann 240
Charles Tilly 246
Immanuel Wallerstein 252

THEORIES OF THE NATION 259
Benedict Anderson 261
Ernest Gellner 266
Anthony D. Smith 270

GUIDE TO FURTHER READING 277

PREFACE

This book follows in the footsteps of Diané Collinson's *Fifty Major Philosophers* (1987) and John Lechte's *Fifty Key Contemporary Thinkers* (1994). It has been a daunting challenge to maintain the high standards set by these authors. Like them, I provide the reader with a summary of each thinker's work, some biographical information where appropriate and a bibliographical guide to further reading. I have tried to be as objective as possible with each thinker, although I have not shied away at times from inserting my own judgements. To assist the reader in navigating the field as a whole as well as the particular schools of thought within it, I include a general guide to further reading at the end of the book.

This book confines its coverage to key thinkers of the twentieth century. There are a number of other, excellent texts on classical thinkers in the discipline (listed in the general guide), and I wanted as little overlap with them as possible. For this reason I also excluded key thinkers in nuclear strategy, and refer the reader to John Baylis and John Garnett (eds), *Makers of Modern Strategy*, London, Pinter, 1991. Some duplication is inevitable, however. The last two decades have been characterised by a series of seemingly endless arguments over the comparative merits of competing 'paradigms' in the field. In the absence of consensus over the appropriate criteria for their identification and evaluation, it is fitting to consider key thinkers in their own right, and this is increasingly the case in the field. Thus a number of the thinkers included in this book are also discussed elsewhere. See, in particular, Iver B. Neumann and Ole Waever (eds), *The Future of International Relations: Masters in the Making*, London, Routledge, 1997; Joseph Kruzel and James N. Rosenau (eds), *Journeys Through World Politics: Autobiographical Reflections of Thirty-Four Academic Travellers*, Lexington, Massachusetts, Lexington Books, 1989; and Michael Smith, *Realist Thought From Weber to Kissinger*, Baton Rouge, Louisiana State University Press, 1986. However, I have tried to minimise such duplication, some of which is inevitable when one is writing about key thinkers in any academic field.

Despite the growing emphasis on the need to discuss individual thinkers rather than disembodied 'schools of thought', I follow the example of John Lechte's volume and so divide the thinkers into particular categories rather than simply list all fifty thinkers in alphabetical order. The categories themselves represent the dominant schools of thought in the contemporary study of international relations, even though there is a substantial range of views and ideas among the thinkers within them. Indeed, it could be argued that the mark of any great thinker is his or her ability to transcend conventional frameworks for analysis. For example, J.A. Hobson's theory of imperialism is highly critical of many liberal arguments concerning the merits of 'free trade', and was inspired by some of the ideas of Karl Marx. Similarly, Robert Keohane is indebted to the insights of many realists, even as he has sought to go beyond their alleged limitations. The use of categories, in my view, is not meant to place these thinkers within some kind of intellectual or ideological cage, but to show how key thinkers, whilst they can be usefully slotted into long-standing traditions of thought, are rarely bound by them. A brief introductory note precedes each group of thinkers within a particular category.

This book covers writers who have made a substantial contribution to the way we think about international relations at the end of the twentieth century, and I have tried to ensure that the book as a whole fairly represents the scope of the field. Thus, in addition to the traditional trilogy of realists, liberals and radicals, I have included thinkers in emerging sub-fields, such as gender and postmodernism. Within the three main categories, I have included one statesman who represents the political embodiment of the category in question. Thus Henry Kissinger as the arch-realist, Woodrow Wilson as the liberal, and V.I. Lenin as the radical. These historical figures also contributed a substantial literature on international relations. The section on theories of the nation may be problematic for some. I believe that in an era when nationalism is resurgent in global politics, it makes sense to include some of the best writers on the phenomenon, even though they may not be considered as 'international relations theorists' in a narrow sense. Within the three dominant categories, I have tried to ensure some balance between political philosophers, students of diplomacy and the use of force among states, as well as international political economists.

Finally, it should be pointed out that most of the thinkers in this book are still thinking and writing, so the reader should not substitute my thumbnail sketches for a more direct encounter with their work. What follows is intended to supplement courses on international relations, and to provide some inspiration for students entering one of most exciting and rapidly changing academic disciplines.

Martin Griffiths

ACKNOWLEDGEMENTS

Kieron Corless first contacted me in 1995 with the initial proposal for this book. He was most helpful in getting it off the ground, and I thank him for all the work he did in the initial stages. I could not have written this book without the research assistance of a number of people along the way. Special thanks to Terry O'Callaghan for his help in researching key bibliographical items. I am also grateful to David Mathieson and Lachlan Pontifex for their aid in collecting material. Several colleagues read and provided useful critical feedback on particular entries. They include George Crowder, Leonard Seabrooke, Tom Martin and David Moore. I am especially indebted to Rick DeAngelis. He read the entire book from beginning to end and his editorial skills were invaluable in improving the final draft. To all those who encouraged me to believe that I could complete this project on time, many thanks.

Finally, my partner Kylie had to endure many late nights listening to the sound of a keyboard in the next room. I thank her for her tolerance and love, and I promise not to work so obsessively on a project like this ever again!

REALISM

Relations among states take place in the absence of a world government. For realists, this means that the international system is anarchical. International relations are best understood by focusing on the distribution of power among states. Despite their formal legal equality, the uneven distribution of power means that the arena of international relations is a form of 'power politics'. Power is hard to measure; its distribution among states changes over time and there is no consensus among states about how it should be distributed. International relations is therefore a realm of necessity (states must seek power to survive in a competitive environment) and continuity over time. When realists contemplate change in the international system, they focus on changes in the balance of power among states, and tend to discount the possibility of fundamental change in the dynamics of the system itself. The following key thinkers all subscribe to these basic assumptions in their explorations of the following questions: (1) What are the main sources of stability and instability in the international system? (2) What is the actual and preferred balance of power among states? (3) How should the great powers behave toward one another and toward weaker states? (4) What are the sources and dynamics of contemporary changes in the balance of power? Despite some shared assumptions about the nature of international relations, realists are not all of one voice in answering these questions, and it would be wrong to believe that shared assumptions lead to similar conclusions among them. In fact, there is sharp disagreement over the relative merits of particular balances of power (unipolarity, bipolarity and multipolarity). There is also much debate over the causal relationship between states and the international pressures upon them, and the relative importance of different kinds of power in contemporary international relations.

RAYMOND ARON

Raymond Aron was born in 1905 in Paris, the same year as John-Paul Sartre. They were both educated at the elite school Ecole Normale Supérieure, which also produced such authors and politicians as Claude Lévi-Strauss, Leon Blum, Georges Pompidou and Michel Foucault. Although Sartre's name was usually much better known, in part because Aron's Gaullism and staunch anti-communism made him a pariah among French left-wing intellectuals from the 1940s to the 1970s, his reputation has risen since his death in 1983 in comparison with that of his old sparring partner.

Aron's work is too complex and extensive to lend itself to a neat summary. He was a journalist as well as a sociologist, and the range of his intellectual interests went far beyond the concerns of most students of international relations. In IR, Aron is best known for his book *Peace and War*, which first appeared in English in 1966. In addition to this book, whose discursive range and historical depth did not make easy reading for students in search of a master key to peer beneath the apparent contingencies of inter-state relations, Aron is also remembered for his incisive analysis of the dilemmas of strategy in the nuclear age. While it is not unfair, as we shall see, to classify him within the realist school of thought, it is also important to appreciate some of the main differences between his approach to the study of international relations and that of North American realist thinkers.

As a French Jew who had spent some time in Germany just before Hitler's rise to power in the 1930s, Aron's reaction to the rise of fascism in Europe and Stalinism in the Soviet Union set him apart from most French intellectuals in the post-war era. Despite his philosophical training in the abstract theories of history contained in the works of Marx and Hegel, his abhorrence of utopian thought and totalitarianism in all its forms lent an air of critical pessimism to his writing and a refusal to entertain the possibility that politics could ever be an appropriate arena for promoting particular versions of the good life by force at the expense of others. In 1978 he wrote that

> [t]he rise of National Socialism . . . and the revelation of politics in its dialogical essence forced me to argue against myself, against my intimate preferences; it inspired in me a sort of revolt against the instruction I had received at the university, against the spirituality of philosophers, and against the tendency of certain sociologists to misconstrue the impact of regimes with the pretext of focusing on permanent realities.[1]

This experience instilled in Aron a commitment to liberalism and an admiration for the work of Max Weber, rather than the utopianism and historical materialism of Marx that inspired other European intellectuals similarly disenchanted with progressive evolutionary theories of history (see in particular his book, *The Opium of the Intellectuals*, published in 1955). A prudent approach to the theory and practice of politics lay in the acknowledgement of different and often incompatible political values and therefore in the availability and competition between divergent interpretations/ideologies that privileged some at the expense of others. Particular interpretations could be critically analysed in terms of their internal consistency, as well as their compatibility with existing social and political structures, but it would be utopian to believe in the use of reason to transcend such competition.

Informed by this outlook, much of Aron's work focused on the nature of industrialisation and the viability of different ways of promoting it in capitalist and allegedly 'socialist' societies. He was one of the first to argue that the Soviet model of central planning, whilst it facilitated forced industrialisation, was not appropriate for running an ever more complicated industrial society.[2]

In principle, he defended Western, liberal capitalism against its leftist critics as the best means of combining economic growth with some measure of political freedom and economic redistribution. Whilst recognising the fact of class conflict, he never believed in the idea that 'the working class' was either sufficiently homogeneous or motivated to revolt against the inequities of capitalist society. If capitalist societies could combine the search for profits with some measure of welfare and redistribution, he saw no reason why the conflict between workers and capitalists should be zero-sum. Indeed, he hoped that in the longer term such societies could moderate ideological competition, although he worried about the dominance of pressure groups in weakening the democratic process and depriving liberal states of sufficient 'steering capacity' in the interests of the society as a whole.

When it came to the study of international relations rather than industrialisation per se, Aron was inspired by the work of Hobbes and Clausewitz. To some extent he shared the realist view that there was a fundamental difference between *domestic* and *international* relations, and that this difference should be the foundation for all international theory. For Aron, foreign policy is constituted by diplomatic-strategic behaviour, and international relations takes place in the shadow of war. By this, he did not mean that war was always likely, but that the legitimacy of violence to secure state goals was shared among states, and it could not be monopolised as it had been within the territorial boundaries of the state. In his most famous phrase, international relations are 'relations between political units, each of which claims the right to take justice into its own hands and to be the sole arbiter of the decision to fight or not to fight'.[3]

Of course, such an argument seems to place Aron squarely within the realist camp, but on closer examination Aron's work is far more subtle than that of, say, Hans Morgenthau or Kenneth Waltz. Whilst he agreed with Morgenthau that international relations was in some respects a struggle for power among states, the concept of power was too nebulous to serve as a master key for understanding international relations. Similarly, whilst he would agree with Waltz that the milieu of international relations was a unique structured environment, the latter did not determine state goals. Indeed, state 'goals' could not be reduced to a simple formula at all:

> Security, power, glory, ideas, are essentially heterogeneous objectives which can be reduced to a single term only by distorting the human meaning of diplomatic-strategic action. If the rivalry of states is comparable to a game, what is 'at stake' cannot be designated by a single concept, valid for all civilisations at all periods. Diplomacy is a game in which the players sometimes risk losing their lives, sometimes prefer victory to the advantages that would result from it.[4]

In the absence of a simple formula to predict state goals, the best one could do as a thinker, diplomat or strategist is to attempt an understanding of state aims and motives on the best evidence available. *Peace and War* may be disappointing for those in search of ahistorical generalisations, since it is at best a collection of partial hypotheses based on the ways in which states influence one another in light of a) different historical eras; b) the 'material' constraints of space (geography), population (demography) and resources (economics); and c) the 'moral' determinants arising from states' 'styles of being and behaving'.[5] International theory, for Aron, ought not to try and privilege any one of these categories over the other, but to blend all three in an historically sensitive attempt to chart processes of change and continuity over time in the interaction of such 'determinants'. If this is the case, whilst it may make sense to compare historical eras characterised by, for example, bipolar and multipolar configurations of power, hypotheses concerning their relevant stability could only be tentative in light of the fact that one cannot ignore the character of particular states within a distinct era. Whether the states share certain values or common interests may be just as important as how they stand in relation to one another on some quantitative scale of 'power'. Similarly, much of *Peace and War* is devoted to reproducing and analysing the weakness of a number of schools of thought that, in Aron's view, exaggerate the influence of environmental factors, such as geopolitics and the Marxist-Leninist theory of economic imperialism, as causes of war. Aron points out, for example, that the 'excess capital' of France – which according to the theory would require overseas colonies to be invested in – usually went to South America and Russia rather than North Africa. Moreover, he suggested that there was no good reason why home markets should not expand indefinitely to absorb any 'excess production' of the advanced capitalist states. In contrast, he emphasised traditional inter-state rivalry as the main 'cause' of war.

The final part of *Peace and War* is taken up with the question of how the international system has changed in the post-1945 era. Here he is particularly interested in whether nuclear weapons have fundamentally changed strategic thinking about the role of force in foreign policy. In this book and elsewhere, Aron showed a keen awareness of just how ambiguous the evidence was, as well as the central dilemmas facing the strategy and ethics of statecraft in the nuclear age.

On the one hand, he recognized that nuclear weapons were fundamentally different from conventional weapons in that their destructiveness, speed of delivery and limited military utility required that they be used to deter war rather than fight one. For the first time in human history, nuclear armed states had the ability to destroy each other without having to defeat their opponents' armed forces. As soon as the superpowers were in a condition of mutually assured destruction (a condition reached by the late 1950s), they were in a condition of what has come to be called 'existential' deterrence. Each side had the capability to destroy the other totally in a retaliatory second nuclear strike, and the extreme sanction and fear of escalation were sufficient to deter each other from ever embarking on a first strike. For Aron, this existential condition was secure as long as neither superpower could destroy the other's retaliatory capability in a nuclear attack, and as long as no iron-clad defence against nuclear weapons could be constructed. The effectiveness or credibility of nuclear deterrence did not rely on complex *strategies* or *doctrines* employed by either side to make the other certain of what would happen should direct conflict break out between them. The credibility of deterrence lay in the weapons themselves, not in the attempts by states to think of nuclear war in conventional terms, and Aron severely criticised nuclear planners and game theorists in the United States for thinking otherwise. As with his exhortations regarding the inherent limitations of international theory in general, Aron insisted that nuclear strategy could never become anything like an exact science.

On the other hand, if Clausewitz was of limited help in thinking about the conditions under which nuclear war could be fought and 'won', the greater stability there was in deterrence between the United States and the Soviet Union (notwithstanding the arms race between them), the less there was at lower levels in the international system. The superpowers themselves could be tempted to use conventional weapons in their 'proxy' wars, unless this gave rise to fears of escalation, and regional conflicts would continue in the shadow of the nuclear stand-off between the big two. Aron concluded that the Cold War was both unprecedented and, in the context of the ideological differences between two superpowers armed with nuclear weapons, inevitable.

Despite, or rather because of, the

unprecedented dangers of the nuclear era, combined with the uncertainty that had always characterised international relations, Aron believed strongly in *prudence* as the most appropriate ethics of statecraft. By this he meant the need to substitute an ethics of consequences over conviction:

> To be prudent is to act in accordance with the particular situation and the concrete data, and not in accordance with some system or out of passive obedience to a norm ... it is to prefer the limitation of violence to the punishment of the presumably guilty party or to a so-called absolute justice; it is to establish concrete accessible objectives ... and not limitless and perhaps meaningless [ones], such as 'a world safe for democracy' or a world from which power politics has disappeared'.[6]

In short, Raymond Aron must be remembered for his sober realism and liberal pluralism as a student of international relations and as a critic of Cold War excesses. In addition, he remorselessly alerted us to the limits that we can expect from theory, the need to base our generalisations on a deep familiarity with the contingencies of history, and to avoid either falling into a permanent cynicism or entertaining utopian hopes for the transcendence of international relations.

Notes

1 'On the historical condition of the sociologist', reprinted in a collection of Aron's essays, *History and Politics*, M.B. Conant (ed.), New York, Free Press, 1978, p. 65.
2 See, in particular, Raymond Aron, *Democracy and Totalitarianism*, London, Weidenfeld & Nicolson, 1968.
3 Raymond Aron, *Peace and War*, New York, Praeger, 1968, p. 5.
4 Ibid., p. 91.
5 Ibid., p. 279.
6 Ibid., p. 585.

See also in this book

Hoffmann, Morgenthau, Waltz

Aron's major writings

The Century of Total War, London, Derek Verschoyle, 1954
The Opium of the Intellectuals, trans. Terence Kilmartin, London, Secker & Warburg, 1957
Diversity of Worlds: France and the United States Look at Their Common Problems, Westport, Connecticut, The Greenwood Press, 1957
France: The New Republic, New York, Oceana Publications, 1960
Introduction to the Philosophy of History: An Essay on the Limits of Historical Objectivity, trans. George J. Irwin, London, Weidenfeld & Nicolson, 1961
The Dawn of Universal History, trans. Dorothy Pickles, London, Weidenfeld & Nicolson, 1961
The Great Debate: Theories of Nuclear Strategy, trans. Ernst Pawel, Garden City, New York, Doubleday, 1965
'What is a theory of international relations?', *Journal of International Affairs* 21 (1967), pp. 185–206
On War, trans. Terence Kilmartin, New York, W.W. Norton, 1968
Peace and War, trans. Richard Howard and Annette Baker-Fox, New York, Praeger, 1968
Progress and Disillusion: The Dialectics of Modern Society, London, Pall Mall Publishers, 1968
Democracy and Totalitarianism, trans. Valence Ionescu, London, Weidenfeld & Nicolson, 1968
Marxism and the Existentialists, New York, Harper & Row, 1969
The Imperial Republic: The United States and the World, 1945–1973, trans. Frank Jellinek, London, Weidenfeld & Nicolson, 1975
Politics and History, ed. Miriam Bernheim, London, The Free Press, 1978
Memoires, Paris, Julliard, 1983
Clausewitz: Philosopher of War, trans. Christine Booker and Norman Stone, London, Routledge & Kegan Paul, 1983
History, Truth, Liberty: Selected Writings of Raymond Aron, ed. Franciszek Draus, with a memoir by Edward Shils, Chicago, University of Chicago Press, 1985
Power, Modernity, and Sociology: Selected Sociological Writings, ed. Dominique Schnapper and trans. Peter Morris, Aldershot, Hants, England, Gower, 1988

Further reading

'Raymond Aron: a critical retrospective and prospective', special edition of *International Studies Quarterly* 29 (1985).

Baverez, Nicolas, *Raymond Aron*, Lyon, Manufacture, 1986

Colquhoun, Robert, *Raymond Aron: Volume One: The Philosopher in History, 1905–1955*, Beverly Hills, California, Sage Publications, 1986

Colquhoun, Robert, *Raymond Aron: Volume Two: The Sociologist in Society, 1955–1983*, Beverly Hills, California, Sage Publications, 1986

Mahony, Daniel J., *The Liberal Political Science of Raymond Aron*, Oxford, Rowman & Littlefield, 1991

EDWARD HALLETT CARR

E.H. Carr is best known for his book *The Twenty Years' Crisis* (1946), which combines a trenchant critique of Western diplomacy between the two world wars with an influential framework of analysis. Carr's work helped to establish the terms on which international theory has been discussed in the twentieth century, namely, as an ongoing debate between 'realists' and 'idealists' or 'utopians'. Carr did not begin this debate, nor did he stake out his own position clearly within it. What he did do was to demonstrate how two contrasting conceptions of historical progress manifested themselves in international thought and practice. Furthermore, the facility with which he combined philosophical reflection, historical analysis and commentary on current affairs ensured that this book remains one of the classics in the field.

Carr was born in 1892, and he graduated from Cambridge University with a first class degree in Classics when the First World War interrupted his studies. He joined the Foreign Office and attended the Paris Peace Conference at the end of the Great War. He returned to academia in 1936, when he was appointed Wilson Professor of International Politics at the University College of Wales at Aberystwyth. When the Second World War broke out, he became assistant editor of *The Times* newspaper in London. He returned to Cambridge in 1953, where he remained to concentrate on his research into the history of the Soviet Union. Although his research into the Soviet Union culminated in the publication of fourteen books on the subject, Carr will always be best known for his contribution to the ascendancy of 'realism' in the study of international relations based on *The Twenty Years Crisis*.

In this book, first published in 1939 (the second edition appeared in 1946), Carr engages in a sustained critique of the 'utopian' thinking that he argues dominated Western intellectual thought and diplomatic practice in the inter-war years. He suggests that all human sciences, particularly when they are young, tend to be somewhat prescriptive, subordinating the analysis of facts to the desire to reform the world. The study of international relations, he argues, was overly influenced by a set of ideas that were themselves products of a particular balance of power in which Britain enjoyed a dominant role. Thus it was committed to efforts to bring about international peace on the basis of norms and principles which were in fact limited to the historical experience of domestic politics and economics in Britain, and they could not be applied internationally in a world divided among states with very different degrees of power and commitment to the international status quo. Chief among these were the beliefs in both the natural harmony of interests (derived from nineteenth-century laissez-faire economics) and collective security. In particular, the latter treated war as a consequence of 'aggression' across borders.

If it were to be abolished, there would need to be an international organisation; states would commit themselves to the rule of law and be prepared to co-operate to deter and, if necessary, punish 'aggressors', with a spectrum of measures ranging from diplomacy and economic sanctions to the use of collective force to assist the victims of aggression. Carr argued that the faith and optimism concerning collective security, as well as the institution of the League of Nations which was designed to implement it, was based on the erroneous assumption that the territorial and political status quo was satisfactory to all the major powers in the international system. In a world of separate sovereign states of unequal power, this was unlikely ever to be the case. Conflict among states, therefore, was not merely a consequence of a failure to understand one another, but an inevitable result of incompatible aspirations that could only be dealt with on the basis of negotiation in light of the balance of power rather than by appealing to 'universal' principles of moral conduct. He therefore dismissed the idea that peace could result from the replication among states of judicial or legislative processes that could be enforced by the state within the domestic arena.

Carr recommended that scholars and diplomats could have avoided some of the problems of the inter-war period if they had adopted a less idealistic and more 'realistic' approach to international affairs. This approach would entail the need to substitute rhetoric with diplomacy, and to subordinate universal principles to the procedural ethics of compromise between status quo and revisionist states in the international system.

> The process of give-and-take must apply to challenges to the existing order. Those who profit most by that order can in the long run only hope to maintain it by making sufficient concessions to make it tolerable to those who profit by it the least, and the responsibility for seeing that these changes take place as far as possible in an orderly way rests as much on the defenders as on the challengers.[1]

Carr argued that the relationship between realism and utopianism was dynamic and dialectical. Although he was a severe critic

of utopian thinking in the 1930s and 1940s, he also acknowledged that realism without utopianism could descend into a cynical *realpolitik*: '[c]onsistent realism excludes four things which appear to be essential ingredients of all effective political thinking: a finite goal, an emotional appeal, a right of moral judgement, and a ground for action.'[2]

There is, however, a tension between Carr's portrayal of the clash between realism and utopianism, and his deeply felt need to mediate between them. On the one hand, his discussion of the theoretical differences between these 'isms' is infused with determinism (the Marxist idea that norms and values are simply epiphenomenal expressions of the ruling class), as well as metaphysical dualism ('the two elements – utopia and reality – belong to two different planes that can never meet').[3] The antithesis between them is analogously identified with a series of dichotomies that Carr posits as free will versus determinism, the relation between theory and practice, the intellectual versus the bureaucrat and ethics versus politics. Carr then collapses the antinomy into an apparent dichotomy of power and morality, the latter subordinate to the former to have any effect. Given such presuppositions, realism and utopianism are both unsound doctrines, but each can only act as a 'corrective' to the other. But they cannot be transcended or synthesised in thought. All one can do, it seems, is see-saw between them, using the strengths of one to attack the other when one of them appears to be getting the upper hand in informing international diplomacy and the conduct of great-power foreign policy.

On the other hand, Carr did argue that 'sound political thought and sound political life will be found only where both have their place'.[4] Whatever the philosophical difficulties involved in his argument, Carr sought to reconcile the competing tendencies in his own diagnoses and prescriptions for international stability. This led to some judgements that have been criticised, although, it must be said, with the luxury of hindsight. The most blatant example was Carr's endorsement of the British government's policy of appeasing Germany in the late 1930s. This was included in the first edition of *The Twenty Years' Crisis* when it was published in 1939, but significantly absent from the second edition published in 1946. As William Fox observed in his excellent examination of Carr's views in the late 1930s, '[a] good big theory does give a handle on the long- and middle-run future, but it does not point directly and ineluctably to the big short-run decisions'.[5]

During and immediately after the Second World War, Carr turned his attention to the prospects for international stability that did not attempt to predict short-term policies or diplomatic episodes. As a man of the Left, Carr hoped that it would be possible to learn from the Soviet experience in social and economic planning, and he hoped that communism and capitalism could coexist without undue antagonism. This was based on his deep suspicion of capitalism to promote equality among people or states, and his belief that, for all its faults, communism rested on the belief in a common moral purpose that was necessary to generate the self-sacrifice that could provide a common bond between the weak and the powerful. Carr was acutely aware of the dramatic changes in foreign affairs brought about since the French Revolution and the growth of democracy. Mass participation in the political process could not be sustained unless Western societies discovered new ways to manage the market and achieve forms of social democracy that required intervention in the marketplace rather than naïve nineteenth-century ideas derived from simplistic readings of Adam Smith. Notwithstanding his own somewhat naïve view of Hitler in the late 1930s, he acknowledged that the Second World War was as much a product of revolutionary ideology as the clash of enduring national interests. Despite the horror of war, he

argued that the experience of fascism and communism had contributed useful lessons to Western democracies, particularly the need for social planning and international intervention to tame the inequities of global capitalism.[6]

In his book *Nationalism and After* (1945), Carr compared the nationalist movements of the nineteenth century with those of the twentieth and, as with his other books of this period, he laments the application of ideas that may have been applicable in the past, but which were now obsolete. For those interested in the problems of nationalism at the end of the Cold War, *Nationalism and After* is still required reading, for many of its arguments and analyses are as relevant today as they were when Carr made them. In this book, he argues that the principle of national self-determination is no longer a recipe for freedom, but guarantees conflict insofar as its interpretation along ethnic lines is incompatible with the ethnic diversity of most states. Furthermore, twentieth-century nationalism is closely linked to the rise of public participation in the political system, which would lead to a dramatic rise in the number of 'nation-states' if the process was not managed. At the same time there was a clear incompatibility between the value of national self-determination as an expression of freedom and the waning economic power of the nation-state to deliver either military or social security to its people. According to Carr, the solution was to create large multinational and regional organisations of states which could better coordinate their policies and sustain a commitment to social justice than either Soviet-style communism or American 'free enterprise'. In light of the experience of the European states during the Cold War, *Nationalism and After* was prophetic in its foresight.

Carr did not write a great deal on international relations per se after his two great works of the 1930s and 1940s. From the early 1950s onwards he devoted his attention to the historical analysis of the Soviet Union, an enormous project in which Carr tried to empathise with the problems faced by Soviet leaders and refused to engage in a 'moralistic' condemnation of the Soviet political system. He always argued, however, that American fears of Soviet 'aggression' toward Western Europe were exaggerated, and that the West had much to learn from the East in its own attempts to reconcile individual freedom and egalitarian social policies:

> The fate of the western world will turn on its ability to meet the Soviet challenge by a successful search for new forms of social and economic action in which all that is valid in the individualist and democratic traditions can be applied to the problems of mass civilisation.[7]

One might argue that the collapse of the Soviet Union has not meant the end of the challenge, merely the end of the need to confront a state whose own attempts to meet it failed so dramatically. Carr himself offered no blueprint for how that challenge might be met. To do so would have been precisely the kind of utopian exercise he deplored.

Carr died in 1982 at the age of 90, and his work continues to inspire debate among students of international relations. Whilst he has been hailed as the author of one of the most important classics of the twentieth century, his portrayal of the continuing theoretical division between realism and utopianism is by no means convincing for many scholars in the field. Some, particularly those associated with the 'English School' of International Relations such as Martin Wight and Hedley Bull, have argued that his dichotomy between realism and utopian is far too rigid and simplistic an attempt to distinguish between theoretical approaches in the study of international relations. Others have condemned Carr's apparent relativism, and his refusal to defend his socialist values in a far more explicit manner than he ever attempted. To some extent this can be attributed to

Carr's Marxist beliefs (themselves never elaborated in his own published work), and his indebtedness to the work of Karl Mannheim on the sociology of knowledge. But whatever its philosophical weakness, Carr's work reminds us that however we justify our commitment to values such as liberty or equality, they remain abstract and somewhat meaningless unless they are embodied in concrete political and economic arrangements whose reform is contingent on a complex historical process in which progress cannot be guaranteed.

For a profound analysis of Carr's view on historical progress, students can look no further than his text *What is History?*, which not only reveals Carr's own views but remains a classic work on the reading and writing of history. Among other issues, Carr examines the notion of progress in history and historiography since the Enlightenment, noting that what began as a secularisation of Christian teleology needed to be continually modified by later historians, and eventually by Carr himself, in order not to succumb to mysticism or to cynicism, but to maintain a constructive view of the past. In this book Carr tries to mediate between a view of progress as an eternal Platonic form standing outside of history and an historically determined goal set in the future, unformed and susceptible to being shaped by attitudes in the present. Carr's early training, it must be remembered, took place within the full flood of Victorian optimism, only later to be reduced by the more pessimistic realities embodied in the world wars. The decline of England as a world power made Carr a spokesman for his generation when he expressed the notion that historical progress could not be true in the Victorian sense, yet might be true in some broader, complex sense. Carr's own notion of historical progress is embodied in the idea that 'man is capable of profiting (not that he necessarily profits) by the experience of his predecessors, that progress in history, unlike evolution in nature, rests on the transmission of acquired assets'.[8] According to Carr, progress is not a straight line to perfection, but it depends on the ability of people to learn from the past, and upon the ability of the historian to transmit that past to his or her culture in a useful way in light of contemporary problems. Human civilisations may rise, fall and stagnate as different groups within society gain and lose power, but 'progress' in Carr's modified sense can still persist. This is because as more and more different events take place, the collective memory of historians becomes richer. This in turn enables them more accurately to glimpse the ever-changing direction in which history is moving, and even to alter that direction to a more favourable course. We may still debate the merits of Carr's own modest attempts to steer the course of international history, but there can be no doubt that among the fifty great thinkers introduced in this particular book, Carr remains among the greatest of them.

Notes

1 E.H. Carr, *The Twenty Years Crisis, 1919–1939*, Second edition, London, Macmillan, 1946, pp. 87–8.
2 Ibid., p. 89.
3 Ibid., p. 93.
4 Ibid., p. 10.
5 William Fox, 'E.H. Carr and political realism: vision and revision', *Review of International Studies*, 11 (1985), p. 5.
6 See, in particular, E.H. Carr, *Nationalism and After*, London, Macmillan, 1945.
7 E.H. Carr, *The Soviet Impact on the Western World*, London, Macmillan, 1947.
8 E.H. Carr, *What is History?*, London, Macmillan, 1961, p. 117.

See also in this book

Bull, Morgenthau, Wight

Carr's major writings

Britain: A Study of Foreign Policy From the Versailles Treaty to the Outbreak of War, London, Longmans Green, 1939
Conditions of Peace, London, Macmillan, 1942

Nationalism and After, London, Macmillan, 1945
The Twenty Years Crisis, 1919–1939, Second edition, London, Macmillan, 1946
The Soviet Impact on the Western World, London, Macmillan, 1947
A History of Soviet Russia (Fourteen Volumes), London, Macmillan, 1950–1978
The New Society, London, Macmillan, 1951
German–Soviet Relations Between the Two World Wars, 1919–1939, Baltimore, Johns Hopkins University Press, 1951
Socialism in One Country, 1924–1926 (Three Volumes), Harmondsworth, Penguin, 1958–64
The Romantic Exiles: A Nineteenth Century Portrait Gallery, Boston, Beacon Press, 1961
What is History?, London, Macmillan, 1961
From Napoleon to Stalin, and Other Essays, New York, St Martin's Press, 1980

Further reading

Abramsky, Chimen, *Essays in Honour of E.H. Carr*, London, Macmillan, 1970
Bull, Hedley, 'The Twenty Years Crisis thirty years on', *International Journal* 24 (1969), pp. 625–38
Evans, Graham, 'E.H. Carr and international relations', *British Journal of International Studies* 1 (1975), pp. 77–97
Fox, William, 'Carr and political realism: vision and revision', *Review of International Studies* 11 (1985), pp. 1–16
Gellner, Ernst, 'Nationalism reconsidered and E.H. Carr', *Review of International Studies* 18 (1992), pp. 285–93
Howe, Paul, 'The utopian realism of E.H. Carr', *Review of International Studies* 20 (1994), pp. 277–97
Morgenthau, Hans J., 'The political science of E.H. Carr', *World Politics* 1 (1949), pp. 127–34
Smith, Michael J., *Realist Thought From Weber to Kissinger*, Baton Rouge, Louisiana State University Press, 1986, pp. 68–98

ROBERT GILPIN

Robert G. Gilpin is Professor of Politics and International Affairs at the Woodrow Wilson School, Princeton University. He has been a congressional fellow and vice president of the American Political Science Association, and he is best known for his work in international political economy. In response to those who argue that realism is overly concerned with the politics of military security and tends to ignore economic forces, Gilpin attempts to reintegrate the study of international politics (concerned with the role of power in shaping relations among states) with international economic forces (concerned with the nature and dynamics of firms in the marketplace). In addition, he is one of the few realists concerned with *change*, particularly in trying to explain the rise and decline of states over time. This has been a growth area in the study of international relations over the last couple of decades. It was inspired both by the concern with the apparent economic decline of the United States in the 1970s and 1980s relative to Europe and Japan and by the arguments of many liberals that the growth of economic interdependence among states was weakening their power and attenuating the historical relationship between military force and the ability to sustain state national interests.

Gilpin's work reveals a consistent concern with the role of power and the management of power by the state. His first major publication was a study of the tensions between American nuclear scientists and the US government on nuclear weapons policies in the 1950s. But his most important work emerged in the mid-1970s and the 1980s in the area of international political economy. Contrary to those who argued that the growth of economic interdependence was undermining the state and reducing the relevance of coercive military power to determine economic influence in world affairs, Gilpin argued that a liberal international trading order depended upon the very factors it was alleged to be undermining, namely, the presence of a powerful state to provide what have come to be called international 'public goods'.

The basic argument is this. Markets cannot flourish in producing and distributing goods and services in the absence of a state to provide certain prerequisites. By definition, markets depend on the transfer, via an efficient price mechanism, of goods and services that can be bought and sold among private actors who exchange ownership rights. But markets themselves depend on the state to provide, via coercion, regulation and taxation, certain 'public goods' that markets themselves cannot generate. These include a legal infrastructure of property rights and laws to make contracts binding, a coercive infrastructure to ensure that laws are obeyed and a stable medium of exchange (money) to ensure a standard of valuation for goods and services. Within the territorial borders of the state, governments provide such goods. Internationally, of course, there is no world state capable of replicating their provision on a global scale. Building on the work of Charles Kindleberger and E.H. Carr's analysis of the role of Great Britain in the international economy of the nineteenth century, Gilpin argues that stability and the 'liberalisation' of international exchange depend on the existence of a 'hegemon' that is both able and willing to provide international 'public goods', such as law and order and a stable currency for financing trade.

The overall direction of Gilpin's argument can be found in his three most important works, *US Power and the Multinational Corporation* (1975), *War and Change in World Politics* (1981) and *The Political Economy of International Relations* (1987). The first of these is an examination of the foreign influence of American multinational corporations in the post-war era. Contrary to some of the conventional wisdom that the spread and autonomy of overseas corporate activity was beyond the control of the US government, Gilpin argues that their overseas activity can only be understood in the context of the open liberal economy established under US auspices at the end of the Second World War. Its hegemonic leadership and anti-Sovietism. was the basis of its commitment to 'liberal internationalism' and the establishment of international institutions to facilitate the dramatic expansion of trade among capitalist states in the 1950s and 1960s.

Gilpin's next two major works were written in the context of a growing debate about the alleged decline of the United States in international relations, particularly in light of the dramatic economic recovery of Europe and Japan from the devastation of the Second World War. Although far more attention was paid to the work of Paul Kennedy in the late 1980s, Gilpin's *War and Change in World Politics* is an important attempt to place the debate within an overall theory of the rise and decline of hegemonic states in international relations. The originality of this work lies in its attempt to integrate propositions both at the level of the international system and at the level of individual states within the system. Starting with certain assumptions about states, he seeks to explain the emergence and change of systems of states within a rational choice framework. In addition, he distinguishes between three kinds of change in international relations. *Interaction* change simply refers to changing inter-state relations within a given balance of power. *Systemic* change refers to the overall governance of the system, the number of great powers within it, and the shift in identity of predominant powers, usually after a systemic war involving challenges to, and attempts to maintain, the existing distribution of power. Finally, and most significantly, *systems* change refers to a fundamental transformation of the actors and thus the nature of the system per se. For example, one could point to the emergence of the state system itself in the fifteenth and sixteenth centuries, or the change from empires to nation-states in the eighteenth and nineteenth centuries.

Gilpin's model of systemic change is based on a number of assumptions about states that he derives from microeconomic, rational choice theory. This is used to postulate a cyclical theory of change in the international system. It consists of five key propositions:

1 An international system is stable (i.e., in a state of equilibrium) if no state believes it profitable to change the system.

2 A state will attempt to change the international system if the expected benefits exceed the expected costs.

3 A state will seek to change the international system through territorial, political and economic expansion until the marginal costs of further change are equal to or greater than the expected benefits.

4 Once equilibrium between the costs and benefits of further change and expansion is reached, the tendency is for the economic costs of maintaining the status quo to rise faster than the economic capacity to sustain the status quo.

5 If the disequilibrium in the international system is not resolved, then the system will be changed, and a new equilibrium reflecting the redistribution of power will be established.[1]

As far as Gilpin is concerned, world history since the Treaty of Westphalia (1648) has been a period of systemic change within a state-centric system, and the stability or otherwise of the system depends upon the existence of a political and economic hegemon. But stability is difficult to sustain because economic and technological change is never evenly distributed among states. Hence over time there is an increasing gap between the status and prestige of particular states and the power they are able to deploy to safeguard their national interests. Despite the need for peaceful change in the system to manage the process of change, Gilpin grimly observes that, up to now, 'the principal mechanism of change . . . has been war, or what we shall call hegemonic war (i.e., a war that determines which state or states will be dominant and will govern the system)'.[2] The factors that lie behind change in the international system are largely environmental, and these structure the array of incentives that states have to try and change the system to their benefit, such as population shifts and the diffusion of military technology throughout the system. Although the decline of empires seems to confirm the obsolescence of territorial expansion and its substitution by hegemonic states (such as Britain in the nineteenth century and the United States after 1945), the attempts by Germany and Japan to expand their territorial control in the first half of this century suggest that the mode of change remains indeterminate.

In the context of the debate over the alleged decline of the United States in international relations, the last two propositions deserve particular attention. Essentially, Gilpin believes that all hegemonies are transient because the costs of maintaining them rise faster than the resources available to do so. On the one hand, the hegemon is unable to prevent the diffusion of its economic skills and techniques to other states. On the other hand, the hegemon must confront the rising expectations of its own citizens. Over time they will privilege consumption over production and resist further sacrifices in order to maintain the supremacy of the hegemon on the international stage. The combination of internal and external factors leads to what Gilpin calls 'a severe fiscal crisis' for the hegemon. It then has a limited choice of options. If it wishes to maintain its power, it can either confront its internal obstacles and reverse the tendency towards complacency, or it can attack rising powers before they mount a challenge of their own. Alternatively, it can seek to reduce its overseas commitments and promote strategic alliances with other states. Gilpin illustrates the former with reference to imperial China, whilst in the 1930s, Britain attempted the latter course of action. Gilpin is sceptical about the lessons of history, however. Whilst

each of these options has been pursued with varying degrees of success in the past, neither has been able to prevent the onset of war to resolve the disequilibrium of global power. In the late twentieth century, such a conclusion raises urgent questions about contemporary stability in the international system and the need to discover means other than war for managing the process of change, since the next 'systemic' war is likely to be the last in the context of nuclear weapons.

The third book, *The Political Economy of International Relations* (1987), is both a major textbook in the field of international political economy and a continuation of the themes addressed in his previous work. After exploring a range of sources of change that encompass finance, trade and investment in the post-war era, Gilpin concludes that the period of American hegemony in the international system is coming to an end and that Japan is emerging as a potential hegemon in the international system. He believes that the decline in American power, caused by a mixture of internal and external forces, is detrimental to the maintenance of a liberal economic order among states. On the one hand, American exports of technology and capital have facilitated the recovery of Europe and Japan, whilst on the other hand the costs of containing the Soviet Union have made it difficult for the United States to maintain its competitive edge over its rivals. In particular, the United States became a major debtor nation in the 1980s, whilst Japan had accrued large capital surpluses that it had invested in the United States. Gilpin believes that this situation has grave consequences for the continuation of a liberal trading system since over time the United States will be reluctant to pay for the public goods whose benefits accrue to 'free riders' in the international system such as Japan. Gilpin argues that the decline of US hegemony is likely to usher in a period of 'new mercantilism', perhaps even the establishment of new trading blocs under the respective regional hegemonies of the United States, Germany and Japan.

Thus in contrast to those who talk of 'globalisation' in the world economy, Gilpin emphasises the fundamental changes in the world economy that are a byproduct of the erosion of American hegemony. He believes that we are now in the midst of a transition from a long period of liberal internationalism to one of mercantilism, and whether the latter will be malign or benign remains a very open question.

Gilpin's work has been subject to a number of criticisms, notwithstanding his novel attempt to adapt realism to account for change in the international system. Some writers have drawn attention to the ambiguity and indeterminacy of the theory, whilst others have argued that Gilpin's pessimism regarding the future of the international system is based almost entirely on his ideological predisposition for realism and that his theory of change is little more than the application of a social Darwinian approach to the study of international relations.

The first type of criticism is particularly pertinent in light of the dramatic changes that have taken place in the last decade. Gilpin did not predict the end of the Cold War, but one could argue that the collapse of the Soviet Union has rendered much of his diagnosis of US decline obsolete, since the hegemon has no further need to engage in an expensive military competition with its arch-rival. The indeterminacy of the theory, particularly insofar as it tends to rely on two case studies (Britain and the United States), leaves much room for debate. As Richardson points out,

If the US *is* in the declining stage of the cycle, then Gilpin's theory can suggest some of the reasons why, and can suggest options and constraints. But is it? How do we know that it is not, like imperial China or eighteenth-century Britain or France, capable of rejuvenation? ... Gilpin's theory is not rigorous enough to specify criteria which would resolve the issue: he assumes that the model of the declining hegemon fits the US, but does not, beyond a comparison with [its] position in the immediate post-war period, spell out the reasoning behind the assumption.[3]

One could well argue that in the last decade of the twentieth century, unipolarity has replaced bipolarity in international relations, and that the economic growth of the United States in the last few years, combined with the relative decline of Japan and other 'newly industrialising countries' in the Asia-Pacific, renders much of the concern with American 'decline' out of date. The issue is difficult to resolve in the absence of agreed criteria either for measuring power in the contemporary international system, or for the selection of relevant timescales. One could also argue that China is the most important emerging hegemon at the end of the twentieth century, rather than Japan.

Others have drawn attention to the way in which Gilpin's theory is informed less by its empirical validity than his underlying assumptions and value judgements rooted in a very pessimistic view of the world. As he has said himself, 'it's a jungle out there!'[4] Gilpin's world view remains state-centric, and he is not convinced that the historic patterns of relations among states in an anarchical world are going to change in the near future. Some critics have suggested that Gilpin's theoretical work is based on a fundamental assumption that the United States is a benign hegemon, but it is quite possible to construe nuclear deterrence as a public 'bad' rather than a 'good'. Despite his attempt to synthesise realism and microeconomic utilitarianism, many remain sceptical about whether this provides an adequate basis on which to justify his underlying pessimism about the possibility of progressive reform in the international system.

Notes

1 Robert Gilpin, *War and Change in World Politics*, Cambridge, Cambridge University Press, 1981, pp. 10–11.
2 Ibid., p. 15.
3 James Richardson, 'Paul Kennedy and international relations theory: a comparison with Robert Gilpin', *Australian Journal of International Affairs* 45 (1991), pp. 73–4. For an attempt to test Gilpin's theory in the context of British hegemony, see K. Edward Spezio, 'British hegemony and major power war: an empirical test of Gilpin's model of hegemonic governance', *International Studies Quarterly* 34 (1990), pp. 165–81.
4 Robert Gilpin, 'The richness of the tradition of political realism', *International Organization* 38 (1984), p. 290. For his most recent articulation and defence of realism, see Robert Gilpin, 'No one loves a political realist', *Security Studies* 5 (1996), pp. 4–26 (special issue edited by Benjamin Frankel, published by Frank Cass, London).

See also in this book

Cox, Keohane, Krasner, Strange

Gilpin's major writings

Scientists and National Policy-Making, New York, Columbia University Press, 1964
France in the Age of the Scientific State, Princeton, New Jersey, Princeton University Press, 1968
'The politics of transnational economic relations', *International Organization* 25 (1971), pp. 398–419. Also in Robert O. Keohane and Joseph S. Nye (eds), *Transnational Relations and World Politics*, Cambridge, Massachusetts, Harvard University Press, 1970, pp. 48–69
US Power and the Multinational Corporation: The Political Economy of Direct Foreign Investment, New York, Basic Books, 1975
'Three models of the future', *International Organization* 29 (1975), pp. 30–67
'Economic interdependence and national security in historical perspective', in Klaus Knorr and Frank N. Trager (eds), *Economic Issues and National Security*, Lawrence, Kansas, Regents Press of Kansas, 1977, pp. 19–66
War and Change in World Politics, Cambridge, Cambridge University Press, 1981
'The richness of the tradition of political realism', *International Organization* 38 (1984), pp. 287–304

The Political Economy of International Relations, Princeton, New Jersey, Princeton University Press, 1987
'The theory of hegemonic war', *Journal of Interdisciplinary History* 18 (1988), pp. 591–613
'The cycle of great powers: has it finally been broken?', in Geir Lundestad (ed.), *The Fall of Great Powers: Peace, Stability, and Legitimacy*, Oslo, Scandinavian University Press, 1994

Further reading

Gowa, Joanne, 'Rational hegemons, excludable goods, and small groups: an epitaph for hegemonic stability theory', *World Politics* 41 (1989), pp. 307–24
Grundberg, Isabelle, 'Exploring the "myth" of hegemonic stability', *International Organisation* 44 (1990), pp. 431–77
Rogowski, Roger, 'Structure, growth, power: three rationalist accounts', *International Organization* 37 (1993), pp. 713–38

JOHN HERZ

As with the work of Susan Strange, the writing of John Herz cannot be placed squarely within a 'realist' school of thought without some qualification. In his first book, he describes his own position as 'realist liberalism', a term which sums up the work of someone who acknowledges all the empirical constraints identified by more traditional 'realists', but who also affirms the need to transcend those constraints in search of a more humane and just world order.[1] In his work on the 'territorial state' in the 1950s, Herz believed that its transcendence was imminent, facilitated by the apparent failure of the state to fulfil its main purpose in the nuclear era – to defend its citizens. By the late 1960s, he acknowledged that the state was unlikely to disappear, despite the arrival of nuclear weapons, and his writing took on a more normative dimension, appealing to the need for more enlightened views of self-interest in foreign policy. In 1981 he wrote that

We live in an age where threats to the survival of all of us – nuclear superarmament, populations outrunning food supplies and energy resources, destruction of man's habitat – concern all nations and people, and thus must affect foreign policy-making as much as views of security.[2]

This shift in emphasis was accompanied by a sustained concern with what might be called an 'immanent critique' of the way in which foreign policy is often framed within what Herz argues are inappropriate 'images' of the world. He urges us (as observers of and participants in international relations) to distinguish between that part of 'reality' which is fixed and immutable and that part which arises from 'the perceptual and conceptual structures that we ... bestow on the world'.[3] In his long career Herz has always tried to do so, and to evaluate dominant perceptions in light of what he once referred to as 'mild internationalism'. In a short essay written for the *International Encyclopaedia of the Social Sciences* in 1968, he distinguishes between a mildly internationalist ideology and more radical forms of internationalism. The former, which is both practical and desirable, aims at a world in which states remain the most important political actors, they are democratic and self-determining, and conflicts are settled by mediation, arbitration and the application of international law in the context of growing interdependence and co-operation. The goal of radical internationalism is to replace the existing system of sovereign states with some kind of world government.[4]

Herz was born in 1908 in Germany. He attended the University of Cologne where he studied legal and political philosophy as well as constitutional and international law. After completing his doctorate under the supervision of the legal theorist Hans Kelsen, Herz moved to Switzerland, where he enrolled in courses in international relations at the Geneva Institut de Hautes Etudes Internationales. As with so many of the key thinkers in this book (Deutsch, Haas, Kissinger, Morgenthau), he came to the United States in order to escape the Nazis shortly before the outbreak of the Second World War. He taught at Howard University, Columbia University, the New School for Social Research in New York and the Fletcher School of Law and Diplomacy (1939–41). He then worked for the Office of Strategic Services and the State Department, and after the war he took up a permanent position as Professor of Political Science at the City College of New York and head of the doctoral programme at the City University of New York. His experience at the State Department taught him 'how little one's work and efforts at a lower level mean for top decision-makers'.[5] He believed that the United States could have done more to establish democratic foundations in Germany in the early post-war years but did not do so because it was so eager to build it up as a bulwark against Soviet Communism. As a teacher, Herz continued to work on German democratisation and the problems of regime change in comparative European politics.[6] Indeed, in addition to his work on international relations, Herz is well regarded as a student of Germany and has edited the journal *Comparative Politics* for a number of years.

In 1951, Herz published his first major book, *Political Realism and Political Idealism*. In it he tries to steer a middle way between 'realism' and 'idealism'. He defines 'realism' as thought which 'takes into consideration the implications for political life of those security and power factors which are inherent in human society'.[7] In contrast, political idealism either ignores such factors or believes that they will disappear once 'rational' solutions to political problems are presented and adopted. However, in contrast to Hans Morgenthau and other 'classical realists' of the period, Herz does not trace the 'power factors' to permanent characteristics of human nature. He acknowledges that the latter has many dimensions – biological, metaphysical and even spiritual – that combine to determine human behaviour, and any adequate account must recognise human ethical properties.

Instead of appealing to metaphysics, Herz posits the existence of a 'security dilemma' as the key factor. It arises from the individual's consciousness that others may be seeking his or her destruction, so there is always some need for self-defence, which in turn may make others insecure. What is true among individuals is equally relevant to understanding group behaviour. In fact, Herz argues that the security dilemma is more acute among groups, for the simple reason that groups can develop means of self-defence that are far more destructive than those available to individuals. Moreover, insofar as individuals come to equate their own identity and worth with that of the group to which they belong, they may be prepared to sacrifice their lives on behalf of the survival of the group. Thus even if one makes the most optimistic assumptions about the nature and motives of individuals and groups, the security dilemma will persist as long as there remain groups that are not subordinate to a higher authority. In the modern world, these are sovereign states.

Of course, this argument is not original to Herz. Hobbes said something very similar in the mid-seventeenth century. Herz has become famous for the label 'security dilemma', however, as well as the skill with which he uses the basic framework to illustrate the history of international relations over the past 200 years. In the body of the book, Herz examines certain movements for democracy, nationalism and internationalism, showing how the 'idealistic' rhetoric behind such movements always ran into 'realistic' problems that doomed them to failure. At the same time he acknowledges that 'ideals' are also part of political and historical 'reality', and that any philosophy that denies ideals engenders lethargy and despair. Robert Berki sums up Herz's argument as follows:

> Political means in the realist perspective must be fashioned so as to combat the 'resistance' of forces that hinder ideals, which means to enter the game that is played imperfectly in politics, with imperfect rules. The promised land lies perpetually over the horizon, and imagined means which derive their value from this promised land are unsuitable.[8]

Over the next two decades Herz continued to elaborate on the nature of the security dilemma in post-war international relations. In 1959 he published his second classic work, *International Politics in the Atomic Age*. This introduced readers to Herz's views on the rise (and imminent collapse) of the 'permeability' of the sovereign state. The book is divided into two parts. The first provides an account of the rise of the state that focuses on the role of military technology, whilst the second describes the crisis of the state in the nuclear era. Whilst the first book focuses on the role of political philosophy in shaping our attitudes to international politics in general, the second is an application of 'liberal internationalism' in the specific context of nuclear bipolarity and the Cold War.

Observing the variety of units that have engaged in 'international relations' throughout history, Herz tries to account for the rise of the modern state in terms of its ability to provide protection and security to its citizens against armed attack from outsiders. As such, Herz engages in a form of 'strategic determinism'. In particular, he focuses on the change from the small and vulnerable political units of the European Middle Ages (such as fortified castles and walled cities) to the larger units that came to be known as nation-states. He claims that the invention and widespread use of gunpowder enabled rulers, along with artillery and standing armies, to destroy feudal authorities within larger areas, which they could then protect by building 'impenetrable' fortifications. Compared to what preceded them, sovereign states were 'territorially impenetrable'.

The crucial change in this situation took place in the twentieth century. First, there was a dramatic increase in the destructive capacity of air power between the two world wars, even though some military strategists had exaggerated its ability to win wars. As the experience of the Second World War demonstrated, the widespread bombing of industrial infrastructure did not incapacitate the states on which it was inflicted, and the targeting of civilians did not promote a general desire to sue for peace regardless of the consequences. For example, the fire-bombing of Tokyo with conventional weapons in early 1945 caused more direct casualties than the dropping of the atom bomb on Hiroshima in August, and there was no evidence at the time to suggest that it would make a conventional invasion by allied troops unnecessary. Herz argues that nuclear weapons have now destroyed the 'impermeability' of the sovereign state, so that traditional 'balance of power' politics are finally obsolete. Of course, the 'realist' in him acknowledges that the security dilemma still operates, even though the means used to tame it undermine the purpose of doing so. Throughout the book Herz laments the way in which the United States and the Soviet Union have failed to adapt to the new situation, building thousands more weapons than are required for the purposes of deterrence. The appalling condition of 'nuclear overkill' and the elaborate schemes of civilian strategists and nuclear weapons designers to escape from the new security dilemma have meant that we have lost sight of the more fundamental problem:

The very fact that technical developments of weapons and armaments in themselves wield such a tremendous impact has meant that they have almost come to dictate policies instead of policies determining type and choice of weapons, their use, amount of armaments, and so forth. In other words, instead of weapons serving policy, policy is becoming the mere servant of a weapon that more and more constitutes its own raison d'être.[9]

In short, the world had become too small for traditional territoriality and the protection it had previously provided. The balance of terror was not the continuation of the old balance of power. War, which had functioned as part of the dynamics of the balance, was no longer a rational means of policy. Herz claimed that what had once been considered 'idealistic' – namely, the dilution of state sovereignty – was now an overriding national interest.

Almost a decade later, Herz acknowledged that 'developments have rendered me doubtful of the correctness of my previous anticipations'.[10] In the late 1950s he had implied that the territorial state was in demise. Technological change, which he had claimed was a crucial factor in determining the rise of the state, would now facilitate the emergence of new forms of transnational and co-operative governance. Herz felt confident that arguments, which in the 1930s were associated with idealism, were now consistent with realism. What caused him to change his mind was not only the failure of political leaders to pay any more attention to him than they had when he worked for the State Department.

Herz identifies three reasons for the continuation of territoriality as a marker of political differentiation. First, decolonisation had led to a remarkable 'creation' of new states, and Herz admitted that he had not anticipated the speed with which 'old empires' had collapsed. Second, Herz admitted that the technological determinism of his earlier argument was in fact deterministic. He had not acknowledged the power of nationalism in sustaining the territorial state regardless of its military permeability in the nuclear age. Third, whilst Herz continued to lament the arms race between the two superpowers, he later claimed that the balance of terror was more robust than he had thought a decade earlier. In 1968 he argued that, if the nuclear arms race was to be controlled in the future, a 'holding operation' was necessary. This would consist of a set of policies such as 'arms control, demarcation of bloc spheres, avoidance of nuclear proliferation ... and reducing the role of the ideologies of communism and anticommunism'.[11]

This is the context in which Herz defended the policies of détente in the late 1960s and early 1970s. He did so by reinforcing the distinction between constraints that were inherent in the security dilemma and misplaced perceptions of those constraints based on inappropriate images of international relations. For example, in 1974 he was vigorous in attacking the idea, then proposed by some conservative critics, that détente was a form of 'appeasement'.[12] Herz argued that there was very little similarity between the international political situation of the 1930s and the 1970s. The United States was negotiating from a position of strength, not weakness. The existence of nuclear weapons ensured that 'aggression' on the part of the (then) Soviet Union would be an act of suicide, not opportunism, and that détente, far from being a radical departure from realism, was in fact merely a prerequisite for more radical policies in the 'common interest' of humankind in survival.

During the 1980s, Herz became increasingly disillusioned with American foreign policy. Détente, upon which he had placed so much hope, collapsed and was replaced by what Fred Halliday famously called the 'second' Cold War.[13] The renewal of the nuclear arms race, the superpowers' intervention in Afghanistan and Central America, and their failure to even begin tackling ecological and demographic problems all helped to impart 'a despairing and anguished romanticism' to his writing.[14]

Herz does not think that the end of the Cold War justifies complacency in the analysis of international relations. The Cold War came to an end because one superpower could no longer sustain its competition with the West, on ideological or economic terms. It did not come to an end as a result of any policy-makers deciding to place the 'human' interest over the 'national' interest. Although the fear of nuclear war between the great powers has lessened, it has been replaced by new fears of nuclear proliferation and the legacy of old images lives on. For example, the United States continues to evoke the legacy 'appeasement' in justifying its policies towards Iraq, and there is no indication that what Herz calls 'a survival ethic' has replaced what he disparages as 'regional parochial' ethics in international relations. In his retirement, Herz has dedicated himself to what he calls 'survival research', less concerned with descriptive and explanatory analyses of contemporary international relations than with urging us to abandon the images of international relations that make 'regional parochialism' possible.

Notes

1 John Herz, *Political Realism and Political Idealism: A Study in Theories and Realities*, Chicago, University of Chicago Press, 1951, p. 129.
2 John Herz, 'Political realism revisited', *International Studies Quarterly* 25 (1981), p. 184.
3 Ibid., p. 185.
4 John Herz, 'International relations: ideological aspects', *International Encyclopaedia of the Social Sciences*, London, Macmillan, 1968, pp. 72–3.
5 John Herz, 'An internationalist's journey through the century', in Joseph Kruzel and James N. Rosenau (eds), *Journeys Through World Politics: Autobiographical Reflections of Thirty-Four Academic Travellers*, Lexington, Massachusetts, Lexington Books, 1989, p. 252.
6 See, for example, John Herz (ed.), *From Dictatorship to Democracy: Coping With the Legacies of Authoritarianism and Totalitarianism*, Westport, Connecticut., Greenwood Press, 1982.

7 John Herz, *Political Realism and Political Idealism*, op. cit., p. 18.
8 Robert N. Berki, *Political Realism*, London, Dent, 1981, p. 29.
9 John Herz, *International Politics in the Atomic Age*, New York, Columbia University Press, 1959, p. 220.
10 John Herz, 'The territorial state revisited – reflections on the future of the nation-state', *Polity* 1 (1968), p. 12.
11 John Herz, 'An internationalist's journey through the century', op. cit., p. 253.
12 John Herz, 'Détente and appeasement from a political scientist's vantage point', in John Herz, *The Nation-State and the Crisis of World Politics: Essays on International Politics in the Twentieth Century*, New York, David McKay, 1976, pp. 279–89.
13 Fred Halliday, *The Making of the Second Cold War*, London, Verso, 1983.
14 Kenneth Thompson, *Masters of International Thought: Major Twentieth-Century Theorists and the World Crisis*, Baton Rouge, Louisiana State University Press, 1980, p. 112.

See also in this book

Carr, Giddens, Mann, Morgenthau

Herz's major writings

'Idealist internationalism and the security dilemma', *World Politics* 2 (1949), pp. 157–80
Political Realism and Political Idealism: A Study in Theories and Realities, Chicago, University of Chicago Press, 1951
'The rise and demise of the territorial state', *World Politics* 9 (1957), pp. 473–93
International Politics in the Atomic Age, New York, Columbia University Press, 1959
Government and Politics in the Twentieth Century (with Gwendolen Margaret Carter), New York, Praeger, 1961
The Government of Germany, New York, Harcourt, Brace & World, 1967
'The territorial state revisited', *Polity* 1 (1968), pp. 11–34
The Nation-State and the Crisis of World Politics: Essays on International Politics in the Twentieth Century, New York, David McKay, 1976
'Technology, ethics, and international relations', *Social Research* 43 (1976), pp. 98–113
'Political realism revisited', *International Studies Quarterly* 25 (1981), pp. 179–83
'An internationalist's journey through the century', in Joseph Kruzel and James N. Rosenau (eds), *Journeys Through World Politics:* *Autobiographical Reflections of Thirty-Four Academic Travellers*, Lexington, Massachusetts, Lexington Books, 1989, pp. 247–61

Further reading

Ashley, Richard K., 'Political realism and human interests', *International Studies Quarterly* 25 (1981), pp. 204–36
Wright, Quincy, 'Realism and idealism in international politics', *World Politics* 5 (1952), pp. 116–28

GEORGE KENNAN

George Frost Kennan was born in Wisconsin in 1904 (the same year, incidentally, as his fellow realist, Hans Morgenthau). He is best known as both a major contributor towards, as well as a trenchant critic of, US foreign policy during the Cold War. Whilst it is not unfair to characterise him as a realist, he is less interested in contributing to international theory than drawing on broad realist principles to analyse and evaluate diplomatic conduct.

In part this is simply a consequence of his background. As a young man he was sent to military school, and then Princeton University, before joining the US Foreign Service in 1926. When President Roosevelt recognised the Soviet Union in 1933, Kennan was sent to the Soviet Union and was stationed in Moscow during the crucial years 1944–6. Perhaps most importantly, he had trained as a Soviet specialist in Riga, the capital of Latvia, in the late 1920s. This was during the brief period of Latvian independence, and Kennan not only came into regular contact with 'White Russian' émigrés, but observed firsthand the rise of Stalin and the ruthless consolidation of his power in the Soviet Union.

Although he was not well known in the United States, this low profile soon changed after he published a famous article in 1947 in the prestigious journal *Foreign Affairs*, although he attempted to maintain his anonymity by signing the article 'Mr X'. It was based on an intensive analysis of 'the sources of Soviet conduct' that he had sent to the State Department in Washington in 1946 (the 'long telegram'). At a time of profound uncertainty and debate over how the United States should conduct relations with the Soviet Union after the end of the Second World War, Kennan's warnings concerning the expansionist drives of the Soviet Union and the need to 'contain' it struck a responsive chord back in the United States, and it led to his appointment as head of the newly created Policy Planning Staff in the State Department, where he remained until retiring as a diplomat in 1950. Although he served briefly as the American ambassador to the Soviet Union in 1952, and again in the early 1960s as the ambassador to Yugoslavia when President Kennedy was trying to improve US relations with Tito, George Kennan spent most of his working life at Princeton University at the Institute for Advanced Study. There he produced a stream of books and articles on US foreign policy, the history of the Soviet Union, and the impact of nuclear weapons on international relations during the Cold War.

What emerges from his work is the outlook of a conservative, aristocratic critic of some of the most revolutionary changes in world politics, with a nostalgic fondness for the relatively more sedate world of Europe in the eighteenth and nineteenth centuries. Despite his fame and the sheer volume of his writing, Kennan has never felt part of the United States. Even at the height of his influence in the late 1940s he lamented the apparent inability of American leaders to understand the subtlety of his thought, and in much of his work he repudiates policies and practices implemented in the name of 'containment', a doctrine that will always be associated with his name.

To understand his disillusionment with American foreign policy, one has to appreciate both the ways in which it departed from Kennan's vision, as well as Kennan's deeply felt regrets about the evolution of international politics from a European-centred multipolar system to a bipolar system based on the dominance of two nuclear superpowers. In the late 1940s, Kennan argued that international stability depended upon a recreation of a multipolar order that had been destroyed by world war. In particular, he advocated that the United States should use its enormous economic strength to help restore Europe and Japan as great powers, so that the burden of containing the Soviet threat could be shared rather than borne alone by a country that Kennan suspected was incapable of behaving in a moderate fashion abroad. As far as he was concerned, the aims of containment should have been limited to the defence and restoration of areas of crucial military–industrial power. In terms of method, he insisted that the best way in which the United States could achieve this was by offering economic aid to the war-torn economies of Europe and Japan. This would enable them both to recover their status and to weaken the appeal of indigenous, radical or communist movements. Although his early writings stressed the revolutionary challenge of communism to international order, he always believed that, if the Soviet Union were geographically 'contained', its appeal to other states would diminish over time and, indeed, it would undergo gradual internal changes that might transform its status from a revolutionary state to a more moderate great power. Unlike others trained at Riga, he never worried about communist 'grand designs' to conquer the globe. In an incisive analysis written as the Cold War was fading into history, Richard Barnet identifies four crucial factors that account for the failure of the Truman administration to follow Kennan's advice.[1]

First, the United States enjoyed a nuclear monopoly in the 1940s that inspired Truman and some of his advisers to believe that nuclear weapons could be used to intimidate Stalin and achieve concrete concessions to American demands. Second, in the absence of any firm means of predicting Soviet foreign policy, the Truman administration relied heavily on the alleged 'lessons of history' of the 1930s, namely, the self-defeating nature of 'appeasement' in the face of authoritarian aggression. Although the Marshall Plan was consistent with Kennan's emphasis on economic aid, he was aghast at the language used in the formulation of the 'Truman Doctrine' in 1947 which appeared to commit the United States to an open-ended support of any regimes confronted with 'internal subversion' supported by the Soviet Union. Third, the United States was very eager to cement Germany in a Western alliance, and this required the presence of American troops on German soil as part of what was to become (in 1949) NATO. Finally, Kennan underestimated the degree of volatility in American public opinion. As Barnet puts it, '[the Truman administration] had run into trouble when they tried to present a nuanced view of the situation in Europe, and a consensus swiftly developed in the administration that scaring the hell out of the American people ... was essential for combating the isolationist mood'.[2]

Consequently, Kennan's original formulation of containment was, in his view, distorted by the conflation of the Soviet threat with communism in general, the emphasis on military means rather than economic ones and the geographical expansion of the Cold War into Asia. In the mid-1960s, like Morgenthau, Kennan was a stern critic of US foreign policy in Vietnam. Consistent with his emphasis on 'strongpoint' as opposed to 'perimeter' defence, in 1967 he testified to the Senate Foreign Relations committee that Vietnam was not vital to the United States' strategic interests, and that the prestige of the country would not be hurt if it withdrew from the conflict. Oddly enough, Kennan

shared the view of many radicals in the peace movement that the American conduct of the Cold War could undermine the very ideals of freedom and democracy that the United States claimed to be defending, both at home and abroad. Such ideals could best be promoted if the United States tried to be an example to the rest of the world and refrained from trying to impose its ideals on other states, or supporting authoritarian regimes simply on the basis of their 'anti-communist' credentials.

Much of Kennan's writing is concerned with the question of whether the United States is capable of behaving like a 'traditional' European great power. In his essays and lectures, particularly in the volume *American Diplomacy, 1900–1950*, he bemoaned what he liked to call American's tendency to adopt 'a legalistic-moralistic approach to international politics'. This was inevitable in a democracy like the United States, but it interfered with a cool calculation of the national interest on the basis of long-term trends in the balance of power rather than short-term fluctuations. A moral reaction is a short-term phenomenon when the public perceives the national interest to be at stake. Having no intensive knowledge of the situation and lacking accurate facts even more than officialdom, citizens often have no option but to express their concerns in crude and moral terms. As a reliable guide to the conduct of foreign affairs, however, such reactions may have disastrous longer-term effects. For example, Kennan argued that the so-called 'fall of China' in 1949 did not represent a golden opportunity for the Soviet Union to cement a communist alliance against the West, but instead represented a major challenge to the Soviet Union as the leader of the communist movement. In an interview in 1972, and just prior to Nixon's attempt to normalise relations with China, Kennan pointed out

the position of Moscow as the 'third Rome' of international communism is essential to the carefully cultivated Soviet image of self. Take it away, and the whole contrived history of Soviet Communism, its whole rationale and sense of legitimacy, is threatened. Moscow must oppose China with real desperation, because China threatens the intactness of its own sense of identity.[3]

Although Kennan was a supporter of the policy of détente between the superpowers in the late 1960s and early 1970s, it would be wrong to argue that the subsequent history of relations between the United States and the Soviet Union fully bears out the validity of Kennan's original vision of containment. Certainly the Soviet Union, as he had predicted, did 'mellow' over time, and the dramatic policies followed by Gorbachev in the late 1980s testify to the inability of the Soviet Union to maintain its competition with the United States on a rapidly shrinking economic base. Yet Kennan takes no pleasure from the ending of the Cold War, which in his view might have occurred many years prior to the late 1980s without the enormous costs of the nuclear arms race. Indeed, the latter is an excellent example of the way in which US foreign policy had been distorted by an irrational fear that the Soviet Union might consider using nuclear weapons as rational means to expand its territory in Europe or engage in some form of nuclear blackmail.

Although the vast bulk of Kennan's work has been devoted to diplomatic statecraft (or rather its lamentable absence during much of the Cold War), the reader must pore though his memoirs to distill the philosophical outlook that informs Kennan's views on foreign policy in the twentieth century. Like many classical 'realists', Kennan has always harboured a tragic view of the human condition. In his latest book *Around the Cragged Hill*, he describes humans as 'cracked vessels', doomed to mediate between our animal nature and an almost divine inspiration to escape the contingency of human limitations. It is always a constant struggle to control our more base passions and cultivate civilisation. Whilst he would agree with other realists that we cannot avoid the struggle for power that is inextricably linked with human nature, we are not animals and our capacity for reason and morality obliges us to develop virtues that cannot be guaranteed to manifest themselves in any political system. His concern with democracies such as the United States is that public officials are always tempted to do what is popular rather than what is right and virtuous. Similarly, in much of his work Kennan is deeply suspicious of free-market capitalism, which thrives on self-interest and greed.

George Kennan will be remembered as one of the most persistent, influential and trenchant critics of US foreign policy in the twentieth century. He has not been without his critics, however. One of the difficulties lies in his constant appeal to *the national interest* as a guide to foreign policy. He often implies that if only governments followed their long-term interests, as opposed to their short-term passions, order and stability would result. Yet this depends upon some consensus among governments, particularly among the great powers, on the values of maintaining some fair distribution of power among them and therefore the limits that they have to respect in seeking to represent the interests of their citizens. As Michael Smith has pointed out, 'Kennan never considered whether, or how, the necessary consensus around those values could be built'.[4] For those who wish to build on Kennan's legacy in the post-Cold War era, this is no less daunting a challenge than it was when Kennan began publishing his work in the 1940s.

Notes

1 Richard J. Barnet, 'A balance sheet: Lippmann, Kennan, and the Cold War', in M. Hogan (ed.) *The End of the Cold War: Its Meaning and*

Implications, Cambridge, Cambridge University Press, 1992, pp. 113–27.
2 Ibid., p. 122.
3 'Interview with George F. Kennan', *Foreign Policy* 7 (1972), p. 10.
4 Michael Smith, *Realist Thought From Weber to Kissinger*, Baton Rouge, Louisiana State University Press, 1986, p. 236.

See also in this book

Aron, Kissinger, Morgenthau

Kennan's major writings

'The sources of Soviet conduct', *Foreign Affairs* 25 (1947), pp. 566–82
American Diplomacy 1900–1950, Chicago, Chicago University Press, 1951
Realities of American Foreign Policy, Princeton, New Jersey, Princeton University Press, 1954
Soviet–American Relations, 1917–1920, London, Faber & Faber, 1958
Russia, the Atom and the West, London, Oxford University Press, 1958
Soviet Foreign Policy, 1917–1941, Princeton, New Jersey, D. Van Nostrand, 1960
Russia and the West Under Lenin and Stalin, Boston, Little, Brown, 1961
Memoirs: 1925–1950, London, Hutchinson, 1968
From Prague After Munich: Diplomatic Papers, 1938–1940, Princeton, New Jersey, Princeton University Press, 1968
Memoirs: 1950–1963, London, Hutchinson, 1973
The Cloud of Danger: Current Realities of American Foreign Policy, Boston, Little, Brown, 1977
The Decline of Bismarck's European Order: Franco–Russian Relations, 1875–1890, Princeton, New Jersey, Princeton University Press, 1979
The Nuclear Delusion: Soviet–American Relations in the Atomic Age, New York, Pantheon Books, 1982
The Fateful Alliance: France, Russia and the Coming of the First World War, Manchester, Manchester University Press, 1984
Around the Cragged Hill: A Personal and Political Philosophy, New York, W.W. Norton, 1993
At a Century's Ending: Reflections, 1982–1995, New York, W.W. Norton, 1996

Further reading

Gaddis, John Lewis, 'Containment: a reassessment', *Foreign Affairs* 60 (1977), pp. 873–88
Gelman, Barton, *Contending With Kennan: Toward a Philosophy of American Power*, New York, Praeger, 1984
Harper, John L., *American Visions of Europe: Franklin D. Roosevelt, George F. Kennan, and Dean G. Acheson*, Cambridge, Cambridge University Press, 1994
Herz, Martin F., *Decline of the West?: George Kennan and his Critics*, Washington DC, Ethics and Public Policy Center, Georgetown University, 1978
Hixson, Walter L., *George F. Kennan: Cold War Iconoclast*, New York, Columbia University Press, 1989
Mayers, David, *George Kennan and the Dilemmas of US Foreign Policy*, New York, Oxford University Press, 1988
Miscamble, Wilson Douglas, *George F. Kennan and the Making of American Foreign Policy, 1947–1950*, Princeton, New Jersey, Princeton University Press, 1992
Smith, Michael J., *Realist Thought From Weber to Kissinger*, Baton Rouge, Louisiana State University Press, 1986, pp.165–91
Stephenson, Anders, *Kennan and the Art of Foreign Policy*, Cambridge, Massachusetts, Harvard University Press, 1989
Travis, Frederick F., *George Kennan and the American–Russian Relationship, 1865–1924*, Athens, Ohio University Press, 1990

HENRY KISSINGER

Henry Kissinger was United States Secretary of State from 1973 to 1977. He was also President Nixon's National Security Advisor in the late 1960s and survived Nixon's fall from power during the Watergate scandal of the early 1970s. At one point he held both posts simultaneously, a reflection of his desire and ability to control American foreign policy and centralise executive power as much as possible. He was the chief architect of the policy of détente in the late 1960s and early 1970s, the opening to China and 'shuttle diplomacy' to the Middle East. Before joining the White House, Kissinger was a member of the Faculty at Harvard University and had written widely and critically on American foreign policy in the Cold War. Indeed, many consider his tenure of office as a period during which Kissinger attempted to implement a new 'realist' approach to the conduct of foreign affairs, and some of the alleged shortcomings of realism are often illustrated by the policies of Henry Kissinger. Since leaving office in 1977, Kissinger has continued to write books and articles and has remained active as a television commentator, lecturer and political consultant.

Kissinger was born in Fuerth, Germany, on 27 May 1923. His family arrived in the United States in 1938, having fled the Nazi persecution of the Jews. During the Second World War, Kissinger served in the US Army Counter-Intelligence Corps. After the war, he began an academic career in political science at Harvard, receiving his BA (1950), PhD (1954), teaching in the Government Department (1957–71) and directing the university's Defense Studies Programme from 1958 to 1969. Whilst at Harvard, Kissinger also served as a consultant to the State Department, the Rand Corporation and the National Security Council.

In his approach to the theory and practice of foreign policy and diplomacy, Kissinger has sought to challenge and recast what he perceives to be the traditional American approach to the world. This is a constant theme in his writing from his doctoral dissertation *A World Restored* (1957) to his latest book, *Diplomacy* (1994). His own approach is based on the European diplomatic tradition, often referred to as *realpolitik*, as it developed from the seventeenth to the nineteenth century. Two ideas are central to this tradition. First, there is the idea of *raison d'état*, or reason of state, where the interests of the state justify the use of external means that would seem repugnant within a well-ordered domestic polity. Second, Kissinger believes that it is the duty of the statesman, particularly of a great power like the United States, to manipulate the balance of power in order to maintain an international order in which no one state dominates the rest. All 'status quo' states

benefit from a 'legitimate' international order in which they can maintain their independence by aligning themselves with, or opposing, other states according to shifts in the balance. As a diplomat, Kissinger follows in the footsteps of Cardinal Richelieu, William of Orange, Frederick the Great, Metternich, Castlereagh and Bismark. As a scholar, he writes in the realist tradition of Max Weber, and he has much in common with Hans Morgenthau and George Kennan. He accepts the view that international relations take place in an arena that lacks a central authority to arbitrate conflicts of interest and value among states. Since states are equal only in a formal, legal sense and very unequal in a military and economic sense, international relations will take the form of a struggle for power between them. However, the struggle may be contained if the great powers are led by individuals who can contrive a 'legitimate' order, and work out between them some consensus on the limits within which the struggle should be controlled.

This is the central theme of one of Kissinger's earliest works, *A World Restored* (1957), based on his doctoral dissertation, which is a careful examination of the nineteenth-century Concert of Europe. In describing how the diplomats managed to contrive such a balance after 1815, Kissinger focuses on two characteristics of the era, which he both admired and to some extent sought to recreate in the very different period of the late 1960s. The first was the existence of a cosmopolitan European culture among the diplomats who met at the Congress of Vienna. They were able to subscribe to a shared system of values that mitigated the clash of national interests. Second, and this helped to sustain such a culture, Kissinger admires the relative autonomy of foreign policymaking from domestic politics. The tension between the creativity of statecraft and the drudgery of bureaucracy and domestic politics is one that recurs throughout his work. As he declares:

Inspiration implies the identification of the self with the meaning of events. Organisation requires discipline, the submission to the will of the group. Inspiration is timeless, its validity inherent in its conception. Organisation is historical, depending on the material available at a given period. Inspiration is a call to greatness; organisation a recognition that mediocrity is the usual pattern of leadership.[1]

The publication of *A World Restored* was made possible by the popularity of Kissinger's first book, *Nuclear Weapons and American Foreign Policy* (1957). In this book, Kissinger argues that the United States can no longer rely on the strategy of 'massive retaliation' followed by Eisenhower and Dulles. Kissinger warned that as soon as the Soviet Union achieved some kind of nuclear parity with the United States, such a strategy would leave the United States no options in the event of Soviet 'adventurism' using conventional weapons. So he argued that the United States should prepare to fight a limited nuclear war with the Soviet Union. In the late 1950s, Kissinger essentially assumed a dangerous, Cold War, bipolar, zero-sum confrontation between the superpowers. His academic interest was in examining how the United States could maintain good relations with Western Europe in light of the confrontation. This was the theme of his next two books, which are of interest today only insofar as their focus of concern was surprisingly absent from Kissinger's conduct of diplomacy when he moved into the White House with Richard Nixon in 1969.

To some extent, it is possible to interpret Kissinger's diplomacy over the next few years as an attempt to recreate certain elements of the Congress of Vienna in the turbulent era of the 1960s. His challenge was two-fold. First, he wanted to extricate the United States from the Vietnam War without damaging the 'credibility' of the United States as a superpower in the eyes of its allies and enemies alike. Second, he wanted to improve relations with the Soviet Union so that the Russians would not try and take advantage of an apparent defeat by the United States, and so that the superpowers could create some 'rules of engagement' that would limit the competition between them. The key to achieving this dual aim was the idea of 'linkage'. The idea was for the United States to 'pursue a carrot and stick approach, ready to impose penalties for adventurism, and to be willing to expand relations in the context of responsible behaviour'.[2] Improvements in superpower relations, according to Kissinger, depended on the American ability and willingness to induce Soviet 'good behaviour' by rewarding co-operation and deterring Soviet 'adventurism', particularly in the Third World. This, in turn, required the United States to be able to manipulate relations of 'interdependence' in arms control, trade and other areas. The 'opening to China' was part of this overall strategy.

Of course, the strategy of linkage ultimately failed in its intended aim of bringing about a more stable balance of power 'managed' by the United States with Kissinger manipulating the levers of influence. By the mid-1970s, détente was a dirty word in American politics, and Gerald Ford refused even to use the term during his presidential campaign in 1975. There were three main reasons for the failure, which illustrate some of the difficulties of realism as a guide to the conduct of foreign policy.

The first problem was that the Soviet Union did not appear to understand the rules of the balance of power as laid down by Kissinger. Although the aging Soviet leadership acknowledged the need for peaceful coexistence with the United States in light of the nuclear threat and its desire for the United States to recognise a Soviet sphere of influence in Eastern Europe, this did not mean the end to competition. For the Soviet Union, détente (relaxation of tensions) was made possible by the Soviet achievements in the arms race and the American recognition of the Soviet Union as a superpower. It did not mean, or require, cohabitation on American terms. So Kissinger was outraged when the Soviet Union did not put enough pressure on North Vietnam to make concessions during the Paris Peace negotiations to end the Vietnam War quickly, and when it appeared to take advantage of better trade relations with the United States to promote Soviet influence in the Third World (for example, in its support for radical 'freedom fighters' in Angola and Chile in the early 1970s). This raised the question of whether the Soviet Union was committed to the status quo, or whether it was still a revolutionary force in international affairs, the leader of the communist world. Depending on one's assessment, the 'manipulation' of the relevant balance of forces could require, and help to bring about, either co-operation or conflict. Philip Windsor summarises the problem as follows:

> If the Russians need American grain-plus-computers ... and are offered help with these as part of a set of agreements leading up to a SALT treaty, then surely they are likely to accept the necessity of calculating their whole range of interests together, and behaving in the prudential and rational manner which would square with the requirements of world order. [But] suppose they feel they can swap good behaviour in SALT for economically advantageous deals, but do not feel any need to extend this pattern of behaviour to the Middle East?[3]

The second major problem was the difficulty Kissinger had in controlling the behaviour of third parties, which was essential if the United States was to carry out a very delicate and complex strategy. To give just some examples, Kissinger was unable to control the pace of co-operation between East and West Germany, which proceeded faster

than he would have liked. He was also unable to convince the South Vietnamese government that the 'Vietnamisation' of the war (by gradually bringing American ground troops home and handing over military responsibility to the South Vietnamese) was not simply to buy time before the United States abandoned its ally. Similarly, he tended to assume that the Soviet Union had more influence over its allies (such as North Vietnam or Cuba) than was actually the case.

The third major problem was his manifest failure to persuade the American people that détente was in the national interest. He was criticised from the Left for secretly escalating the war in Vietnam and Cambodia as he and Nixon relied increasingly on devastating air strikes to achieve greater 'progress' during the protracted peace negotiations. He was criticised from the Right for his refusal to extend the process of 'linkage' to the Soviet Union's respect for human rights within its own country. However, Kissinger argued that the United States should focus on Soviet foreign policy and subordinate issues such as Jewish emigration and the treatment of political prisoners to the more important quest for international stability as defined by him. Also, despite Kissinger's attempt to centralise the control of American foreign policy in the White House, he had to confront a suspicious Congress increasingly intent on weakening executive power and autonomy.

In his memoirs, Kissinger acknowledges these and other problems, but he still believes that his fundamental strategy for détente was sound, and he blames Watergate and the failure of the American people to understand the art of realist statecraft. He did have some success, however. For a while in the early 1970s he achieved more popularity than any other modern American diplomat. The Gallup poll listed him as the most admired man in America in 1972 and 1973. He received the Nobel Peace Prize in 1973 for his negotiations leading to the Paris peace accords that ended American military involvement in Vietnam, but his reputation soon faded. During the Watergate scandal, congressional investigators discovered that he had ordered the FBI to tap the telephones of subordinates on the staff of the National Security Council. By the mid-1970s, his achievements in foreign policy were also being re-evaluated. The communist victory in Vietnam, and the rise to power of Pol Pot in Cambodia, destroyed the Paris peace accords. There was little progress being made on arms control talks with the Soviet Union, and President-elect Carter accused him of engaging in ineffective 'lone ranger diplomacy' during the presidential campaign of 1976. The 'structure of peace' that he had promised to deliver in 1969 was giving way to a 'new' Cold War between the superpowers, and by 1977 Kissinger had lost control over American foreign policy.

In his latest book, *Diplomacy* (1994), Kissinger reflects on the challenges for the United States in the post-Cold War era. Much of the book is taken up with the practice of realist statecraft, exemplified by Cardinal Richelieu, the First Minister of France in the seventeenth century. Kissinger traces the history of diplomacy over the last couple of centuries, and many of the themes developed in *A World Restored* are reproduced. He points out that the 'European tradition' of diplomacy is not totally alien to the United States since he regards the American Founders, Theodore Roosevelt and Richard Nixon in his pantheon of practitioners of balance-of-power politics. In the 1990s and into the next century, Kissinger argues that the need for a legitimate international order is as great as it has ever been and the United States needs to guard against an unwarranted resumption of Wilsonian 'idealism'. The dominant 'American tradition', he argues, sees foreign policy only as a means to protecting and promoting individual freedom and well being. In Kissinger's account, the United States sees itself as an exceptional nation due to its republican form of government, the benign circumstances attending its development and the innate virtue of its citizenry. He argues that this tradition points in two opposite and equally unfortunate directions. The first response is the isolationist withdrawal of America from international affairs, so as to perfect its own democratic institutions and serve as a beacon for the rest of humanity. The second, more recent response is to engage in crusades for democracy around the world, as a means to transform the old international system into a global international order based on democracy, free commerce and international law. In such a world peace will be the natural outcome of relations among peoples and nations, rather than as the result of a flexible if often unstable and unjust balance of power.

For most of its history, Kissinger argues, the United States chose the first course, isolationism. But during the second half of the twentieth century, the second American path, that of crusading internationalism, dominated. For Kissinger, as for Kennan and Morgenthau, Woodrow Wilson is the exemplar of American internationalism. He acknowledges and celebrates the fact that the United States did succeed in bringing down the Soviet Union. Nevertheless, he believes that American foreign policy during the Cold War was excessively moralistic and insufficiently attuned to the realities of the balance of power. He particularly criticises the view that the former Soviet Union was an ideological rather than a geopolitical threat. As a result of this misperception, Kissinger argues, America's Cold War success was far more costly than it could have been. The tragedy of Vietnam, rather than the triumph of the fall of the Berlin Wall, dominates his reflections on American policy during the Cold War.

The lesson to be learnt, he argues, is that the United States should not expect the end of the Cold War to result in a radically new international system. In what he believes to be an emerging multipolar world, the relative decline of American power since 1945 precludes the United States from dominating the world, just as its interdependence with the rest of the world precludes withdrawal. To summarise his views, he identifies two areas where the balance of power should be applied. In Europe, Russia and Germany are the powers that the United States needs to focus upon. The United States has an interest in ensuring that a united Germany and a resurgent Russia do not compete over the centre of the Europe, as they did in the first half of the century. This requires the continuation of the American presence in Europe and the enlargement of NATO to the east. In Asia, Kissinger argues that the United States must balance China against Japan and help them to coexist despite their suspicion of each other.

There is much value in Kissinger's analysis of the international system at the end of the twentieth century, although his critique of American foreign policy is simply conventional wisdom among realists. As usual, he stresses the distinction between the 'high' politics of military and geopolitical issues and the 'low' politics of trade and economics, which many scholars would argue is becoming increasingly blurred. Ironically, however, his emphasis on the primacy of national interests and power balances may turn out to be more politically palatable in the United States today than when he was the architect of American foreign policy in the midst of the Cold War and Vietnam.

Notes

1 Henry Kissinger, *A World Restored: Metternich, Castlereagh and the Problems of Peace, 1812–22*, London, Weidenfeld & Nicolson, 1957, p. 317.
2 Henry Kissinger, *White House Years*, Boston, Little, Brown, 1979, p. 120.
3 Philip Windsor, 'Henry Kissinger's scholarly contribution', *British Journal of International Studies* 1 (1975), p. 35.

See also in this book

Kennan, Morgenthau, Wilson

Kissinger's major writings

Nuclear Weapons and Foreign Policy, New York, Harper, 1957
A World Restored: Metternich, Castlereagh and the Problems of Peace, 1812–22, London, Weidenfeld & Nicolson, 1957
The Necessity for Choice: Prospects of American Foreign Policy, New York, Harper, 1961
The Troubled Partnership: A Re-appraisal of the Atlantic Alliance, New York, McGraw-Hill, 1965
American Foreign Policy: Three Essays, London, Weidenfeld & Nicolson, 1969
White House Years, Boston, Little, Brown, 1979
Years of Upheaval, Boston, Little, Brown, 1982
Observations: Selected Speeches and Essays, 1982–1984, London, Michael Joseph, 1985
Diplomacy, New York, Simon & Schuster, 1994

Further reading

Bell, Coral, *The Diplomacy of Détente: The Kissinger Era*, London, Martin Robertson, 1977
Brodine, Virginia and Selden, Mark (eds), *Open Secret: The Kissinger–Nixon Doctrine in Asia*, New York, Harper & Row, 1972
Chomsky, Noam, *Towards a New Cold War: Essays on the Current Crisis and How We Got There*, New York, Pantheon Books, 1982
Cleva, Gregory D., *Henry Kissinger and the American Approach to Foreign Policy*, London, Associated University Press, 1989
Dickson, Peter W., *Kissinger and the Meaning of History*, New York, Cambridge University Press, 1978
Hersh, Seymour M., *The Price of Power: Kissinger in the Nixon White House*, New York, Summit Books, 1983
Isaacson, Walter, *Kissinger: A Biography*, London, Faber & Faber, 1992
Landau, David, *Kissinger: The Uses of Power*, Boston, Houghton, 1972
McDougall, Walter, 'Oh Henry! Kissinger and his critics', *Orbis* 38 (1994), pp. 657–72
Mazlish, Bruce, *Kissinger: The European Mind in American Policy*, New York, Basic Books, 1976
Morris, Roger, *Uncertain Greatness: Henry Kissinger and American Foreign Policy*, New York, Harper & Row, 1977
Schulzinger, Robert D., *Henry Kissinger: Doctor of Diplomacy*, New York, Columbia University Press, 1989

Shawcross, William, *Sideshow: Kissinger, Nixon, and the Destruction of Cambodia*, New York, Simon & Schuster, 1979

Smith, Michael J., *Realist Thought From Weber to Kissinger*, Baton Rouge, Louisiana State University Press, 1986

Stoessinger, John G., *Henry Kissinger: The Anguish of Power*, New York, W.W. Norton, 1976

STEPHEN KRASNER

At the end of his autobiographical reflections on his career thus far, Stephen Krasner urges students 'to resist succumbing to the fashion of the moment and to try to develop a mode of inquiry that does lend itself to some form of empirical validation, even if such validation can never be fully compelling'.[1] These are virtues which Krasner's work exhibits in abundance. They also explain his stature in the field as a scholar who refuses to follow the conventional wisdom of the day and whose fidelity to the ideals of empirical social science provides a model for others to emulate, even if they may dissent from his arguments. In an era when realism seemed to be under constant criticism from so many quarters, and in a sub-field of inquiry whose *raison d'être* is often alleged to be the absence of inquiry into economics by classical realists concerned with military security, Krasner's work has helped to breathe new life into the realist paradigm. Along with the work of Kenneth Waltz and Robert Gilpin, his contribution to the study of international political economy has helped to entice some liberal scholars (such as Robert Keohane) to present their own work as a modification of structural realism rather than a direct challenge to its core assumptions:

> Realism is a theory about *international* politics. It is an effort to explain both the behavior of individual states and the characteristics of the international system as a

whole. The ontological given for realism is that sovereign states are the constitutive components of the international system. Sovereignty is a political order based on territorial control. The international system is anarchical. It is a self-help system. There is no higher authority that can constrain or channel the behavior of states. Sovereign states are rational self-seeking actors resolutely if not exclusively concerned with relative gains because they must function in an anarchical environment in which their security and well-being ultimately rest on their ability to mobilize their own resources against external threats.[2]

In the 1960s and early 1970s, when Krasner was a young graduate student engaged in his doctoral research and later a faculty member of the Department of Political Science at Harvard University, all these assumptions were being questioned. In particular, there was a perception that insofar as they had ever been correct, international politics was undergoing immense structural change. The United States' failure to win the Vietnam War, the oil crisis and looming trade problems with Japan occurred at the same time as many observers began to suggest that 'anarchy' was being replaced by a phenomenon of 'complex interdependence' among states. The traditional agenda of international relations, it was often claimed, was shifting from issues of 'high politics' (military security and nuclear deterrence) to what were sometimes regarded as the 'low politics' of trade and international finance. It was also a period when the state itself was no longer regarded as a unitary, rational actor among foreign policy analysts. In particular, the work of Graham Allison suggested that this assumption was often an inadequate guide to understanding governmental decision making in the United States and, by implication, other states as well.[3]

This was the context in which Krasner, who at the time saw himself as 'something of a gadfly' in his own Department at Harvard, wrote his pathbreaking article 'State power and the structure of international trade' (1976) which, according to Robert Keohane, 'defined the agenda [of IPE in the United States] for years of scholarship'.[4] Krasner's argument is an attempt to account for variations in the 'openness' of the world economy, focusing on trade as his criterion of openness/closure, and measured in terms of tariff levels between states, trade as a proportion of gross national product and the degree to which trade is concentrated at a regional level. An open world economy is one in which tariffs are low; there is a high ratio of trade to national income, and a low regional concentration of trade. Having established his dependent variable, Krasner then examines variations in the distribution of economic power among states over the last 200 years, measured in terms of per capita income, gross national product and shares of world trade and investment. On the basis of his careful analysis of the empirical data, Krasner then makes a number of bold propositions and explains them by appealing to the continuing importance of the realist approach. He argues that periods of openness in the world economy correlate with periods in which one state is clearly predominant. In the nineteenth century it was Great Britain. In the period 1945–60, it was the United States. Consequently, the degree of openness is itself dependent on the distribution of power among states. Economic 'interdependence' is subordinate to the political and economic balance of power among states, not the other way round.

Krasner's explanation for his findings relies on realist assumptions about state interests. A powerful state with a technological advantage over other states will desire an open trading system as it seeks new export markets. Furthermore, large, powerful, states are less exposed to the international economy than small ones, so what Krasner called 'the opportunity costs of closure' will be lower too. Furthermore,

they are less vulnerable to changes from abroad and can use this power to maintain their access to overseas markets. On the other hand, if power is more evenly distributed among states, they are less likely to support an open trading system. The less economically developed states will try to avoid the political danger of becoming vulnerable to pressure from others, whilst states whose hegemony may be declining fear a loss of power to their rivals and find it hard to resist domestic pressures for protection from cheap imports. A crucial factor in Krasner's argument is his claim that states do not always privilege wealth over other goals. Political power and social stability are also crucial and this means that, although open trade may well provide absolute gains for all states who engage in it, some states will gain more than others. What is rational for the collective good of states is not necessarily the case for individual states. In his appraisal of Krasner's argument and its contribution to the evolution of IPE, Keohane makes the interesting point that it was powerful not only because it subverted the conventional wisdom of liberals, but because it contained flaws and suggested further avenues for research that inspired a whole generation of scholars in the late 1970s and 1980s.

Since the publication of his seminal 1976 article, Krasner has continued to elaborate its arguments and apply them across a range of issues in IPE. In 1978 he published his first book *Defending the National Interest*. Here, in contrast to liberals and Marxists, Krasner examines the United States' policy towards raw material investments abroad during the twentieth century. His core argument is that the state is an autonomous entity that seeks to implement the 'national interest' against both domestic and international actors. In particular, he looks at those acts and statements of central decision makers in the White House and the State Department that aim to improve the general welfare and show a persistent rank-ordering in time. What emerges from this study is that the American national interest in the international commodity markets has three components, ranked in order of increasing importance: stimulating economic competition; insuring security of supply; and promoting broader foreign policy goals, such as general material interests and ideological objectives. His claim is that while smaller states focus on preserving their territorial and political integrity and their narrow economic interests, only great powers will try to remake the world in their own image. Since 1945 the United States has been such a great power, and the key to its foreign policy is ideology, namely, anti-communism. Although this policy has been generally conducive to the growth of multinational corporations based in the United States, it cannot be fully explained merely as the long-term preservation of capitalism. Krasner attacks Marxist structuralists for their failure to explain the United States' involvement in the Vietnam War, which caused so much domestic dissent for so little economic gain. On the basis of his analysis of the evidence, Krasner concludes that United States decision makers were often willing to protect the interests of American corporations, but they reserved the large-scale use of force for ideological reasons. This explains the use of force against Vietnam, an area of negligible economic importance to the United States, and the reluctance to use force during the oil crises of the 1970s, which threatened the oil supply to the entire capitalist world.

In a recent defence of the book's argument, Krasner makes it clear that the main focus of *Defending the National Interest* was not a direct defence of realism and its portrayal of the international system, but rather 'an effort to demonstrate the empirical plausibility of an important realist assertion: namely, that states could be treated as unified rational actors'.[5] The national interest is a term that has been used very vaguely both by defenders of realism as well as its critics. For Krasner, it refers to 'an empirically validated set of transitively ordered objectives that did not disproportionately benefit any particular group in a society'.[6] The normative implications of Krasner's book, insofar as there were any, were that statism is not only consistent with realism, but something to be welcomed because it frustrates the ability of populist, economically privileged or other self-serving groups from capturing the state and shaping its policies for their own ends.

In the late 1970s and early 1980s, Krasner turned his analytical and theoretical skills back to the debate that was in part inspired by his 1976 article. As already noted, many of those who argued that interdependence was eroding the 'anarchy' of the states modified their position in light of Krasner's arguments. But he himself had noted that there was not a perfect fit between periods of hegemony and open trade in the world economy. Significantly, there were important gaps in the causal argument and some empirical anomalies. As Keohane points out, '[t]he anomalies – Britain's support of openness after 1900, the failure of the United States to exercise leadership after 1919, and arguably ... U.S. support of openness after 1960 – practically leap off the page'.[7]

Of course, Keohane himself has done a great deal of research into such anomalies. During the early 1980s, he and a number of other scholars were responsible for popularising the idea of 'regimes' as intervening variables between state power on the one hand and international outcomes on the other. Regimes are principles and rules that regulate the interaction of states and other actors across a range of issue-areas and they impart a degree of 'governance' to the international system. Krasner's contribution to the debate on regimes, particularly regarding their capacity to transform state interests and maintain co-operation despite changes in the balance of power, is contained in his provocative book *Structural Conflict: The Third World Against Global Liberalism* (1985).

In this book Krasner argues that small, poor states in the South tend to support those regimes that allocate resources authoritatively, while the richer states in the North will favour those regimes whose principles and rules give priority to market mechanisms. By 'authoritative' regimes, Krasner refers to principles, rules and procedures that increase the sovereign powers of individual states or that give states acting together the right to regulate international flows (such as migration or radio signals) or allocate access to international resources (such as the ocean seabed). In part, the reasons for this difference are straightforward. Third World states try to protect themselves against the operation of markets in which they are at a disadvantage. Transportation is a good example. The Third World has supported the persistence of an authoritative regime governing civil aviation against pressure from the United States to move toward a more market-orientated regime. As a result, Third World states enjoy 'a market share that is more or less proportional to their share of world airline passengers'.[8] In shipping, however, the Third World has not been able to modify significantly the existing market-oriented regime. Consequently, most states in the Third World have a diproportionately low share of world shipping (often less than one-tenth) compared to their share of world cargo.

Krasner's explanation for this marked difference of preferences goes far beyond conventional economics, however. As in all his previous work, he rejects the assumption that states pursue merely wealth and he argues that Third World states are also involved in a struggle for power. They want to reduce their vulnerability to the market by exerting greater state control over it. In this endeavour poorer states are able to use the power of the principle of state sovereignty, according to which all states are equal in a formal, legal sense. Sovereignty provides Third World states with a form of 'metapower', that of a coherent ideology to attack the legitimacy of international market regimes and the inequities of global capitalism. Krasner argues that the Third World's challenge to global liberalism is really an attack on the rules of the game rather than a direct response to economic poverty. For example, he produces evidence to show that poorer countries are collectively better off economically than they were in the past, and that their calls for a New International Economic Order (NIEO) came at a time when their growth and income were at a post-war high. Furthermore, his argument is strengthened by the support of many Third World states for authoritative regimes that conform to the principle of sovereignty but which are also not in the economic interests of individual Third World states. For example, Third World states supported OPEC oil price rises in the 1970s despite their devastating effects on the budgets of those that imported oil.

The upshot of Krasner's realist analysis is that the attempt to establish regimes as a means of overcoming or even attenuating the effects of anarchy is not likely to work. The existence of universal regimes cannot disguise the inequalities of power in international relations, nor can such regimes modify the importance of state sovereignty. Rather, they provide a structural setting in which clashes between North and South are inevitable. Moreover, any clash between the rich and poor states is likely to be resolved in favour of the former. Thus the 'success' of UNESCO in adopting an anti-liberal international information policy was followed by the withdrawal of the United States and its financial support from the organisation. Also, the United States simply refused to sign drafts of the Law of the Sea Treaty that included authoritative mechanisms to regulate deep-sea mining. Krasner is somewhat pessimistic about the ability of regimes to moderate conflicts of interest between North and South, but his work on this issue is a necessary corrective to more benign evaluations that ignore the continuing importance of sovereignty in world politics.

Since 1981, Stephen Krasner has worked at Stanford University as Graham A. Stuart Professor of International Relations. He was the editor of the journal *International Organization* between 1987 and 1992, and is a Fellow of the American Academy of Arts and Sciences. In the 1990s, Krasner has continued to publish important work on the nature of state sovereignty and changes in the global political economy. It testifies to the continuing relevance of realist insights into international relations at the end of the twentieth century. Unlike those who are content to give their allegiance to theoretical approaches on ideological or personal grounds, Krasner is committed to the use of evidence to support his claims, and thereby 'to discipline power with truth'.[9] His work is a good example of how to avoid two academic vices: the manipulation of data in the absence of any larger theoretical context and the temptation to dwell in the realm of meta-theory without relating it to the empirical world.

Notes

1 Stephen Krasner, 'Fortune, virtue, and systematic versus scientific inquiry', in Joseph Kruzel and James N. Rosenau, *Journeys Through World Politics*, Massachusetts, Lexington Books, 1989, p. 426.
2 Stephen Krasner, 'Realism, imperialism, and democracy', *Political Theory* 20 (1992), p. 39.
3 Graham T. Allison, *Essence of Decision: Explaining the Cuban Missile Crisis*, Boston, Little, Brown, 1971.
4 Robert O. Keohane, 'Problematic lucidity: Stephen Krasner's "state power and the structure of international trade"', *World Politics* 50 (1997), p. 151.
5 Stephen Krasner, 'Realism, imperialism, and democracy', op. cit., p. 46.
6 Ibid., p. 47.
7 Robert Keohane, op. cit., p. 153.
8 Stephen Krasner, *Structural Conflict: The Third World against Global Liberalism*, Berkeley, University of California Press, 1985, p. 197.
9 Stephen Krasner, 'The accomplishments of International Political Economy', in Steve

Smith, Ken Booth and Marysia Zalewski (eds), *International Theory: Positivism and Beyond*, Cambridge, Cambridge University Press, 1996, p. 125.

See also in this book

Gilpin, Keohane, Strange, Waltz

Krasner's major writings

'Are bureaucracies important? (or Allison in wonderland)', *Foreign Policy* 7 (1972), pp. 159–79
'State power and the structure of international trade', *World Politics* 28 (1976), pp. 317–46
Defending the National Interest: Raw Material Investment and U.S. Foreign Policy, Princeton, New Jersey, Princeton University Press, 1978
'Transforming international regimes: what the Third World wants and why', *International Studies Quarterly* 25 (1981), pp. 119–48
'American policy and global economic stability', in William P. Avery and David P. Rapkin (eds), *America in a Changing World Political Economy*, New York, Longman, 1982, pp. 29–48
'Structural causes and regime consequences: regimes as intervening variables', *International Organization* 36 (1982), pp. 1–21
'Regimes and the limits of realism: regimes as autonomous variables', *International Organization* 36 (1982), pp. 355–68
'Approaches to the state: alternative conceptions and historical dynamics', *Comparative Politics* 6 (1984), pp. 223–46
Structural Conflict: The Third World Against Global Liberalism, Berkeley, University of California Press, 1985
'Toward understanding in International Relations', *International Studies Quarterly* 29 (1985), pp. 137–45
'Trade conflicts and the common defence: the United States and Japan', *Political Science Quarterly* 101 (1986), pp. 787–806
Asymmetries in Japanese–American Trade: The Case for Specific Reciprocity, Berkeley University of California Press, 1987
'Fortune, virtue, and systematic versus scientific inquiry', in Joseph Kruzel and James N. Rosenau (eds), *Journeys Through World Politics: Autobiographical Reflections of Thirty-Four Academic Travellers*, Lexington, Massachusetts, Lexington Books, 1989, pp. 417–27
'Global communications and national power: life on the Pareto frontier', in David A. Baldwin (ed.), *Neoliberalism and Neorealism*, New York, Columbia University Press, 1993, pp. 234–49

'Economic interdependence and independent statehood', in Robert H. Jackson and Alan James (eds), *States in a Changing World: A Contemporary Analysis*, Oxford, Clarendon Press, 1993, pp. 301–21

'International political economy: abiding discord', *Review of International Political Economy* 1 (1994), pp. 13–19

'Compromising Westphalia', *International Security* 20 (1996/97), pp. 115–51

'The accomplishments of International Political Economy', in Steve Smith, Ken Booth and Marysia Zalewski (eds), *International Theory: Positivism and Beyond*, Cambridge, Cambridge University Press, 1996, pp. 108–27

Further reading

Keohane, Robert, 'Problematic lucidity: Stephen Krasner's "State power and the structure of international trade"', *World Politics* 50 (1997), pp. 150–70

Thompson, Janice E., 'State sovereignty in international relations: bridging the gap between theory and empirical research', *International Studies Quarterly* 39 (1995), pp. 213–33

HANS MORGENTHAU

Hans Morgenthau, who died in 1980 at the age of 76, has been dubbed 'the Pope' of international relations. He is certainly the best known, even though he often claimed to be the least understood, of the classical, realist thinkers in the twentieth century. Along with E.H. Carr and George Kennan, Morgenthau is best remembered as one who tried to develop a comprehensive theory of 'power politics' on the philosophical basis of realist principles of human nature, the essence of politics, the balance of power and the role of ethics in foreign policy. As a Jewish refugee from Nazi Germany, he sought to educate Americans in these principles so that the United States could learn how to conduct its foreign policy as an active, great power in the international system. Like Kennan, in the 1950s he acknowledged that he had failed to shape

US foreign policy to any great extent. But his influence on the study of international relations, notwithstanding the vehemence with which his arguments have often been criticised, has been greater than that of any other 'key thinker' covered in this book.

Morgenthau was born in 1904 in Germany. As an only child of a somewhat authoritarian father, he was a shy and introverted boy who also had to cope with growing anti-semitism and discrimination at school. Not surprisingly, he found solace in books and enjoyed reading history as well as philosophy and literature. In the 1920s he studied at the Universities of Frankfurt and Munich, specialising in law and diplomacy. It was during this period that he discovered and devoured the work of Max Weber, who became both a personal as well as an intellectual role model. In particular, he admired Weber's juxtaposition of rigorous detached scholarship with impassioned social and political activism, a combination that he sought to emulate throughout his life. In the early 1930s Morgenthau taught public law at the University of Geneva. He also worked in Spain before fleeing Europe for the United States as Hitler consolidated his power in Germany.

He arrived in the United States in 1937 and managed to find academic work despite the anti-semitism confronting many Jews in academia at the time. Although he taught for short periods at Brooklyn College (1937–9) and at the University of Kansas City (1939–43), his academic career was spent mostly at the University of Chicago (1943–71) and, after his retirement, at the City College of New York (1968–75) and the New School for Social Research in New York (1975–80). Although he worked for short periods for the government (as a consultant to the Policy Planning Staff in the State Department in the late 1940s and again in the early 1960s as an advisor to the Pentagon), he devoted most of his working life to writing and teaching. In addition to his theoretical work, Morgenthau was a prolific contributor to more popular journals and magazines. Indeed, he published no less than four separate volumes of collected articles in his lifetime.

As a theorist, Morgenthau made his reputation in the late 1940s and early 1950s. His first book, *Scientific Man Versus Power Politics* (1946), represents his most systematic exposition of a realist philosophy and it constitutes an incisive critique of what he called 'rational liberalism'. In contrast to what he claims is the dominant liberal belief in progress, based on an optimistic set of assumptions regarding human nature, Morgenthau asserts the more traditional metaphysical and religious conception of 'fallen man'. All politics is a struggle for power because what he calls 'political man' is an innately selfish creature with an insatiable urge to dominate others. Human nature has three dimensions, biological, rational and spiritual. Although Morgenthau acknowledges that all three combine to determine human behaviour in different contexts, he focuses on the 'will-to-power' as the defining characteristic of politics, distinguishing it from economics (the rational pursuit of wealth) and religion (the spiritual realm of morality). Since the defining character of politics is the use of power to dominate others, morality and reason are subordinate virtues in politics, mere instruments for attaining and justifying power.

Morgenthau's basis for positing international politics as a realm of continuity and necessity invokes a contextual dimension to political autonomy in addition to its substantive elements, thus revealing as naïve the possibility of domesticating international politics via disarmament or the establishment of international parliamentary bodies. Within the territorial boundaries of the state, the struggle for power is mitigated through pluralistic loyalties, constitutional arrangements and culturally relative 'rules of the game'. These both disguise and direct the struggle for power toward competing conceptions of the good life. The legitimated coercive power of the state, combined with a network of social norms and community bonds, distinguishes domestic politics as an arena of potential progress. In contrast, all these factors are much weaker internationally. Here, not only is the 'will-to-power' allowed virtually free reign, but it is accentuated by the multiplicity of states, whose individual sovereignty elevates each as the secular pinnacle of political and moral authority. Consequently,

> [c]ontinuity in foreign policy is not a matter of choice but a necessity; for it derives from [factors] which no government is able to control but which it can neglect only at the risk of failure ... the question of war and peace is decided in consideration of these permanent factors, regardless of the form of government ... and its domestic policies. Nations are 'peace-loving' under certain conditions and are warlike under others.[1]

For Morgenthau, the function of international theory is to discover these conditions and, on the basis of an intensive examination of history, examine patterns of continuity and change in them. His massive textbook *Politics Among Nations*, first published in 1948, remains the most systematic attempt to employ 'realist' principles in constructing an empirical theory of international politics. Such a theory is made possible both by the role of power in delimiting the scope and nature of the field of study and the recurrent patterns of activity among states that the struggle for power produces throughout history. Furthermore, although Morgenthau claimed that his theory was applicable to all states, he focused directly on the most powerful of them, arguing that only the great powers determine the character of international politics at any one period of history.

On the basis of his interpretation of the historical evidence, Morgenthau argues that all foreign policies tend to conform to and reflect one of three patterns of activity: maintaining the balance of power, imperialism and what he called the politics of prestige (impressing other states with the extent of one's power). He outlines the conditions that determine which policy will be pursued, the proximate goals they are aimed at, the methods employed to achieve them and the appropriate policies to counteract them. Whilst he never discovers any firm 'laws' of the balance of power, the latter serves as a key organising device in which he examines the difficulties of measuring power and the relative stability of various configurations of power. Although some kind of 'balance' is in the long run inevitable in the anarchical system, its stability is a function of the ability and willingness of statesmen accurately to assess its character and then to work within the constraints that it imposes on their freedom of action abroad. This is particularly important in the post-1945 system, whose stability is threatened by historical changes that have made the uniquely new 'bipolar' structure much more difficult to manage. Morgenthau highlights four changes in particular.

First, he argues that the number of great powers has declined since the eighteenth century. In the past, when peace depended upon a stable balance among five or six great powers in Europe, the loose alliance structure among them induced caution and prudence in the foreign policy of each. The bipolarity of the second half of the twentieth century had robbed diplomacy of a necessary flexibility, and it resembled a zero-sum game in which marginal shifts in power could lead to war. Second, there was no great power to act as a buffer between the superpowers, and Morgenthau argued that this had been a key ingredient of European politics in the past when Britain could act as a neutral 'arbiter' in continental conflicts. Third, in the era of decolonisation, territorial compensation was no longer available to maintain the central balance. In the past, the territorial division and distribution of

colonies and lesser powers in Europe (such as Poland) had been an important technique for negotiating concessions in European diplomacy. Finally, the application of new technologies of transport, communication and war had transformed the twentieth century into an era of what Morgenthau called 'total mechanisation, total war, and total domination'.[2]

In short, Morgenthau was very pessimistic about the capacities of the United States and the Soviet Union to maintain international peace. Although the struggle for power was kept within barely tolerable limits by the mutual deterrence provided by nuclear weapons, he had no faith in their ability to maintain the peace. Since weapons were not the source of instability in the Cold War, neither could they be a cure. At the same time, Morgenthau had little faith in any liberal, or 'idealist', reforms of the international system. He devoted long chapters to the futility of international law, public opinion, disarmament and the United Nations. Given his metaphysical beliefs regarding human nature and the centrality of power, he condemned all attempts either to avoid the roots of the problem or to discover answers outside the existing framework of the states system. Such attempts were worse than useless – ultimately their failure led to cynicism and despair.

Morgenthau himself avoided such despair by suggesting that, despite the difficulties, there was still some scope for statesmen to moderate the instabilities inherent in contemporary international politics. However, the United States would have to learn to rid itself of some deep-seated illusions about international politics. Morgenthau's third major book, *In Defence of the National Interest* (1951), is a sustained critique of what Morgenthau described as 'certain deeply ingrained habits of thought, and preconceptions as to the nature of foreign policy' in the United States.[3] He believed that American foreign policy was continually plagued by four main flaws (legalism, uto-pianism, sentimentalism and isolationism) that arise from the fortuitous geographical, historical and diplomatic separation of the United States from the European balance of power. If the United States were to play a constructive role in stabilising the new balance of power after 1945, it would have to rid itself of these preconceptions and engage in a sober analysis of the new balance of power and the concomitant requirement to promote the national interest. In particular, Morgenthau was eager to demolish the 'moralistic' assumptions that he argued had characterised the diplomacy of Woodrow Wilson after the First World War. Instead, he urged a return to the 'realistic' diplomacy of George Washington and Alexander Hamilton in the eighteenth century, when the United States recognised and acted on behalf of the national interest – to prevent France or Britain from establishing sufficient power in Europe to threaten the security of the United States.

Stanley Hoffmann has written that Morgenthau 'provided both an explanation [of international politics] and a road map' for the conduct of American foreign policy.[4] However, in seeking to unite the realm of theory with that of policy, it must be said that Morgenthau did not succeed in his ambitious attempt. Whilst he is a key figure in helping to establish 'realism' as a dominant 'paradigm' in the study of international relations, the links between theory and policy have moved in the opposite direction, whilst Morgenthau himself, like George Kennan, became increasingly disenchanted with the conduct of American policy during the Cold War. Although the reasons for this failure cannot be entirely attributed to flaws in Morgenthau's approach, neither can those flaws be overlooked.

Morgenthau's international theory, whilst it remains impressive in terms of its historical reach, is beset by a number of tensions and contradictions that Morgenthau never succeeded in resolving. Three in particular are worth noting.

First, he never clearly distinguished between power as an end in itself and power as a means to achieve an end. On the one hand, Morgenthau's 'second principle' of political realism, in addition to other remarks in *Politics Among Nations*, affirms that 'statesmen think and act in terms of interest defined as power, and the evidence of history bears that assumption out'.[5] On the other hand, his distinction between status quo and imperial states presupposes that the degree to which international politics is a struggle for power is dependent on the (in)compatibility of state interests. The struggle for power is not therefore a given, but is variable. Whether or not, and to what extent and under what conditions, states seek power then becomes a matter of empirical and historical study to discover the determinants of state interests. As John Vasquez points out, 'power politics is not so much an explanation as a description of one type of behaviour found in the global political system [which] itself must be explained; it does not explain'.[6]

Second, as Kenneth Waltz and others have pointed out, there is an important 'level-of-analysis' problem in Morgenthau's work. It is never clear whether his pessimism about the nature of international politics derives from his metaphysical assumptions about 'human nature' or the anarchical nature of the international system per se. Insofar as human nature is the source of power politics among states, this is to commit the ecological fallacy in reverse – the analysis of individual behaviour used uncritically to explain group behaviour. As Waltz points out, one cannot explain both war and peace by arguing that humans are wicked.[7] Insofar as the context of international politics is deemed to be the source of power politics, this presupposes what Morgenthau is often at pains to refute, namely, that the international system has been characterised by change as well as continuity, and that the key change is from a relatively stable Eurocentric system to a global system whose central players cannot agree on the rules of the game. Finally, there is a real tension between Morgenthau's commitment to theory as a description of reality and as an instrument of advocacy for American foreign policy. In addition to claiming that *Politics Among Nations* contained an empirical theory to be tested against 'the facts' and the 'evidence of history', Morgenthau was fond of invoking the metaphors of a painted portrait and a photograph to illustrate the relationship between theory and practice.

> Political realism wants the photographic picture of the political world to resemble as much as possible its painted portrait. Aware of the inevitable gap between good – that is, rational – foreign policy and foreign policy as it actually is, political realism maintains not only that theory must focus upon the rational elements of political reality, but also that foreign policy ought to be rational.[8]

The problem with trying to unite theory and practice on the basis of a somewhat dogmatic and determinist theory of the balance of power was one of inconsistency. Insofar as the theory is empirical, its claims to truth require that its key propositions be tested against the evidence. But this was rather difficult to do since Morgenthau was reluctant to operationalise his key variable of power so that it could be measured in any quantitative sense. More importantly, insofar as his critique of American foreign policy presupposed that it had failed to act in accordance with the requirements of 'the national interest', this undermined Morgenthau's claims that international politics was not a realm of choice and contingency, but one of necessity and determinism. If international politics is indeed governed by 'objective laws rooted in human nature', which apply regardless of historical change and their recognition by those whose behaviour they explain, it

should not matter whether statesmen recognise these laws or not. On the other hand, if their application depends on their prior recognition and conscious embodiment in 'rational' policymaking, they are not objective empirical 'laws' at all, and therefore cannot be invoked as part of a metatheoretical *deus ex machina* determining either state behaviour or patterns of activity arising from such behaviour.

From the 1950s onwards, whilst Morgenthau continued to publish successive editions of his *magnum opus*, he turned his attention away from theory to focus on American foreign policy and relations with the Soviet Union. Like Kennan, he became disenchanted with American foreign policy in the 1960s, particularly its involvement in Vietnam, which he courageously opposed on the classic principle of diplomacy that statesmen should never commit themselves or the prestige of their country to positions from which they cannot retreat without damaging their credibility or advance without risking a direct clash with other great powers. In light of the generality of his theory, and its ambiguity regarding the nature of power in international politics, his views on the nature of the Soviet Union were not consistent, but he was acutely aware of the limits of American diplomacy in an era of decolonisation, and his articles on the limits of nuclear weapons in foreign policy are among the best on the subject.

Notes

1 Hans Morgenthau, *Scientific Man Versus Power Politics*, Chicago, University of Chicago Press, 1946, p. 66.
2 Ibid., p. 383.
3 Hans Morgenthau, *In Defence of the National Interest*, New York, Alfred Knopf, 1951, p. 91.
4 Stanley Hoffmann, 'Hans Morgenthau: the limits and influence of realism', in his collection of essays, *Janus and Minerva*, Boulder, Westview Press, 1987, p. 76.
5 Hans Morgenthau, *Politics Among Nations*, New York, Alfred Knopf, 1948, p. 5.

6 John A. Vasquez, *The Power of Power Politics*, New Jersey, Rutgers University Press, 1983, p. 216.
7 Kenneth N. Waltz, *Man, The State, and War*, New York, Columbia University Press, 1959.
8 Hans Morgenthau, *Politics Among Nations*, op. cit., p. 8.

See also in this book

Carr, Herz, Kennan, Kissinger

Morgenthau's major writings

Scientific Man Versus Power Politics, Chicago, Chicago University Press, 1946

Politics Among Nations: The Struggle for Power and Peace, New York, Alfred Knopf, 1948.

In Defence of the National Interest: A Critical Examination of American Foreign Policy, New York, Alfred Knopf, 1951

Dilemmas of Politics, Chicago, University of Chicago Press, 1958

The Purpose of American Politics, New York, Alfred Knopf, 1960

Politics in the Twentieth Century (Three Volumes), Chicago, University of Chicago Press, 1962

The Crossroad Papers: A Look into the American Future, New York, W.W. Norton, 1965

Vietnam and the United States, Washington DC, Public Affairs Press, 1965

A New Foreign Policy for the United States, London, Pall Mall Press, 1969

Truth and Power: Essays of a Decade, 1960–70, New York, Praeger, 1970

Science: Servant or Master?, New York, W.W. Norton, 1972

Further reading

Claude, Inis, L. jr., *Power and International Relations*, New York, Random House, 1966

Gardiner, Lloyd, C., *The Origins of the Cold War*, Waltham, Massachusetts, Ginn-Blaisdell, 1970

Gelman, Peter, 'Hans J. Morgenthau and the legacy of political realism', *Review of International Studies* 14 (1988), pp. 247–66

Griffiths, Martin, *Realism, Idealism and International Politics: A Reinterpretation*, London, Routledge, 1995

Hoffmann, Stanley, 'Notes on the limits of realism', *Social Research* 48 (1981), pp. 653–9

Jervis, Robert, 'Hans Morgenthau, realism, and the scientific study of international politics', *Social Research* 61 (1994), pp. 856–76

Mastny, Vojtech, *Power and Policy in Transition: Essays Presented on the Tenth Anniversary of the National Committee on American Foreign Policy in Honor of its Founder Hans J. Morgenthau*, Westport, Connecticut, 1984.

Nobel, Jaap W., 'Morgenthau's theory and practice: a response to Peter Gelman', *Review of International Studies* 15 (1989), pp. 281–93

Nobel, Jaap W., 'Morgenthau's struggle with power: the theory of power politics and the Cold War', *Review of International Studies* 21 (1995), pp. 61–85

Russell, Greg, *Hans J. Morgenthau and the Ethics of American Statecraft*, Baton Rouge, Louisiana State University, 1990

Smith, Michael J., *Realist Thought From Weber to Kissinger*, Baton Rouge, Louisiana State University Press, 1996, pp. 134–64

Social Research, 48, 4, (Winter 1981). Special Issue on the Work of Hans Morgenthau with essays by George Liska, Kenneth Thompson, Michael Joseph Smith, Stanley Hoffmann, Richard Rosecrance, Hedley Bull and others.

Thompson, Kenneth and Myers, Robert J., *Truth and Tragedy: A Tribute to Hans Morgenthau*, New Bruswick, Transaction Books, 1984

Tickner, J. Ann, 'Hans Morgenthau's principles of political realism: a feminist reformulation', in Rebecca Grant and Kathleen J. Newland (eds), *Gender and International Relations*, Bloomington, Indiana University Press, 1991, pp. 27–40

Tucker, Robert, 'Professor Morgenthau's theory of political "realism"', *American Political Science Review* 46 (1952), pp. 214–24

SUSAN STRANGE

Of all the thinkers classified under the label 'realism', Susan Strange is the most unconventional. Although her work has been very critical of neorealism, she still describes herself as a 'new realist' in the sub-field of international political economy (IPE). Strange is unconventional for the further reason that she has always been what Robert Cox calls 'a loner' rather than 'a groupie'. Rather than start with an existing set of agreed theoretical or ideological dispositions, Strange develops her theoretical concepts to answer the empirical questions that she asks and to respond to her dissatisfaction with the way those questions have been answered in the existing literature. As Cox observes,

[h]er realism is a search for the effective entities of world politics, whatever they may turn out to be. Instead of defining the world exclusively in terms of states, she sees power as the basic concern of realism and asks: Where does power lie? With states certainly, to some degree, but also with markets. With firms, too, and possibly with some other entities. The answer is not given with the question, and the answer is subject to change.[1]

This is particularly true in IPE, a field that Strange has helped to establish and develop.

Susan Strange was born in 1923 and completed her undergraduate studies at the London School of Economics. After spending some time at Cambridge during the Second World War, she became a journalist, working for *The Economist* and, in 1946, for *The Observer* newspaper as its Washington correspondent. Strange's experience in journalism was invaluable in exposing her to contemporary politics, and it has also contributed to her style of writing – direct, clear and unpretentious. In 1948 she took up her first teaching post at University College, London. After falling out with the university administration over the length of her maternity leave, Strange joined the Royal Institute of International Affairs at Chatham House as a research fellow.[2] It was during this period that she wrote her famous article attacking the way in which politics and economics were treated as separate domains in the study of international relations, as well as her first book *Sterling and British Policy* (1971). In it she placed the blame for Britain's economic decline upon its political and economic leaders. She claimed that they had been obsessed with maintaining the British currency as an international mark of prestige. In 1978 she returned to the London School of Economics, this time as Montague Burton Professor of International Relations. For the next decade she established her reputation as a leading scholar of international finance and trade, as well as a tough-minded critic of the way in which IPE was evolving in the United States. In the 1970s Strange played a leading role in establishing courses on international political economy at the LSE, and she also established the British chapter of the International Studies Association (BISA). Over the last decade Susan Strange worked at the European University Institute in Florence. In 1993 she joined the University of Warwick. She died after a year-long fight with cancer on 25 October 1998.

In 1970, Strange led the charge in criticising IR scholars' ignorance of the ways in which economic forces were altering traditional power politics, and she also criticised economists for relying too heavily on abstract calculations in determining politico-economic action. The events that followed the collapse of the Bretton Woods system for governing the global economy provided a good example of Strange's complaints. For example, according to pure economic logic, a shift from fixed to floating exchange rates should allow states to equilibrate their basic accounts, yet deficit states fell into more debt and creditors accumulated more capital. In trying to account for this and other anomalies in IPE, Strange has explicitly drawn from more than one school of thought. In the 1970s the discipline of international relations was often portrayed in terms of three such schools: realists, who have continued the mercantilist tradition and emphasised the need for state control of the marketplace; liberals, who maintain the ideal of a 'free' market and value competition as a means to promote global welfare; and Marxists, who argue that capitalism is inherently exploitative. Strange argues that the field is unnecessarily divided 'like three toy trains on separate tracks, travelling from different starting-points and ending at different (predetermined) destinations, and never crossing each other's paths'.[3] Strange draws from all three in developing the idea of *structural power* as a concept in IPE that can enable students to bring politics and economics together. Structural power

> [c]onfers the power to decide how things shall be done, the power to shape frameworks within which states relate to each other, relate to people, or relate to corporate enterprises. The relative power of each party in a relationship is more, or less, if one party is also determining the surrounding structure of the relationship.[4]

Strange argues that the study of any issue-area within IPE should begin with a set of empirical questions: 'By what political and economic processes, and thanks to what political and economic structures, did this outcome come about? After causes, come consequences: Who benefited? Who paid? Who carried the risks? Who enjoyed new opportunities?'[5] Such questions should then be answered by examining decisions taken and bargains struck between the relevant actors, including but not limited to governments. But the analysis should not be limited to explicit bargains (the outcome of relational power between actors), for it should acknowledge the constraints of and interaction between four analytically distinct structures of power as well, 'the power to influence the ideas of others [the knowledge structure], their access to credit [the financial structure], their prospects for security [the security structure], their chances of a better life as producers and as consumers [the production structure]'.[6] For Strange, these four structures interact and change over time. No single structure always predominates over the others, but the ways in which they interact help to shed light on the bargains struck between political and economic actors in different issue-areas in IPE.

Strange's distinction between the four kinds of structural power is most fully developed in *States and Markets* (1988), and her analysis of each illustrates well her theoretical eclecticism. For example, her description of the security structure is consistent with conventional realism, in which the authoritative power of the state derives from its provision of security for its citizens against threats from other states. The production structure refers to the basic source of wealth creation in society and to the ways in which technologies of production structure the distribution of power among and between states and markets. The financial structure refers to the ways in which credit is created, distributed and managed (or mismanaged) in international relations. Finally, the knowledge structure concerns, as May puts it, 'what is believed, what is known (and perceived as understood or given) and the channels by which these beliefs, ideas and knowledge are communicated or confined'.[7]

Strange's work on structural power in international political economy arose from her dissatisfaction with the inadequacy of existing theoretical tools in the study of politics and economics in the 1970s. It was also inspired by her disagreement with those scholars who argued that the United States' politico-economic power over other states was on the wane in the same decade. The conventional argument was that Japan and Europe had recovered from the destruction of their economies in the Second World War. The Bretton Woods arrangements that the United States had put in place to ensure an open trading system were inadequate to stop the alleged growth of protectionism among states. Furthermore, the apparent inability of the United States to maintain a trading surplus over its main competitors indicated that there was a growing imbalance between its military power and commitments, and its economic base. Consequently, its willingness to provide authoritative international 'public goods', such as a stable, international currency and extended nuclear deterrence to Europe and Japan, was under threat. For Susan Strange, such analysis is a classic example of the failure to distinguish between relational and structural power. As far as protectionism is concerned, she insists that global capitalism is not really suffering as the result of an increase in protectionist measures. This is because the production structure will ensure that they will not work. Although states have an interest in protecting their industries from 'unfair' competition from abroad, they also have an interest in limiting such measures because their industries will stagnate if they are too insulated from the pressures of international competition. Furthermore, the production structure has undergone enormous change, since over one-third of world trade occurs not between separate firms in states per se, but between branches of multinational corporations.

Strange has focused most of her empirical analysis on changes in the world financial structure, concluding that those who bemoan the United States' hegemonic decline conflate relational and structural power. Rather than the United States losing power to other states as a consequence of the latter's 'free-riding' on privileged access to the American market:

> The US government has lost power ... to the market – and the loss has been largely self-inflicted. In order to make the rest of the world safe and welcoming to American capitalism, successive US governments have broken down barriers to foreign investment and promoted capital mobility, have destroyed the Bretton Woods agreements, abused the GATT with unilateralised Trade Acts; [and] deregulated markets for air transport and finance. And even this list is not exhaustive. All these political decisions by the US have promoted structural change in the world economy, and from many of them the US government has shared with others a deterioration in the legitimate authority of the state over the economy.[8]

In her most provocative book *Casino Capitalism* (1986), which resonates with themes of political irresponsibility flagged in her earliest work, Strange argues that the global capitalist system does suffer from a lack of order in the financial structure. In particular, the move from fixed to floating exchange rates has made it difficult for states to manage their economies and has created a climate in which economic growth is very hard to achieve. As far as the Third World is concerned, she argues that the real problem here is not merely the high levels of debt but the lack of an assured supply of credit for long-term development.

Strange is very clear about who is responsible for creating the 'casino capitalism' of the 1970s and 1980s – the United States. She identifies a series of instances when the American government refused to act as a responsible hegemon (for example, the creation of floating exchange rates, the refusal to negotiate directly with OPEC and the refusal to establish an international lender of last resort after the bank failures of 1975). In contrast to realists such as Stephen Krasner, Strange alleges that the American state is weak and unwilling to resist economic group interests in the United States. She insists, however, that neorealist/neoliberal arguments that the United States is so economically weak that it cannot establish international financial order are just excuses for bad policy and judgement. Despite its loss of power to the market, the United States retains vast structural power compared to other states in the international system, and Strange believes that it should be held accountable for its actions.

However, it is not clear, from *Casino Capitalism* at least, what the cure is for the disease she diagnoses. She suggests that the United States could put its own house in order by tackling its enormous budget deficit, which gave rise to the volatile eurocurrency markets in the first place, and by controlling international banks through regulating their access to New York. But such reforms will not take place without pressure and, since this is unlikely from within the United States, it must come from other states. Strange thus endorses a version of balance-of-power diplomacy, arguing that Europeans in particular must develop a common currency and take much greater responsibility for their security needs than they have thus far. Despite borrowing liberally from the Marxist school in elaborating the nature of the production structure, Strange dismisses any lingering hopes that the working classes, trapped as they are within nation-states, can be realistic agents of reform or revolution.

In her most recent work, Strange is less concerned with the debate about hegemonic decline in the United States and more interested in the degree to which structural power has changed so as to diffuse authority away from the territorial state. Rather than compete over territory, states now compete for market shares in the world economy. Consequently, their priorities have shifted away from defence and foreign policy towards trade and industrial policy, and they must now share authority with other actors. '[S]tate authority has leaked away, upwards, sideways, and downwards. In some matters, it seems even to have gone nowhere, just evaporated'.[9] Strange argues that the reason for this is primarily the rate of technological change in the production structure. It is not just that we live in a world where the speed of communication across borders is unprecedented, but that technological advance is so rapid that the amount of capital needed to develop competitive goods and services cannot be recouped on the basis of domestic sales alone. The changes have not only complicated the identity of actors engaged in the international economy, but also the range of bargaining between states and firms. One disturbing trend is that, as states compete for shares in the global market, offering inducements to foreign firms to invest and manufacture products in their territory, their capacity to tax and regulate markets is declining, and this process magnifies the difficulties of managing the global economy. All this is a result of structural changes in the nature of power that cannot

be understood if one confines one's analysis to inter-state relations. The shift in power is from states to markets, which is not necessarily reflected in a shift in power between states. The United States still possesses enormous structural power in security, finance and knowledge, as reflected in the dominance of American universities in attracting overseas students compared to other states.

The implications of Strange's work are two-fold. First, she has done more than any other scholar to promote theoretical fertilisation across the central 'paradigms' of international relations thought, particularly in IPE. Second, she has alerted scholars to the need for, and difficulties of, central management of what she describes as a shift from the world of nation-states to a 'new medievalism' in international relations. The first is essential if the second is to be attempted. '[U]nless the intellectuals can find the courage to abandon the impedimenta of a fast-vanishing past and can start thinking anew about some of the basic issues of society, polity, and economy, progress of any kind toward a sustainable system will be impossible'.[10] A new realist, indeed!

Notes

1 Robert Cox, *Approaches to World Order*, Cambridge, Cambridge University Press, 1996, p. 183.
2 As she remarks of the period, 'the feminist case in the professions still had to be made, and with four young children at home, I didn't relish a fight'. Joseph Kruzel and James N. Rosenau (eds), *Journeys Through World Politics: Autobiographical Reflections of Thirty-Four Academic Travellers*, Lexington, Massachusetts, Lexington Books, 1989, p. 433.
3 Susan Strange, *States and Markets: An Introduction to International Political Economy*, London, Pinter, 1988, p. 16.
4 Ibid., pp. 24–5.
5 Susan Strange, 'Political economy and international relations', in Ken Booth and Steve Smith (eds), *International Relations Theory Today*, Cambridge, Polity Press, 1995, p. 172.
6 Ibid.

7 Chris May, 'Strange fruit: Susan Strange's theory of structural power in the international political economy', *Global Society* 10 (1996), p. 182. May raises the interesting possibility that the knowledge structure should be treated much more seriously as prior to the other structures, but this is a topic that needs further research. See Susan Strange, 'A reply to Chris May', *Global Society* 10 (1996), pp. 303–6.

8 Susan Strange, 'Wake up, Krasner! The world *has* changed', *Review of International Political Economy* 1 (1994), p. 213.

9 Susan Strange, 'The defective state', *Daedalus* 24 (1995), p. 56.

10 Ibid., p. 72.

See also in this book

Keohane, Krasner

Strange's major writings

'International economics and international politics: a case of mutual neglect', *International Affairs* 46 (1970), pp. 304–15

'Cave, hic dragones: a critique of regime analysis', *International Organization* 36 (1982), pp. 479–96

'Still an extraordinary power: America's role in a global monetary system', in Raymond E. Lombra and Willard E. Witte (eds), *Political Economy of International and Domestic Monetary Relations*, Ames, Iowa, Iowa State University Press, 1982, pp. 73–103

Paths to International Political Economy (ed.), London, Allen & Unwin, 1984

'The global political economy: 1958–1994', *International Journal* 34 (1984), pp. 333–45

'Protectionism and world politics', *International Organization* 39 (1985), pp. 233–59

Casino Capitalism, Oxford, Oxford University Press, 1986

'Supranationals and the state', in John A. Hall (ed.), *States in History*, Oxford, Basil Blackwell, 1986, pp. 289–305

'The persistent myth of lost hegemony', *International Organization* 41 (1987), pp. 551–74

States and Markets: An Introduction to International Political Economy, London, Pinter, 1988

'The future of the American empire', *Journal of International Affairs* 42 (1988), pp. 1–17

'Towards a theory of transnational empire', in James N. Rosenau and Ernst-Otto Czempiel (eds), *Global Changes and Theoretical Challenges: Approaches to World Politics for the 1990's*, Toronto, D.C. Heath & Co., 1989, pp. 161–76

'Finance, information and power', *Review of International Studies* 16 (1990), pp. 259–74

Rival States, Rival Firms: Competition for World Market Shares (with John M. Stopford), Cambridge, Cambridge University Press, 1991

'An eclectic approach', in Craig N. Murphy and Roger Tooze (eds), *The New International Political Economy*, Boulder, Colorado, Lynne Reinner, 1991, pp. 33–50

'Rethinking structural change in the international political economy: states, firms and diplomacy', in Richard Stubbs and Geoffrey R.D. Underhill (eds), *Political Economy and the Changing Global Order*, Toronto, McClelland & Stewart, 1994, pp. 103–15

'Political economy and international relations', in Ken Booth and Steve Smith (eds), *International Relations Theory Today*, Cambridge, Polity Press, 1995, pp. 154–74

The Retreat of the State: The Diffusion of Power in the World Economy, Cambridge, Cambridge University Press, 1996

Further reading

Calleo, David P., *The Imperious Economy*, Cambridge, Massachusetts, Harvard University Press, 1982

Gill, Stephen and Law, David, *The Global Political Economy: Perspectives, Problems and Policies*, Brighton, Harvester Wheatsheaf, 1988

Lukes, Stephen, *Power: A Radical View*, Basingstoke, Macmillan, 1974

May, Christopher, 'Strange fruit: Susan Strange's theory of structural power in the international political economy', *Global Society* 10 (1996), pp. 167–89. May has provided a comprehensive bibliography of Strange's published work on the Internet at the following address: http://human.ntu.ac.uk/foh/is/ipebib.html

KENNETH WALTZ

Kenneth Waltz was born in 1924. He completed his MA at Columbia University in 1950, and in 1954 he finished his doctorate, which was published that year to great acclaim. *Man, The State and War* was not only a superb exercise in the history of ideas on the causes of war between states – it also contained the germs of an idea that Waltz only fully developed a quarter of a century later. At one level his first book is simply an attempt to examine systematically the answers given by philosophers, statesmen, historians and political scientists to the fundamental question, what is the cause of war? He argued that they could be classified as either optimists or pessimists whose answers could be located among three levels of analysis or 'images'. These were human nature, the domestic economic and political systems of states, and the anarchical environment in which all states coexist without a supreme power authoritatively to arbitrate conflicts between them. Waltz argued that it was necessary to be aware of the interaction between these images and not to exaggerate the importance of any one of them.

The third image describes the framework of world politics, but without the first and second images there can be no knowledge of the forces that determine policy; the first and second images describe the forces in world politics, but without the third image it is impossible to assess their importance or predict their results.[1]

Over the next twenty-five years Waltz wrestled with the problem of how to evaluate the empirical relationship between the images he had identified in his first book. He became a full professor at the age of 33 and was appointed Ford Professor of Political Science at Berkeley in 1971, having taught at Harvard and Brandeis in the intervening years. He contributed important articles on the merits of bipolar versus multipolar balances of power among the great powers, and in 1967 published a book comparing the foreign policies of the United States and Britain in light of their different political systems.

In 1979, on the eve of the election of Ronald Reagan and just as détente between the superpowers was giving way to a new (and as it turned out, terminal) phase of tension between the United States and the Soviet Union, Waltz published the book that has been described as 'the single most widely read contribution to neorealism, establishing [Waltz] as the paradigmatic successor to Morgenthau'.[2] *Theory of International Politics* is a key text in the field. There are several reasons for this success.

First, although its timing was in some respects accidental, the coincidence between its publication and the onset of a new Cold War ensured that its main argument would be particularly controversial. Waltz's defence of the continued domination of the superpowers as the best guarantor of order and stability in world politics was put forward at a time when many believed that a nuclear war could break out in Europe as a result of the nuclear arms race. Second, unlike the early post-war realists (such as Carr or Morgenthau), Waltz claimed that he had achieved the equivalent of a 'Copernican revolution' in the study of world politics by finally unravelling the level-of-analysis problem that he had revealed in the 1950s. Third, Waltz claimed that *Theory* was the first *scientifically defensible* theory of the balance of power in international relations. In marked contrast to all those scholars who were arguing that international relations were undergoing a radical transformation as a result of growing interdependence in the international economy as well as the limitations of force in the nuclear age, Kenneth Waltz reaffirmed the salience of the state as the main actor in international politics and castigated his opponents' arguments as reductionist and non-falsifiable. During the so-called inter-paradigm debate that dominated international relations in the 1980s, Waltz was a key figure, and his book continues to be a critical reference point for supporters and opponents of neorealism in IR.

The argument of *Theory* is both a continuation of some of the ideas first presented in *Man, The State and War*, as well as a repudiation of the latter's conclusions. Rather than explore the inter-relationship between the levels of analysis that he had identified in his earlier work, Waltz focuses on the autonomy and influence of the structural component of the international system. This third level influences state behaviour, and hence outcomes such as the incidence of war, by constraining states from certain policies and predisposing them toward others. He defines the international political structure by two criteria. The first is a principle of arrangement by which states relate to one another. The inter-state system is a self-help, or anarchical, one. This principle, he argues, is constant over time, and severely constrains the degree to which a division of labour can take place between states. They are, as Waltz puts it, functionally undifferentiated. Multiple sovereignty, therefore, limits the scope for interdependence among states. While anarchy is a constant, the second criterion of the structure, the distribution of capabilities, varies among states. States are similar in the tasks they face, although not in their abilities to perform them. The empirical referent for this latter variable is the number of great powers who dominate the system. Given the small number of such states, and Waltz suggests that no more than eight have ever been consequential, international politics 'can be studied in terms of the logic of small number systems'.[3] This logic, he argues, can be understood without making any untestable and vague assumptions about whether and to what extent states seek to pursue power. '[B]alance-of-power politics prevail whenever two, and only two, conditions are met: that the order be anarchic and that it be populated by units wishing to survive.'[4]

Having isolated the structure, Waltz then argues that a bipolar structure dominated by two great powers is more stable than a multipolar structure dominated by three or more great powers. It is more likely to endure without system-wide wars. Again, in contrast to earlier realists who were concerned about the ideological confrontation of the superpowers in a nuclear era, Waltz claims that there are striking differences between multipolarity and bipolarity in terms of strategic behaviour. Under multipolarity, states rely on alliances to maintain their security. This is inherently unstable, since 'there are too many powers to permit any of them to draw clear and fixed lines between allies and adversaries'.[5] In contrast, the inequality between the superpowers and every other state ensures that the threat to each is easier to identify, and both the Soviet Union and the United States maintain the central balance by relying on their own devices rather than allies. The dangers of miscalculation and defection are thereby minimised. Nuclear deterrence, and the inability of either superpower to overcome the retaliatory forces of the other, enhances the stability of the system. In the terms laid down by his earlier work, by the late 1970s Waltz had finally identified himself as a third image optimist.

For over a decade since its publication, *Theory* and its author were at the heart of an intense and sometimes vitriolic debate in international relations. Some scholars praised Waltz for having overturned the liberal belief that international relations was undergoing structural change and for having provided the most systematic attempt yet to articulate a testable theory of the balance of power. At the other extreme, he was accused of legitimating 'an authoritarian project of global proportions'.[6]

Among those who admired the rigour of Waltz's book, the debate revolved around his attempt to isolate the nature and effects of the structure of the international system, the degree to which his substantive conclusions were consistent with his premises, and the relationship between change and continuity in the international system.

The first issue is the degree to which Waltz succeeds in isolating the structure as a cause of state behaviour. He argues that it functions rather like the human liver or a progressive income tax system, working its effects by socialisation and competition among states. Waltz admits that he was inspired by Durkheim as well as sociological studies of crowd behaviour, but the extent to which the structure functions independently of states' perception of the balance of power is not clear. Attention has also been drawn to the inconsistencies between Waltz's substantive arguments on the merits of bipolarity in the 1970s and his theory of the balance of power. Some of his critics have argued that the 'stability' of the Cold War had much more to do with nuclear weapons (a 'unit level' phenomenon) than bipolarity. Just because the superpowers were more powerful than other states in the system did not mean that they were equally as powerful as each other and had become successfully 'socialised' to the prevailing structure. Again, the explanatory and predictive power of Waltz's theory was compromised by the difficulty of separating levels of analysis and determining the content of each. Finally, a number of critics have argued that Waltz's model is too static and deterministic. It lacks any dimension of structural change. States are condemned to reproduce the logic of anarchy and any co-operation that takes place between them is subordinate to the distribution of power. Waltz's assumptions regarding the nature of states has been hotly contested by neoliberals who believe that it exaggerates the degree to which states are obsessed with the distribution of power and ignores the collective benefits to be achieved via co-operation.

Rather than seek to amend or reconstruct Waltz's theory to deal with some of its alleged shortcomings, others have regarded *Theory* with much more suspicion as a scarcely disguised attempt to legitimate the Cold War under the mantle of science. Much of the book is concerned with problems of theory construction, the relationship between laws of behaviour and theories that explain those laws, and how to test a theory so that it conforms to proper behavioural scientific standards. For Waltz, a theory is

an instrument to explain patterns of state behaviour within a circumscribed realm of human activity. Although explanation is a necessary precondition for successful purposeful action, theoretical inquiry is a politically value-free activity. Given his rigid distinction between international political theory and foreign policy analysis, the former cannot evaluate and prescribe for the latter. 'The problem is not to say how to manage the world, but to say how the possibility that great powers will constructively manage international affairs varies as systems change.'[7] Ironically, the system has changed dramatically with the end of the Cold War and the collapse of one pole of the structure, the Soviet Union. This dramatic turn of events was not consistent with the expectations of *Theory*, according to which the superpowers were maturing into 'sensible duopolists' at the head of an increasingly stable structure.

Since the end of the Cold War, Waltz has turned his attention to the consequences of what he sees as a shift from bipolarity to unipolarity. As one might expect, his recent work reflects some of the concerns he articulated in the 1960s regarding the undesirable consequences that flow from an imbalance of power. In particular, he argues that in the absence of effective countervailing pressures, the United States is likely to become increasingly unilateral in seeking to secure its foreign policy interests, and in so doing rely on its military preponderance to secure any vision of a new world order. In this context, he is remarkably sanguine about the consequences of nuclear proliferation in international politics. In the early 1980s, he had argued that nuclear deterrence was a force for stability in world affairs, inducing states to pursue their goals without risking all-out nuclear conflict. He still holds to that argument, believing that the 'managed spread' of nuclear weapons may succeed in replicating the merits of nuclear deterrence in a multipolar world, and counter-acting its inherent dangers. This argument, however, assumes that the complex dynamics of the nuclear relationship between the super-powers can be unproblematically duplicated. Waltz has not responded to his more radical critics for whom *Theory* is a testimony to the impoverishment of IR theory in a neo-realist, positivist mode.

Notes

1 Kenneth Waltz, *Man, The State, and War*, New York, Columbia University Press, 1959, p. 238.
2 Michael Banks, 'The inter-paradigm debate', in M. Light and A.J.R. Groom (eds), *International Relations: A Handbook of Current Theory*, London, Frances Pinter, 1985, p. 14.
3 Kenneth Waltz, *Theory of International Politics*, Reading, Massachusetts, Addison-Wesley, 1979, p. 131.
4 Ibid., p. 121.
5 Ibid., p. 168.
6 Richard Ashley, 'The poverty of neorealism', *International Organization* 38 (1981), p. 226.
7 Kenneth Waltz, *Theory of International Politics*, op. cit., p. 210.

See also in this book

Gilpin, Keohane, Morgenthau, Wendt

Waltz's major writings

Man, The State, and War, New York, Columbia University Press, 1959
'Political philosophy and the study of international relations' in William Fox (ed.), *Theoretical Aspects of International Relations*, Notre Dame, Indiana, University of Notre Dame Press, 1959, pp. 51–69
'The stability of a bipolar world', *Daedalus* 93 (1964), pp. 881–909
Foreign Policy and Democratic Politics, Boston, Little, Brown, 1967
Theory of International Politics, Reading, Massachesetts, Addison-Wesley, 1979
'The spread of nuclear weapons: more may be better', *Adelphi Paper* 171, London, International Institute of Strategic Studies, 1981
'The origins of war in neorealist theory', *Journal of Interdisciplinary History,* 18 (1988), pp. 615–28
'Realist thought and neorealist theory', *Journal of International Affairs* 44 (1990), pp. 21–37
'The emerging structure of international politics', *International Security* 18 (1993), pp. 44–79

Further reading

Buzan, B., Jones, C. and Little, R., *The Logic of Anarchy: Neorealism to Structural Realism,* New York, Columbia University Press, 1993
Halliday, F. and Rosenberg, J. 'Interview with Ken Waltz', *Review of International Studies* (1998), pp. 371–86
Keohane, Robert (ed.), *Neorealism and its Critics,* New York, Columbia University Press, 1986
Linklater, Andrew, 'Neo-realism in theory and practice', in Ken Booth and Steve Smith (eds), *International Relations Theory Today,* Cambridge, Polity Press, 1995
Mouritzen, Hans, 'Kenneth Waltz: a critical rationalist between international politics and foreign policy', in Iver B. Neumann and Ole Waever (eds), *The Future of International Relations: Masters in the Making*, London, Routledge, 1997, pp. 66–89. This assessment of Waltz's work contains a complete bibliography of his work.

LIBERALISM

In contrast to realists, liberals see international relations as a potential realm of progress and purposive change. They value individual freedom above all else, and they believe that the state ought to be constrained from acting in ways that undermine that freedom. Domestically, the power of the liberal constitutional state is limited by its democratic accountability to its citizens, the need to respect the demands of the economic marketplace and the rule of law. Liberals believe that, despite the difficulties of replicating these constraints at the international level, they must be established to promote stability among, as well as within, sovereign states. Among the key thinkers included in this section, there are differences of emphasis between the priority to be given to democracy, economic interdependence and the international legal regulation of security and economic issue-areas. Republican, commercial and regulatory forms of the liberal tradition are represented here, as liberals debate both the merits of these forms and the degree to which (in isolation or combination) they affect international relations. In the 1920s and 1930s, liberalism was disparaged as a form of 'idealism' or 'utopianism' by the self-proclaimed 'realists' of the time. This was the label that was indiscriminately applied to the work of Norman Angell, Woodrow Wilson and Alfred Zimmern. Today, liberalism is no longer marginalised in the study of international relations. The collapse of the Soviet Union, and therefore communism as a global competitor to capitalism, has provided an opportunity for contemporary liberals to assess the legacy of their intellectual tradition and its relevance at the end of the twentieth century. However, although some contemporary trends may appear to vindicate the insights of the 'idealists', liberalism must respond to new challenges as the forces of global capitalism undermine the apparent 'victory' of liberal democracy in the Cold War.

NORMAN ANGELL

Norman Angell published his famous book *The Great Illusion* just two years before the outbreak of the First World War. He argued that the economic interdependence of advanced industrialised states had become so great that territorial control was obsolete as a prerequisite for economic wealth and that war was therefore irrational. Unfortunately, the perception that Angell was predicting the obsolescence of war has helped strengthen the impression of this key thinker as an 'idealist' who was either fundamentally mistaken or (a more charitable interpretation) way ahead of his time. The attribution of the label is, however, erroneous if based on such a perception. Angell was not the victim of his own 'illusion' that war would not break out simply because it was no longer economically rational. Indeed, he was inspired to write his book precisely because he feared the onset of war and he wanted to repudiate the conventional wisdom that he believed contributed to the willingness of the public to support policies that were not in their own self-interest. Now that the Cold War is over, and realism no longer dominates the study of international relations, students can return to the pre-1914 era with less prejudice than in the past, and, in so doing, appreciate the work of 'a theorist of whom everyone has heard and few take seriously'.[1]

Norman Angell was born in 1874 in Lincolnshire, England, into a middle-class family, and he learnt to read at an early age, absorbing the works of Voltaire, Tom Paine, Walt Whitman and, in particular, John Stuart Mill. His formal education was not extensive. He spent a few years in France and Switzerland, where he took a few courses at the University of Geneva. At the age of 17 he decided to emigrate to the United States, convinced that Europe's problems were insoluble. In the United States he travelled around the West Coast, working as a farm-hand, cowboy, vine planter and eventually a reporter for the St Louis *Globe-Democrat* and later the San Francisco *Chronicle*. When he ran out of money, he returned to Paris and found work as a sub-editor of the English language *Daily Messenger*, and he was finally selected by Lord Northcliffe to manage the French edition of the *Daily Mail*.

In 1903 he published his first book *Patriotism Under Three Flags: A Plea for Rationalism in Politics*. In his autobiography, Angell points out that 'the book was in fact a blunt challenge to materialistic and economic determinism ... men are not guided by facts but by their opinion about the facts, opinions which may or may not be correct; and usually are not'.[2] As a journalist, Angell was acutely aware of the way in which the press could shape and distort public opinion and he was committed to using his position to change public opinion through the press. Although his first effort at educating the people did not draw a great deal of attention, the theme of irrationality was to dominate everything he subsequently wrote. In 1909 he wrote a short pamphlet entitled *Europe's Optical Illusion*, which was generally ignored until Angell expanded the argument of the book and published it as *The Great Illusion*. His talent for self-advertisement, and the free distribution of the book to eminent statesmen and other journalists, helped to establish it eventually as a bestseller. It sold over 2 million copies prior to the outbreak of the Great War and was translated into twenty-five languages. It even gave rise to a theory of 'Norman Angellism', and its success enabled him to devote the rest of his life to writing, teaching and organising political movements to promote policies consistent with his vision of liberal internationalism. Before his death in 1967, Angell published over forty books on international relations, revisiting and expanding the arguments first put forward in 1909. He also continued to write for newspapers and edited the journal *Foreign Affairs* from 1928 to 1931. For a short period in the late 1920s he was a Labour Member of Parliament and was knighted for public service in 1931. He was a member of the Council of the Royal Institute for International Affairs in London, as well as the Executive Committee of the League of Nations Union. In 1933, Angell was awarded the Nobel Peace Prize, for which he was formally nominated by such figures as Bertrand Russell, J.M. Keynes, Harold Laski, John Dewey and John Hobson.

Angell is an important precursor to the work of 'interdependence' theorists that emerged in the late 1960s and early 1970s. The core of Angell's analysis is that a central feature of modernity after the mid-nineteenth century is the incompatibility between war and the pursuit of economic wealth. In the era of mercantilism, territorial expansion through colonialism and war contributed to economic wealth. Other things being equal, territorial acquisition enabled states to increase their resources, particularly gold. However, the transition to highly developed commercial societies, accompanied by an emerging world market and the growing division of labour on a universal scale, produced a situation which makes war futile as a means of resolving conflicts of material interest. Angell did not believe that the new era reflected some utopian 'harmony of interests' among those who participated in the international division of labour. As he illustrates in the following passage, his basic argument is that, if we wish to preserve the advantages of economic interdependence, we have to find new ways of resolving the conflicts that do take place:

> The boat was leaky, the sea heavy, and the shore a long way off. It took all the efforts of one man to row, and of the other to bale. If either had ceased both would have drowned. At one point the rower threatened the baler that if he did not bale with more energy he would throw him

overboard; to which the baler made the obvious reply, that if he did, he (the rower) would certainly drown also. And as the rower was really dependent upon the baler, and the baler upon the rower, neither could use force against the other.[3]

This did not mean that war would cease to exist or that interdependence was inevitable. But he did believe that the latter would increase over time, even if he and others would have to engage in a great deal of effort to eradicate the former. In particular, he argued that colonialism was unnecessary, and that financial interdependence among the great European powers made it irrational for them to compete for territory or even to demand indemnities from those they had defeated in war. Angell hoped that, once this message was understood, political leaders would seek co-operation rather than war to resolve their differences. The process of interdependence itself would facilitate this. As the division of labour increased, the state would be unable to control the emergence of transnational organisations whose co-operation cut across territorial borders and could lead to what we would today call an emerging international civil society.

Of course, Angell's fears were confirmed by the outbreak of the First World War. After the war he acknowledged that it had required him to change some of his views, but he persisted with the central thesis of *The Great Illusion*. He had believed, for example, that the war would be limited to Germany and Britain, and that their ability to finance the conflict would be constrained by the refusal of other states to extend credit and financial assistance. He acknowledged that he had also underestimated the power of the state to safeguard its own currency and marshal its own resources to mobilise for war. This illustrated the capacity of the state to intervene in the division of labour and to control the degree of interdependence even though such political intervention could have very high economic costs. But Angell thought that the war had confirmed his basic thesis, and he bitterly opposed the decision at Versailles to impose huge reparation costs on the defeated Germany. For Angell, this was futile in an era when wealth was measured not in gold but goods and their exchange. By 'punishing' Germany, the Allies were only hurting themselves, since Germany would have to be rehabilitated if it was to pay the reparations demanded by the victors. As Navari points out,

> it was the one postulate upon which he could unreservedly congratulate himself ... during the negotiations for the peace following the First World War, French unions refused to receive German goods as reparations because of competition; the only way Germany eventually 'paid' was by a tax on its trade; and it was essentially American loans which rehabilitated the German economy so that it could pay.[4]

Later, in addition to reflecting on the adequacy of his thesis in light of the First World War and its broader lessons, Angell turned his attention increasingly to the need for international political reforms to prevent another world war. Since war obviously had already broken out, one could not rely on economic processes alone to prevent violent conflict. In addition to the constant need to educate, Angell was a staunch supporter of international efforts to promote disarmament and promote the rule of international law through the League of Nations.

Angell was never a pacifist. He did not believe that force should never be used in international affairs. In his major study of pacifism in Britain in the first half of the twentieth century, Martin Ceadel distinguishes between pacifism and what he calls *pacificism*, the view 'that war, though *sometimes necessary*, is always an irrational and inhumane way to solve disputes, and that its prevention should always be an over-riding political priority'.[5] Angell was a pacificist and

a keen supporter of collective security in international relations. He believed that since the rule of law is crucial in maintaining peace within states, it should be accorded a similar role at the international level. Thus, while he supported the principle of disarmament, he never joined those pacifists who argued in favour of unilateral disarmament. He regretted the way in which Germany had been treated at Versailles and in the early 1930s he wanted to recreate something like the nineteenth-century Concert of Europe. In particular, Germany and Italy should be accorded equal status and rights with the other great powers in Europe, and the League of Nations should seek to be as universal as possible in terms of its membership. The need to contain Germany and Italy by the late 1930s was itself in part a consequence of their treatment by the Allies at the end of the First World War. In his defence of Angell as a 'realist' rather than as the 'idealist' he was accused of being (particularly by E.H. Carr in *The Twenty Years' Crisis*), J.D.B. Miller shows how, in practice, these labels are problematic in distinguishing between the two ways of thinking:

> 'Utopians' [like Angell] had no doubt suggested that there could be a painless issue out of the difficulties created by the demands of Italy and Germany; but they also proposed an alliance [between the United States and the Soviet Union, Britain and France] which eventually came into being. The 'realists' [Carr] had scorned the possibility of an alliance, but had failed to recognise that Hitler was not just a routine politician who could be bought off with a loan and the fuzzy possibility of trade and colonial concessions.[6]

Angell, although he always opposed the idea that formal colonialism was important to maintain the economic prosperity of the colonial power, was not an opponent of empire per se.[7] Unlike other liberals, such as Hobson, Angell did not believe that decolonisation and non-intervention were important in themselves as instruments of political freedom and as contributions to international stability. Angell was an ardent opponent of nationalism wherever it may be found and he argued that decolonisation was consistent with the spread of nationalism rather than antithetical to it. He believed that the illusion of political and economic sovereignty was less important than the provision of political order and the extension of the rule of law to all people, whether they were formally independent or not. Angell was always very skeptical about 'the public mind' in so-called democracies. He believed, as did Hobson, that war often occurred because of jingoism, distorted nationalism and the ability of military elites to distort their citizens' views of other states. If this was the case in the First World, it was likely to be more so in the Third World, where leaders were even less constrained by the press than they were in modern industrialised states.

In her excellent review of Angell's contribution to the study of international relations in the twentieth century, Cornelia Navari focuses on three major weaknesses of his work. First, while his analysis of interdependence as a function of the division of labour is an advance on eighteenth-century liberalism (which traced the necessity of economic markets to natural law), it is still flawed. Although his empirical analysis was confined to Europe, and particularly to Germany and Britain, Angell was prone to making generalisations that were not justified by the evidence. Interdependence, as so many writers have argued since, should never be understood to mean equality of dependence between states. The metaphor of the leaky boat is, therefore, misleading. At best, interdependence is limited to particular regions of the world; it is not universal and rarely are states equally vulnerable to the costs of war. Insofar as they are not equally vulnerable, in a world where 'relative gains' from trade and co-operation are unevenly distributed, it may be rational for

states to forego the absolute gains from co-operation to insure their relative security.

Second, Angell did not contribute a great deal to our understanding of nationalism. He hated nationalism in all its forms, but he tended to make general assertions about the weakness and vulnerability of 'the public mind' to manipulation rather than grant any moral legitimacy to national identity. As a result, whilst he never predicted that war would end as a result of economic interdependence, he certainly thought that it ought to. He therefore failed to consider the possibility that there may be defensible reasons for going to war despite its economic costs. As Colin Gray observes,

> [the] central problem is that although Man is Economic, he is also Political, Religious, and just possibly also Military (and perhaps Warlike) in nature ... even if one could define, measure and achieve economic well-being, what would be achieved? If, *ab extensio*, economic well-being has to incorporate the values of physical and political security, possibly security of conscience as well, what utility remains in this concept-value?[8]

Third, Angell tended to assume that there was an inverse relationship between economic interdependence across territorial borders and the power of governments to control what went on inside them. He never made a systematic distinction between states and governments, nor did he acknowledge that the state

> is constituted by more than the formal governing apparatus. Institutions such as the press, research institutes and lobbies have been absorbed into the structure of modern governance. While [the] government may be losing determinate power over individual policies, it is gaining more as co-ordinator, intervener in and ultimate legitimator of the activities of the many informal agents that make up the modern state.[9]

Despite these problems with Angell's views, they should not detract from his immense contribution to the study of international relations, understood in the context of his own time and place. We know much more now than we did in his time about the nature and scope of interdependence in world politics, and the debate about its relationship with war is far more sophisticated than in his day. Angell did much to lay the foundations for liberal internationalism and he helped to exorcise the myth, still alive in some circles, that war is a profitable enterprise. His appeal to rationality and the need for education in the area of international relations were also very important. Whatever one thinks of the content of some of his arguments, his attempt to apply ideas of enlightened self-interest to international relations is still a powerful inspiration for the rest of us.

Notes

1 Cornelia Navari, 'The great illusion revisited: the international theory of Norman Angell', *Review of International Studies* 15 (1989), p. 341.
2 Norman Angell, *After All*, London, Hamish Hamilton, 1951, p. 107. A good summary of Angell's life can be found in J.D.B. Miller, *Norman Angell and the Futility of War*, Basingstoke, Macmillan, 1986, pp. 1–24.
3 Norman Angell, *The Foundations of International Polity*, London, Heinemann, 1914, p. 17.
4 Cornelia Navari, op. cit., p. 350.
5 Martin Ceadel, *Pacificism in Britain 1914–45*, Oxford, Clarendon Press, 1980, p. 3.
6 J.D.B. Miller, op. cit., p. 72.
7 See, in particular, Norman Angell, *The Defence of the Empire*, London, Hamish Hamilton, 1937.
8 Colin Gray, 'Global security and economic well-being: a strategic perspective', *Political Studies* 42 (1994), p. 30.
9 Cornelia Navari, op. cit., p. 354.

See also in this book

Carr, Hobson, Wilson

Angell's major writings

Patriotism Under Three Flags: A Plea for Rationalism in Politics, London, Fisher Unwin, 1903
The Great Illusion: A Study of Relations of Military Power in Nations to Their Economic and Social Advantage, London, William Heinemann, 1912
The Foundations of International Polity, London, William Heinemann, 1914
Human Nature and the Peace Problem, Glasgow, W. Collins Sons & Co., 1925
From Chaos to Control, New York, Century Co., 1933
'The international anarchy', in Leonard Woolf, *The Intelligent Man's Way to Prevent War*, London, Gollancz, 1933, pp. 19–66
The Press and the Organization of Society, Cambridge, Minority Press, 1933
Preface to Peace, New York, Harper & Brothers Ltd, 1935
The Unseen Assassins, London, Hamish Hamilton, 1935
This Have and Have-not Business: Political Fantasy and Economic Fact, London, Hamish Hamilton, 1936
The Defence of the Empire, London, Hamish Hamilton, 1937
Peace with the Dictators?: A Symposium and Some Conclusions, London, Hamish Hamilton, 1938
The Great Illusion – Now, Harmondsworth, Penguin, 1938
Let the People Know, New York, Viking Press, 1943
Steep Places: An Examination of Political Tendencies, London, Hamish Hamilton, 1947
After All: The Autobiography of Norman Angell, London, Hamilton, 1951

Further reading

Bisceglia, Louis, *Norman Angell and the Liberal Internationalism in Britain, 1931–1939*, New York, Garland, 1982
Howard, Michael, *War and the Liberal Conscience*, London, Temple Smith, 1978
Miller, John D.B., *Norman Angell and the Futility of War: Peace and the Public Mind*, London, Macmillan, 1986. Contains a comprehensive bibliography of Angell's publications.
Navari, Cornelia, 'The Great Illusion revisited: the international political theory of Norman Angell', *Review of International Studies* 15 (1989), pp. 341–58
Weinroth, H., 'Norman Angell and "The Great Illusion": an episode in pre-1914 pacifism', *Historical Journal* 17 (1974), pp. 551–74

CHARLES BEITZ

Most of the liberals in this part of the book are empirical theorists. Although they are motivated by liberal values of individual freedom, political equality and democracy, they are primarily concerned with the ways in which international relations promote or impede those values. Beitz is an important theorist who is interested in the justification of the values themselves and the problem of how to give individuals reasons to behave in accordance with them on a global scale. In other words, he wants to elaborate principles of justice desirable in themselves and to which we can reasonably conform, given that individuals and states are motivationally complex. His book *Political Theory and International Relations* (1979) is an attempt to pursue two basic goals of political theory – the elaboration of an ideal of collective life and a persuasive argument as to why we should try to promote it. As Thomas Nagel points out, '[a]n ideal, however attractive it may be to contemplate, is utopian if real individuals cannot be motivated to live by it. But a political system that is completely tied down to individual motives may fail to embody any ideal at all.'[1] These two dimensions of Beitz's project are inextricably connected to each other, since he is just as concerned to avoid the tag of 'idealism' as he is to defend his liberal principles.

Political Theory and International Relations arose out of Beitz's doctoral work at Princeton University in the mid-1970s. This was an interesting period, both intellectually and politically. On the one hand, political theory in the United States was emerging from a long period of slumber and marginalisation in light of the dominance of positivism and behaviouralism in American political science. 'Values' were often associated with the emotions or 'preferences' of individuals, relegating morality to the realm of 'opinions'. The dominant political philosophy in the academy was utilitarianism, which asserted the seemingly simple principle, 'maximise social welfare and happiness'. This principle coexisted with the liberal intuition that the rights of individuals should not be sacrificed for the sake of social welfare, but those who believed in such rights lacked systematic philosophical arguments against the prevailing utilitarian wisdom. On the other hand, in the study of international relations, there were signs that the dominant framework of realism was inadequate for studying a world of 'complex interdependence'. Writers such as Robert Keohane and Joseph Nye were claiming that the image of 'power politics' among self-contained states, if not entirely obsolete, was inappropriate for analysing important issues and emerging trends in international political economy. Actors other than states needed to be examined in their own right, such as multinational corporations and transnational social movements. The distribution of military power was increasingly irrelevant, they argued, whilst the image of 'anarchy' was being replaced by what Wolfram Hanreider called a 'new convergence' of international and domestic political processes. The politics of economic distribution was often as, and sometimes more important than, the politics of military security.[2]

The renaissance of political theory in the United States was due in large part to one man, John Rawls, and his book, *A Theory of Justice* (1971). Beitz took advantage of the moment and claimed that the 'principles of justice' elaborated by Rawls could perform the two functions of political theory on a global scale now that 'realists' had allegedly lost one of their main arguments against the integration of political theory and international relations. The latter was no longer an arena of 'continuity and necessity' in the form of power politics, whilst (or so Beitz believed) the collective ideals of liberal political theory could be defended in terms of universal self-interest. To understand the reasons for Beitz's argument, a brief summary of Rawls's book is required. Rawls provided a unique *method* for discovering principles of justice that protected individual rights. He then developed principles of justice that defended not only the traditional list of civil and political liberties but also a more equal distribution of income, wealth, education, job opportunities, health care and other 'goods' essential to secure the wealth and dignity of all, including the disadvantaged.

The method that Rawls used to generate his principles of justice is based on the social contract tradition employed by Hobbes, Rousseau and Kant. But instead of postulating certain characteristics of 'human nature' to fix the terms of the contract, Rawls suggests the idea of an 'original position'. This is a hypothetical situation in which a 'veil of ignorance' deprives us of knowledge of our natural talents, moral views and place in the social order so that we can rationally choose principles of justice that are not biased in our own favour. Not knowing your own religion, you will choose a principle of religious toleration to govern society. Ignorant of your social class, you will choose principles that guarantee fair equality of opportunity and maximise your life chances if you turn out to be one of the least advantaged citizens. Every 'rational' person will choose these principles, because there is nothing to distinguish us from each other in the original position, where we are all rational choosers. Here, we are 'free and equal moral persons', led by our sense of 'justice as fairness' to develop principles binding on each of us and society as a whole.

The political substance of Rawls's theory attempts to integrate socialist criticism into liberalism. The first principle of justice is equal liberty, giving priority to securing basic liberal freedoms of thought, conscience, speech, assembly, universal suffrage, freedom from arbitrary arrest and the right to hold property. The second principle of justice is divided into two parts. First, there is the 'difference principle'. Social and economic inequalities are justified only if they increase benefits to the least advantaged citizens. The second part requires fair equality of opportunity for all, equalising not only job opportunities, but also life chances irrespective of social class. Thus Rawlsian justice is liberalism for the least advantaged that pays tribute to the socialist critique. The difference principle prevents the poor from falling so long as it is possible to raise their life prospects higher. Similarly, *fair* equality of opportunities goes beyond classical liberalism in requiring compensatory education and limits on economic inequality.

The importance of Rawls in the history of political theory is now acknowledged. Beitz claims that he is equally important in the study of international relations, despite the fact that Rawls himself says very little about the subject. He does not ignore it, but argues that at a global level, the consequences of proceeding from an original position *among states* would generate 'familiar' principles already contained in international law:

> The basic principle of the law of nations is a principle of equality. Independent peoples *organised as states* have certain fundamental equal rights. This principle is analogous to the equal rights of citizens in a constitutional regime. One consequence of this equality of nations is the principle of self-determination, the right of a people to settle its own affairs without the intervention of foreign powers. Another ... is the right of self-defence against attack, including the right to form defensive alliances to protect this right. A further principle is that treaties are to be kept ... but agreements to cooperate in an unjustified attack are void *ab initio*.[3]

Rawls himself is ambiguous in failing to distinguish between nations and states. Either way, Beitz sees no reason to confine the original position to individuals within a nation or a state. He defends a radically cosmopolitan conception of international justice against what he calls a 'morality of states' conception. The rights of states are themselves derivative from the rights of human beings, and Beitz sees no reason to confine the second principle, pertaining to distributive justice, to relations among citizens within the territorial borders of the sovereign state. From a moral point of view, territorial boundaries are arbitrary, the consequence of historical contingency rather than ethical deliberation. He is somewhat sceptical, therefore, of the principle of 'self-determination' being limited to those states that happen to exist at any particular moment in history. Who is the relevant 'self'? What is the scope of 'self-determination'? Political 'autonomy' for particular groups, or fully-fledged sovereign statehood? What counts for Beitz is the ethical primacy of individuals, not the murky 'shared' characteristics of groups:

> The idea that states should be respected as autonomous sources of ends, and hence should not be interfered with, arises as an analogue of the idea that individual persons should be respected as autonomous beings. But the analogy is faulty. *The analogue of individual autonomy, at the level of states, is conformity of their basic institutions with appropriate principle of justice . . . the principle of state autonomy . . . cannot be interpreted correctly without bringing in considerations of social justice usually thought to belong to the political theory of the state.*[4]

If Beitz is right, and Rawlsian principles of justice are indeed appropriate at a global level, then much of what passes for the study of international ethics must be rethought completely. Indeed, Beitz is very clear on this point. The Hobbesian analogy between individuals and states, which most students are taught in their first undergraduate lecture on international relations, is wrong. He devotes a great deal of space in his book to relentlessly exposing the extent to which the study of international relations is fundamentally flawed, since Rawls provides us –

at last – with universal principles of justice that ought to be implemented at a global level. What is more, they can be, or at least, the condition of interdependence makes it more possible to do so now than ever before, and Beitz makes a strong case on contracterian grounds that 'persons of diverse citizenship have distributive obligations to one another analogous to those of citizens of the same state. International distributive obligations are founded on justice and not merely on mutual aid.'[5]

With one book, Charles Beitz succeeded in awakening a new generation of students to the value of political theory for international relations. He was able to use Rawls to rebut epistemological arguments that equate morality with emotions or custom (ethical skepticism), and he could appeal to economic interdependence to attack substantive arguments about international relations being an inappropriate realm for applied ethics (what might be called ethical impossibility). In many ways, *Political Theory and International Relations* is therefore a very important book for students of political theory and international relations. It seeks to integrate two sub-fields in political science that have traditionally evolved along separate tracks. Martin Wight had argued that political theory was confined to the state, and that the closest analogue to political theory in the study of international relations was the philosophy of history. If Beitz was right, that situation was about to change.

To some extent, the situation has changed thanks in part to Beitz. But it would be wrong to suggest that his argument has been widely accepted and that one can simply move on to consider the complexity of the details of global distributive justice along Rawlsian lines. To be sure, just how one would go about implementing the distributive principle at a global level is a daunting task in itself. Of course, Beitz acknowledges that his theory should be seen as an ideal to which individuals and states ought to aspire, and should be motivated to work towards.

It is not a fault of the theory that such a gap exists between its injunctions and contemporary practice, although Janna Thompson gives some idea of what would be involved:

> There is, for one thing, no world political body capable of taxing rich individuals for the sake of the least well-off; no world body capable of ensuring that resources actually benefit needy individuals. To make this theory practical it seems that we need, at the very least, an organisation capable of administering and enforcing a universal system of social distribution.[6]

Needless to say, we have nothing of the sort in the world today, and it is doubtful whether distributive justice can ever be achieved along Rawlsian lines without more drastic restraints on global capitalism than either Rawls or Beitz would be prepared to accept. The reason is that political interventions in the 'free market' would undermine other values that liberals hold dear, such as freedom from state (or supranational!) coercion and the right to hold property.

One could, then, conclude that Beitz has succeeded in integrating political theory and international relations, even if the task of achieving his practical goals is immense. However, the theory itself has been subject to a number of criticisms, which need to be considered by those who support the kind of cosmopolitan vision Beitz has articulated. Two, in particular, stand out.

First, it may be that Rawls has good philosophical reasons for being reluctant to endorse a global version of his theory of justice, quite apart from the obvious difficulties of implementation. If he succeeded in placing a discourse of rights back into political theory and dislodging the intellectual dominance of Benthamite utilitarianism, Rawls now concedes that the original position is not as innocent as it first appeared to be. This is in response to the views of 'communitarian' political philosophers who have attacked the 'abstract universalism' of the veil of ignorance. It is argued that the theory rests upon a mistaken and incoherent conception of people as unencumbered by shared, socially determined and 'constitutive' ends. In more recent essays Rawls denies that his theory presupposes any *metaphysical* conception of the person. As a 'political', rather than a metaphysical, theory it aims to achieve a consensus among citizens of a pluralistic democracy who can nonetheless stand back from their social practices and reflect on their reasonableness. If that is the case, then there are good reasons for limiting the scope of the theory to particular societies like the United States. Rawls thinks societies should be thought of as 'co-operative ventures for mutual advantage', and it is difficult to see how one could characterise the globe in such terms. As Chris Brown points out,

> World 'society', so-called, is not a society in this sense because it does not co-operatively create a surplus that has to be divided; thus principles of distributive justice are not required on a world scale because there is nothing to distribute. Individual societies do not co-operate but they do have to coexist. International justice is about this co-existence.[7]

So perhaps Rawls is right to exclude the second principle of justice from the international arena, and Beitz is mistaken to imagine a global 'veil of ignorance' generating anything but a lot of noise. It is hard enough to imagine consensus within national societies on a list of 'basic goods' to distribute, let alone global society.

A second criticism of Beitz is the way in which he appeals to international interdependence to justify his theory. There are a couple of problems. First, if the appeal is supposed to justify calling international society a 'co-operative venture', the power of the appeal is subject to change. Interdependence, after all, is a variable in international relations, not a constant. As Andrew Linklater notes, 'any ... theory which specifies interdependence as the key to its development generates very substantial limitations; for it would be a regional theory and perhaps even an ephemeral one'.[8] Would the theory have greatest application in those regions that were most 'interdependent'? If so, then as Brown points out, Beitz's theory 'works best where it is least needed and most irrelevant', within areas such as Western Europe rather than between Western Europe and the Third World.

These are powerful criticisms directed at both elements of Beitz's project – its appeal to philosophical universalism in justifying political and economic rights, and its empirical claims regarding the scope of the theory in international relations. Nevertheless, although Beitz has acknowledged the force of these criticisms, his work remains of value as a bold attempt to integrate political theory with the study of international relations. Whilst it fails to offer an escape from the conflict between particularism and universalism in the study of international ethics, the legitimacy of the quest itself is now acknowledged to be a legitimate one in international relations. *Political Theory and International Relations* is an important book which helped to shift the nature of debate in international relations in a new direction. Beitz was quite right to observe that 'such systematic moral debate about international relations as has taken place has been between adherents of international scepticism and the morality of states. However . . . the more pressing issues are those that divide the morality of states from a cosmopolitan morality.'[9] Charles Beitz is presently Professor and Dean of Faculty at Bowdoin College in the United States. He has taught political philosophy and international relations at Princeton University and Swarthmore College, Pennsylvania. He is also a member of the editorial board of the journal *Philosophy and Public Affairs*.

Notes

1 Thomas Nagel, 'What makes a political theory utopian?', *Social Research* 56 (1989), p. 904.

2 Wolfram F. Hanreider, 'Dissolving international politics: reflections on the nation-state', *American Political Science Review* 72 (1978), pp. 1276–87. See also Robert Keohane and Joseph Nye, *Power and Interdependence: World Politics in Transition*, Boston, Little, Brown, 1977.
3 John Rawls, *A Theory of Justice*, Cambridge, Massachusetts, Harvard University Press, 1971, pp. 378–9.
4 Charles Beitz, *Political Theory and International Relations*, Princeton, New Jersey, Princeton University Press, 1979, p. 122. Emphasis added.
5 Ibid., p. 128.
6 Janna Thompson, *Justice and World Order*, London, Routledge, 1992, p. 15.
7 Chris Brown, *International Relations Theory: New Normative Approaches*, London, Harvester Wheatsheaf, 1992, pp. 173–4.
8 Andrew Linklater, *Men and Citizens in the Theory of International Relations*, Second Edition, London, Macmillan, 1990, p. 6.
9 Charles Beitz, *Political Theory and International Relations*, op. cit., p. 183.

See also in this book

Wight, Walzer

Beitz's major writings

'Justice and international relations', *Philosophy and Public Affairs* 4 (1975), pp. 360–89
Political Theory and International Relations, Princeton, New Jersey, Princeton University Press, 1979
'Bounded morality: justice and the state in world politics', *International Organization* 33 (1979), pp. 405–24
'Nonintervention and communal integrity', *Philosophy and Public Affairs* 9 (1980), pp. 385–403
Law, Economics, and Philosophy: A Critical Introduction, With Applications to the Law of Torts (with Mark Kuperberg), Totowa, New Jersey, Rowman & Allenheld, 1983
Political Equality: An Essay in Democratic Theory, Princeton, New Jersey, Princeton University Press, 1990
'Sovereignty and morality in international affairs', in David Held (ed.), *Political Theory Today*, Stanford, Stanford University Press, 1991, pp. 236–54

Further reading

Brown, Chris, *International Relations Theory: New Normative Approaches*, London, Harvester Wheatsheaf, 1992

Malnes, Raino, 'Philosophers crossing borders: recent literature on ethics and international relations', *Journal of Peace Research* 20 (1983), pp. 193–200

Rawls, John, *A Theory of Justice*, Cambridge, Massachusetts, Harvard University Press, 1971

Rawls, John, 'Justice as fairness: political not metaphysical', *Philosophy and Public Affairs* 14 (1985), pp. 223–51

Suganami, Hidemi, 'Reflections on the domestic analogy: the case of Bull, Beitz, and Linklater', *Review of International Studies* 12 (1986), pp. 145–58

Thompson, Janna, *Justice and World Order: A Philosophical Inquiry*, London, Routledge, 1992

MICHAEL DOYLE

Two factors have militated against the systematic study of history in the Anglo-American study of international relations. First, there is the impact of what might be called 'current affairs' in determining the focus of study. In the desire for 'policy relevance' and an understandable urge to stay abreast of the issues of the day, students can easily become hostages to the daily headlines, unable and perhaps unwilling to stand back and try to assess longer-term patterns of behaviour among states. Second, and this is almost a ritual complaint in the field, the search for 'laws of state behaviour' in the 1950s and 1960s has left an indelible mark in the field. History was studied only insofar as it could generate 'testable hypotheses' or provide the equivalent of a laboratory for the testing of hypotheses themselves generated by logic and deductive reason.

The main reason for including Michael Doyle in this book is his appreciation for the 'internal' history of the field. In his recent critique of the way international relations and its history is presented in much of the literature, Brian Schmidt laments what he regards as its overwhelming 'presentism':

> The present theoretical consensus of the discipline, or possibly some polemical version of what that consensus should be, is in effect taken as definitive, and the past is then reconstructed as a teleology leading up to and fully manifested in it ... the net result of this presentist orientation is that the historical talk of faithfully reconstructing past ideas, practices and conversations becomes subservient to demonstrating a thesis about the contemporary nature of the discipline.[1]

Schmidt's article was published in 1994, three years before the publication of what is, in my view, the best undergraduate textbook in contemporary international relations theory, Michael Doyle's *Ways of War and Peace* (1997). When this book landed on my desk in mid-1997, I must confess to an inward groan. My first reaction was that here was yet another American 'blockbuster' of a textbook for gullible undergraduates, packed with contemporary 'data', a cornucopia of complicated models with arrows sprinkled liberally across the page, and hundreds of historical 'snapshots' illustrating the empirical 'relevance' of suggestive but unprovable generalisations. It is, however, a unique text, far superior to most books that seek to introduce students to the field in a theoretically rigorous manner. Its value arises from Doyle's ability to combine two tasks. On the one hand, he is able to reproduce the 'classics' of the field whilst remaining sensitive to the context in which they were written. On the other hand, he demonstrates their contemporary relevance by extracting the relevant empirical generalisations contained within them and subjecting them to a rigorous examination in light of the historical evidence. This is the method that Doyle has used to great effect in the past, particularly in his work on Kant and Thucydides, and in his major study on imperialism.

Michael Doyle is Professor of Politics and International Affairs at the Woodrow Wilson School, the Director of the Center for International Studies and Director of Graduate Studies in the Politics Department at Princeton University. Born in Honolulu, Hawaii, Doyle was educated in France and Switzerland and graduated from Jesuit High School in Tampa, Florida. He studied at the US Air Force Academy before transferring to Harvard University, where he earned his BA, MA and PhD degrees in political science. Prior to taking up his present position at Princeton, he taught at the University of Warwick and the Johns Hopkins University. In 1993 he served as Vice President of the International Peace Academy and currently he is a Senior Fellow of the International Peace Academy in New York. He is the North American editor of *International Peacekeeping* and a member of the Council on Foreign Relations in New York.

Prior to the publication of *Ways of War and Peace*, Doyle was best known for his work on nineteenth-century European imperialism, as well as for his rigorous examination of the alleged connection between the prevalence of liberal democracy within states and the absence of war between them. In 1986 he published *Empires*, which is a fully multicausal analysis of European imperialism. The latter, he argues, has been poorly defined within the literature, making it difficult to generate testable hypotheses on the causes of this elusive phenomenon. Doyle defines imperialism as 'a relationship, formal or informal, in which one state controls the effective political sovereignty of another'.[2] A comprehensive explanation of empire, therefore, should demonstrate the nature of such effective control, explain the motives for seeking control and explain either the submission or ineffective resistance of the peripheral society. Any theory intended to describe and explain imperial relationships should, he argues, take into account four factors: the interests and capabilities of the metropole; the interests and capabilities of the periphery; the dynamics of transnational forces; and the nature of international systemic relations. Transnational forces are the means through which the imperial power affects the periphery. These may be military, trade, missionary or some combination of all three. International systemic relations refer to the balance of power among imperial states.

Doyle criticises theories such as those of Lenin, Hobson and Schumpeter that blame imperialism primarily on the needs of the metropolitan states to expand. He also criticises theories that blame imperialism chiefly on the weakness and collapse of the peripheral states. For Doyle, imperialism is not merely the consequence of forces in one or another part of the international system. Instead, nations and societies come into contact with one another through transnational forces. Imperialism is one possible result, depending on the relative capacities and interests of the societies involved.

In particular, three characteristics separate imperial states or those with imperial potential from states liable to imperial rule. Size and wealth, interestingly enough, are not the key factors, although these may affect the struggle between imperial states and have an effect on the scope of empire. More important are political centralisation, unity and differentiation. Thus a highly centralised, unified, differentiated state, such as England, is likely to overwhelm decentralised, fragmented, less differentiated states with which it comes into contact, resulting in imperialism even when the target states – such as China and India – are larger and even wealthier in aggregate terms.

Doyle also suggests that imperialism has important variations that need to be explained. Some empires exercised direct rule whilst others ruled indirectly through indigenous leaders in the colonies. Doyle claims that the kind of rule does not depend mainly on the goals of the imperial power. He notes that European powers generally preferred informal rule, where at all possible, as a less expensive way of obtaining the trading rights they valued. Yet trade required security, law enforcement and adjudication of interests between representatives of the imperial power and members of the peripheral states. Where the latter were weakly differentiated tribes of people, the peripheral state could not perform these tasks. The imperial state was then drawn, sometimes reluctantly, to exercise direct rule and undertake the necessary services itself through consular authority. State making in the periphery was thus a consequence of imperial activity.

In contrast, where the peripheral state had a more differentiated patrimonial or feudal structure, the peripheral state could perform many of these duties, at least in controlling its own population. The metropolitan power could then make agreements with the peripheral state regarding trade and protection of its emissaries. The relationship that initially developed could be described as unequal, or dependent, but it was still not empire. This structure was often broken by the growth of indebtedness on the part of the peripheral state. The latter borrowed for a variety of reasons, from investment to state consumption. But in most cases the government invested too rashly to be able to repay its debts. In this event, the imperial state was drawn to exercise more control over the economy and budget of the peripheral state. Indirect rule developed as the 'effective sovereignty' of the peripheral state weakened.

Peripheral characteristics thus explain much regarding the contours of imperial rule. Yet they do not suggest when the pace of imperialism is likely to accelerate, or which colonies are considered the most important, or which great power is likely to be the leader in the process. For these issues, Doyle turns to systemic and domestic considerations within the imperial state. Systemic factors help account for the acceleration of imperialism after 1870. Up to that point, when British naval supremacy and

industrial domination were widely acknowledged, European states were happy to use trading stations protected by Pax Britannica. After 1870, however, Bismarck's orchestration of European alliances and European powers' attempts to gain secure markets for their own efforts at industrialisation led to a scramble for territorial control overseas, mainly in the unclaimed regions of Africa. Following a general consideration of how the multipolar international system shaped the *pace* of imperialism, Doyle examines more closely how domestic considerations shaped the imperial efforts of France, Britain, Germany and Spain. Doyle concludes his book by arguing that a combination of the weakening of imperial interests among the European powers and a growing coherence in the peripheral states meant the end of empire in the twentieth century.

Empires is a fine example of the way Doyle engages with classical international theory. First, he reads the conventional theorists on the issue, re-presenting their arguments with due regard to the particular contexts within which they were arguing. Next, he extracts from their work a set of empirical generalisations. Third, he carefully examines the evidence to see how well classical theories stand up under the test of time. The approach is a cautious one and the conclusion to his book is not particularly surprising. 'No one explanation [of imperialism] was sufficient ... [t]he foundations of empires remained a combination of causes'.[3] At the same time, Doyle's book makes clear the need to avoid simplistic, unicausal explanations of complex transnational and international processes.

In 1983, Doyle engaged in a similarly thorough analysis of the work of Immanuel Kant. Doyle was among the first of a number of theorists who discovered, after an exhaustive empirical analysis of the historical record, what Kant had predicted and hoped for, an emerging 'zone of peace' among liberal democratic states. Doyle stated the proposition as follows:

Even though liberal states have become involved in numerous wars with nonliberal states, constitutionally secure liberal states have yet to engage in war with one another. No one should argue that such wars are impossible; but preliminary evidence does appear to indicate that there exists a significant predisposition against warfare between liberal states ... a liberal zone of peace, a pacific union, has been maintained and has expanded despite numerous particular conflicts of economic and strategic interest.[4]

This finding has been seized on by a number of liberal theorists of international relations, particularly Fukuyama, to proclaim that, with the end of the Cold War, the collapse of communism, and the alleged expansion of liberal democracies around the world, war between states has become 'obsolescent'. Doyle is far more cautious. Whilst he welcomes the legacy of liberalism in creating a 'zone of peace' between liberal states, the very success of liberalism, for reasons outlined by Kant in the eighteenth century, give cause for concern in a 'mixed' system of liberal and nonliberal states:

The very constitutional restraint, shared commercial interests, and international respect for individual rights that promote peace among liberal states can exacerbate conflicts in relations between liberal and non-liberal societies. ... According to liberal practice, some nonliberal states ... do not acquire the right to be free from foreign intervention, nor are they assumed to respect the political independence and territorial integrity of other states. Instead conflicts of interest become interpreted as steps in a campaign of aggression against the liberal state.[5]

To simplify greatly, if the explanation for the separate peace between liberal states is due to their liberalism, it is tempting to argue that relations between liberal and nonliberal states *cannot* be peaceful, for the latter are,

in a sense, at war with their own people. Lacking internal legitimacy, nonliberal states will be more willing (other things being equal) to engage in aggression against other states when it is in the interests of their leaders to do so. Doyle does not argue that this is the case, merely that liberal states, such as the United States, may act on this presupposition, and therefore be unwilling to accord nonliberal states the same degree of respect that they give to other liberal states. Indeed, the use of 'appeasement' as a term of abuse, whether applied to Britain in the 1930s or to the United States during the years of détente with the former Soviet Union in the late 1960s, owes something to this way of thinking. Consequently, when liberal states do go to war with nonliberal states, Doyle suggests that they are prone to what he calls 'liberal imprudence', as well as 'liberal imperialism', seeking to 'export' their liberal democratic doctrine to the rest of the world. In short, a world that includes liberal and nonliberal states is not necessarily a very stable one and requires a healthy dose of realist prudence by liberal statesmen.

Doyle's work on Kant and the liberal peace is included in his latest work, *Ways of War and Peace*. As with his book on the theory and practice of imperialism, Doyle applies contemporary social science methodologies to a review of classical theories of international relations. This is a great work of theoretical synthesis, for three reasons.

First, it is a superb analytic survey of classical approaches in the discipline. Indeed, if the reader is looking for a companion volume to the one you are presently reading, which focuses on key thinkers *before* the twentieth century, then Doyle's book is highly recommended for this reason alone. There is simply no other volume that can provide as good a summary of the following: Thucydides, Machiavelli, Hobbes, Rousseau, Locke, Bentham, Smith, Schumpeter, Kant, Marx, Engels and Lenin. Doyle's summaries of each are very well written, with extensive reference to key sources on each writer. They are also, at times, very amusing. For example, Rousseau:

> He revealed late in life the deep psychological and sexual frustrations from which he had long suffered in his extraordinarily frank psychological memoir, *Confessions*. Can you imagine Henry Kissinger or Alexander Haig or some other contemporary proponent of Realism confessing in public that he went through life craving to be spanked? A bit of a con artist, he proceeded to set himself up as a teacher of music to young girls in Geneva before he could read a note. But above all he was a genius.[6]

Second, although Doyle uses what is now a somewhat old-fashioned typology of realists, liberals and socialist thinkers, he is appropriately sensitive to the important differences between thinkers in each category. As he rightly puts it, 'worldviews align themselves on spectrums; they do not fall into neat boxes'.[7] Appropriately, Doyle's categorisation of writers within each of his main groups is determined by their own arguments, not by some predetermined epistemological criteria invoked from on high by the author. There is a refreshing absence of any mention of the philosophy of science, positivism, postmodernism or 'perspectivism'. In other words, Doyle does exactly what Schmidt called for in 1994, and he provides us with what Schmidt calls a 'critical internal discursive history':

> The task . . . is to describe the evolution of conceptual forms the discipline has taken by examining the discursive practices that led to the different historical configurations. The concern of such a history is to re-assemble the internal academic discourse of international relations by following a relatively coherent conversation.[8]

The delineation of differences among realists is original and useful. Doyle distinguishes between fundamentalist, structural and constitutional realists. He also has some interesting points to make about the members of the so-called English School, preferring to locate liberalism between realism and socialism rather than in the idea of 'international society', *à la* Martin Wight and Hedley Bull.

Finally, Doyle does not rest content with reconstructing a conversation among dead giants. He also elaborates their empirical generalisations and evaluates them against the available empirical evidence. Since so many of his classical mentors are political philosophers, translating their normative arguments solely into the language of empirical social science is inadequate, so the book contains two comprehensive chapters on the ethics of international intervention and distribution. It concludes with a tentative gaze into the future through the lenses of each normative framework of analysis and, quite properly, Doyle does not pretend to be able either to conclude or transcend the conversation. His plea for pluralism in international relations theory is a suitable justification for greater toleration among students for, although he himself is a liberal, he acknowledges the need for realist prudence and he is also sensitive to the inequality that inspires socialist visions of world order:

> A pluralistic model of world politics is not a contradiction to theoretical knowledge, but a basis for it. We as thinking human beings need not be, and for the most part are not, singular selves. Our modern identities are pluralistic, found in individual identity, nation, and class, as well as religion, race, and gender. We cannot escape multiplicities entering into our policy choices, nor, if we want to be true to ourselves, should we try to.[9]

Notes

1 Brian Schmidt, 'The historiography of academic international relations', *Review of International Studies* 20 (1994), p. 363.

2 Michael Doyle, *Empires*, Ithaca, New York, Cornell University Press, 1986, p. 45.
3 Ibid., p. 341.
4 Michael Doyle, 'Kant, liberal legacies, and foreign affairs: Part 1', *Philosophy and Public Affairs* 12 (1983), p. 213–15.
5 Michael Doyle, 'Kant, liberal legacies, and foreign affairs: Part 2', *Philosophy and Public Affairs* 12 (1983), pp. 324–5, emphasis in original.
6 Michael Doyle, *Ways of War and Peace*, New York, Norton, 1997, pp. 139–40.
7 Ibid., p. 210.
8 Schmidt, op. cit., p. 365
9 Michael Doyle, *Ways of War and Peace*, op. cit., pp. 499–500.

See also in this book

Fukuyama, Hobson, Lenin

Doyle's major writings

'Kant, liberal legacies, and foreign affairs: Part 1', *Philosophy and Public Affairs* 12 (1983), pp. 205–34
'Kant, liberal legacies, and foreign affairs: Part 2', *Philosophy and Public Affairs* 12 (1983), pp. 323–53
'Liberalism and world politics', *American Political Science Review* 80 (1986), pp. 1151–69
Empires, Ithaca, New York, Cornell University Press, 1986
'Thucydidean realism', *Review of International Relations* 16 (1990), pp. 223–37
'An international liberal community', in Graham Allison and Gregory Treverton (eds), *Rethinking America's Security: Beyond Cold War to New World Order*, New York, W.W. Norton, 1992, pp. 307–33
'Liberalism and world politics revisited', in Charles W. Kegley (ed.), *Controversies in International Relations Theory: Realism and the Neoliberal Challenge*, New York, St Martin's Press, 1996, pp. 83–106
Ways of War and Peace, New York, Norton, 1997

Further reading

Brown, Chris, 'Really existing liberalism and international order', *Millennium: Journal of International Studies* 21 (1992), pp. 313–28
Lake, David, 'Powerful pacifists: democratic states and war', *American Political Science Review* 86 (1992), pp. 24–37

Meuller, John, *Retreat From Doomsday: On The Obsolescence of Major War*, New York, Basic Books, 1989
Smith, Michael Joseph, 'Liberalism and international reform', in Terry Nardin and David R. Mapel (eds), *Traditions of International Ethics*, Cambridge, Cambridge University Press, 1993, pp. 201–24

FRANCIS FUKUYAMA

Rather like E.H. Carr's *The Twenty Years' Crisis* (1945), Fukuyama's book *The End of History and the Last Man* (1992) provided an interpretation of the significance of the end of the Cold War that captured an enormous amount of public attention. Almost overnight, the phrase 'end of history' was used as a synonym for the 'post-Cold War era' and Fukuyama, hitherto almost unknown amongst students of international relations, became an instant intellectual celebrity. In a sense, this was unfortunate. Fukuyama did *not* say that 'history' had come to an end in the sense that politics, war and conflict would no longer take place. Nor did he argue that the collapse of communism would guarantee that all states would become liberal democracies. These misconceptions are perhaps a consequence of Fukuyama's overexposure in the media. The subtleties of his argument, an ingenious blend of political philosophy, historical analysis and tentative futurology, can only be gleaned from a careful reading of the text, something that too many commentators have neglected to do. Ironically, however, once one abandons some of the more simplistic interpretations of Fukuyama's argument, it remains unclear why the book did attract so much attention in the last decade of the twentieth century. The most interesting aspects of the book, in my view, were the ones least commented on, having to do with the characteristics of 'the last man' rather than the 'end of history' per se. Again, those who have focused on the first part of the book have downplayed these aspects. Only if one grasps the underlying pessimism of Fukuyama's argument is it possible to avoid the temptation to celebrate or condemn him on the erroneous assumption that his book is merely an exercise in liberal 'triumphalism' at the end of the Cold War.

Francis Fukuyama was born in 1953. He was raised in the United States, but he is Japanese by descent. His grandfather on his father's side fled from Japan in 1905 when Japan was at war with Russia and his mother came for a well-known intellectual family in Japan. Both parents were academically inclined. His father was a Protestant minister and Fukuyama describes himself as 'a sort of open-minded agnostic but without any anti-clericalism'.[1] He went to Cornell University as an undergraduate and he received his PhD in political science from Harvard University. His thesis was on Soviet foreign policy in the Middle East, but he also spent some time in France studying post-structuralism under Jacques Derrida. When he left Harvard, Fukuyama joined the Rand Corporation (an influential private think tank in the United States) as a policy analyst specialising in Middle Eastern political-military affairs and the foreign policy of the former Soviet Union. He has held a variety of positions with Rand and with the US State Department over the last fifteen years. At present he is the Hirst Professor of Public Policy at George Mason University.

In the summer of 1989, Fukuyama published a short article in the conservative journal *The National Interest*, entitled 'The end of History?' His major book was written in response to the debate that followed, although the book itself has continued to attract widely divergent opinions from across the ideological spectrum in the United States and elsewhere. For example, John Dunn describes it as a 'puerile volume' and compares it to 'the worst sort of American undergraduate term-paper'.[2] In contrast, Wayne Cristaudo judges it to be 'the most

important defence of liberal democracy since John Rawls' *A Theory of Justice*'.[3]

The book operates at a number of levels. In the words of Perry Anderson, 'no one has ever attempted a comparable synthesis – at once so deep in ontological premise and so close to the surface of global politics'.[4] Given the scope of Fukuyama's ambition, I can only sketch the main contours of his argument in the hope that readers will not substitute what follows for a thorough examination of the text itself. Any book that can attract such divergent opinions as those expressed by Dunn and Cristaudo deserves to be read with some care.

By the phrase 'end of History', Fukuyama is referring to the history of thought about legitimate first principles governing political and social organisation. His argument is primarily a normative one. At the end of the twentieth century, the combination of liberal democracy and capitalism has proved superior to any alternative political/economic system, and the reason lies in its ability to satisfy the basic drives of human nature. The latter is composed of two fundamental desires. One is the desire for material goods and wealth and the other (more fundamental) desire is for recognition of our worth as human beings by those around us. Capitalism is the best economic system for maximising the production of goods and services and for exploiting scientific technology to generate wealth. However, economic growth is only part of the story. Fukuyama appeals to Hegel's concept of recognition to account for the superiority of liberal democracy over its rivals in the political arena. Whilst economic growth can be promoted under a variety of political regimes, including fascist ones, only liberal democracies can meet the fundamental human need for recognition, political freedom and equality. It was Hegel who contended that the end of history would arrive when humans had achieved the kind of civilisation that satisfied their fundamental longings. For Hegel, that end point was the constitutional state. In his version, Hegel appointed Napoleon as the harbinger of the end of history at the beginning of the nineteenth century. Fukuyama argues that we need to recover the philosophical idealism of Hegel and abandon the philosophical materialism of Marx and his followers who believed that socialism was necessary to overcome the economic inequality of capitalist societies. Fukuyama also finds in Hegel a more profound understanding of human nature than can be gleaned from the ideas of such philosophers as Thomas Hobbes and John Locke, who privileged self-preservation above recognition.

In addition to Hegel, Fukuyama invokes Plato and Alexandre Kojève, Hegel's most famous interpreter. From Plato, Fukuyama borrows the notion of *thymos*, variously translated as 'spiritedness', 'courage' or 'desire'. *Megalothymia* is the *thymos* of great men, the great movers of history such as Caesar and Stalin. In contrast, *isothymia* is the humble demand for recognition in the form of equality rather than superiority. History is a struggle between these thymotic passions. The genius of liberal democracy is that it represents the end point of the struggle. The master–slave dialectic is a primary motor of history, which can never be stable as long as human beings are divided between masters and slaves. The latter will never accept their subordinate status and the genius of capitalist liberal democracy is its ability to reconcile the thymotic passions. Shadia Drury sums up Fukuyama's argument as follows:

Liberalism pacifies and de-politicises the aristocratic world of mastery by turning politics into economics. Liberalism pacifies the masterful *thymos* of the first man and replaces it with the slavish *thymos* of the last man. Instead of superiority and dominance, society strives for equality. Those who still long for dominance have the capitalist pursuit of wealth as their outlet.[5]

Fukuyama also relies on the interpretation of Hegel by Alexandre Kojève, the Russian exile and political philosopher. In a series of lectures delivered in Paris in the 1940s, Kojève argued that the welfare state had solved the problems of capitalism identified by Marx.[6] Thus capitalism has managed to suppress its own internal contradictions. Furthermore, it not only provides material prosperity, but also homogenises ideas and values, thus undermining the clash of ideology between states, thereby reducing the threat of war. Hegel did not believe that the end of war within states could be replicated at the international level. Kojève and Fukuyama argue that whilst wars will not disappear, the homogenisation of values among the great powers will promote peace among the most powerful states, and these are the ones that matter in a long-term historical perspective.

Fukuyama's philosophical views are elaborated in conjunction with a detailed examination of the inexorable trend towards liberal democratic forms of government in the twentieth century. He argues that, in Southern Europe, Latin America, parts of Asia and Eastern Europe, free-market economics and parliamentary democracy are, with some important exceptions, becoming the norm. He claims that there were only thirteen liberal democracies in 1940, thirty-seven in 1960 and sixty-two in 1990. He also traces the decline of war among democratic states over time, arguing that peace between states correlates closely with their internal convergence towards liberal democratic norms.

But the 'end of History', according to Fukuyama, is not necessarily welcome news. Despite the victory of liberal democracy as a normative model over its rivals, Fukuyama is concerned that the subordination of *megalothymia* to *isothymia* may be also the pursuit of equality at the expense of the pursuit of excellence. If there is too much equality, and no great issues to struggle for, people may revolt at the very system that has brought them peace and security. We cannot subsist merely on equal rights and material comfort alone, and those that satisfy themselves with these become what Nietzsche called 'last men' or, as C.S. Lewis put it, 'men without chests'. At the end of the book Fukuyama sounds a note of warning. Unless there are ways to express *megalothymia* in those societies lucky enough to have reached the 'end of History' (and according to his own statistics, less than one-third of all states have arrived thus far), liberal democracy may atrophy and die. At one point Fukuyama argues that perhaps Japan may offer an alternative to American liberal democracy and combine a successful economy with social bonds strong enough to withstand the fragmentary forces of liberal democracy. Many Asian societies, he claims, have 'paid lip service to Western principles of liberal democracy, accepting the form while modifying the content to accommodate Asian cultural traditions'.[7] This is a theme Fukuyama pursues in his second book, *Trust: The Social Virtues and the Creation of Prosperity* (1995). Before considering the argument of that book, it is important to note some of the main criticisms levelled at *The End of History*.

First, Fukuyama's appeal to Hegel and Plato has been called into question by some commentators, outraged by Fukuyama's attempt to integrate Platonism with Hegelian dialectics. Shadia Drury, for example, points out that it is not possible to '[reconcile] Plato's objectivist views with [an] intersubjective concept of recognition'.[8] She argues that Fukuyama's invocation of Plato is designed to avoid the awkward fact that Hegel himself never predicted that history would end, even in the sense that Fukuyama uses the term 'end'. Nor could Hegel do so, given his commitment to the idea that history is inherently dialectical. John O'Neill, who attacks Fukuyama with Hegelian tools of analysis, makes a similar criticism. According to O'Neill, Hegel argued that

'recognition cannot be its own end since it is parasitic on other goods' which provide the appropriate criteria for recognition:

> Recognition is required to confirm my self-worth as a being with powers of rationality and the capacities to stand above and shape particular desires. It is only from beings that I recognise themselves as having such powers and capacities that recognition counts ... it is in virtue of this parasitic nature of recognition on prior goods that Hegel *ultimately rejects an individualised market economy as satisfactory as means of recognition even with civil society itself.*[9]

It is unclear, therefore, how Fukuyama can coherently use Hegel to defend capitalism and liberal democracy when Hegel explicitly denied that such a combination could adequately achieve the goal of recognition. For all his criticisms of Hobbes and Locke, Fukuyama fails to make a sufficient break with their atomistic conceptions of human nature.

A second set of criticisms has been levelled at Fukuyama's substantive empirical claims regarding the spread of liberal democracy around the globe and the inherently pacific nature of relations among liberal democratic states. On the one hand, Fukuyama defines liberal democracies in somewhat vague, formal, terms. A liberal democracy is one whose constitution respects some basic political rights and requires the government to rule on the basis of explicit consent from its citizens through regular competitive and fair elections. Whilst a broad definition facilitates some rough measurement of the 'march of democracy', such a crude indicator is hardly adequate for any firm conclusions to be made about the extent of freedom in the contemporary world. For example, according to Fukuyama, El Salvador and the United States both count as liberal democracies. The term itself becomes less clear now that there are, in his view, no alternatives against which to define it. In light of the historical mission that Fukuyama believes liberal democratic states to have fulfilled, the failure to distinguish between states within his broad category is a major weakness of the book as a whole. There is simply no analysis of the enormous differences in the way states that he lumps together manage the tensions between freedom and equality in politics and economics. As for his argument that 'liberal democracies' do not go to war with each other *because* they are liberal democracies, Fukuyama fails to explore the possibility of other explanations in the literature on the causes of war.

Finally, there are problems with Fukuyama's presumption that political and economic liberalism – the twin engines of his unidirectional historical motor – can coexist comfortably within the territorial boundaries of the sovereign state. By contrast, much of the literature in search of a substantive term to describe the post-Cold War era is concerned with the contradictory dynamics of 'globalisation' versus 'fragmentation', of which ethnic nationalism is a prime example. Globalisation is a blanket term that conveys the limits to state power arising from the myriad dynamics of a global economy in which the state seems to be relatively powerless to manage its domestic economy. In particular, the integration of global capital, much of it speculative, tends to subordinate domestic politics to the demand for flexibility, efficiency and competitiveness on a global playing field that is anything but level.

Consequently, as governments become less accountable to those they claim to represent over a broader range of issues, so the spectrum of democratic choice before citizens narrows considerably. To the extent that economic globalisation and political fragmentation are operating at different levels of social, political and economic organisation, one could plausibly accept much of Fukuyama's philosophical assumptions and reach opposite conclusions to the ones that

he draws. On the reasonable assumption that global capitalism is exacerbating economic inequality both within and between states whilst simultaneously denying them a redistributive capacity to moderate its impact, the 'struggle for recognition' may take reactive forms such as ethnic nationalism.[10] It is not clear how this problem can be solved merely by appealing to the virtues of capitalism and liberal democracy, since the main difficulty lies in striking the right balance between them, an issue that Fukuyama does not deal with in his book.

Since the publication of *The End of History and the Last Man* in 1992, Fukuyama has moved on to examine in more detail the cultural dimensions of comparative political economy. In 1995, he published his second book, *Trust: The Social Virtues and the Creation of Prosperity*. Having dealt with history, Fukuyama focuses on the social prerequisites of economic prosperity. He argues that economic success depends only in part on the factors emphasised by economists, competition, technology and skills. Fully as important is a supporting culture of trust or 'spontaneous sociability' – a readiness to get on with one's fellow citizens in economically productive ways:

> Virtually all economic activity in the contemporary world is carried out not by individuals but by organisations that require a high degree of social cooperation. Property rights, contracts, and commercial law are all indispensable institutions for creating a modern market-oriented economic system, but it is possible to economise substantially on transaction costs if such institutions are supplemented by social capital and trust. Trust, in turn, is the product of preexisting communities of shared moral codes or values. These communities ... are not the product of rational choice.[11]

At the core of the book is an examination of two contrasting groups of countries. The first comprises three economies in which civil society flourishes; that is, social institutions of many different kinds that play a large role in people's lives, mediating between the family and the state. These 'high trust' economies are the United States, Germany and Japan. The economies of the second group, in contrast, lack strong civil societies, according to Fukuyama. They have strong families and strong governments at the centre, but little else. As examples of such 'low trust' economies, he chooses China, France and Italy.

The book is provocative for two reasons. First, although the idea of the importance of 'social capital' is not new (indeed, it can be found in the work of Hegel), Fukuyama's categorisation of states is unconventional, to say the least. Fukuyama argues that his lists reflect the degree to which states have or have not adopted corporate forms of organisation as they underwent industrialisation over the last 200 years. 'High trust' economies are better able to develop corporate structures than 'low trust' economies, in which family-sized businesses dominate the economy. Second, Fukuyama is keen to dispel the idea that it is useful to generalise about 'Asian' economic growth. He argues that, along the spectrum of 'trust', Japan and China are very different from one another. He argues that China's allegedly low level of non-kin trust will impede economic growth. Apart from large corporate state companies, which suffer from high levels of debt, the lack of *spontaneous* tendencies to create large companies makes it difficult for China to create major strategic industries where scale is a crucial factor in success. Furthermore, it remains debatable whether a country without stable property rights and a reliable code of commercial law can maintain high rates of growth indefinitely.

To some extent, there is continuity between the two books. The underlying paradox of liberalism is the same. If you universalise liberal individualism, extending its premises to all spheres of life, liberal institutions (including the market) will eventually malfunction and then liberal democratic society will itself decay. As with the first book, however, there are at least a couple of major problems. First, just as Fukuyama's dichotomy between liberal democracies and the rest is somewhat crude, so is the basic division between 'high' and 'low trust' economies. On most indices of comparison (such as crime, lifetime employment, distribution of wealth, geographical and occupational mobility), the United States and Japan are far apart. Few commentators have been persuaded by Fukuyama's typology linking them together. Similarly, there are doubts about his views on China. Constance Lever-Tracy, for example, argues that Fukuyama misunderstands the cultural dimensions of wealth-creation in China, where 'family fortunes grow by multiplication of small units, not by expansion of large bureaucratic structures'.[12] She suggests that the transnational 'networking' between family firms, based on personal 'trust', perform the same functions that Fukuyama attributes to large bureaucratic structures.

In addition, even if the states he studies do fit into the categories of 'low trust' and 'high trust' economies, the bigger question is, so what? Whilst 'the social virtues' may have something to do with the creation of prosperity, it remains unclear just how much they contribute to economic growth compared to other factors. Over the last two decades, for example, China has been the fastest-growing economy in the world and not, it seems, because of a sudden outbreak of trust. Just as there are different kinds of 'liberal democracy', so there are many subtly different forms of capitalism, which suggests that it is somewhat simplistic to search for and attempt to isolate a single factor contributing to economic growth.

In summary, the work of Francis Fukuyama is both provocative and infuriating. He is, to use Isaiah Berlin's famous metaphor, neither a hedgehog (who knows one big thing) nor a fox (who knows many things), but both at the same time. The scope and ambition of his writing is large, and his ability to illustrate abstract philosophical arguments with a vast array of contemporary empirical data is enviable. Fukuyama is not a triumphal liberal at the end of the twentieth century. He is deeply worried about the apparent decline of 'social capital' in the United States, and his work suggests that the achievements of liberal democracy and capitalism are fragile. They depend on cultural factors that are crucial to the success of the liberal project. As Ross Poole argues,

despite its concern with the individual, liberalism has never been very good at supplying the individual with a reason or motive for accepting its principles. In assuming the existence of a social world which is devoid of values, liberalism has assigned the task of creating them to the vagaries of individual choice. It then discovers that it has no strong argument against the individual who chooses values antithetical to liberalism.[13]

However, Fukuyama's solution to this problem is, to say the least, controversial. Whilst he is a firm opponent of cultural and moral relativism in all its forms, it remains to be seen whether he will provide an explicit defence of the communitarian values that underpin his recent work.

Notes

1 Henry Porter, 'Fukuyama worried about the future' (interview with Francis Fukuyama), *The Guardian Weekly*, 22 March, 1992, p. 27.
2 John Dunn, 'In the glare of recognition', *Times Literary Supplement*, 24 April, 1992, p. 6.
3 Wayne Cristaudo, 'The end of History?', *Current Affairs Bulletin* 69 (1992), p. 29.
4 Perry Anderson, *A Zone of Engagement*, London, Verso Press, 1992, p. 341.
5 Shadia B. Drury, 'The end of History and the new world order', *International Journal* 48 (1992/93), p. 95.
6 Alexandre Kojève, *Introduction to the Reading of Hegel*, New York, Basic Books, 1969.
7 Francis Fukuyama, *The End of History and the Last Man*, London, Hamish Hamilton, 1992, p. 243.

8 Drury, op. cit., p. 93.
9 John O'Neill, 'Hegel against Fukuyama: associations, markets and recognition', *Politics* 17 (1997), p. 193, emphasis in original.
10 For an extended argument along such lines, see Perry Anderson, *A Zone of Engagement*, London, Verso, 1992, pp. 331–75.
11 Francis Fukuyama, *Trust: The Social Virtues and the Creation of Prosperity*, London, Hamish Hamilton, 1995, p. 335–6.
12 Constance Lever-Tracy, 'Fukuyama's hijacking of Chinese trust', *Policy, Organisation and Society* 12 (1996), p. 94.
13 Ross Poole, *Morality and Modernity*, London, Routledge, 1991, p. 91.

See also in this book

Angell, Doyle, Rosecrance

Fukuyama's major writings

'The end of History?: After the Battle of Jena', *The National Interest* 18 (1989), pp. 15–25
'Reply to my critics', *The National Interest* 18 (1989), pp. 21–8
The End of History and the Last Man, London, Hamish Hamilton, 1992
Trust: The Social Virtues and the Creation of Prosperity, London, Hamish Hamilton, 1995
'Social capital and the global economy', *Foreign Affairs* 74 (September/October 1995), pp. 91–103

Further reading

Anderson, Perry, *A Zone of Engagement*, London, Verso Press, 1992
Bertram, Christopher and Chitty, Alan (eds), *Has History Ended?: Fukuyama, Marx, Modernity*, Aldershot, Edward Elgar, 1994
Drury, Shadia, 'The end of History and the new world order', *International Journal* 48 (Winter 1992/93), pp. 80–99
Halliday, Fred, 'An encounter with Fukuyama', *New Left Review* 193 (May/June 1992), pp. 89–95
Halliday, Fred, 'International society as homogeneity: Burke, Marx, and Fukuyama', *Millennium: Journal of International Studies* 21 (1992), pp. 435–61
Milliband, Ralph, 'Fukuyama and the socialist alternative', *New Left Review* 193 (May/June 1992), pp. 108–13
Poole, Ross, *Morality and Modernity*, London, Routledge, 1991

Rustin, Michael, 'No exit from capitalism', *New Left Review* 193 (May/June 1992), pp. 96–107

DAVID HELD

David Held is Professor of Politics and Sociology at the Open University in Britain. Over the past twenty years he has written widely on political and social theory in the modern era, focusing on the nature of democracy and on its prospects in an era of 'globalisation'. His work is a useful corrective to that of Fukuyama, who argues that the 'end of History' occurs when 'liberal democracy' is the only legitimate form of governance in international relations. It can also be seen as an important contribution to the practical implementation of critical approaches to the problem of global governance beyond the territorial limits of the nation-state. Held seeks to integrate what he views as the most important contributions of both liberalism and Marxism to the promotion of human freedom and equality, assesses the difficulties of achieving the goal of human autonomy in the post-Cold War era, and offers practical proposals to achieve cosmopolitan democracy in the twenty-first century. In his view, globalisation is both a threat to democracy as well as an opportunity. The inadequacy of the nation-state as the container of democratic forms of government requires the extension of democracy into the international arena. This summary of his work will discuss each element of his overall project.

Held first argues that democracy provides the means by which it may be possible to integrate the best insights of liberalism and Marxism. It may be useful to summarise Held's understanding of the liberal and Marxist projects.[1] He reduces each to a small number of key elements to emphasise the ways in which they appear to be incompatible with each other. Liberalism is hostile to state power, and it emphasises the

importance of a diversity of power centres in society, particularly economic ones. Marxism, on the other hand, is hostile to the concentration of economic power and private ownership of the means of production. Liberals believe in the separation of the state from civil society as an essential pre-requisite of a democratic order. Marxists, on the other hand, believe in the eventual restructuring of civil society and the abolition of private ownership as an essential pre-requisite of true democracy. Liberals argue that the most desirable form of the state is an impersonal structure of power embedded in the rule of law. Marxists argue that the liberal idea of 'neutrality' cannot be achieved in the context of capitalism. Liberals emphasise the importance of separating the private and the public spheres. The former is a realm of protected space in which individual autonomy and initiative may flourish. Marxists argue that freedom without equality is not worth having. Liberals see the market as a mechanism for coordinating the diverse activities of producers and consumers. Marxists believe that in the absence of careful public planning of investment, production will be anarchic, wasteful and remain geared to the pursuit of profit, not need.

On the face of it, it is difficult to see any means of reconciling liberalism and Marxism. But Held argues that they share a number of concerns, which he expresses as a commitment to the principle of autonomy:

> Individuals should be free and equal in the determination of the rules by which they live; that is, they should enjoy equal rights (and, accordingly, equal obligations) in the specification of the framework which generates and limits the opportunities available to them throughout their lives.[2]

By extracting what he claims is common to each political ideology, Held believes that it may be possible to integrate them if one can also acknowledge their respective limits and flaws. To some extent, the weaknesses of one are reflected in the strengths of the other. Once this is acknowledged, it may be possible to appreciate the potential complementarity of liberals' scepticism about political power and Marxists' scepticism about economic power. Held suggests that the key to integrating these apparently irreconcilable doctrines lies in the implementation of radical democracy, at the level of civil society as well as the state. Held is a great advocate of participatory democracy at all levels of political life. However, whilst he has much to say about the virtue of participatory democracy, he shies away from indicating what the desired outcome of democratic deliberation should amount to. He does not believe that capitalism either can or should be overcome, or at least he recognises the political price that would be paid for such an abstract goal. In order to mitigate its inherent inegalitarianism, he believes that the state should play an active role in managing the economy.

On the other hand, he is suspicious of state power and agrees with the liberal claim that the distinction between the public and the private domain should be preserved. In order to exploit the strengths of liberalism and Marxism, he thinks that 'civil society and the state must become the condition for the other's democratisation'.[3] Thus, although he supports the maintenance of representative democracy at the level of the polity, the precise boundary between the state and civil society is one that must be negotiated in 'a multiplicity of social spheres – including socially-owned enterprises, housing cooperatives, [and] independent communications media and health centres'.[4] This is an argument that recurs throughout Held's work, the emphasis on democracy per se as a public good, whose inherent value transcends competing perspectives on the appropriate role and purpose of government:

Democracy is, I think, the only 'grand' or 'meta'-narrative that can legitimately frame and delimit the competing narratives of the contemporary age. The *idea* of democracy is important because it does not just represent one value among many, such as liberty, equality, and justice, but is the value that can link and mediate among competing prescriptive concerns . . . democracy does not presuppose agreement on diverse values. Rather, it suggests a way of relating values to each other and of leaving the resolution of value conflicts open to participants in a political dialogue.[5]

With the end of the Cold War, Held's interest in exploring the potential for 'democracy' to synthesise the best of liberalism and Marxism has shifted to focus on the threats posed to democracy by the forces of economic globalisation. This term embraces a variety of phenomena such as the development of a global economy in which global economic actors operate in conjunction with increasingly integrated capital and finance markets, global information processes and the increasing awareness of global environmental problems. Conceptually, globalisation is a process that not only undermines, and sometimes overrides, the nation-state, but more importantly that also calls into question the importance of territory per se. Power and influence flow between many actors, of which the nation-state is but one, who are increasingly defined independently of any territorial reference. In this context, Held argues that we are confronted with a strange paradox at the end of the twentieth century. On the one hand, the end of the Cold War has been accompanied by a celebration of the victory of 'democracy' over communism. On the other hand, there is little recognition of the variety of democratic systems in theory and practice as well as the enormous challenges posed to the future health of democracy by globalisation.

Held suggests that political theorists are prevented from contributing to the new global agenda by their statist predisposition to view the state as a 'community of fate'. They have assumed that a 'symmetrical and congruent' relationship exists between political decision makers and the recipients of their decisions. In principle, politicians are supposed to be accountable to the citizens who elect them, and who are the major 'recipients' of political 'outputs'. Because democratic theory has not questioned the arbitrary role of territorial borders in determining the relevant constituencies of sovereign states, it is unable to respond adequately to the challenges of the late modern era. With the increase in global interconnectedness, states are finding it difficult to control activities within and beyond their borders. Their range of policy instruments, particularly for the purpose of macroeconomic policy, is shrinking, and states cannot solve a growing number of transnational problems unless they co-operate with other states and non-state actors. Held argues that states find themselves enmeshed in a host of collaborative arrangements to manage transnational issues, the result being a growing disjuncture 'between, on the one hand, the formal domain of political authority [states] claim for themselves and, on the other, the actual practices and structures of the state and the economic system at the national, regional and global levels'.[6]

He identifies four such 'disjunctures' that are worthy of note. First and most obviously, the formal authority of the state does not correspond with the actual system of global production, distribution and exchange. Second, states are increasingly enmeshed in international 'regimes' of coordinated agreements to regulate transnational forces and issue-areas. This has given rise to a number of important organisations and decision-making bodies that have enormous power, but over which there is little democratic accountability, such as the United Nations or the International Monetary Fund. A third arena is that of international law, which has expanded in the post-war era to bestow new rights and obligations on states and individuals that diminish the effective sovereignty of the territorial state. Particularly in Western Europe, individuals can appeal to the European Court of Human Rights and even initiate legal proceedings against their own government. Finally, Held reminds us that, in the security arena, there continues to be a disjuncture between democratic accountability and the operation of alliances such as NATO.

In short, the assumption of state sovereignty that informs contemporary democratic theory is obsolete. Held is severely critical of Fukuyama's thesis that, with the end of the Cold War, we have arrived at the philosophical 'end of History'. He criticises him on three counts. First, Held argues that Fukuyama treats liberalism as a unity and ignores distinctive differences between different models of democracy. Second, Fukuyama fails to consider tensions between liberalism and democracy. Finally, Fukuyama fails to question whether liberal democracy can continue to flourish in the context of globalisation. Held argues that, in order to re-assert and extend democratic control, we need to think of democracy in a cosmopolitan rather than a national context. The challenge is not how one might replicate particular models of democracy between states with very different cultures, economies and political systems. The challenge is to correct the 'democratic deficit' between the limited scope of contemporary democracy and the dispersion of political authority away from the formal centres of national governance.

Held's recipe for rethinking the democratic project in the 1990s is similar to the prescriptions he offered for transcending liberalism and Marxism in the mid-1980s. The key features of his model for cosmopolitan democracy are as follows:

1 The global order consists of multiple and overlapping networks of power including the political, social and economic.

2 All groups and associations are attributed rights of self-determination specified by a commitment to individual autonomy and a

specific cluster of rights. The cluster is composed of rights within and across each network of power. Together, these rights constitute the basis of an empowering legal order – a 'democratic international law'.

3 Law-making and law-enforcement can be developed within this framework at a variety of locations and levels, along with an expansion of the influence of regional and international courts to monitor and check political and social authority.

4 Legal principles are adopted which delimit the form and scope of individual and collective action within the organisations and associations of state *and* civil society. Certain standards are specified for the treatment of all, which no political regime or civil association can legitimately violate.

5 As a consequence, the principle of non-coercive relations governs the settlements of disputes, though the use of force remains a collective option in the last resort in the face of tyrannical attacks to eradicate democratic international law.

6 The defence of self-determination, the creation of a common structure of action and preservation of the democratic good are the overall collective priorities.

7 Determinate principles of social justice follow: the *modus operandi* of the production, distribution and the exploitation of resources must be compatible with the democratic process and a common framework of action.[7]

How should we assess Held's contribution to international relations theory? It has both strengths and weaknesses. On the one hand, it is refreshing to read a political theorist who takes international relations seriously and refuses to accept the traditional distinction between politics within the state and international 'relations' between states. He is quite right to question this traditional dichotomy within political science.

Furthermore, his work on models of 'liberal democracy' is useful in reminding us that there is no single model 'for export', so to speak, so we should be cautious in celebrating the alleged victory of democracy in the post-Cold War era. On the other hand, I would suggest that there are two flaws in Held's defence of 'cosmopolitan democracy'.

The first is the underdeveloped defence of democracy itself at a philosophical level. Held argues that democracy is the best 'meta-narrative' because it transcends substantive disagreements about particular political goods. One might argue that this view has a number of problems. Why does it follow that if individuals and groups disagree on how to rank substantive ideals such as political liberty and economic equality, they either will or should agree to debate the merits of each in a democratic fashion? Held does not answer this question; he tends to assume that 'reasonable' people will agree on neutral procedures to decide the ranking of political goods in the absence of any substantive consensus. Will they? Should they? In his analysis of the relationship between philosophical pluralism and political liberalism, George Crowder identifies a major difficulty in using the former to justify the latter:

> The mere fact that values are 'plural' [in that there is no common currency to compute their respective merits] tells us . . . we must choose but not what to choose. It gives no reason not to embrace values that have, by themselves or in combination with others, illiberal implications. We have no reason, as [philosophical] pluralists, not to prefer order and hierarchy to liberty and equality.[8]

It is incumbent on Held to justify his defence of democracy as a legitimate meta-narrative more clearly, particularly if he wants to promote it as a global value.

Second, Held's work is part of a solid, Left–Liberal, social democratic tradition. He wants to preserve the distinction between the state and civil society, as well as the basic values of political and economic liberalism. At the same time, he not only wants to curb the undemocratic and inegalitarian consequences of global capitalism, but to do so by a radical transformation of the allegedly obsolete Westphalian system. One might argue that Held cannot have it both ways. In the absence of a far more radical curtailment of the global 'free market', it is highly unlikely that any of the political changes that he desires will come about. This is not a criticism of Held's 'utopianism' per se. As Alex Callinicos notes:

> The eclipse over the past twenty years of any distinctive social-democratic policies, in the face of the resurgence throughout the West of laissez-faire economics, poses the question of whether the two constraints Held places on his project – preserving the separation of state and civil society and regulating capitalism – are in fact compatible.[9]

Having said that, it remains the case that Held is an important exception to the 'liberal triumphalism' that sounded so loudly in the immediate post-Cold War era. Whatever the achievements of liberalism in the modern world, Held reminds us that there remains much to be done if these achievements are to be preserved and shared more widely in the international system.

Notes

1 This summary is taken from David Held, 'Beyond liberalism and Marxism?' in Gregor McLennan, David Held and Stuart Hall (eds), *The Idea of the Modern State*, Milton Keynes, Open University Press, 1984, pp. 223–40.
2 Ibid., p. 231.
3 Ibid., p. 236.
4 Ibid.
5 David Held, 'Liberalism, Marxism, and democracy', *Theory and Society* 22 (1993), p. 274, emphasis in original.
6 David Held, 'Democracy, the nation-state and the global system', *Economy and Society* 20 (1991), p. 150.
7 David Held, 'Democracy: from city-states to a

cosmopolitan order?', *Political Studies* 40 (1992), p. 36, emphasis in original.
8 George Crowder, 'Pluralism and liberalism', *Political Studies* 42 (1994), p. 303.
9 Alex Callinicos, 'Liberalism, Marxism, and democracy: a response to David Held', *Economy and Society* 22 (1992), p. 285.

See also in this book

Cox, Falk, Fukuyama, Linklater, Ruggie

Held's major writings

Introduction to Critical Theory: Horkheimer to Habermas, London, Hutchinson, 1980
New Forms of Democracy (with Christopher Pollitt), London, Sage Publications in association with Open University, 1986
Models of Democracy, Cambridge, Polity Press, 1987
'Sovereignty, national politics and the global system', in David Held (ed.), *Political Theory and the Modern State: Essays on State, Power and Democracy*, Stanford, Stanford University Press, 1989, pp. 214–42
Political Theory Today (ed.), Cambridge, Cambridge University Press, 1991
'Democracy, the nation-state and the global system', *Economy and Society* 20 (1991), pp. 138–72
Modernity and its Futures (with Stuart Hall and Tony McGrew), Cambridge, Polity Press in association with Open University, 1992
'Democracy: from city-states to a cosmopolitan order?', *Political Studies* 40 (1992), pp. 10–39
Prospects for Democracy: North, South, East, West, Cambridge, Polity Press, 1993
Foundations of Democracy: the Principle of Autonomy and the Global Order, Cambridge, Polity Press, 1993
'Globalization and the liberal democratic state', *Government and Opposition* 28 (1993), pp. 261–88 (with Anthony McGrew)
'Liberalism, Marxism and democracy', *Theory and Society* 22 (1993), pp. 249–81
Cosmopolitan Democracy: An Agenda for a New World Order (with Daniele Archibugi), Cambridge, Polity Press, 1995
Democracy and the Global Order: From the Modern State to Cosmopolitan Governance, Cambridge, Polity Press, 1995

Further reading

Archibugi, Daniele, 'Models of international organisation in perpetual peace projects',

Review of International Studies 18 (1992), 295–317

Thompson, Janna, *Justice and World Order: A Philosophical Inquiry*, London, Routledge, 1992

JOHN HOBSON

John A. Hobson was born in Derbyshire, England, in 1858, and died on April Fools' Day in 1940, which, as David Long wryly points out, 'might appear to be enough to justify the portrayal of Hobson as an idealist'.[1] In the study of international relations, his name is associated with Norman Angell and Alfred Zimmern as the most important liberal critics of the First World War. Hobson was perhaps the most radical of them. He is often (incorrectly) considered as part of the Marxist tradition because some of his views, particularly on imperialism, directly influenced Lenin. However, although Hobson was inspired by some of Marx's work, he did not accept Marx's materialistic view of history and regarded Marx as an economic reductionist. A more accurate description of Hobson is the term 'new liberal'. In contrast to the classical liberals of the late eighteenth and early nineteenth century, new liberals such as Hobson were characterised by three fundamental beliefs. First, they refused to accept that there was an inevitable trade-off between liberty and equality. They wanted to apply the egalitarian goals of socialism within a political system that also promoted private property and liberal political values. This could be achieved by taxing economic rent, the 'unearned income' that accrued to individuals as a result of their ownership of a scarce resource (such as land) rather than their direct contribution to production. Second, they repudiated the utilitarian idea that individuals exist prior to civil society, and did not accept the classical liberal idea that the social good is the sum of individual or private satisfactions. Third, they argued that the idea of reason is not exhausted by

the rational calculation of means to achieve given ends. Instead, they held an evolutionary view of historical progress and, while they remained suspicious of state power, believed that the state had an important role to play in improving social welfare and enhancing the collective good.[2] Hobson's work illustrates all three beliefs, and the tag of 'idealism' that was attached to him by the realists of the 1930s and 1940s should not detract from his contribution to the liberal tradition in political economy and international relations.

Hobson was educated in Derby and went to Oxford University in 1876 on an open scholarship, where he studied Classics. In 1880 he left Oxford to become a schoolteacher and then, in 1887, he followed in his father's footsteps to take up a career in journalism. He moved to London, and managed to write a weekly column for *The Derbyshire Advertiser and North Staffordshire Journal* as well as giving lectures in English literature and political economy. In 1889 he published his first book (with A.F. Mummery, a businessman), *The Physiology of Industry*, which outlined his radical ideas on underconsumption in capitalist society and made him very unpopular among orthodox economists of the classical school. When his father died in 1897, Hobson was able to give up lecturing for a living and his inheritance allowed him to devote himself to his research and writing. He was an active campaigner for social reform in Britain and continued writing articles for the general public as well as more academic books and articles.

When the First World War broke out, Hobson was instrumental in the formation of the British Neutrality Committee, as well as the Union of Democratic Control, which campaigned for an end to 'secret diplomacy' among the great powers. He resigned from the Liberal Party in 1916 over the issue of import duties (Hobson was a firm believer in free trade) and was narrowly beaten in the 1918 election, when he stood as an

Independent member of the House of Commons. After his defeat he joined the Independent Labour Party, and he served on a number of committees dealing with economic and social reform. Not only did his work inspire Lenin in the early years of this century, his economic analysis of underconsumption and unemployment also inspired John Maynard Keynes in the inter-war period.[3]

Hobson is best known among students of international relations for his analysis and critique of imperialism in the late nineteenth century. His own unique theory of imperialism, first published in 1902 and reprinted many times since, is best understood in contrast to the most influential rival theories. Of these, four are particularly noteworthy.

Conservative thinkers, such as Benjamin Disraeli, Cecil Rhodes and Rudyard Kipling, claim that imperialism is necessary to preserve the existing social order in the more developed states. It is necessary to secure trade and markets, to maintain employment and to channel the energies and social conflicts of metropolitan citizens into foreign lands. There is a very strong ideological and racial assumption of Western superiority within this body of thought. Among *realists* such as Hans Morgenthau, imperialism is simply a manifestation of the balance of power and is one of the processes by which states try to achieve a favourable change in the status quo. The purpose of imperialism is to reduce the strategic and political vulnerability of a state. For *Marxist radicals* such as Lenin, imperialism arises because increased concentration of wealth in capitalist society leads to underconsumption. However, since the state represents the capitalist class it is not possible to redistribute wealth. Ultimately, according to Lenin, the world would be completely divided up and the capitalist states would then fight over the redivision of the world. This analysis served as his basic explanation for the First World War. Finally, *social-psychological* theories, as in the work of Joseph Schumpeter,

conceive of imperialism as 'objectless expansion', a pattern learned from the behaviour of other states and institutionalised into domestic political processes by a warrior class. The latter may be created initially because of the need for defence and security, but, over time, the class will manufacture reasons to perpetuate its existence, usually through the manipulation of public and elite opinion.

Hobson's own views, whilst they do not preclude elements from the other dominant schools, explain imperialism as a policy choice, not as an inevitable consequence of the balance of power, capitalism, the need for new markets to export manufactured goods to or social pathology. For Hobson, the 'economic taproot' of late nineteenth-century imperialism lay in domestic underconsumption. He identified a vicious circle in which the economic concentration of power supports an oligarchic political elite, which in turn facilitates further economic inequality. The increase in productive efficiency under capitalism has produced a great deal of wealth that is channelled to owners of capital in the form of profits rather than to workers in the form of wages. The pressure of over-saving from profits among the capitalist rich, combined with forced underconsumption among the exploited poor, leads to the accumulation by the rich of vast sums of money. This can neither be spent nor reinvested domestically (given low interest rates produced by fierce domestic competition and the lack of domestic markets created by underconsumption). Consequently, investors in search of a high rate of return invest their money overseas. In turn, foreign investments have to be protected to ensure their profits, and this creates the economic pressure for political and military intervention in those markets where capital is growing. Imperial pressure may arise from a number of groups, not just from financiers (as Lenin argued), but also from 'an ambitious statesman, a frontier soldier, an overzealous missionary, a pushing trader'. In his most famous phrase, he argued that, ultimately, imperialism constituted 'a vast system of outdoor relief for the upper classes'.[4] Whilst Hobson never denied the influence of a number of factors contributing to imperial behaviour, he believed firmly that surplus elite wealth was the ultimate determinant.

To some extent, Hobson's argument was limited both by the scarcity of empirical data and by his focus on Great Britain in the last quarter of the nineteenth century. Certainly, the period from 1870 to the First World War, in most of the advanced industrialised states in Europe was one of massive capital accumulation and its export abroad. As Gilpin puts it:

> The City of London increased its foreign holdings more than five times between 1870 and 1914. By 1914, over one-quarter of British wealth was invested in foreign government securities and foreign railroads. Britain was, in fact, investing far more abroad than it was at home [and] ran a chronic trade deficit during this period ... [but] the massive outflow of capital undoubtedly contributed to the industrial and overall decline of the British economy and accelerated the eclipse of Britain by rising industrial powers.[5]

For Hobson, it makes no sense to study the international political economy by treating domestic and international relations separately from one another. In order to bring an end to imperialism, it is necessary to undertake major economic and political reforms at the domestic level. Unlike Lenin, who regarded this as impossible in capitalist states, Hobson regarded imperialism as a policy choice; he did not view it as an inevitable companion to capitalist systems of private property. He believed that a state can tackle the problem of underconsumption at home by raising the income levels of the majority of the population either through legislation concerning wage laws, child labour laws and the legalisation of trade unions, or through income transfers by taxing the economic rent of the wealthy and redistributing wealth through unemployment compensation and social welfare. Capitalism can be socially 'benign' if liberal states move in a more social democratic direction. This is why he endorsed the view that a policy of free trade would be a force for peace. The political and economic elites whose behaviour was at the heart of imperialism objected to open trade because it would threaten their protected domestic position at the top of the economic hierarchy. Hobson argued that import duties and tariffs not only reduced economic competition, but they were also unlikely to increase domestic consumption because the gains from protection would be enjoyed by the wealthy (agricultural landlords and industrial magnates) rather than the poor. Hobson was also very suspicious of the Leninist thesis that in order to bring an end to imperialism, there would need to be a revolutionary overthrow of capitalism. He argued that the Leninist doctrine was incompatible with social democratic reforms and would simply empower a new elite and therefore new types of imperialism.

Was Hobson an idealist? Kenneth Waltz, in his criticism of Hobson's ideas, describes him as a 'second image optimist'.[6] It is worth noting Waltz's comments since most students are likely to encounter Hobson via Waltz's well-known text *Man, The State, and War* (1959). According to Waltz, Hobson's views on international relations were based on the optimistic idea that the problem of war could be best dealt with by 'perfecting' the domestic political and economic arrangements of states. Only if social, economic and political reform occurs within states will it be possible to end conflict between them. He sums up Hobson's recipe for peace as follows:

> First socialism, Hobson is saying, and then the virtues extolled by the nineteenth-century liberals will operate effectively to produce a world at peace. Frictions in

trade will no longer inflame the relations of states; trade will instead bind them together in a mutuality of interest. Reason will no longer devise new deceits and new ways to outsmart other countries or, if that fails, to overpower them; reason will instead be the means by which the relations of states are adjusted to the mutual advantage of all of them.[7]

Of course, as far as Waltz is concerned, Hobson's recipe for peace is naïve, since it fails to take into account the structural anarchy among states that promotes war-like behaviour, regardless of states' internal economic and political arrangements. Thus the tag 'idealism' is appropriate for Hobson and others like him.

David Long, however, in his excellent analysis of Hobson's 'idealism', provides grounds for pausing before we rush to premature judgement. If idealism is another term for naïveté, then Hobson's work deserves further attention. Long agrees that Hobson was an idealist in the sense that he believed in the power of ideas to change the world in a progressive direction, but his work on international relations is a great deal more sophisticated than the crude summary by Waltz. Hobson wrote on the difficulties of reforming the international anarchy and he did not confine himself to issues of domestic reform alone. Long distinguishes between three forms of idealism, all of which can be found in the work of Hobson, and which operate at the domestic, transnational and international levels of analysis. In addition to his domestic reforms, Hobson acknowledged the continuing importance of state sovereignty, but he hoped that the growth of trade and interdependence would undermine the links between sovereignty as a legal status and the search for autonomy and independence from other states, promoting common interests among states on behalf of peace. Long also draws attention to Hobson's work on international law and organisation. He supported the strengthening of legal obligations among states, which would require the establishment of much stronger legal instruments at the international level, including the creation of some form of international governance. As Long points out,

> Hobson supported collective security, the need for military sanctions to back up international arbitration and the call for an international police force. [He] proposed a strong League of Nations, in effect an international government with a Court, Executive and Legislature to which states would bring their disputes; and a collective security system whereby the use of legitimate force was concentrated in the hands of the society of states' representative, the international government. This League would have to be as inclusive and as powerful as possible in order to avoid the possible reinstatement of the balance of power within the League and between the League and outside powers.[8]

In short, it is a disservice to the subtlety and 'realism' of Hobson's ideas to label them pejoratively as 'idealist'. During the First World War, Hobson exhibited considerable foresight in warning the Allies against the dangers of German revenge that would only be encouraged by the imposition of punitive sanctions against Germany at the end of the war. Indeed, it could be argued that the problem of appeasement in the 1930s lay in its timing rather than the attempt to co-operate with Germany per se. Had the Allies taken Hobson's advice in 1918 and not inflicted such huge reparation payments on Germany at that time, it is possible that the conditions that gave rise to Hitler in the 1920s and 1930s would not have existed.

It is important to stress the multidimensional quality of Hobson's thought on international relations, not only to counter simplistic descriptions of it, but also to indicate its continuing relevance at the end of the twentieth century. One could, of course, argue that his treatment of imperialism, however accurate for the period he was studying, is not relevant today. Overseas investment is no longer a precursor to the imperial practices of the 1870s and 1880s. However, one reason for that is precisely because many of the reforms than Hobson proposed in the early part of the twentieth century have indeed taken place, at least in the advanced industrialised parts of the world. The rise of the welfare state, trade unionism, the expansion of the electoral franchise and the enormous expansion of trade in the post-1945 era have all reduced the constituency for imperialism that was the target of Hobson's wrath. Of course, all these achievements of social democracy have been under threat for a number of years now. Hobson's work reminds us that, contrary to many neoliberal recipes for world order in the 1990s, in the absence of democratic and economic constraints, we cannot put our faith in 'open' markets and unrestrained capital movements if we wish to preserve a peaceful world order. Crucial to Hobson's thinking was the desire and attempt to preserve the integrity of the nation-state whilst simultaneously enveloping it in a cocoon of overriding considerations of supranational importance, political, social and economic. The project remains as vital today as it was in his own time.

Notes

1 David Long, 'J.A. Hobson and idealism in international relations', *Review of International Studies* 17 (1991), p. 285.
2 John Allet, *New Liberalism: The Political Economy of J.A. Hobson*, Toronto, University of Toronto Press, 1981, pp. 15–22.
3 For more autobiographical detail, see Michael Schneider, *J.A. Hobson*, Basingstoke, Macmillan, 1996, pp. 2–20.
4 J.A. Hobson, *Imperialism: A Study*, Ann Arbor, Michigan University Press, 1965, pp. 59, 50–1.
5 Robert Gilpin, *The Political Economy of International Relations*, Princeton, Princeton University Press, 1987, pp. 308–9.
6 Kenneth Waltz, *Man, The State, and War*, Second edition, New York, Columbia University Press, 1959, pp. 45–56.

7 Ibid., p. 153.
8 David Long, op. cit., p. 294.

See also in this book

Angell, Lenin, Waltz, Zimmern

Hobson's major writings

The Physiology of Industry (with A.F. Mummery), London, Murray, 1889
The War in South Africa: Its Causes and Effects, London, J. Nisbet, 1900
Imperialism: A Study (1902) Ann Arbor, Michigan University Press, 1965
Toward International Government, London, Macmillan, 1915
The Economics of Unemployment, London, George Allen & Unwin, 1922
The Evolution of Modern Capitalism: A Study of Machine Production (1926), London, George Allen & Unwin, 1954
Conditions of Industrial Peace, London, George Allen & Unwin, 1927
Rationalization and Unemployment: An Economic Dilemma, London, George Allen & Unwin, 1930
Democracy and a Changing Civilization, London, Lane, 1934
The Crisis of Liberalism: New Issues of Democracy (1909), Brighton, Harvester Press, 1974
Veblen (1936), New York, A.M. Kelley, 1963
Confessions of an Economic Heretic: The Autobiography of J.A. Hobson (1938), Sussex, Harvester Press, 1976

Further reading

Allett, John, *New Liberalism: The Political Economy of J.A. Hobson*, Toronto, University of Toronto Press, 1981. This book contains a comprehensive bibliography of Hobson's published work.
Brailsford, Henry Noel, *The Life Work of J.A. Hobson*, London, Oxford University Press, 1948
Freeden, Michael (ed.), *J.A. Hobson: A Reader*, London, Allen & Unwin, 1988
Freeden, Michael (ed.), *Reappraising J.A. Hobson: Humanism and Welfare*, Boston, Unwin Hyman, 1990
Long, David, 'J.A. Hobson and idealism in international relations', *Review of International Studies* 17 (1991), pp. 285–304
Long, David, *Towards a New Liberal Internationalism: The International Theory of J.A. Hobson*, Cambridge, Cambridge University Press, 1996

Schneider, Michael, *J.A. Hobson*, Basingstoke, Macmillan, 1996

STANLEY HOFFMANN

Stanley Hoffmann is an important figure in the study of French politics and comparative European politics as well as American foreign policy and international relations theory. His intellectual mentor is the French thinker Raymond Aron, and he shares with Aron a tragic, liberal, Weberian outlook. As a student of American foreign policy and international ethics, Hoffmann has engaged in an ongoing argument with policymakers as well as realists. Hoffmann's values are liberal and he strives to prescribe ways in which liberal values of individual freedom can be promoted in a world that constantly threatens to undermine them. In some ways he is very similar to realists such as Kennan, Morgenthau and Henry Kissinger. Like them, he has written long books and many articles on what is wrong with American foreign policy. Also, his analysis focuses, like theirs, on the often naïve preconceptions that American policymakers harbour about foreign affairs.

Unlike the realists, however, Hoffmann does not believe that the answer is to try and educate Americans in the art of nineteenth-century European statecraft. He is a trenchant critic of realists, whose advice he believes only exacerbates the least desirable aspects of American practice. Instead, his work tries to persuade students and policymakers alike of the sheer complexity of world politics, the ethical dilemmas of foreign policy and the risks of applying inappropriate models of state behaviour. In some ways Hoffmann can be seen as an American version of Hedley Bull, whom he admired and whose general outlook he shared.[1] Unlike Bull, Hoffmann does not construct an identifiable theoretical edifice that would somehow synthesise the tensions between

realism and idealism in the study of international affairs. Instead, he moves between them at the level of theory and foreign policy analysis. As he puts it,

> [l]ike Aron, I tend naturally to think 'against'. Utopians tempt me into demonstrating (gleefully) that their recipes are worthless. Cross realists provoke me into trying to show that they have overlooked some exits.[2]

In light of the volume of work from someone who constantly articulates his views 'against' the theoretical and political currents of the day, I will focus on the fruitful tension between Hoffmann's realism and idealism in his work on American foreign policy.

Stanley Hoffmann was born in Vienna in 1928, and he was raised in France in the 1930s. As a child in France, Hoffmann describes himself as a 'little Austrian, partly Jewish, rootless pupil' whose family suffered all the traumas associated with the rise of fascism and the invasion of France by Germany in May 1940. He remained in France during the years of the Vichy regime, living in Nice. The family returned to Paris in 1945, and Hoffmann enrolled at the Institut d'Etudes Politiques and the Paris University Law School. He graduated in 1948 and pursued his doctoral studies in international law. He spent a year at Harvard in 1951. After completing his doctoral thesis (which he describes as 'quite unreadable'), Hoffmann returned to Harvard to take up an instructorship in the Department of Government in 1955. Today, Hoffmann is C. Douglas Dillon Professor of the Civilisation of France at Harvard, where he combines his teaching and research interests in French politics and international relations.

Hoffmann has written three major books on American foreign policy. In 1968, he published *Gulliver's Troubles, Or, The Setting of American Foreign Policy*. This is a thorough examination of the changing international environment confronting United States' policymakers in the late

1960s, as well as a perceptive analysis of the preconceptions of those policymakers in reacting to their environment in the past. It is a large and ambitious book that attempts to integrate the internal and external constraints on American foreign policy. As with his other books on the same subject, Hoffmann is concerned to elaborate, often in great detail, the appropriate purpose of American foreign policy, and to establish

> [w]hat the United States can or cannot do, given the kind of nation it is, in the kind of world we have. Purposes that go against the grain of a nation's deepest beliefs or habits, or against the grain of the world in which it is trying to fulfill such purposes, are not sound. Power at a nation's disposal ought to be used in full awareness of the external conditions that define which uses are productive and which are not, as well as of the domestic predispositions and institutions that channel national energies in certain directions or inhibit the country from applying them in other ways.[3]

Given the task he sets himself in his books, as well as his refusal to use theoretical models that he regards as unduly simplistic, it is no surprise that Hoffmann's books tend to be rather long and, to be honest, hard to read at one sitting. He tends to reproduce the complexity of the world for his readers rather than simplify it. Nonetheless, they do repay the effort. In this book he argues that the contemporary international system (in the 1960s) is characterised by revolutionary dynamism, qualified or muted bipolarity, and ideological clashes. He distinguishes between three related levels of the system, each of which exhibits different structural attributes. Most fundamentally, the system is bipolar in terms of the nuclear destruction the superpowers can unleash, but the very restraints imposed by the nuclear stalemate have given the nation-state a new lease on life and have allowed, on a second systemic level, the emergence of political polycentricism. This,

in turn, has encouraged the trend toward nuclear proliferation, which lends a multipolar attribute to the third 'systemic' level.

In light of such a complexity of relations within and across the systemic levels, Hoffmann diagnoses the peculiar national disabilities that make it so difficult for the United States to operate effectively to promote world order. The complexity of the world is especially challenging to the United States because of a debilitating set of attitudes that stem from the American 'national style' (a function of America's past and principles) and American governmental institutions. The major institutional problem is the dispersal of power among and within the governmental structure and bureaucracy. Deficiencies in foreign policy 'style' are reflected in legalism, reliance on formulas, short-range planning and the conflict between quietism and activism.

In the last part of the book, Hoffmann argues that the United States should make a modest withdrawal from Europe that would allow the emergence of a 'European Europe', integrated along confederal lines and protected by a Franco-British nuclear umbrella with American and Soviet guarantees. The programme is essentially a Gaullist blueprint for Europe. Aside from furthering the establishment of a relatively independent Europe, this programme would free up American resources for more urgent containment projects, such as the restraint of China. Hoffmann argues against overly relying on military force as an instrument of policy, but he recognises that, in its absence, revolutionary forces are likely to undermine international order. In short, the book is an appeal for the United States to adapt to an increasingly 'multi-hierarchical' international system and to allow Eastern and Western Europe to emerge from the Cold War as part of a united political entity.

Hoffmann renews the appeal in his next book, *Primacy or World Order* (1978). He distinguishes between two cycles of American foreign policy after 1945, the Cold

War cycle (1945–68) and what he calls the Kissinger cycle (1968–76). Hoffmann is particularly critical of his former colleague at Harvard, accusing him of failing to extricate Gulliver from overseas entanglements and of bringing to his office a set of realist dogmas whose application is limited in a world of growing interdependence, in which economic relations are just as important as military ones. The contradictions of Kissinger's diplomacy arise out of the gap between abstract notions of the requirements of the balance of power and geopolitical reality. Hoffmann argues that Kissinger's diplomacy was based on the illusion that the United States could enjoy primacy *and* world order, whereas for Hoffmann there is a trade-off between them. He urges (once again) US policymakers to conduct their rivalry with the Soviet Union at benign levels of parity and to abandon any attempt to achieve world order on the basis of imperial control.

Hoffmann's third major book on American foreign policy, *Dead Ends* (1983), continues to develop familiar themes in Hoffmann's writing: the growing complexity of the international system, the demands and opportunities of global interdependence, the multi-dimensional and nonfungible nature of power, the limited utility of military force, the relative decline of the United States, the weakness of American diplomacy, and the need for a 'mixed' strategy toward the Soviet Union. But at the heart of the book, a revised collection of a number of Hoffmann's essays, lies his assertion that the foreign policies of Kissinger, Carter and especially Reagan have led to a series of 'dead ends'. Whereas Kissinger's grand design suffered from the fatal flaw of hegemonic pretension, Carter understood that the diffusion of power to new actors insistent on asserting themselves and on rejecting neocolonial dependencies had created a world in which American leadership 'without hegemony' could be its only possible role. Furthermore, Hoffmann

applauds Carter's early emphasis on such long-term global issues as human rights, nuclear proliferation, arms sales and the law of the sea, and he credits the administration with appreciating 'that this ever more complex world could be neither managed by the superpowers nor reduced to the relationship between them'.[4] But in its eagerness to reduce America's traditional obsession with communism, Carter's administration never offered a strategy for dealing with the Soviet Union. This omission constituted 'the hole in the doughnut' of Carter's world order outlook. It failed 'to communicate . . . which Soviet activities were intolerable, and which were compatible with Washington's conception of the global contest [and failed] to integrate its excellent intuitions and assumptions into a strategy'.[5] In the angriest essay in the book, Hoffmann ridicules Reagan for his dangerous attempt to recreate a global containment strategy that once again reduces the world to an ideological and military confrontation between the superpowers and for his dubious claim that the United States had merely lost the *will* to employ its power. In 1983, Hoffmann argued that Reagan's nostalgia for the world of the 1950s would result in another dead end – alienated allies, a spiralling arms race and an obstinate Soviet Union.

Well, Hoffmann got the last point wrong, of course. The Soviet Union did capitulate. But the end of the Cold War and the short-term success of the Reagan/Bush administrations in bringing the Cold War to an end (which they did not anticipate any more than Stanley Hoffmann) does not invalidate Hoffmann's arguments, nor should they detract from appreciating the broader wisdom of his commentary on American foreign policy, which extends over the last thirty years. Unlike his former colleague Henry Kissinger, Hoffmann has never openly sought to play a major role in the active formulation of American foreign policy, preferring to play the role of a concerned critic of its overall direction.

In the late 1970s and early 1980s, in addition to his ongoing commentaries on American foreign affairs, Hoffmann turned his critical attention to the difficulties and potential of reconciling the realist approach to international relations with the demands of liberal morality and ethics. His most well-known book on this issue is *Duties Beyond Borders: On The Limits and Possibilities of Ethical International Politics* (1981). This book consists of five essays first delivered in 1980 as the Frank W. Abrams lectures at Syracuse University. Hoffmann addresses concerns that have been dismissed as peripheral or inappropriate by some realists and that have often been handled in a 'utopian' fashion by liberals.

In particular, he examines three issues that have provided the grounds for so much debate between realists and liberals: the use of force, human rights and distributive justice. The first is focused primarily on war, particularly through an examination of Michael Walzer's *Just and Unjust Wars* and its critics. He delves into the thorny problem of what moral criteria statespersons might apply in the development of decisions involving the application of force. On the second topic, human rights, Hoffmann provides an impressive list of pitfalls for any universal definition of human rights and acknowledges the difficulties in promoting them as an explicit value in foreign policy:

> The structure of the international milieu which limits possibilities for moral action, the conflicts of value systems which result in very sharp disagreements on conceptions of human rights and on priorities, the difficulties of assessment and evaluation are all manifest here and lead repeatedly to failure, or to confrontation, or to distorted uses of the human rights issues for purposes of political warfare at home or abroad.[6]

Despite these problems, Hoffmann argues that the United States would not be true to its conception of itself if it did not promote the pursuit of human rights, and he endorses a policy of liberal internationalism. At the same time he warns that such a policy must coexist with the realisation that emphasising political and civil human rights at the expense of economic and social rights can often appear as neocolonialism in another guise.

Since the end of the Cold War, Hoffmann has continued to publish widely on the themes that have concerned him for over thirty years as a student of international relations. These include the possibility of constructing a liberal world order in a pluralistic, anarchical environment, the responsibility of the United States as the world's leading superpower, and the 'dead ends' of international theory as well as American statecraft.

Personally, I am not a great admirer of Hoffmann's books, even though their arguments have been the basis of this summary of his work. The books are too long and all too often contain innumerable policy guidelines whose connection to the underlying central themes is less than clear. On the other hand, I regard him as the finest essayist on the study of international relations and American foreign policy this century. Two volumes of his essays are available. The first was published in 1965 and consists of a number of his revised lectures on war and peace delivered at Harvard and Geneva in the early 1960s, and the second volume, appropriately titled *Janus and Minerva*, was published in 1987. As a whole they represent a body of thought on international relations that is remarkably consistent even as it has evolved over the years. They are, I think, required reading for any serious student of international relations. His essay on Kant and Rousseau remains unsurpassed as a comparative analysis of these classical theorists in the field, and his essays on the limits of realism in international relations theory remain as relevant today as when he first wrote them in the late 1950s and 1960s. At the end of the twentieth century,

Hoffmann remains 'an unhappy Sisyphus' in the field. As he recently commented,

[t]he tension between morality and politics will always remain – because morality is always at war not only with egotistical or asocial interests, but also with the will to power and domination. In the world of international relations, it's going to be an uphill struggle. Albert Camus wanted us to imagine a happy Sisyphus. In international affairs, this simply is not possible.[7]

Notes

1 See Stanley Hoffmann, 'Hedley Bull and his contribution to international relations', *International Affairs* 62 (1986), pp. 179–95.
2 Stanley Hoffmann, 'A retrospective', in Joseph Kruzel and James N. Rosenau (eds), *Journeys Through World Politics: Autobiographical Reflections of Thirty-Four Academic Travellers*, Lexington, Massachusetts, Lexington Books, 1989, p. 269.
3 Stanley Hoffmann, *Gulliver's Troubles, Or, The Setting of American Foreign Policy*, New York, McGraw-Hill, 1968, p. xiii.
4 Stanley Hoffmann, *Dead Ends: American Foreign Policy in the New Cold War*, Cambridge, Massachusetts, Ballinger, 1983, p. 69.
5 Ibid., pp. 73–4.
6 Stanley Hoffmann, *Duties Beyond Borders: On the Limits and Possibilities of Ethical International Politics*, Syracuse, New York, Syracuse University Press, 1981, p. 95.
7 Stanley Hoffmann, 'Democracy and society', *World Policy Journal* 12 (1995), p. 39.

See also in this book

Aron, Kennan, Kissinger, Morgenthau, Walzer

Hoffmann's major writings

'International relations: the long road to theory', *World Politics* 11 (1959), pp. 346–77
Contemporary Theory in International Relations, Englewood Cliffs, New Jersey, Prentice-Hall, 1960
The State of War: Essays on the Theory and Practice of International Politics, New York, Pall Mall Press, 1965
'Obstinate or obsolete? The fate of the nation-state and the case of Western Europe', *Daedelus*

3 (1966), pp. 862–913
Gulliver's Troubles, Or, The Setting of American Foreign Policy, New York, McGraw-Hill, 1968
Decline or Renewal?: France Since the 1930s, New York, The Viking Press, 1974
Primacy or World Order: American Foreign Policy Since the Cold War, New York, McGraw-Hill, 1978
Duties Beyond Borders: On the Limits and Possibilities of Ethical International Politics, Syracuse, New York, Syracuse University Press, 1981
The Mitterrand Experiment: Continuity and Change in Modern France (edited with George Ross and Sylvia Malzacher), New York, Oxford University Press, 1987
Janus and Minerva: Essays in the Theory and Practice of International Relations, Boulder, Colorado, Westview Press, 1987
'A retrospective', in Joseph Kruzel and James N. Rosenau (eds), *Journeys Through World Politics: Autobiographical Reflections of Thirty-Four Academic Travellers*, Lexington, Massachusetts, Lexington Books, 1989, pp. 263–78
'International Society', in J.D.B. Miller and R.J. Vincent (eds), *Order and Violence: Hedley Bull and International Relations*, Oxford, Clarendon Press, 1990, pp. 13–37
The New European Community: Decision-Making and Institutional Change (edited with Robert O. Keohane), Boulder, Colorado, Westview Press, 1991
After the Cold War: International Institutions and State Strategies in Europe, 1989–1991 (edited with Robert O. Keohane), Cambridge, Massachusetts, Harvard University Press, 1993
'The crisis of liberal internationalism', *Foreign Policy* 98 (1995), pp. 159–77
World Disorders, Oxford, Rowman & Littlefield, 1998

Further reading

Miller, Lynda B., 'America, Europe, and the international system', *World Politics* 21 (1969), pp. 315–41
Miller, Lynda, B. and Smith, Michael, J. *Ideas and Ideals: Essays on Politics in Honour of Stanley Hoffmann*, Boulder, Colorado, Westview Press, 1993. Contains a full bibliography of the work of Stanley Hoffmann.

RICHARD ROSECRANCE

In 1986, when a major international concern was Ronald Reagan's Star Wars programme and the risks this raised of turning the new Cold War into a hot one, Richard Rosecrance published *The Rise of the Trading State*: *Commerce and Conquest in the Modern World*. In it he argued that the classic geopolitical preoccupations of territory and military power which dated from the Peace of Westphalia at the end of the Thirty Years War in 1648, symbolising the transition from the medieval to the modern era, were – at last – nearly obsolete. Despite the key exceptions of the (then) Soviet Union and the United States, trade had replaced territorial expansion and military might, he argued, as the key to international prestige, power and wealth. The balance of trade was supplanting the balance of power. What appeared to be a novel proposition in the mid-1980s, has, with the end of the Cold War, become more broadly accepted. In the 1990s, Rosecrance has continued to develop and apply the argument he presented in 1986, building on the thesis and exploring its implications for peace and democracy in the twenty-first century.

Of course, the proposition was not entirely novel, since Norman Angell made very similar arguments in the early years of this century. Unlike Angell, however, Rosecrance writes at a level of theoretical sophistication that reflects his long-standing academic interest in the development of international relations theory and, in particular, in the relationship between domestic and foreign policy. At the same time, Rosecrance has the enviable ability (which he shares with Angell) to write for an informed general public, as well as fellow academics in international relations. Whereas Angell was a journalist, Rosecrance has spent most of his career in a university setting, although he came to academia via the US State Department, working on the Policy Planning Council. At present he is Professor of International Relations in the Department of Political Science at UCLA, and also the Director of its Center for International Relations. Although

Rosecrance now teaches and writes at the university from which he received his BA in 1952, he has taught at a number of American universities. He was awarded his MA in 1954 from Swarthmore College and completed his doctoral thesis at Harvard University in 1957. Before taking up his present position, for many years Rosecrance was Carpenter Professor of International and Comparative Politics at Cornell.

Rosecrance established his reputation in the field in the 1960s and early 1970s for his work on systems theory. He combined his extensive historical knowledge of European statecraft since the eighteenth century with formal explanatory models to explain state behaviour and the stability of different historical systems. He published *Action and Reaction in World Politics* in 1963, and a decade later, *International Relations: Peace or War?* (1973). The latter summarises the historical analyses of the earlier work and elaborates on its general discussion of foreign policy making. In *Action and Reaction* Rosecrance is concerned with long-term developments in international relations and the way in which fundamental changes in both the nature of states and the international environment have altered the nature of *relations* between states. These themes have evolved throughout his career and are reflected in his writing on interdependence, the balance of power, the adequacy of existing theories and the dynamics of the post-Cold War era.

In his first book Rosecrance divides the history from 1740 to the present (circa early 1960s) into nine historical systems. In general he uses the outbreak of war to delimit the end of one system and the beginning of another. Unlike those who use the term 'system' to refer to a continuous process of political relations at the international level, Rosecrance refers to what might be called the 'diplomatic constellations' or the patterns of power and diplomatic relations which characterise a given historical period. Major changes in these patterns, often accompanied by conflict, indicate the development of a new system. On average, each system only lasts for a couple of decades.

Rosecrance claims the stability of any system is determined by the relationship between four major variables or 'determinants'. Interestingly, three of them refer to the actions of states that compose the system. These are the *direction* which elite groups give to foreign policy (and the compatibility of direction and objectives between states), the degree of *control* of elites over foreign policy within their respective states, and the *resources* ('persuasive skills, the quantity of mobilizable resources and the speed of mobilization') which can be used in support of foreign policy. Of these determinants, he argues that the second is most crucial in explaining systemic stability. Four of the nine systems were in 'disequilibrium' when there were major changes in the security of tenure of national elites, suggesting that the latter often attempt to solidify support by aggressive behaviour in the international system. However, in the final analysis, the stability of any particular system depends most upon the fourth determinant, the *capacity* of the environment to absorb or placate the objectives of states. In turn, capacity can be analysed in terms of the interplay between *regulative* forces (direct preventative action against disruptive policies) and more passive environmental factors.[1]

Rosecrance's argument in the 1960s and early 1970s is a direct challenge to structural realism, according to which the international system can be treated as a separable entity from the interactions of the states within it, rather than a network of relations among sub-system actors. According to Rosecrance, it is not possible to isolate domestic from foreign policy in evaluating systemic stability. System-wide action is brought into play only in response to policy initiatives of member states. In *Action and Reaction*, Rosecrance leaves little doubt that he believes the chief causes of foreign policy behaviour lie within domestic political

systems. Serious international instability and upheaval arise from the inability of the existing international system to cope with the disturbances from domestic causes. Thus, on the one hand, the wars of 1792–1815 can be explained by the attempt to export the domestic ideology of Revolutionary and Napoleonic France and, on the other, the need of conservative regimes to protect or restore their domestic positions.[2]

Similarly, the upsurge of nationalism and the wars of national unification which destabilised mid-nineteenth-century Europe and led to the final collapse of the Concert of Europe arose from the successful attempts of conservative elites to outbid their liberal opponents in domestic struggles for political power. The liberals had used democracy to rally the people against conservative rule, but the conservatives won back support by appealing to nationalism, thereby combining traditionalism and democracy. The environmental capacity of the system in Europe was limited by the absence of open territory and the result was a great deal of unregulated conflict. The great age of nineteenth-century imperialism, which began to develop after the collapse of the Concert of Europe, was directly related to it. Within Europe, Bismarck re-established a form of the Concert under Germany as a unilateral regulator. But a continuation of conservative-nationalist political control and a more general background of social and political unrest accompanied this. Even when more liberal governments achieved power, as in Britain and France, they could only maintain themselves in office by fulfilling nationalist expectations. At the same time, the international environment offered vast territories available for conquest outside Europe where expansion had been made difficult by the rise of 'national' populations eager to defend the territorial integrity of 'their' states. Rosecrance argues that this is the fundamental cause of European imperial expansion. For as soon as the new extra-European territories available for conquest had all been taken, these mutual national antagonisms, which arose originally within states, turned back inward upon Europe, leading ultimately to the First World War. In his later book, and in response to criticism that he had exaggerated the degree to which international stability depended on domestic variables, Rosecrance modifies the force of his earlier arguments. He admits that there is no conclusive link between domestic upheaval and international violence and instability, but maintains his basic argument that the former will tend to promote the latter and that nineteenth-century imperialism is a classic example of the close link between foreign and domestic policy.[3]

During the 1970s and 1980s, Rosecrance shifted his focus and began to study the degree to which the international environment was changing and the consequences of such change for American foreign policy. The arguments of *The Rise of the Trading State* emerged in part from Rosecrance's examination of the empirical data on the degree to which states were becoming more interdependent in international relations and the varying interpretations of this data by realists and liberals in the late 1970s. He believed that the data itself was ambiguous. There was some evidence that states were becoming more 'interconnected' in that one could identify increasingly common movements in such factors as prices in a number of countries. Rosecrance investigated the degree to which variations in wholesale prices, consumer prices, interest rates and wage rates showed similarities in the major industrialised economies from 1890 to 1975. Similarities in variation were established by correlating indices of the four factors and he discovered that neither realists nor liberals were correct. The evidence was mixed, suggesting both sharp discontinuities between phases of growth and diminishing interconnectedness over the last century.[4] In 1981, in a critical review of Kenneth Waltz, Rosecrance argued that the international

system could not be understood solely with the analytical tools of either realism or liberalism, we need both.

The future study of international politics will have to take account of the failure of [each]. Power and [the number of great powers] are sufficient criteria neither of international politics nor international stability. Instead, international politics exists on a continuum that ranges from Waltz's extreme structural formulation at one end, in which all units are homogeneous, to an extreme formulation at the other, in which all units are heterogeneous. Neither is sufficient by itself and neither, like the model of pure competition in formal economics, applies consistently. Most cases exist toward the middle of a continuum.[5]

Five years later, Rosecrance published his most well-known book, *The Rise of the Trading State*. In it he rejects 'monistic' explanatory frameworks for the study of international relations. Instead, he proposes a 'dualistic' approach, suggesting that the international system is characterised by the presence of two worlds, the 'military-political world' and the 'trading world'.

In part, Rosecrance was inspired by the experience of Japan. In the first half of this century, Japan rose as a political-military state, pursuing mercantilist policies of territorial expansion in Asia that were overcome (or 'regulated' to use the term from Rosecrance's earlier work) only after a very destructive world war. In contrast, since 1945 Japan has become a trading state, relying on trade and specialisation in the global division of labour to generate wealth and economic growth. Like Angell in the first decade of the twentieth century, Rosecrance supports a version of commercial liberalism, although unlike Angell he does not imply that interdependence will inevitably triumph over the logic of territoriality. However, on balance, he suggests that the future of international relations will be characterised by a shift in states' priorities from the logic of military competition to the logic of trade and interdependence.

The reasons for this switch are very simple and can be understood on the basis of rational choice. In the nuclear era, the costs of territorial expansion and military defence are rising exponentially, whilst the benefits are declining. Since the Second World War, the benefits of trade have risen in comparison to the costs, and those states (such as Japan) that understand the advantages of trade are benefiting at the expense of states such as the United States and the Soviet Union. Moreover, as war has become more costly and dangerous, domestic support for militarism and high defence expenditure has declined. Finally, since 1945, the previous trend toward fewer states in the international system has been reversed. From the Middle Ages to the end of the nineteenth century, the number of states in Europe had shrunk from about 500 to fewer than twenty-five. But after the Second World War, when European empires finally collapsed and decolonisation proceeded apace, the number of states in the world grew to about 150 by the mid-1960s. Of course, after the Cold War and the collapse of the Soviet Union, there are at present 187 member states in the United Nations, and that number may be close to 200 in the early years of the twenty-first century. In this context, the importance of trade between states becomes crucial for their continued survival. In response to those who argue that similar optimistic predictions about the peaceful consequences of trade in the late nineteenth century did not prevent the First World War, Rosecrance argues that the logic of the trading system is much more powerful today than ever before. Whilst he does not discount the possibility of nuclear war between the behemoths of the international system, the alleged 'superpowers', he argues that they are capable of change and can adapt to the requirements of the trading state.

Rosecrance's key book was published when Reagan was still in power. Gorbachev had yet to embark on his policies of *perestroika* and *glasnost*, and many observers were still fearful that the 'second Cold War' of the 1980s could end in a nuclear holocaust. If anything, then, Rosecrance's analysis has been strengthened by events over the last decade. The number of states has continued to rise, and both Russia and China are trying hard to join the capitalist trading system from which they were excluded for much of the Cold War era. The collapse of the ideological competition between communism and capitalism has been replaced by the hegemony of the world market as the only 'civilisation' at the end of the twentieth century.

In his more recent writing, Rosecrance argues that we are now in the era of the 'virtual state'. Although the process is not universal, and while less developed countries still rely on land to produce foodstuffs and crops for export, capital, labour and information are more mobile factors of production than ever before. In this environment, developed states would rather compete in the world market than acquire territory. The 'virtual state' is one that does not try to increase its territorially-based productive capability. Instead, like the headquarters of a giant corporation, it invests in services and people rather than amassing expensive production capacity, and contracts out other functions to states that specialise in them. Equally, it may play host to the capital and labour of other states. To promote economic growth, the virtual state specialises in modern technical and research services and derives its income not just from high-value manufacturing, but from product design, marketing and financing.

Whilst Rosecrance continues to argue that his own version of commercial liberalism will dominate international relations in the future, he is not unaware of the continuation of the military-political world and the need for some 'regulation' of the new international system emerging from the Cold War. He argues that there is still a need for some version of the nineteenth-century Concert system. Today, the United States, Russia, China, Japan and the European Union must co-operate to ensure the stability of the system. Progress is not automatic, the balance of power is not a 'self-regulating' system and the dynamics of global capitalism are likely to promote inequality between (and within) states, at least in the short term. Any coalition of states can only be sustained on the basis of three principles, 'involvement of all, ideological agreement, and renunciation of war and territorial expansion, giving liberal democratic and economic development first priority'.[6] In the absence of agreement on such principles, the benign consequences of the new system may not materialise, and Rosecrance is aware that there is an inherent tension between the demands of commercial liberalism in the 1990s and the prospects for democratic liberalism. In successful virtual states the traditional demands of advanced democracies – high government spending, larger deficits and more social benefits – have to be subordinated to the demands of the international marketplace – low inflation, rising productivity, a strong currency and a flexible and trained workforce. The social instability that accompanied the recent collapse of many Asian currencies testifies to the difficulties of reconciling the demands of economic growth and political participation.

Despite these difficulties, Rosecrance remains convinced that the contemporary international system can be a stable one. In addition to the need for international regulation to deal with the complex problems of transition from one system to another, he has written a great deal on the need for the United States to adapt to the demands of change. In 1976, he edited a book entitled *America as an Ordinary Country*, in which he argued that the United States could no longer be expected to take on special responsibilities in the international system. It

needed to become an 'average' state whose relative decline required it to play the role of balancer in the international system rather than the state others looked up to for leadership. In 1990 he published *America's Economic Resurgence*, a wide-ranging examination of the ways in which the United States needs to reform its domestic and foreign policies, particularly with Japan, if it is to take advantage of international systemic change in the next century.

Notes

1 Richard Rosecrance, *Action and Reaction in World Politics: International Systems in Perspective*, Boston, Little, Brown, 1963, pp. 79–93.
2 Ibid., pp. 236–9.
3 Richard Rosecrance, *International Relations: Peace or War?*, New York, McGraw-Hill, 1973, pp. 33–6.
4 Richard Rosecrance, Arthur Stein and Alan Alexandroff, 'Whither interdependence?', *International Organization* 31 (1977), pp. 425–72.
5 Richard Rosecrance, 'International theory revisited', *International Organization* 35 (Autumn 1981), p. 713.
6 Richard Rosecrance, 'A new concert of powers', *Foreign Affairs* 71 (Spring 1992), p. 75.

See also in this book

Angell, Keohane, Waltz

Rosecrance's major writings

Action and Reaction in World Politics: International Systems in Perspective, Boston, Little, Brown, 1963
'Bipolarity, multipolarity and the future', *Journal of Conflict Resolution* 10 (1966), pp. 314–27
Defence of the Realm: British Strategy in the Nuclear Epoch, New York, Columbia University Press, 1967
International Relations: Peace or War?, New York, McGraw-Hill, 1973
America as an Ordinary Country: U.S. Foreign Policy and Future (ed.), Ithaca, New York, Cornell University Press, 1976
'Whither interdependence?', *International Organization* 31 (1977), pp. 425–72 (with Arthur Stein and Alan Alexandroff)
'International theory revisited', *International Organization* 35 (1981), pp. 691–713

The Rise of the Trading State: Commerce and Conquest in the Modern World, New York, Basic Books, 1986
America's Economic Resurgence: A Bold New Strategy, New York, Harper & Row, 1990
'A new Concert of powers', *Foreign Affairs* 71 (1992), pp. 64–82
'The rise of the virtual state', *Foreign Affairs* 75 (July/August 1996), pp. 45–61
The Costs of Conflict: Prevention and Cure in the Global Arena, Oxford, Rowman & Littlefield, 1998 (with Michael E. Brown)

Further reading

Barry Jones, R.J. and Willetts, Peter (eds), *Interdependence on Trial*, London, Pinter, 1984
Crawford, Beverly, 'The new security dilemma under international economic interdependence', *Millennium: Journal of International Studies* 23 (1994), pp. 25–55

WOODROW WILSON

The phrase 'liberal internationalism', which was characterised as 'utopianism' or 'idealism' in the 1930s and after the Second World War, has enjoyed a resurgence in the post-Cold War era. At least for a short period of time in the early 1990s, particularly after the Gulf War and the collapse of the Soviet Union as well as communism, it seemed to many that the dream of world order espoused by President Wilson was becoming a reality. In particular, the 'New World Order' announced by President Bush in 1991 bore a striking resemblance to the vision of international stability held by Woodrow Wilson in the first two decades of the twentieth century. Of course, that vision failed in the 1920s, and it could be argued that its successor in the late twentieth century has already failed to transform international relations from a realm of conflict to one of co-operation. For those inspired by liberal internationalism in the 1990s and beyond, the fate of Wilson's attempts to reform global politics in the 1920s still merit serious analysis.

The project of liberal internationalism is to transform international relations so that they conform to models of peace, freedom and prosperity allegedly enjoyed in constitutional liberal democracies such as the United States and Western Europe. Robert Keohane distinguishes between three forms of liberal internationalism, all of which can be found in the thought and diplomacy of Woodrow Wilson. *Commercial* liberalism promotes trade and commerce across state borders, in the belief that economic interdependence among states will reduce incentives to use force and raise the costs of doing so. According to this strand of the doctrine, territorial divisions among states need not cause conflict if territorial control is dissociated from power. *Republican* liberalism endorses the spread of democracy among states in order that governments will be accountable to their citizens and find it difficult to promote policies that protect the interests of economic and military elites. In the 1990s there is extensive debate on the extent to which democracies are more peaceful than non-democratic states, and the reasons behind the alleged link between the domestic character of states and their foreign policies. Finally, *regulatory* liberalism seeks to promote the rule of law in international relations, as well as organisations and practices that moderate the security dilemma among states. This would help to modify international anarchy and reduce incentives for states to engage in behaviour that privileges their short-term interests over the collective interest of the society of states.[1] Looking back at the experience of President Wilson during and after the First World War, contemporary liberals are better able to assess the feasibility of all these forms of liberal internationalism than the liberals of his day.

Woodrow Wilson was born in December 1856 in the town of Staunton, Virginia. His father was a pastor at the Presbyterian Church. The family moved to Georgia soon after Wilson's birth and then moved to South

Carolina in 1870. Wilson himself joined the church in 1873, and he enrolled at the College of New Jersey (now Princeton University) in 1875, where he studied history and classics. He then studied law at the University of Virginia and opened his own law office in Atlanta in 1880. However, the business did not succeed as he had hoped, and in 1883 he enrolled at the Johns Hopkins University to begin a career in teaching. There he wrote his first book, *Congressional Government*, for which he was awarded his doctorate in 1886. He published his second book, *The State*, in 1886, and four years later was appointed Professor at Princeton University, where he remained until 1910. Wilson advanced rapidly as a young professor of political science, and in 1902 he became President of Princeton. Throughout this period Wilson was a dedicated Christian, attending services regularly and reading the Bible on a daily basis.

Wilson was elected Governor of New Jersey in 1911, and he began a series of radical reforms whose success would take him to the White House in 1912. As Governor, he transformed New Jersey from a somewhat conservative state into a progressive one. As a champion of democracy, Wilson's administration passed new laws establishing direct primary elections to the state legislature, regulation of state public utilities, anti-trust laws against industrial monopolies, as well as reform of the state educational system. The zeal with which he campaigned for what he called The New Freedom on a national level swept him to the Presidency in the campaign of 1912. Once elected, he embarked on a national programme of reform. Under his leadership, the government passed the Underwood Act in October 1913, which reduced tariffs on imports from a level of about 40 per cent to 25 per cent and expanded the list of goods that could be imported without tariffs. He was also responsible for reforming the banking system, as well as passing radical anti-trust legislation to prevent national monopolies in industry.

In 1914 he created a Federal Trade Commission with sweeping powers to prevent unfair economic competition.

In foreign affairs, Wilson emphasised the importance of human rights, including the right of self-government and the illegitimacy of formal empire. He also believed that the United States had no interest in following European imperial practices and that the United States had a key role to play as a mediator of disputes between other states. Wilson supported the independence of the Philippines in 1916 and was quite prepared to use force to defend democracy in Mexico and to restore 'order' in Nicaragua and Haiti. In 1916, United States troops occupied the Dominican Republic and placed it under direct control of the United States. Nonetheless, Wilson rejected all notions of Manifest Destiny and territorial expansionism. He believed that trade and commerce had superseded annexation as a key US concern. If the profits of trade could be gained, then formal control of territory was no longer necessary.

Wilson's readiness to use force in Central America on behalf of stable government and against dictatorships did not extend to Europe when war broke out there in 1914. He declared that the United States would remain neutral in the conflict and impartial, since the United States had no interest in a war that he believed to the outcome of imperial rivalries and arms races among states with weak constitutional democracies. As long as the United States could continue to trade without hindrance, it should act as a mediator rather than as a participant. Unfortunately, this became impossible after German submarines attacked American ships and, in 1917, Wilson asked Congress for a declaration of war against Germany and its allies. The involvement of the United States in the war helped to turn the tide against Germany in 1918, and the Great War came to an end in November.

Wilson's reputation as a liberal internationalist is based on his grand vision for a peace settlement in Europe at the end of the war, as well as his role in helping to establish the League of Nations to promote collective security and prevent another war from ever taking place. His vision was contained in his Fourteen Points, a series of principles and proposals that he announced in January 1918, and took with him to the Versailles Conference in December:

1 Open convenants (agreements) of peace openly arrived at, with no secret agreements.

2 Freedom of the seas outside territorial waters.

3 Removal of all economic barriers to trade.

4 Reduction of national armaments to the lowest level consistent with domestic safety.

5 Free, open-minded and impartial adjustments of colonial claims.

6 Evacuation of German troops from Russia and respect for Russian independence.

7 Evacuation of German troops from Belgium.

8 Evacuation of German troops from France, including the contested Alsace-Lorraine region.

9 Readjustment of Italian borders along clearly recognised lines of nationality.

10 Limited self-government for the people of Austria-Hungary.

11 Evacuation of German troops from the Balkans and independence for the Balkan people.

12 Independence for Turkey and limited self-government for other nationalities formerly living under the Ottoman Empire.

13 Independence for Poland.

14 The formation of a general association of nations under specific covenants for the purpose of affording mutual guarantees of political independence and territorial integrity for large and small states alike.

To ensure that his principles were implemented at Versailles, Wilson attended the Conference, but he failed to ensure that members of the US Senate were included in the peace delegation; he also excluded Republicans. Wilson returned to the United States in early 1919 after securing international agreement to set up the League of Nations, the first international organisation dedicated to the promotion of collective security at a global level. Despite the attraction of Wilson's vision, it contained a number of flaws and failed to be implemented to his own satisfaction.

The principle of collective security presupposes a world of status quo states that are generally satisfied with the distribution of territorial control. According to the principle, states should not use force against one another and are obliged to use force collectively if any state commits 'aggression' against another state. Paradoxically, states are most likely to be in favour of such a principle when it is least necessary and unlikely to support it if to do so requires them to go to war on behalf of other states. This was the situation in 1919 when the human cost of war was unprecedented. (Germany, 1.8 million dead; Russia, 1.7 million; France, 1.4 million; Britain, 0.9 million. In comparison, approximately 50,000 Americans were killed.) The carnage of war persuaded European statesmen to subscribe to the idea that peace is indivisible (i.e. the prevention of particular wars is in the general interest of 'the community of states'), but not to the extent of sacrificing their own freedom of choice in decisions of national security. Consequently, as Gabriel points out,

> The League was a modest body. There was no institution comparable to the Security Council where binding and authoritative decisions were made, and there were no provisions for joint enforcement mechanisms. The sovereign independence of its members was in no way restricted, there

was no trace of supranationality . . . [it] was merely a mechanism to postpone war. There was much reliance on dialogue, on investigating and publishing facts. Given the proper information and the necessary time, a learning process was expected to set in and rationality was expected to emerge victorious. The peoples of the world would peer over the shoulders of the assembled diplomats; world public opinion would make itself felt.[2]

Unfortunately, such an organisation was inadequate to secure peace in Europe or elsewhere. Part of the reason for this is that in addition to creating a new security organisation, the statesmen at Versailles were also imposing a punitive peace on Germany, ensuring its deep dissatisfaction with the territorial redistributions determined on the dubious basis that Germany was solely responsible for the outbreak of the First World War. France, in particular, was determined to use the Conference not as an opportunity to end balance of power politics, but as part of its ambition and self-interest to ensure that Germany remained weak. Although Wilson was able to prevent the dismemberment of Germany at the Conference, he was unable to stop the demand for some loss of territory, huge reparations from Germany and its enforced disarmament at the hands of the Allied Powers. Thus Wilson's Fourth Point was applied selectively at Versailles as the winners refused to surrender their arms to a world body over which they could not exercise control, and they used Wilson's points to impose a *diktat* over their conquered enemy.

Other elements of Wilson's vision were only partially implemented by the so-called Big Four powers at the Conference (Britain, France, the United States and Italy). An independent Poland was created, and the principle of national self-determination was implemented on behalf of Czechoslovakia, Finland and the Baltic states of Lithuania, Latvia and Estonia. But there were major problems in determining the scope and criteria of the principle in so many states that contained a plurality of different 'nations'. The question of what constituted a nation was never dealt with, and it proved impossible to reconcile the goal of European stability and territorial integrity with the principle of national self-determination. For example, differences among the Balkan nations were ignored in the interests of setting up an independent Yugoslavia, whilst the Great Powers were reluctant to surrender their own colonial possessions. Again, Germany was stripped of its own colonies in Africa and the Pacific, but they were merely transferred to other Allied Powers as mandates – territories controlled by them under varying degrees of supervision by the League of Nations. No agreement was reached on the future of Russia, which at the time was in the midst of a civil war, and Britain simply refused to discuss the prospect of independence for India. A merger of the new German-speaking Austria with Germany was prohibited despite popular wishes. Tragically, Hitler himself later used the language of national self-determination in the 1930s to ensure the break-up of Czechoslovakia and the unification of all German-speaking people in the Reich.

Faced with all these problems, Wilson was convinced that only if the United States joined the League could it hope to influence the future of international relations in a manner consistent with liberal ideals. After he returned from Versailles in 1919, he engaged in an intense campaign to ensure that the Senate would not reject the Peace Settlement. But many Americans were unprepared to undertake the international obligations that the Covenant of the League seemed to require. Although Wilson himself was convinced that American leadership and the passing of time could rectify some of the apparent injustices of the settlement, the US Senate was particularly concerned at what appeared to be a blanket commitment to collective security contained in Article 10 of the League Covenant. This committed member states to 'respect and preserve' the territorial integrity of other states, and Wilson had insisted that this Article was a crucial component of the organisation. But it also appeared to contradict the isolationist tradition in American foreign policy, according to which the United States should never get involved in any 'entangling alliances' overseas that could not be justified in the national interest. For over 200 years the United States had enjoyed a unique geographical, historical and ideological separation from the European balance of power, and many Americans did not understand why they could not return to this state of affairs now that the war had been won. But Woodrow Wilson had not justified war in terms of the balance of power and the need to contain Germany. Instead, he had insisted on justifying the involvement of the United States in wholly moralistic terms, hoping to end war for all time and to replace the European balance of power with a new set of legal and global parliamentary procedures. He failed to do so, and his rhetoric helped to ensure that he could not achieve even the limited goal of United States' membership in the League.

Wilson refused on principle to compromise with the peace settlement signed at Versailles. He believed that he could appeal over the head of Congress to the good sense of the American people and was totally intransigent as he engaged in long travels across the United States hoping to persuade the American people to his point of view. Yet he was unable to secure the two-thirds majority approval by the Senate necessary to ratify the treaty. The Republicans continued to insist on clarifications and changes to Article 10 and believed that their success in the congressional elections in 1918 reflected their growing popularity. The treaty failed in a crucial vote on 19 November, 1919. 'Wilsonism' became a term of abuse in the United States, and 'Wilsonian internationalism' became a synonym for 'utopianism' in the study of international relations for the next seventy years. Wilson himself fell seriously ill whilst on a speaking tour in support of the League in October 1919, and he died in February 1923. In 1920, meanwhile, the Democrats were soundly defeated in the presidential election, which brought Warren Harding to power. The United States never joined the League, which in turn failed to secure international peace. In December 1920, Woodrow Wilson was awarded the Nobel Peace Prize for his efforts in seeking a fair political settlement to the Great War and in founding the League of Nations. The Second World War broke out less than twenty years later.

Notes

1 Robert O. Keohane, 'International liberalism reconsidered', in John Dunn (ed.), *The Economic Limits to Modern Politics*, Cambridge, Cambridge University Press, 1990, pp. 165–95.
2 Jurg Martin Gabriel, *Worldviews and Theories of International Relations*, London, Macmillan, 1994, p. 79.

See also in this book

Angell, Zimmerman, Doyle

Wilson's major writings

George Washington, New York, Harper, 1896
The State: Elements of Historical and Practical Politics (Revised edition), Boston, Heath, 1898
A History of the American People, New York, Harper, 1906
The New Freedom, London, Dent, 1916
Congressional Government: A Study in American Politics (introduced by Walter Lippman), New York, Meridian Press, 1956
Constitutional Government in the United States, New York, Columbia Unversity Press, 1961
Woodrow Wilson's Case for the League of Nations, (1923), compiled with his approval by Hamilton Foley, New York, Kraus Reprints, 1969
The Public Papers of Woodrow Wilson: Authorized Edition (1925), New York, Kraus Reprints, 1970

Further reading

Ambrosius, Lloyd E., *Woodrow Wilson and the American Diplomatic Tradition: The Treaty Fight in Perspective*, New York, Cambridge University Press, 1987

Ambrosius, Lloyd E., *Wilsonian Statecraft: Theory and Practice of Liberal Internationalism During World War I*, Wilmington, Delaware, SR Books, 1991

Anderson, David D., *Woodrow Wilson*, Boston, Twayne Publishers, 1978

Bell, Herbert and Clifford, Francis, *Woodrow Wilson and the People*, Hamden, Connecticut, Archon Books, 1968

Buckingham, Peter H., *Woodrow Wilson: A Bibliography of his Times and Presidency*, Wilmington, Delaware, Scholarly Resources, 1990

Greene, Theodore P., *Wilson at Versailles*, Boston, Heath, 1957

Knock, Thomas J., *To End all Wars: Woodrow Wilson and the Quest for a New World Order*, New York, Oxford University Press, 1992

Walworth, Arthur, *Woodrow Wilson*, New York, W.W. Norton, 1978

ALFRED ZIMMERN

There are two related reasons for including Sir Alfred Zimmern in this book. First, his work is a good example of the kind of 'idealism' that was subject to so much criticism from 'realists' such as Carr and Morgenthau in the 1930s and 1940s. Although I have argued that such criticisms are unwarranted if one examines the work of, say, John Hobson or Norman Angell, the same cannot be said of Zimmern. Although his ideas are not representative of all the 'idealist' liberals in the inter-war period, it is a good example of what Carr and others set out to demolish. Second, the fact that Zimmern failed so spectacularly to persuade students and diplomats of the merits of international law and the League of Nations in the 1930s is itself interesting. It helps to explain the way in which the study of 'international organisation' has developed in the post-1945 era. J. Martin Rochester observes that, after the First World War, students of international relations were concerned with building effective international institutions 'to an extent that international organisation was viewed not so much as a subfield as practically the core of the discipline'.[1] After the Second World War, disillusionment with the performance of the League as well as the views of its main supporters (including Zimmern) relegated the study of international organisation to the realm of 'low politics'. The United Nations, although it sought to build on and modify the institutional design of its predecessor, could not function effectively in 'maintaining international peace and security' as long as the Cold War existed. In contrast to the League, the Security Council privileges the role of great powers, providing them with permanent seats and the ability to veto any resolution. In the absence of any agreement among them, the United Nations is handicapped, at least in the management of international security. Even when the sub-field of 'international organisation' began to expand in the 1970s, it did so because of developments in international relations theory, not because of any great change in the performance of international institutions per se, particularly the United Nations. In 1986, in a major review of the sub-field, Kratochwil and Ruggie noted that 'international organisation as a field of study is where the action is; few would so characterise international organisations as a field of practice ... the doctors [are] thriving when the patient is moribund [because] the leading doctors have become biochemists and have stopped treating and in most cases even seeing patients'.[2]

Zimmern was in part responsible for the woeful reputation of the earlier generation of 'doctors'. He is a key thinker in international relations not because he is a great thinker, but because his work imparts important lessons in how *not* to think about international law and international organisation. If students of international organisation have gone too far in privileging theory at the expense of practice in recent years, they can at least begin to rectify the imbalance without repeating the errors of some of their intellectual forefathers.

Alfred Zimmern was born in 1879. His father was a German Jew, although Zimmern was brought up as a Christian, and he took his spiritual values very seriously, becoming actively involved with the World Council of Churches in the 1940s. He went to school at Winchester and read Classics at New College, Oxford University, from where he graduated with a first class degree in 1902. He remained there until 1909, lecturing in the field of ancient history. In 1909 he went to Greece to study, and in 1911 he published his first book, *The Greek Commonwealth*. When he returned to Britain he worked for the Board of Education as a school inspector and was active in the growing Labour movement, stressing the need for working-class education in national and international affairs. With the outbreak of the First World War, Zimmern began to play a more important role in international relations. He contributed short articles to the journal *The New Europe*, edited by R.W. Seton-Watson, calling for the establishment of a new international institution, the League of Nations, the abolition of war and the need to respect the principle of national self-determination.

As the First World War drew to a close in 1918, the Ministry of Reconstruction employed Zimmern, where he worked in the Political Intelligence Department of the Foreign Office. This gave him the opportunity to shape British policy toward the League of Nations and advocate the liberation of 'subject people' in Europe. He served on the League of Nations Union research committee and contributed to the so-called 'Cecil draft' that was tabled in Paris by the British delegation. He attended the Versailles Conference, which set up the League, and was very pleased with the final Covenant despite his reservations about the scale of reparations demanded from Germany by France.

In 1919, at the age of only 40, Alfred Zimmern was appointed to the Woodrow Wilson Chair of International Politics at the University of Wales in Aberystwyth. Thus, he became the first Professor in the new discipline, appointed less for the scale and reputation of his publications than for what Brian Porter described as 'his cosmopolitan outlook ... as well as his easy familiarity with ruling circles'.[3] His 'cosmopolitanism' was reflected in his insistence that the new professor be allowed to devote every third term to overseas travel. At Aberystwyth, Zimmern designed the undergraduate curriculum around the study of the League of Nations Covenant and delivered weekly lectures on contemporary topics in the news of the day, which attracted many students. Zimmern also managed to attract the wife of one of his colleagues. When they eventually got married, the new professor was 'prevailed upon' to resign and did so in 1921.

For the next decade, until his appointment as the first Montague Burton Professor of International Relations at Oxford in 1930, Zimmern attended sessions of the League in Geneva and taught at Cornell University in the United States. He joined the Labour Party in 1924 and even ran for election against Lloyd George that same year. Between 1926 and 1930, he was Deputy Director of the League's Institute of Intellectual Co-operation in Paris, and devoted himself to the task of developing higher education in the study of inter-national relations. He was instrumental in the establishment of the Royal Institute for International Affairs in London and an ardent supporter of the need to educate students in the management of 'international co-operation'.

At Oxford, Zimmern finally finished the book for which he is best known, *The League of Nations and the Rule of Law*, published in 1936. Hedley Bull describes the book as 'the most polished' work of the writers later condemned for their 'idealism'. Indeed, it suffers from all the flaws that Bull attributes to 'idealists' in general:

The distinctive characteristic of these writers was their belief in progress: the belief, in particular, that the system of international relations that had given rise to the First World War was capable of being transformed into a fundamentally more peaceful and just world order; that under the impact of the awakening of democracy, the growth of the 'international mind', the development of the League of Nations, the good works of men of peace or the enlightenment spread by their own teachings, it was in fact being transformed; and that their responsibility as students ... was to assist this march of progress to overcome the ignorance, the prejudices, the ill-will, and the sinister interests that stood in its way.[4]

As a summary of all 'idealists', Bull's words are perhaps unfair, but they adequately summarise the dominant themes of Zimmern's major work in international relations. The book itself is divided into two parts. The first is entitled 'The Pre-War System', and the second part focuses on the Covenant and 'The Working of the League'. What Zimmern refers to as 'the past' is rejected as a guide to the present and the future, 'the possibilities of which were not limited by the test of previous experience but were deducible from the needs of the present'.[5] In his excellent analysis of Zimmern, Markwell singles out 'five main strands' of Zimmern's account of the Covenant, which Zimmern relies upon to maintain international stability:

1 An improved and enlarged Concert of the Powers, using the method of regular Conference.

2 Mutual guarantees of territorial integrity and independence.

3 An improved Hague Conference system of Mediation, Conciliation and Inquiry.

4 An improvement and co-ordination of the Universal Postal Union and similar arrangements for the carrying on of world services and ... public utilities.

5 An agency for the mobilisation of the Hue and Cry against war as a matter of universal concern and a crime against the world community.[6]

In his analysis of the power of these 'strands' to transform international relations, all Zimmern's idealism comes to the fore, which provides such an easy target for Carr and Morgenthau to destroy in later years. Markwell singles out a number of idealistic themes in Zimmern's writing.

He notes that Zimmern had originally intended to entitle his book *Towards the Rule of Law*. Zimmern believed that international relations were progressing from the balance of power to the rule of law. He distinguished between an 'old order' and a 'new one', and between 'power politics' and 'responsibility politics'. Another favourite distinction was between 'welfare' politics and 'power' politics, and Zimmern believed that the latter was becoming subordinate to the former as international relations moved from anarchy to enlightenment. E.H. Carr is withering in his contempt for such distinctions:

> For many years prior to 1933, Great Britain, being satisfied with her power, was a 'welfare' state. After 1935, feeling her power contested and inadequate, she became a 'power state'. The contrast is not one between 'power' and 'welfare', and still less between 'politics' and 'economics', but between different degrees of power.[7]

Of course, Zimmern's belief in progress was itself made possible by his underlying faith in the 'harmony of interests' among individuals and states, itself informed by liberal economic doctrines of the eighteenth century. If states did not appear to understand this, there could only be two possible reasons. It could be that they simply lacked intelligence, in which case it was the duty of professors such as Zimmern to educate political leaders and their citizens. As he once put it, 'it is not because men are ill disposed that they cannot be educated into a world social consciousness. It is because they – let us be honest and say "we" – are beings of ... limited intelligence'.[8] In the late 1920s, Zimmern suggested the establishment of an international lending library, subsidised by governments, which could make expensive books available to the poor and assist in the development of an 'international public opinion' on behalf of peace.

The development of an effective public opinion was also crucial in counteracting another motive for states to go to war despite the evidence of progress in international law, which is the absence of democratic constraints against the dictatorial leaders of 'power states'. The principle of 'Hue and Cry' in the League was supposed to be the international equivalent of an electoral 'backlash' in constitutional democracies against unpopular governments. A common complaint about international law is that it is not 'really' law at all, since there is no authoritative body to enforce it. In the absence of a world state, there is nothing to stop states either from invoking the law to justify acts that are motivated primarily by self-interest or from ignoring the law for the same reason. Thus Iraq flouted international law in 1991 when it invaded Kuwait. It then appealed to the core principles of international law (i.e. state sovereignty) in trying to expel American nuclear weapons inspectors as spies in 1997.

Zimmern was not unaware of this problem, but he hoped that the League could become a crucial forum for dealing with it. On the one hand, conflicts between states could themselves be resolved peacefully if the rule of law was strengthened between states. On the other hand, those 'power states' that flouted the law could be deterred and, if necessary, punished by the mechanisms of 'collective security'. Within a system of collective security, states are obligated to renounce the use of force in solving their disputes. So Zimmern was delighted when the United States and France tabled the Kellogg–Briand pact to the League in 1928, a document that outlawed war. On the other hand, states are equally obligated to use force if necessary against any state that refuses to obey international law. Zimmern's optimism in 1928 was soon dispelled when, during the 1930s, the great powers refused to implement the provisions of the Covenant against Japan (after its invasion of Manchuria), and again against Italy after its invasion of Abyssinia. To Zimmern, the failure to implement the principle of 'hue and cry' confirmed the degree to which governments, still wedded to the 'Old Diplomacy', lagged behind the enlightened segments of public opinion within their countries.

The events of the 1930s demonstrate that international law cannot itself bring about a just world order. It may be the expression of a legitimate international order, which is accepted by the great powers, but whether that order is a just one is another matter entirely. Zimmern did not acknowledge this, in part because (as Carr never hesitates to point out in *The Twenty Years' Crisis*) Zimmern himself came from a status quo power. His form of liberalism, stressing its constitutional or regulatory dimensions, was the international manifestation of his analysis of the source of order in Britain and the United States. If international politics were not *inherently* distinct from the domestic politics of the Anglo-Saxon states, he did not see any reason why the rule of law could not be extended to the international arena. If this appears to be quite naïve in the 1990s, one might reflect on the continuing influence of such idealism today. For example, just as Iraq flouted international law in 1991, President Bush also exaggerated the importance of restoring Kuwait's sovereignty for the so-called 'New World Order' in the early 1990s. Whatever justifiable reasons there were for expelling Iraqi forces from Kuwait on strategic grounds, the success of Operation Desert Storm did not inaugurate a new era in international politics. As in the 1930s, there can be no stable international order that is divided between status quo and revisionist states, particularly if the latter are powerful ones. Unless international law includes legitimate procedures for the negotiation of peaceful change in international relations, which is unlikely given the inequality of power and wealth among states and the absence of any consensus on the meaning of a just world order, disillusionment is inevitable.

It is tempting to conclude this summary of Zimmern's life and work with some polite words about the worthiness of his contribution, despite its evident failings. One should resist the temptation to judge Zimmern as well-meaning if somewhat naïve. The reason is that his disenchantment with the League of Nations in the 1930s led him to become a fervent Cold Warrior later in life. In 1944 he retired from his chair at Oxford. After working for a short period as secretary-general of the constituent conference of UNESCO, he was appointed visiting professor at Trinity College, Hartford, Connecticut. In 1953 he published his last book, *The American Road to World Peace*. It would not be true to say that he had learned nothing from the criticisms heaped upon him by the realists. He had, but the lessons he learned were the wrong ones. Instead of acknowledging the subordination of international law to the balance of power, and seeking to tame its manifestation as a balance of terror, Zimmern threw all his support behind the United States in the Cold War. Now the Soviet Union was the 'power state' rather than Germany. In his earlier book, Zimmern admitted that international law in the absence of enforcement was merely 'an array of wigs and gowns vociferating in emptiness'.[9] If it were to be effective in the Cold War then it would have to be enforced by the United States. So Zimmern the 'idealist' became a firm supporter of the atomic bomb in the hands of the United States, the world's

first police officer. Unfortunately, Zimmern died in 1957 and so did not live long enough to see the emergence of a rival police force similarly armed.

Notes

1 J. Martin Rochester, 'The rise and fall of international organisation as a field of study', *International Organization* 40 (1986), p. 780.
2 Friedrich Kratochwil and John Gerard Ruggie, 'International organisation: a state of the art on an art of the state', *International Organization* 40 (1986), p. 753.
3 Brian Porter (ed.), *The Aberystwyth Papers: International Politics 1919–69*, London, Oxford University Press, 1972, p. 361.
4 Hedley Bull, 'The theory of international politics 1919–69', in Porter, ibid., p. 34.
5 Ibid., p. 35.
6 D. Markwell, 'Sir Alfred Zimmern: fifty years on', *Review of International Studies* 12 (1986), p. 282.
7 E.H. Carr, *The Twenty Years' Crisis*, London, Macmillan, 1946, p. 120.
8 Alfred Zimmern, *Neutrality and Collective Security*, Chicago, University of Chicago Press, 1936, p. 8.
9 Alfred Zimmern, *The League of Nations and the Rule of Law, 1918–1935*, London, Macmillan, 1936, p. 252.

See also in this book

Angell, Bull, Carr, Hobson, Wilson

Zimmern's major writings

The Greek Commonwealth: Politics and Economics in Fifth-Century Athens, Oxford, Clarendon Press, 1915

Europe in Convalescence, London, Mills & Boon, 1922

The Third British Empire: Being a Course of Lectures Delivered at Columbia University New York, London, Oxford University Press, 1926

Learning and Leadership: A Study of the Needs and Possibilities of International Intellectual Co-operation, London, Oxford University Press, 1928

The League of Nations and the Rule of Law, 1918–1935, London, Macmillan, 1936

Spiritual Values and World Affairs, Oxford, Clarendon Press, 1939

Modern Political Doctrines, London, Oxford University Press, 1939

University Teaching of International Relations, Paris, International Institute of Intellectual Cooperation, League of Nations, 1939

The American Road to World Peace, New York, E.P. Dutton, 1953

Further reading

Claude, Inis, *Power and International Relations*, New York, Random House, 1962

Markwell, D.J., 'Sir Alfred Zimmern: fifty years on', *Review of International Studies* 12 (1986), pp. 272–92

Parkinson, F., *The Philosophy of International Relations*, London, Sage, 1977

RADICAL/CRITICAL THEORY

The following thinkers are concerned with the sources of structural inequality inherent in the international system, as well as the ways in which it might be overcome. Often inspired by, but not limited to, the Marxist tradition of thought, they illuminate how international relations among states makes possible (and tends to conceal) the inequities of a global capitalist system. These thinkers are radical in two ways. First, they believe that theory and practice are not separate and autonomous realms of thought and action. Second, they are not content with international reforms that are limited to regulating relations among states, particularly if they rely on the capacity and the will of the so-called 'great powers'. They believe that both realism and liberalism serve to maintain the basic distribution of power and wealth. They think that we need to reflect critically on the historical conditions underlying inequality, the material and ideological forces that sustain it and the potential for radical reform of the system in favour of a more just world order. If students are to remain faithful to the emancipatory social interest of promoting 'human needs' on a global scale, these thinkers urge them to explore the complex connections between a formal 'anarchy' among states and an economic 'hierarchy' among social and economic classes. The rigid distinction between politics within states and 'relations' among social classes must be dispensed with. These thinkers expand the scope of international relations to include the forces at work in 'global society', whose practical achievement requires that we question our traditional allegiance to the sovereign state. Of course, none of these thinkers believe that the latter's obsolescence is imminent, and they disagree on the relative potency of 'new social movements' as substitutes for Marx and Lenin's transnational revolutionary working-class proletarians.

JOHN BURTON

John Burton's work cannot be classified easily within the conventional frameworks of analysis in the study of international relations. In part this is because he is a trenchant critic of the view that international relations can stand apart from other disciplines in the social sciences. It is also a result both of his eclectic attempt to develop a holistic approach to the analysis of conflict in global politics and of his determination to promote the idea of 'world society' as the necessary concept within which relations among states are seen as but one part of a broader system of connections and links across territorial boundaries.

> In practice, there are so many direct communications, or systems, that a world map which represented them would look like a mass of cobwebs superimposed on one another, strands converging at some points more than others and being concentrated between some points more than between others. The boundaries of states would be hidden from view.[1]

Although the idea that we live in an increasingly 'globalised' world has become popular in the 1990s, John Burton has been studying this phenomenon since the early 1960s and has developed a unique corpus of work that continues to inspire students of world society today.

John Burton was born in 1915 in Australia. His life and career have not followed the usual path from school to university and then into academia. Instead, Burton has moved between academic and diplomatic posts. This helps to account for his criticism of scholarly models divorced from changes in the real world as well as his desire to engage in academic work that would improve decision making. Burton joined the Australian Commonwealth Public Service in 1937 after completing his undergraduate work, and he won a scholarship to

the University of London in 1938. He received his doctorate from the London School of Economics in 1942 and played an active role in Australian diplomacy at the end of the Second World War. However, he was not content to remain a functionary in the Australian diplomatic corps, and many of his ideas were already unconventional at the time. He did some academic work at the Australian National University in the late 1950s and in 1963 he was offered an academic post at University College London. He remained there until the early 1970s, when he moved to the University of Kent at Canterbury. With a number of other, younger colleagues, such as Michael Banks at LSE, Burton was instrumental in setting up the Centre for the Analysis of Conflict based at Kent, which provided a forum for the dissemination and further exploration of his work. In the early 1980s, Burton moved to the United States, where he worked and taught at the George Mason University in Fairfax, Virginia. He now lives in Australia, formally retired but still active as a thinker and writer.

Burton's first major book, *International Relations: A General Theory* (1965), was an ambitious attempt to use systems theory as part of a broader critique of what Burton considered to be the orthodox realist model of international relations. The latter portrayed states as billiard balls, whose interactions could best be understood as the consequence of enduring hierarchies of power. A clear distinction was made between domestic and foreign policy, and states were treated as sealed units. Even in the 1960s, Burton was claiming that the orthodox wisdom on international politics and international organisation – relating to national power, national interests, balance of power, collective security and world government – did not fit contemporary international conditions and situations. For example, one critical weakness of the orthodoxy was its failure to distinguish between power as a means to achieve other goals (such as security) and power as an end in itself.

Instead, Burton used models of cybernetics and systems theory to shed more light on international relations in general and the analysis of conflict in particular. Of course, Burton was not the first to employ the notion of a 'system' to study international relations.[2] But his conception of the international system was original in its attempt both to reintroduce domestic 'inputs' into the study of international order and to substitute power with 'legitimacy' as a crucial variable in accounting for inter-state conflict. Inspired by the work of Karl Deutsch, among others, Burton used concepts from the study of decision making and cybernetics to make his central argument. As he observed,

In terms of communication needs, power is unimportant. When a system is fully integrated, receiving information, classifying it, and reacting, and is subject to feed-back controls, and when through this process it can change its goals and adapt itself to changing situations, power is seen as of incidental importance, no matter how important it might happen to appear at any point in history'.[3]

He also argued that power and the use of force in inter-state relations was at one end of a spectrum, at the opposite of which was mutual decision making in conflict resolution, 'an interest in each state in the responses of other states to its policies, in processes of change, in goal-changing, and in national adjustment to change elsewhere'.[4]

However, the title of Burton's first book was misleading insofar as its theoretical claims were more suggestive than systematic, and Burton's review of the existing state of theory in international relations was marred by his tendency to engage in polemical criticisms against what he perceived to be the limits of orthodoxy. The book is more noteworthy for its analysis and promotion of nonalignment in the context of the ongoing Cold War between the

superpowers. He suggested that unpopular regimes in new states emerging from the process of decolonisation sought alignment with the superpowers not because of ideological sympathy, but because they desire intervention from the superpowers to protect them from domestic upheaval and domestic challenges to their authority. On the other hand, governments that enjoy greater support and legitimacy from their citizens were more likely to choose nonalignment because they do not need outside support and can therefore safely avoid exposure of the new state to intervention from the superpowers.

This insight helps to account for the weakness of so many regimes in the Third World after the Cold War. Now that one superpower no longer exists, and the United States is reluctant to intervene in areas that have no strategic significance for its security, many regimes (particular in Africa) can no longer maintain their tyrannical rule over their people. In 1965, Burton presented nonalignment as a path to peace if adopted by a sufficient number of states. With nuclear deterrence providing a necessary but not sufficient basis for international order, nonalignment could create an international system 'in which all sovereign states regardless of size can live together in a competitive, but not aggressive, relationship'.[5] Burton's ideals are reflected in his vision of the impartial, passive and nonaligned state, which perhaps summed up his view of the appropriate role for such 'middle powers' as Australia. However, the connection between Burton's policy prescriptions and his use of systems theory was not clearly articulated in this work.

In 1968, Burton published his second major text, *Systems, States, Diplomacy and Rules*. He continued his concern with systems theory and decision making, arguing that conflict between states often arises from dysfunctional decision making within them. This might arise from inadequate education and lack of perfect knowledge of conditions abroad, from ideologies that stimulate ambitions and fears or from erroneous perceptions of other states. Burton argued that national leaders often prefer to transfer their domestic challenges to the international realm, even at the price of tension and war. Again, his conception of the ideal world begins with each state unified internally. Delivered of overdemanding and fear-laden domestic pressures, a state could then pursue more flexible policies abroad, base its decision making on accurate perceptions and coordinate its activities with other states through international institutions.

Burton's framework of analysis of world society resembles a triangle. At the top angle is his central proposition derived from general systems theory: the conduct of states is preconditioned by their need either to adjust to changes in their environment or to alter the environment. For Burton the ideal type of world society would be 'one which is fully permissive of change and never requires adjustment by a state or its systems other than that which is slow-moving and continuous'.[6]

At one base of the triangle lies the concept of legitimacy in the behaviour of states. It tries to account for the difference between reciprocal and coordinated behaviour, which is systemic and functional, and power behaviour, which is non-systemic and hence dysfunctional. One needs also to distinguish between legality and legitimacy. Legitimised government is based on the support of citizens for its authority so that coercion is minimal. Burton argued that governments had to reflect the values and satisfy the needs and demands of their people in order to become legitimate. 'Whenever there is a difference between systemic interests, on the one hand, and the goals and values of authorities, on the other, there is . . . a reduced level of social legitimation'.[7]

The second base angle of Burton's structure is occupied by his theory of decision making. The links between the three angles of his triangle are defined by the inner logic of Burton's theory. The needs of states (conceived as systems of action rather than independent actors) can be satisfied only by legitimised behaviour; decision making 'bridges the gap between legitimacy in the sense of representing the values and interests of the state, and legitimacy in the sense of acting in accordance with agreements and demands made on the state'.[8] As David Dunn points out, by the time this book was published, Burton's frame of reference was very wide indeed:

[H]uman relationships are cast in terms of transactions, relationships, systems, patterns, perceptions, and definitions of the situation. There is an international system, comprised of states, but it is one of many and, in terms of the nature of behaviour, authority, legitimacy, loyalty, conflict and control, it may not be the most important system for many people. Increasingly, his vocabulary is about participation, relationships, authority, control, deviance, conflict, and legitimacy.[9]

By the early 1970s, John Burton had established his reputation as a student of world society. Increasingly, he devoted his attention to the nature of conflict and its complex origins in the absence of institutions and behavioural patterns to meet human needs. The focus on systems analysis lessened, although Burton still insisted on the utility of scientific analysis to describe world society rather than political philosophy or normative theory per se. He remained a firm opponent of realism and 'power politics' in general, and he made an important distinction between *puzzle-solving* and *problem-solving*. The former approach to conflict resolution operates within established constraints, employing means (such as the use of force) that have been tried in the past. Since they fail to tackle the roots of the problem of violence, and only work against its symptoms (terrorism would be a good example), they not only fail to eradicate violence, but also often perpetuate it. On the other hand, problem-solving is an approach that tries to transform what may appear to be a zero-sum conflict between parties into a positive-sum relationship. Since states often use means that perpetuate conflict, Burton argued that conflict resolution, whether between states or within them, could not be left in their hands. Instead, he advocated the use of third parties that could assist in the process, widening the participation of those with stakes in the resolution of particular conflicts and facilitating the search for more creative solutions.

Underlying Burton's shift of focus in the 1970s and 1980s was his conviction that once we understood the roots of violence as the failure to meet human needs in world society, we would be better able to create institutions and practices that could improve the global condition. In his search for a value-free concept of human needs, consistent with his positivist commitment to the scientific study of politics, Burton's work displays an enviable multidisciplinary capacity to draw on disparate sources in the social sciences, such as biology, psychology and sociology. In 1972 he referred to human needs as social-biological values, and argued that they were universal characteristics of all human beings. Differing cultural systems merely employ different means to satisfy them and the rank of importance also varies across cultures. In *Conflict: Resolution and Prevention* (1990), Burton argued that conflicts can only be resolved when eight basic needs of the antagonists have been satisfied. They were 'a need for response, a need for security, a need for recognition, a need for stimulation, a need for redistributive justice, a need for meaning, a need to be seen as rational . . . and a need to control'.[10] Once these needs have been satisfied, we take on roles that enable us to defend our needs, and often conflate the needs themselves with the roles designed to defend them. Nonetheless, Burton remains convinced that 'needs frustration' is the basic cause of violence and conflict in contemporary world society. Furthermore,

'[n]eeds theory move[s] the focus away from the individual as miscreant and aim[s] it at the absence of the legitimisation of structures, institutions and policies as the primary source of conflict'.[11]

Of course, Burton's work on conflict resolution, whilst it has inspired many followers, has also attracted some criticism. In particular, the attempt by social scientists to identify some objective list of human needs has not been successful. The list of 'human needs' is often expressed in very vague terms, the debate between those who see them as universal and those who see them as culturally specific remains unresolved, and it must be said that Burton himself fails to specify the conditions under which it would be possible to meet all these needs simultaneously. In part this is a problem with Burton's belief in the utility of social science to solve problems that have traditionally been examined within the field of political philosophy. Whilst much of Burton's work, particularly on the nature of 'world society' is a useful corrective to realism, Richard Little's challenge to Burton and those inspired by him remains as relevant today as when it was mounted in 1984:

[T]here is a choice about the kind of world we want to live in. As a consequence, the social scientist can never be a mere spectator. The possibility of reshaping the world which is being analysed must affect the nature of the analysis. Analogies with the natural sciences, therefore, are inappropriate because any analysis of the social world will be infused with the values of the analyst. In a world of competing values, the merits of any particular model, therefore, are not self-evident. No model is free from ideology. Since John Burton wishes to change the world, he has no alternative but to make the argument for change in ideological terms. It is counter-productive to dress one's values in natural science garb. A non-ideological model of social order is a chimera which it is a mistake to claim or pursue.[12]

Notes

1 John Burton, *World Society*, Cambridge, Cambridge University Press, 1972, p. 43.
2 For a useful overview of the origins and use of systems theory in the study of international relations, see C. R. Mitchell 'Systems theory and international relations', in A.J.R. Groom and C.R. Mitchell (eds), *International Relations Theory*, London, Pinter, 1978, pp. 33–48.
3 John Burton, *International Relations: A General Theory*, Cambridge, Cambridge University Press, 1965, p. 147.
4 Ibid., p. 274.
5 Ibid., p. 231.
6 John Burton, *Systems, States, Diplomacy and Rules*, Cambridge, Cambridge University Press, 1968, p. 36.
7 Ibid., p. 47.
8 Ibid., p. 57.
9 David J. Dunn, 'Articulating an alternative: the contribution of John Burton', *Review of International Studies* 21 (1995), p. 200.
10 John Burton, Frank Dukes and George Mason, *Conflict: Resolution and Prevention*, Basingstoke, Macmillan, 1990, p. 95.
11 John Burton (ed.), *Conflict: Human Needs Theory*, London, Macmillan, 1990, p. xv.
12 Richard Little, 'The decision maker and social order: the end of ideology or the pursuit of a chimera?', in Michael Banks (ed.), *Conflict in World Society*, Brighton, Wheatsheaf Books, 1984, p. 95.

See also in this book

Deutsch, Galtung

Burton's major writings

The Alternative: A Dynamic Approach to Our Relations With Asia, Sydney, Morgan Publications, 1954
International Relations: A General Theory, Cambridge, Cambridge University Press, 1965
Systems, States, Diplomacy and Rules, Cambridge, Cambridge University Press, 1968
Conflict and Communication: The Use of Controlled Communication in International Relations, London, Macmillan, 1969
World Society, Cambridge, Cambridge University Press, 1972

'Resolution of conflict', *International Studies Quarterly* 16 (1972), pp. 5–30
Deviance, Terrorism and War: The Process of Solving Unsolved Social and Political Problems, Oxford, Martin Robertson Press, 1979
'The role of authorities in world society', *Millennium: Journal of International Studies* 8 (1979), pp. 73–9
Dear Survivors: Planning After Nuclear Holocaust: War Avoidance, Boulder, Colorado, Westview Press, 1982
Global Conflict: The Domestic Sources of International Crisis, Brighton, Wheatsheaf Books, 1984
Conflict: Resolution and Prevention (co-authored by Frank Dukes and George Mason), London, Macmillan, 1990
Conflict: Human Needs Theory (ed.), London, Macmillan, 1990

Further reading

Banks, Michael (ed.), *Conflict in World Society: A New Perspective on International Relations*, New York, St Martin's Press, 1984
Banks, Michael, 'Where we are now?', *Review of International Studies* 11 (1985), pp. 215–33
Dunn, David J., 'Articulating an alternative: the contribution of John Burton', *Review of International Studies* 21 (1995), pp. 197–208

ROBERT COX

'Theory is always *for* someone and *for* some purpose.'[1] This is the sentence most often quoted from the writing of Robert Cox, whose work has become far more widely read in the 1990s than it was prior to the end of the Cold War. This is so for two reasons. First, Cox has published a great deal on the phenomenon of 'globalisation' in international relations. Second, he is at the forefront of a growing number of scholars who he has inspired over the years and who represent the emergence of post-Marxian 'critical theory' in the field. Cox's path-breaking article on the nature of critical theory was published in 1981 and appeared to offer a radical alternative to neorealist positivism, which at that time dominated the study of international relations, particularly in the United States.

Cox himself started to write about international relations and the international political economy rather late in life. He was never socialised into the academic conventions of the discipline, and this gives his writing a certain freshness and originality that is very different from most theoretical contributions in the field. Cox's worldview has developed over many years and it has been shaped in important ways by his unconventional career. His biography is perhaps more crucial for understanding his approach to the study of international relations than for most of the key thinkers surveyed in this book.

Robert Cox was born in 1926 in Quebec, Canada and raised in the city of Montreal. Although (or perhaps, because) his parents were both English-speaking conservatives, Cox became a keen student of radical politics in French Canada, but his interest in international relations did not begin until the end of the Second World War. When Cox completed his undergraduate degree at McGill University, he joined the International Labor Organisation at the United Nations, which was based at McGill during the war years. In 1945 Cox left Canada to take up his new appointment in Geneva. He remained with the ILO for the next twenty-five years, first as principal staff officer and then as Chief of the Program and Planning Division. The experience of working with the ILO during the Cold War left an indelible mark on Cox. As he explains:

There were three inherently contradictory but essential bases for political survival in this context: (1) to maintain the support of the United States (especially to an American head who was recurrently being attacked as 'soft on communism' by Cold War hard-liners in the US labor movement and as a cover for 'creeping socialism' by the more reactionary elements of American business); (2) to maintain the

principle of 'universality' which meant trying to make Soviet bloc membership acceptable to the West ... (3) to achieve and maintain a reasonable degree of program coherence in a bureaucracy that was segmented into feudal-type baronies.[2]

In the early 1970s, when Cox felt unable to sustain his intellectual freedom to write and publish his work as a member of the organisation, he resigned from the ILO and took up an academic career based at Columbia University. In 1977, he returned to Canada to take up a post at York University in Toronto, where he remains as Professor of Political Science.

There are three crucial elements of Cox's work that must be understood if one is to engage further with the writing of this theoretical iconoclast: his commitment to critical theory; the influence of Antonio Gramsci and Karl Polanyi on his substantive arguments regarding world order; and his particular analysis of globalisation in the late twentieth century.

First, Cox regards himself as a critical theorist. The term *critical theory* is no doubt inadequate to encompass all the alternatives that can be swept into this category of theory. Perhaps a more adequate label would be 'ideologically oriented inquiry', including neo-Marxism, some forms of feminism and other radical schools of thought. These perspectives are properly placed together, however, because they converge in rejecting the claim of value freedom made by more positivist forms of inquiry. Nature cannot be seen as it 'really is' or 'really works' except through a value window. Since values enter into every inquiry, then the question immediately arises as to what values and whose values shall govern. If the findings of studies can vary depending on the values chosen, then the choice of a *particular* value system tends to empower and enfranchise certain individuals and groups while disempowering and disenfranchising others. Inquiry thereby becomes a political act.

This does not mean that critical theorists are in any sense relativists. Their concern with the phenomenon of 'false consciousness' discloses a belief in the possibility of 'true consciousness', and it is the self-appointed task of critical theorists to reveal the material and social forces that prevent people from achieving their 'real' interests in a world which manipulates their desires and limits their potential. The task of critical inquiry is, by definition, to raise people to a level of 'true' consciousness. This is a necessary, although not sufficient, precondition for them to act to transform the world. Cox contrasts critical theory with what he often refers to as 'problem-solving' theory, a term used to describe theories that take for granted the persistence of the system whose internal dynamics they seek to explain. Critical theory focuses on large-scale historical change of the system itself, and the contradictions and conflicts that may provide the potential for emancipatory systemic change.

Cox's most systematic attempt to construct a substantive critical theory of international relations can be found in his book *Production, Power, and World Order: Social Forces in the Making of History* (1987). The book provides the basic conceptual framework that Cox uses to examine the relationship between material forces of production, ideas, and institutions in particular historical periods in international relations. The basic assumption of the book is that forces of production create the material base for social relations, generating the capacity to exercise power in institutions, but power and production are related dialectically. Power, in turn, determines how production takes place and is organised. The book is divided into three related parts.

In the first, Cox distinguishes between no less than twelve 'patterns' of production relations, which he calls 'modes of social relations of production'. They include subsistence, peasant–lord, primitive labour market, household, self-employment, enterprise labour market, bipartist, enterprise corporatist, tripartist, state corporatist, communal and central planning. Each of these 'modes' is explored as a self-contained structure with its own developmental potential and ideational/institutional perspective. Social relations of production arise in three analytically distinct ways: the accumulated social power that determines the nature of production; the structure of authority that is shaped by the internal dynamics of the production process; and the distributive consequences of production. Cox demonstrates how these aspects of social relations are related to each other in a dialectical manner and he is particularly interested in the ways in which contradictions and conflicts arise between them in particular historical phases.

Despite his panoramic survey of these patterns of production relations, Cox quickly focuses on two basic modes of development, which he calls capitalist and redistributive. Development is associated with and made possible by the generation of an economic surplus within a mode of social relations. Simple reproduction, in which the mode is merely reconstituted over successive production cycles, cannot produce meaningful development. Both capitalist and redistributive forms of development accumulate in order to grow and both may organise production in similar ways to generate a surplus for further development. But the mechanisms and underlying rationale for accumulation in the two modes is different. Capitalism is based on the pursuit of profit in the market, whilst in redistributive societies what is produced is determined by political decision making.

Cox argues that any meaningful comparison between capitalist and redistributive modes of development must be located in a global context, taking into account the relations among states within which these two modes are concentrated. For example, the initial dynamics and repression of redistributive development are explained in large part by the international pressures on regimes whose predominantly agricultural economies had to compete with leading industrial states in Europe and the United States. Although redistributive development began by combining central planning and communalism, more recent developments revealed different patterns of change in the Soviet Union and China. In the Soviet Union, communalism became totally subordinate to the requirements of central planning, whilst in China it has been dismantled in agriculture and replaced by forms of the enterprise labour market.

In the second part of the book, Cox surveys the development of the modern state system and in particular the constraints imposed on states by the global political economy. Such constraints help to explain the transformation and contradictions of different modes of the social relations of production. Whilst Cox stresses the importance of material forces of production in the determination of social relations, he also recognises the key role played by states, and relations among states:

> States create the conditions in which particular modes of social relations achieve dominance over coexisting modes, they structure either purposively or by inadvertence the dominant–subordinate linkages of the accumulation process ... each state is constrained by its position and its relative power in the world order, which places limits on its will and its ability to change production relations.[3]

Cox's worldview owes a great deal to the work of the Italian communist writer, Antonio Gramsci.[4] In particular, he draws upon Gramsci's ideas on hegemonic control in capitalist societies to explain the way in which dominant ideas about world order help to sustain particular patterns of relations among material forces, ideas and institutions at a global level. Gramsci always located his work in the Marxist schema, in which the 'economic base' sets the limiting conditions for politics, ideology and the state. But the underlying thrust of Gramsci's work is consistently away from simple forms of reductionism. What he centrally addressed was the complex nature of the relations between structure and superstructure, which, he argued, could not be reduced to a mere reflection of 'economic' conditions narrowly construed. His theoretical originality lay in the series of novel concepts that he used to expand and transform our understanding of politics. He was greatly preoccupied with the character of state and civil society relations prevailing in relatively modern societies, especially capitalist democracies. Gramsci challenged the reductionist conception of the state as exclusively a 'class' state, an instrument of ruling class coercion and domination. He insisted on the 'educative' role of the state, its significance in constructing those alliances that could win support from different social strata and its role in providing cultural and moral 'leadership'. Although the economic structure may be, in the last instance, determinative, Gramsci gave much greater autonomy to the effects of the actual conduct of the struggle for leadership, across a wide front and on a variety of sites and institutions. He argued that the role of the communist party was to engage and lead in a broad, multi-faceted struggle for 'hegemony'. A shift in socialist political strategy was necessary, away from an outright frontal assault on the state to the winning of strategic positions on a number of fronts. Socialist struggle was conceived as a 'war of position' in the first instance against the forces of capitalist hegemony in civil society and culture.

Thus for Gramsci, and for Cox, hegemony at a global level is not to be equated with mere material or military dominance (as in realism), nor is it to be regarded as a desirable public 'good' (as in neoliberal institutionalism):

> Gramsci used the concept of hegemony to express a unity between objective material forces and ethico-political ideas

– in Marxian terms, a unity of structure and superstructure – in which power based on dominance over production is rationalised through an ideology incorporating compromise or consensus between dominant and subordinate groups.[5]

In much of his writing, Cox is concerned with the rise and decline of hegemonic world orders over time. In his book he distinguishes between three 'successive structures of world order': the liberal international economy (1789–1873); the era of rival imperialisms (1873–1945); and the neoliberal world order (post-1945). The third and final part of the book focuses on the global economic crisis of 1973–4. He argues that the industrial and financial restructuring of the last twenty years has led to the weakening of labour's autonomous collective social power and the increasing peripheralisation of the labour force. This is the context in which Cox examines globalisation in the late twentieth century. Drawing on the work of Karl Polanyi, Cox focuses on what he terms 'the internationalisation of the state'. By this Cox refers to the process whereby national institutions, policies and practices become adjusted to the evolving structures and dynamics of a world economy of capitalist production.

Cox identifies three dimensions of this process. First, 'there is a process of interstate consensus formation regarding the needs or requirements of the world economy that takes place within a common ideological framework'. Second, participation in the negotiation of this consensus is hierarchical. Third, 'the internal structures of states are adjusted so that each can best transform the global consensus into national policy and practice'.[6] He also identifies three historic stages in the process whereby the state has become increasingly internationalised. The first of these was characteristic of the 1930s when states were strong relative to the world economy and protected their populations from it. The second occurred after 1945 with the establishment of the Bretton Woods system, which represented a compromise between the accountability of governments to the institutions of the world economy (particularly its sources of liquidity), and their accountability to domestic opinion for their economic performance and for maintaining the welfare state. The third stage involves the globalisation of the state. It marks a restructuring of the relationship between the state and the world economy and the national/international compromise in favour of the transnational institutions and networks of power that dominate the current world economy. The internationalisation of the state marks a further erosion of its role as a buffer against the world economy and an intensification of trans-state sources of power, authority and decision making.

Thus Cox alerts us to an alternative perspective on the post-Cold War era to those most often discussed by realists and liberals. Changes in the balance of power between states and the alleged ascendancy of democracy over authoritarianism are subservient to what Cox calls 'global perestroika'. He argues that the dramatic changes inspired by Gorbachev's 'revolution from above' were by no means confined to the former USSR. Over a much longer period, a similar structural transformation has been taking place in the capitalist world, namely, the disembedding of global liberalism. For Cox, the globalisation of capital, production and debt is not part of some inevitable trend to a postindustrial, postmodern world caused solely by exponential advances in the technology of manufacturing and communications. It has been enormously facilitated by a neoconservative hegemonic ideology of deregulation designed to disempower traditional oppositional forces, particularly the trade union movement. Its evisceration by the likes of Reagan and Thatcher in the 1980s has contributed to

a revival of the nineteenth-century separation of economy and politics. Key aspects of economic management are therefore to be shielded from politics, that is to say, from popular pressures. This is achieved by confirmed practices, by treaty, by legislation, and by formal constitutional provisions.[7]

Thus the dominant image of contemporary international relations for Cox is radically at odds with some of the more benign interpretations one finds in the field. He believes that our era of 'hyper-liberal globalising capitalism' is the site of some major contradictions and struggles: between the rhetoric of democracy and the 'democratic deficit' caused by the internationalisation of the state; between the growing demands for international protection of the environment and the surrender of state authority to international corporate finance and business; and between the rhetoric of victory in the Cold War over socialism and the accelerating inequality both within and between states.

What is to be done? Cox calls for what he describes as a new form of multilateralism, which should not be limited to regulating relations horizontally between state elites. It should be conceived as:

> The locus of interactions for the transformation of the existing order [on behalf of] an enlarged conception of global society . . . multilateralism must be considered from the standpoint of its ability to represent the forces at work in the world at the local level as well as at the global level.[8]

Since states have played a major role in facilitating the process of globalisation, Cox argues that counter-hegemonic social forces should engage in a 'war of position'. His thoughts on this are, for the moment, merely suggestive. He argues, for example, that the labour movement must mobilise at a global level and build alliances and coalitions with a variety of new social movements. Globalisation 'from above' must be countered with 'globalisation from below'. Cox recognises that this will not be easy. It will be difficult for Western 'progressives' to unite with Islamic social movements to construct some kind of global counterforce. Nonetheless, he claims that the difficulties must be faced and overcome if the juggernaut of globalisation is to be slowed down and even reversed.

The work of Robert Cox is, in conclusion, a major contribution to the rise of critical theory in the study of international relations. From his base at York University, he has inspired many students to rethink the way in which we should study international political economy, and it is fair to say that Gramscian historical materialism is perhaps the most important alternative to realist and liberal perspectives in the field today.

Notes

1 Robert Cox, 'Social forces, states and world orders: beyond international relations theory', *Millennium: Journal of International Studies* 10 (1981), p. 128.
2 Robert Cox, *Approaches to World Order*, Cambridge, Cambridge University Press, 1996, p. 23.
3 Robert Cox, *Production, Power, and World Order: Social Forces in the Making of History*, New York, Columbia University Press, 1987, p. 399.
4 See, in particular, Robert Cox, 'Gramsci, hegemony, and international relations: an essay in method', *Millennium: Journal of International Studies* 12 (1983), pp. 162–75.
5 Robert Cox, 'Labour and hegemony', *International Organisation* 31 (1977), p. 387.
6 Robert Cox, *Production, Power, and World Order*, op. cit., p. 254.
7 Robert Cox, 'Global *perestroika*', in Ralph Miliband and Leo Panitch (eds), *The Socialist Register 1992*, London, Merlin Press, 1992, p. 32.
8 Robert Cox, 'Multilateralism and world order', *Review of International Studies* 18 (1994), pp. 162–3.

See also in this book

Gilpin, Krasner, Keohane, Ruggie

Cox's major writings

International Organisation: World Politics: Studies in Economic and Social Agencies, London, Macmillan, 1969

The Anatomy of Influence: Decision Making in International Organization (with Harold Jacobson *et al.*), New Haven, Yale University Press, 1972

'Social forces, states and world orders: beyond international relations theory', *Millennium: Journal of International Studies* 10 (1981), pp. 126–55

'Gramsci, hegemony and international relations: an essay in method', *Millennium: Journal of International Studies* 12 (1983), pp. 162–75

Production, Power, and World Order: Social Forces in the Making of History, New York, Columbia University Press, 1987

'Global perestroika', in Ralph Miliband and Leo Panitch (eds), *The Socialist Register*, London, The Merlin Press, 1992, pp. 26–43

Approaches to World Order (with Timothy J. Sinclair), Cambridge, Cambridge University Press, 1996. This book is an edited collection of Cox's most important articles. For a complete bibliography of his work, see pp. 537–44

Further reading

Cafruny, Alan Weston, 'A Gramscian concept of declining hegemony: stages of U.S. power and the evolution of international economic relations', in David P. Rapkin (ed.), *World Leadership and Hegemony*, Boulder, Colorado, Westview Press, 1990, pp. 97–118

Gill, Stephen, 'Historical materialism, Gramsci, and international political economy', in Craig N. Murphy and Roger Tooze (eds), *The New International Political Economy*, Boulder, Colorado, Lynne Reinner, 1991, pp. 51–75

Gill, Stephen (ed.), *Gramsci, Historical Materialism, and International Relations*, Cambridge, Cambridge University Press, 1991

Gill, Stephen and Law, David, 'Global hegemony and the structural power of capital', *International Studies Quarterly* 33 (1989), pp. 475–99

Gill, Stephen and Mittelman, James (eds), *Innovation and Transformation in International Studies*, Cambridge, Cambridge University Press, 1997

Polanyi, Karl, *The Great Transformation*, Boston, Massachusetts, Beacon Press, 1944

RICHARD A. FALK

The work of Richard Falk defies easy classification within the established typology according to which key thinkers in the field are often sorted. There are two main reasons for this. First, Falk is not a self-conscious theorist who tries to construct elaborate models that claim to illuminate patterns of relations among states. This is not to say that his work ignores theory, merely that he employs the work of others for his own evaluative purposes. Second, Richard Falk straddles ideological boundaries in his attempt both to criticise the foreign policies of states (particularly the United States) and to offer proposals for reforming the states system that lie within what he considers to be the realm of the possible. It is possible, however, to describe Falk as a critical analyst of the role of international law in global politics who still appeals to legal and constitutional principles through which the states system can evolve in a more cosmopolitan direction.

Not only is Falk difficult to classify, his work also defies neat summary. Many of the thinkers covered in this book are well known for their invention and elaboration of particular theories or concepts. This is not the case with Richard Falk. Instead, the reader will be struck by an enduring concern with normative questions of world order, the role of law in sustaining and potentially transforming the states system and the sheer variety and volume of Falk's written work.[1]

Since 1961, Richard Falk has taught and worked at Princeton University. In 1965 he was appointed Albert G. Milbank Professor of International Law and Practice. Falk was born in 1930 in New York and describes his own family background as 'assimilationist Jewish with a virtual denial of even the ethnic side of Jewishness'.[2] By his own admission, Falk's status as an outsider contributed to his feeling of not quite belonging to American society and may have

119

influenced his future role as a sustained critic of American foreign policy from the early 1960s onwards. Falk graduated from the University of Pennsylvania in 1952 with a degree in economics before deciding to study law. He graduated from Yale Law School in 1955 (LLB) and completed his doctoral studies at Harvard University in 1962. After some teaching at Ohio State University and Harvard in the late 1950s, he joined the law faculty at Princeton, which has been his academic home for the past three decades. He has also taught at Stanford and at the University of Stockholm. In 1985 he was a Guggenheim Fellow.

Falk's awareness of, and interest in, politics did not flourish until he had begun to teach law in Ohio in the heady days of the 1960s, where he witnessed racism against black students and was exposed to a radical group of graduate students and young faculty members who read and discussed the work of Marx, C. Wright Mills and Herbert Marcuse. He was fortunate in moving to Princeton in the early 1960s, where the teaching of international law was not divorced from the study of politics, international relations and other social sciences. This enabled Falk to situate his work within a broader concern for issues of global order and injustice and provided a useful base from which to integrate his expertise in international law with his normative values. Unlike many academics, Falk has sought to fulfil the role of what he calls a 'citizen-pilgrim', and to fuse his academic work with political activism:

> The essential inquiry of a citizen-pilgrim is to discover how to make desirable, yet unlikely, social movements succeed. The movements against slavery, colonialism, racial discrimination, and patriarchy are some instances. My overriding concern is to foster an abolitionist movement against war and aggression as social institutions, which implies the gradual construction of a new world order that assures basic

human needs of all people, that safeguards the environment, that protects the fundamental human rights of all individuals and groups without encroaching upon the precarious resources of cultural diversity, and that works toward the non-violent resolution of intersocietal conflicts.[3]

In the 1960s, Falk was an active opponent of US intervention overseas, particularly in Vietnam. In the late 1960s, Falk began his ongoing involvement with the World Order Models Project (WOMP) with a number of other radical scholars. The purpose of the project is exploring ways in which a new world order can be organised so that: (1) large-scale collective violence is minimised; (2) social and economic well being are maximised; (3) fundamental human rights and conditions of political justice are realised; and (4) ecological quality is maintained and rehabilitated. Falk interpreted his own task as prescribing an order that would enhance these values and the transition processes that may lead to the creation of such an order.

In the 1970s, he was a pioneer in examining ways in which the Westphalian system of separate sovereign states could be transcended. He acknowledged the difficulties and he urged the mobilisation of public opinion, especially in the industrialised world and specifically in the United States. Of particular concern was the persistent resort by states to force as an instrument of national policy in the face of what Falk perceived as the real threat of nuclear disaster. At times he despaired of the prospects for the emergence of an effective legal order in a violent world, short of the coming of a Third World War; such a catastrophe might serve as the catalyst for the general adoption of international institutional changes which would lead to a more centralised, hence supranational, control of the use of force. On the other hand, he did 'acknowledge that there has been a gradual strengthening of moral consciousness and human compassion so as to make the reorganisation of the political basis of human existence on a global scale a meaningful goal'.[4] In the 1970s, Falk argued that the United Nations should play a much more active role as a third party to assist in the resolution of civil wars that were often promoted and supported by the superpowers as part of the Cold War's expansion into the Third World.

In 1981 he published *Human Rights and State Sovereignty*. In this work he argued that the advancement of human rights must proceed by transforming traditional structures, especially by supporting populist movements opposing imperialist forces represented by the United States. He claimed that international capitalism is the greatest impediment to reform and that socialism is ideologically superior to capitalism because it seeks to distribute wealth equally. Capitalism exploits particular classes, and the horizontal division of the world politically makes it very difficult for those at the bottom of the economic hierarchy to mobilise across territorial borders. He suggested that global reform would have to begin by defeating imperialism and subsequently establishing political and economic human rights within them. It should be noted that Falk's advocacy of socialism is based on its promises as opposed to the actual performance of 'really existing' allegedly socialist states.

Since the end of the Cold War in the late 1980s, and the apparent diminution of the threat of nuclear war, Falk has continued to argue the case for the transformation of the Westphalian system of states in order to promote his more cosmopolitan goals. For Falk, the 'stability' of the states system must not be evaluated by the mere absence of war between states (what may be called international order), but by criteria of world order in which the interests of states are subordinate to those of the human beings who live in them. In short, the national interest is less important than the global interest, and the end of the Cold War does not diminish the need for structural transformation. In its absence, the international system will continue to promote the pursuit of 'statist imperatives'. These include pursuit by nation-states of economic growth measured solely in terms of gross national product, economic and technological competition, the diversion of international institutions to the service of domestic goals, political barriers against the movement of people across state boundaries and the reluctance to pursue effective international demographic and environmental policies. Falk describes the post-1989 era not in triumphalist terms as the 'end of History' and the victory of democracy over its rivals, but as a period of history that facilitates the widening of 'the horizon of plausible aspirations' to include far more ambitious extensions of law and institutions in relation to the governance of political and economic life. The post-Cold War era is characterised by new dangers as well as new opportunities for structural change.

The dangers are both geopolitical and economic. Geopolitically, Falk is unconvinced that the collapse of the Soviet challenge to the United States spells an end to balance of power politics. In particular, he points to the way in which some policymakers and American strategists are beginning to portray China as a rising superpower that may pursue policies in the Asia-Pacific region that threaten US interests. North Korea's pursuit of a nuclear weapons capability, Chinese threats to reunify Taiwan with China by force and ongoing territorial disputes between China, Japan and Vietnam are all possible 'flashpoints' for a new Cold War between the United States and China. This would be less an ideological conflict than a traditional great power rivalry overlaid with cultural and racial overtones. Economically, Falk is concerned with what he perceives to be the continuing inequality engendered by global capitalism which he regards as totally antithetical to the promotion of participatory democracy. 'A market-driven alternative, as represented by the effort to constitute free trade regimes in Europe and North America, will accentuate the gaps between North and South and neglect the plight of the disadvantaged everywhere.'[5]

On the other hand, the same technological forces that are reducing the salience of territorial boundaries (such as the Internet), are also potentially empowering for grassroots movements active in promoting WOMP values. This should encourage the project of 'global constitutionalism' as a vehicle leading to some kind of 'transnational democracy' rooted in the efficacy of a dynamic international law that manages to embrace human interests as well as those of states. In the 1990s, Falk's earlier enthusiasm for revolutionary liberation movements and socialism has given way to an embrace of what he calls an emerging 'global civil society'.[6] The latter is comprised of shifting coalitions of individuals and groups who are active in promoting the very goals likely to be ignored if geopolitical and/or economic elites are allowed to pursue their own agendas.

> There is hope and political space for creative initiative. The endorsement of human rights and constitutionalism establishes a foundation on which globalisation-from-below can evolve to balance and neutralise the negative features of globalisation-from-above. It is from this inter-active play of opposing forces that one can envision a new world order that serves the human interest, and yet is rooted in the realities of political trends. To envisage a future world order entirely shaped by transnational democratic forces would be naïve and utopian. To conceive of a creative tension emerging out of various beneficial and detrimental globalising tendencies seems sensible, although the outcome is by no means certain to be positive.[7]

This is the appropriate context in which to understand Falk's cautious embrace of post-modernism in social theory as well as his most recent proposals for United Nations reform. In *Explorations at the Edge of Time* (1992), Falk engages in a lively critique of modern notions of reason, truth and progress. These privilege narratives of Rational Man (the knowing subject) encountering and mastering a single knowable reality (the known object). The result of this encounter is the belief in the possibility of unambiguous knowledge of the 'real world' in order to facilitate its control and mastery. Essentialist, unitary and universal discourses of modernity exclude and devaluate difference, plurality and forms of knowledge that cannot meet 'scientific' standards of rationality. Falk is wary of postmodern repudiations of the Enlightenment that promote a facile relativism and undermine the idea of universal human rights, but he also supports those who identify the 'dark side' of modernity and highlight the environmental and human costs of our search for control over ourselves and our environment. In this book he once again invokes the ideas of the 'citizen-pilgrim' and identifies his own beliefs as a form of 'rooted utopianism' that aims at global reform along 'Highway D-5' (denuclearisation, demilitarisation, dealignment-depolarisation, democratisation and development).

In the 1990s Falk has also been at the forefront of debate on the question of UN reform. He was a vigorous opponent of the Gulf War, because he claims that the UN was being used to legitimate the interests of the United States rather than those of global order. On the one hand, Iraq's invasion of Kuwait in 1990 represented a challenge to the will and ability of the UN to respond effectively to despotism and aggression in the name of collective security. For the first time in the history of modern international institutions a prompt and effective response was given which also displayed a high degree of consensus. The United States 'displayed the initiative and muscle to confront Iraq with effective challenge and to mobilise a common front within the Security Council behind the demand that Iraq withdraw unconditionally from Kuwait'.[8] But he also argues, on the other hand, that the effect of a number of Security Council Resolutions during the crisis gave official backing to a war which the United Nations was unable to control and whose objectives exceeded the simple restoration of Kuwait's sovereignty. In his view, the practical problems of expelling Iraq from Kuwait would have been better handled by using the military forces of the United States and its allies under the strict supervision of the Security Council, as is in fact required by the UN Charter (Chapter VII). This would have facilitated much tighter control over the number and deployment of troops and the way in which force was used.

In Falk's view, the UN will be unable to escape the 'statist imperatives' of the states system unless it becomes more financially independent of the most powerful states and the Security Council more accountable both to the rest of the international community of states in the General Assembly, as well as non-governmental actors in the international system. Similarly, Falk is wary of arguments that in the 1990s either the United States or the UN should embrace policies of assertive humanitarian intervention to deal with the growing number of civil wars. He argues that the record of allegedly 'humanitarian' interventions is not a good one, and that it is never possible for a great power to act on behalf of the oppressed. More typically, great powers focus selectively on the victims of civil war and authoritarian governments to advance their own interests.[9] Consistent with his overall worldview, Richard Falk argues that it is very dangerous to rely on states to resolve problems that are themselves manifestations of the pathology of the states system itself.

Of course, it is possible to criticise Richard Falk as a confused idealist. In the 1960s he was criticised for what some writers interpreted as an anti-American bias in much of his work, and his naïveté concerning human nature as well as the benefits of socialism. Falk has admitted that some of his gloomy predictions concerning the future of the planet were based on faulty statistics coming out of the Club of Rome's analysis, and some may regard his faith in legal cosmopolitanism as merely utopian. Nevertheless, Falk has demonstrated the importance of international law in the study of international relations, not merely as a static body of rules, but as a crucial and dynamic instrument of social change.

Notes

1 Richard Falk's curriculum vitae is more than forty pages, and those interested in a complete list of his published work can find his c.v. on the internet at the following address: http://www.wws.princeton.edu/faculty/falk-papers/cv.html
2 Richard Falk, 'Manifesting world order', in Joseph Kruzel and James N. Rosenau (eds), *Journeys Through World Politics*, Toronto, Lexington Books, 1989, p. 161.
3 Ibid., p. 163.
4 Richard Falk, *Legal Order in a Violent World*, Princeton, New Jersey, Princeton University Press, 1968, pp. x–xi.
5 Richard Falk, 'In search of a new world model', *Current History* 92 (1993), p. 149.
6 See, in particular, 'Evasions of sovereignty', in R.B.J. Walker and Saul H. Mendlovitz (eds), *Contending Sovereignties: Redefining Political Community*, Boulder, Colorado, Lynne Rienner, 1990, pp. 61–78.
7 Richard Falk, 'In search of a new world model', op. cit., p. 149.
8 Richard Falk, 'Reflections on the Gulf War experience', *Juridisk Tidskrift* 3 (1991), p. 182.
9 See in particular, Richard Falk, 'Grounds to reject intervention', *Peace Review* 8 (1996), pp. 467–70.

See also in this book

Bull, Galtung

Falk's major writings

Law, Morality, and War in the Contemporary World, New York, Frederick A. Praeger, 1963

Legal Order in a Violent World, Princeton, New Jersey, Princeton University Press, 1968

This Endangered Planet: Prospects and Proposals for Human Survival, New York, Random House, 1971

A Global Approach to National Policy, Cambridge, Massachusetts, Harvard University Press, 1975

A Study of Future Worlds, New York, Free Press, 1975

'The world order models project and its critics: a reply', *International Organization* 31 (1978), pp. 531–45

'Anarchism and world order', in Richard A. Falk and Samuel S. Sim (eds), *The War System: An Interdisciplinary Approach*, Boulder, Colorado, Westview Press, 1980, pp. 37–57

Human Rights and State Sovereignty, New York, Holmes & Meier, 1981

The End of World Order: Essays on Normative International Relations, New York, Holmes & Meier, 1983

Reviving the World Court, Charlottesville, University Press of Virginia, 1986

The Promise of World Order: Essays in Normative International Relations, Brighton, Wheatsheaf Books, 1987.

Revolutionaries and Functionaries: The Dual Face of Terrorism, New York, Dutton, 1988

Economic Aspects of Global Civilization: The Unmet Challenges of World Poverty, Princeton, New Jersey, Princeton University Press, 1992

Explorations at the Edge of Time: The Prospects for World Order, Philadelphia, Temple University Press, 1992.

The Western State System, Princeton, New Jersey, Princeton University Press, 1992

On Humane Governance: Toward a New Global Politics: The World Order Models Project Report of the Global Civilization Initiative, Cambridge, Polity Press, 1995

Further Reading

Bull, Hedley, *The Anarchical Society*, London, Macmillan, 1977

Franck, Thomas, *The Power of Legitimacy Among Nations*, Oxford, Oxford University Press, 1990

Kruzel, Joseph and Rosenau, James (eds), *Journeys Through World Politics*, Lexington, Massachusetts, Lexington Books, 1989, pp. 153–64

ANDRÉ GUNDER FRANK

Frank is best known as one of the leading scholars of 'dependency theory' in the study of development. Dependency theory is a radical rejection of post-war diagnoses of and prescriptions for Third World development based on liberal modernisation approaches, although today dependency theory has itself been absorbed into world systems theory by radical scholars in the study of international political economy.

Frank was born in 1929 in Germany and his family moved to the United States in the early 1930s to escape Nazi Germany. He attended Swarthmore College, studying economics, and began a PhD at the University of Chicago in 1950. This took some years to complete as Frank began to question the economic orthodoxies of Keynesian theory and to attract the opposition of his supervisors. He eventually completed his doctoral dissertation on the comparative measurement of productivity in agriculture and industry in the Ukraine, and he began to focus on the shortcomings of conventional developmental thought. In the early 1960s, he left his academic post at Michigan State University to live and work in Latin America (based in Chile), where he produced most of his original research, analysing the nature and dynamics of 'development' from a radical perspective.

Throughout the 1960s Frank wrote prodigiously and his work became very popular in North America as the Vietnam war escalated. After the overthrow of the Allende regime in Chile in a successful coup orchestrated by General Pinochet, Frank returned to Germany in 1973 to take up a position at the Latin America Institute of the Free University of Berlin. In 1978 he secured a Professorship in the School of Development Studies at the University of East Anglia, where he began systematic research on the state socialist economies of Eastern Europe and continued his work on the history of global capitalism. For many years he taught and wrote at the University of Amsterdam in the Netherlands, and he is presently a member of the Graduate Faculty at the University of Toronto.

Frank's work in the late 1950s and the 1960s has to be understood as a reaction to and deconstruction of the conventional wisdom on the requirements for 'development' in the Third World. This orthodoxy was characterised by two key assumptions that Frank has done much to undermine. First, mainstream economics tended to equate economic development with economic growth, measured in simple static terms as an increase in gross national product. Problems and questions relevant to the dynamics of institutional development and to the transformation of values were kept outside the boundaries of analysis and policy formulation. In the post-Second World War era, it was often assumed that, since the 'developed countries' of North America and Western Europe were already developed, the challenge was for poor states to implement similar policies that would assist them also to achieve rapid growth. If a country grows, it will also 'develop'. Thus underdevelopment was defined by a comparison of rich and poor countries, and development meant bridging the gap by means of an imitative process until the 'undeveloped' became more like the 'developed'.

Second, even those writers who questioned the equation of growth and development presupposed that obstacles to development were primarily internal to the country being studied, rather than external. In the 1950s, development thinking was dominated by Durkheimian assumptions of social change as increasing rationalisation and consensus. This required the application of objective, impersonal judgements in the construction of human relationships rather than subjective ones. The sociologist Talcott Parsons distinguished between 'modern' and 'traditional' societies. In general, the latter tend to emphasise collective interests over individual self-interest, relations between individuals are based on particular ascriptive attributes rather than universal values according to which all are equal regardless of status, and societal obligations are diffused throughout a network of groups rather than being specific to contractual obligations explicitly undertaken for limited periods and purposes.

Perhaps the most well-known text in the modernisation paradigm is Walt Rostow's *Stages of Economic Growth* (1960). Rostow believed that traditional societies in China, the Middle East and medieval Europe shared a ceiling on the level of attainable output because the potential of science and technology were either not available or not systematically applied. In order to develop or, in his words, 'take off', they had to be introduced to modern ideas of progress, education had to be available to the masses, financial infrastructure had to be established, and there had to be a pool of entrepreneurial individuals prepared to take risks for profit. Traditional societies could only take off down the road to modernisation after a number of stages of industrialisation, when incomes would rise to a point where people could consume beyond the basic necessities, the proportion of people in skilled or office jobs rose, and surplus funds could be reinvested for future growth. In short, whilst economic growth was an important criterion for development, the latter involved a number of sequential structural and behavioural changes. Modernisation came to be understood in terms of an 'upward movement' of the entire social and cultural system from one stage of economic evolution to the next, necessary for and related to ultimate democratisation. In the context of the Cold War, the modernisation paradigm provided a diagnosis and prescription that provided an alternative model of economic growth to that endorsed by the Soviet Union or China, and justified a massive expenditure of US aid to poorer countries to assist the process.

In his work on Latin America in the 1960s, Frank, along with other radical scholars such as Rudolfo Stavenhagen and Fernando Cardoso, turned much of the conventional wisdom on its head. He argued that the Parsonian dualisms were exaggerated and that there was no empirical evidence to back up Rostow's claims concerning the stages of growth. Indeed, he claimed that 'underdevelopment', far from being a characteristic of countries and regions insufficiently integrated into the global economy, was in fact a consequence of their incorporation into what later became known as the capitalist world system.

In order to understand contemporary underdevelopment, we have to focus on the historical roots of 'metropolis–satellite' relations that exist on an international level *and within* 'underdeveloped' nations; for the very same cities that are considered satellites on an international level are themselves the metropoles of the satellite nation. To briefly summarise his argument, it consists of a number of complementary propositions.

First, the 'development' of national and other subordinate metropoles is limited by their satellite status. Second, satellites experience the greatest amount of economic development when their ties to the metropolis are the weakest, not the strongest. Third, the areas which are the most underdeveloped today are in general those that have had the closest ties to the metropolis in the past. Fourth, commercial enterprises that had the power to respond to increased demand for the world market rather than the domestic market were the ones that were often established in satellite countries to take advantage of access to raw materials and low production/labour costs. Finally, economic institutions which today appear the most feudal were the ones which were successful in the past but have since declined with the incorporation of the satellite into the world system. Thus, in order to understand the process of 'underdevelopment', we must see it as an epiphenomenal manifestation of the expansion of capitalism. Contrary to the modernisation paradigm, capitalism is the disease rather than the cure. As for economic aid as a means to establish some of the preconditions for 'take off', Frank argued the opposite. He argued that satellite states were in fact net exporters of capital to metropolitan countries, who exploited the satellites whilst pretending that their economic policies were 'aiding' them.

By the mid-1960s Frank was a revolutionary who believed that positive change could only come about if the satellites, either together or separately, broke away from their incorporation into the capitalist world economy, and this in turn required radical political change within them. He was a strong supporter of the Cuban revolution led by Fidel Castro and also admired Mao Tse Tung's radical economic reforms in China:

> The upshot of all these theoretical and political reflections . . . was that continued participation in the world capitalist system could only mean continued development of underdevelopment. That is, there would be neither equity, nor efficiency, nor economic development. The political conclusions, therefore, were to de-link from the system externally and to transit to self-reliant socialism internally (or some undefined international socialist cooperation) in order to make in- or non-dependent economic development possible.[1]

In the 1970s, Frank clarified, revised and extended his analysis of the way in which the capitalist world system produced underdevelopment in the Third World, and the reader should refer to two major texts published toward the end of that decade for a summary of his work, *Dependent Accumulation and Underdevelopment* (1978) and *World Accumulation 1492–1789*, also published in 1978. In these works he distinguishes between three stages of world capitalist accumulation: mercantilism (1500–1770), industrial capitalism (1770–1870) and imperialism (1870–1930). He also synthesises radical historical research to demonstrate the existence of *long cycles* of successive expansion and stagnation in the evolution of the world capitalist system. In the transition from mercantilism to industrialisation Frank argues that the triumph of the commercial revolution was a product of colonial conquest as well as the hugely profitable slave trade. This was the centre of two trade triangles, the Atlantic and the Oriental, joined together by the role that Europe (and Britain in particular) played in each. Thus the industrial revolution was not simply a European phenomenon, for it also involved substantial transfers of colonial precious metals and raw materials to certain countries which comprised the funds later invested as capital with the onset of industrial and manufacturing capitalism. Thus an accumulating position in the various triangular trades was critical in deciding whether a country would become a developing or an underdeveloping one in the course of the next 200 years.

Frank also analysed the role of growth and stagnation over long cycles of the accumulation process in world history. Stagnation and crisis were, he argued, the consequence of the limitations of productive forces, which over time tended to run up against decreasing returns to scale. The ensuing depressions led to a predominance of 'internal' pressures within individual countries to reorganise production: the successful, such as England, managed to establish their dominance over other countries in the next phase of the economic cycle. Frank argued that the United States became a developing rather than an underdeveloping country for two main reasons. On the one hand, it benefited from a substantial mercantile accumulation of money through its key position in the Atlantic trade triangle of the eighteenth century. On the other, the colonising power, Britain, treated its colony with benign neglect, allowing local yeoman farming to develop and generate surplus funds to finance further growth. By contrast, Frank devoted a great deal of attention to British colonial policies in India. There, he stressed the way in which the British exploited peasants via the taxation system, and organised production almost exclusively for the export of raw materials and the import of British manufactured goods. This was all part of his broader contention that underdeveloping countries become such owing to their particular position in a global expansionary capitalist system.

In situating 'the development of underdevelopment' within a much broader historical analysis of the evolution of global capitalism, Frank argued that the very meaning of 'development' has to be understood as a product of a very specific historical period, namely, the post-1945 'long boom' era as seen from the perspective of Latin America. Now that this era is over, we need to shift our attention from the problem of development within a specific contemporary time period to try and understand the successive phases of development within a much broader historical context. Only this will enable us to study the process of combined and uneven development of capitalism on a global scale, as it has impinged on particular countries at particular times.

Over the last decade or so, Frank has devoted himself to the continued analysis of the world capitalist system, although his 'pessimism of the intellect' remains undiminished. In terms of his own ideals, he still values 'development' not as a simple expression or outcome of economic growth, but as a multi-faceted process of economic, social and technological change by which human welfare may be improved. In turn, human welfare is itself complex, and should not be seen merely in terms of the capacity to consume more goods, regardless of the impact on, for example, the environment. In the late twentieth century, Frank is no longer very confident about the prospects for socialism, particularly if a socialist process is confined to one particular country. Nonetheless, he argues that although the binary divide between traditional and modern societies was always a mythological construction of liberal political economy in the 1950s, today we are seeing the emergence of a new form of dualism, between those regions and sectors that are integrated into the global market economy and those that are systematically (and increasingly) marginalised from it. This is not a process that can be represented geographically by comparing the fate of different countries, for it transcends territorial borders to include/exclude particular regions and sectors of the global economy within so-called 'developed' countries.

In light of the failure of 'really existing' socialism to 'de-link' from the global market, Frank has joined those who see some progressive potential in what have become known as new social movements arising from those marginalised from the global capitalist system. Of course, it remains to be seen whether such movements based on gender or the environment can either achieve their limited aims or unite to represent a broader counter-hegemonic force in contemporary world politics. Frank himself sees them as an essential part of the pursuit of a more participatory civil democracy at the global level.

Note

1 André Gunder Frank, 'The underdevelopment of development', *Scandinavian Journal of Development Alternatives* 10 (1991), p. 28. This is an excellent autobiographical essay in which Frank relates the way in which his life and work have developed since the 1950s.

See also in this book

Cox, Wallerstein

Gunder Frank's major writings

Capitalism and Underdevelopment in Latin America: Historical Studies of Chile and Brazil, New York, Monthly Review Press, 1967
Latin America: Underdevelopment or Revolution: Essays on the Development of Underdevelopment and the Immediate Enemy, New York, Monthly Review Press, 1970

Lumpenbourgeoisie: Lumpendevelopment; Dependence, Class, and Politics in Latin America, trans. Marion Davis Berdecio, New York, Monthly Review Press, 1973
On Capitalist Underdevelopment, New York, Oxford University Press, 1975
'Dependence is dead, long live dependence and the class struggle: an answer to critics', *World Development* 5 (1977), pp. 355–70
World Accumulation, 1492–1789, New York, Monthly Review Press, 1978
Mexican Agriculture 1521–1630: Transformation of the Mode of Production, Cambridge, Cambridge University Press, 1979
Dependent Accumulation and Underdevelopment, New York, Monthly Review Press, 1978
Crisis in the World Economy, London, Heinemann, 1980
Crisis in the Third World, London, Heinemann, 1981
Reflections on the World Economic Crisis, London, Hutchinson, 1981
Critique and Anticritique: Essays on Dependence and Reformism, London, Macmillan, 1984
ReOrient: Global Economy in the Asian Age, Berkeley, University of California Press, 1998

Further reading

Booth, D., 'Andre Gunder Frank: an introduction and appreciation', in Ivar Oxaal, Tony Barnett and David Booth (eds), *Beyond the Sociology of Development*, London, Routledge & Kegan Paul, 1975, pp. 50–85
Chew, Sing C. and Denemark, Robert A. (eds), *The Underdevelopment of Development: Essays in Honor of Andre Gunder Frank*, New York, Sage, 1996.
Foster-Carter, Aiden, 'From Rostow to Gunder Frank: conflicting paradigms in the analysis of underdevelopment', *World Development* 4 (1976), pp. 167–80
Higgott, Richard L., *Political Development Theory: The Contemporary Debate*, London, Croom Helm, 1983
Leys, Colin, *The Rise and Fall of Development Theory*, Indiana, Indiana University Press, 1996.
Nove, Alex, 'On reading Andre Gunder Frank', *Journal of Development Studies* 10 (1974), pp. 445–55
Rostow, Walt W., *The Stages of Economic Growth*, New York, Cambridge University Press, 1960
Smith, Tony, 'The underdevelopment of development literature: the case of dependency theory', *World Politics* 31 (1979), pp. 247–88

JOHAN GALTUNG

Johan Galtung is one of the leading figures in international peace research. He is best known for his analysis of what he calls 'structural violence' in global politics, as well as his attempts to develop a 'structural' theory of imperialism that is inspired by, but is not limited to, Marxism. As with some other key thinkers described in this book, such as Anthony Giddens and John Burton, Galtung's work draws on a number of disciplines in the social sciences and this is appropriate for a scholar whose conception of peace research is holistic and explicitly normative. Galtung's work can be seen as an extended attempt to fuse methods of social science within an emancipatory ethics of world order.

Johan Galtung was born in 1930 in Norway into an upper-class family. His father, a physician, provided him with an important role model from a very early age, combining a variety of skills with a commitment to healing that Galtung absorbed and sought to replicate in his own work. He did not enjoy his school years, feeling constrained by the rigidity of the curriculum. During the Second World War the Germans placed Galtung's father in a concentration camp and, although his father survived the experience, Galtung emerged from the war as a committed pacifist. He refused to be conscripted into Norwegian military service and was sent to jail in Oslo as a conscientious objector in 1951. Although his parents wanted Galtung to follow in his father's footsteps and become a doctor, he refused to specialise at university, studying instead sociology, mathematics and philosophy at two different faculties. In particular, Galtung was inspired by Gandhi's pacifist ethics and began publishing articles in magazines and newspapers at an early age. Galtung moved temporarily to the United States in 1958 to take up a post as Assistant Professor in Sociology at Columbia University in New York, but he returned to Oslo in 1960. He played a key role in setting up the International Peace Research Institute (PRIO), which has published much of his work over the last thirty years. In 1964 Galtung also helped to establish the *Journal of Peace Research* and was its editor for ten years. He has taught in a number of countries, including some in Latin America and in Japan, and he is currently Professor of Peace Studies at the University of Hawaii. He set up the first Master of Peace Studies postgraduate degree in Hawaii and received the Right Livelihood Award in 1987 for his work in the field.

Most of us think of peace intuitively in negative terms, as the absence of war or armed conflict. For example, throughout the Cold War between the United States and the Soviet Union, those who supported the notion of nuclear deterrence and the condition of mutually assured destruction (MAD) claimed that it maintained 'the peace' between the two superpowers. Galtung's conception of peace is also defined as the opposite of violence, but his idea of violence (and hence peace) is not merely the observable use of force between human beings, but 'anything avoidable that impedes human self-realisation'.[1] In turn, Galtung conceives of the latter in terms of the satisfaction of fundamental human needs, which can be physiological, ecological, economic and even spiritual. Thus his idea of 'structural violence' is much broader than the conventional focus of most students in the Anglo-American study of international relations on war and the use of direct, physical armed force between states.

Furthermore, not only is Galtung's focus broader, it is also concerned with the effects of structural violence on its victims. In this context, he distinguishes between four types of violence in global politics. First, there is the 'classical' violence of the conventional literature, which refers to the deliberate infliction of pain, such as in war, torture or inhuman and degrading punishment. Second,

Galtung refers to 'misery' as the deprivation of our fundamental material needs for shelter, clothing, food and water. Third, 'repression' refers to the loss of human freedoms to choose our beliefs and speak out on their behalf. Finally, Galtung refers to 'alienation' as a form of structural violence against our identity and our non-material needs for community and relations with others. Structural violence refers to the second, third and fourth types of violence. For Galtung, such violence does not need to be observed taking place between a perpetrator and a victim. It may be built into a social order or political and economic structure. Insofar as structural violence is not necessary, Galtung sees it as the goal of peace research to understand how it works so that it may ultimately be eradicated.

As a direct consequence of Galtung's interest in structural violence, he has examined the way in which social structures, within and between states, maintain and perpetuate such violence. In 1971, he published the results of his analysis of imperialism, presenting a structural theory that, although inspired by his experiences in Latin America and his exposure to radical dependency theory, attempted to incorporate non-economic variables and could apply to socialist as well as capitalist states. In examining the dynamics of imperialism that sustain the enormous inequality within and between states, Galtung differs from Marx and Lenin and claims that imperialism is not just an economic relationship based on the inherent need of capitalism to expand. Imperialism is a structural relationship of dominance defined in political, economic, military, cultural and communication terms. Just as violence is not limited to direct forms of aggression, neither is imperialism limited to political colonialism or economic neocolonialism. Control over the production and dissemination of news, access to advanced technologies of weaponry, availability of education, participation in decision making: structural inequalities in these and related

areas also qualify as aspects of imperialism as a multi-dimensional phenomenon.

Galtung argues that the world can be divided between Centre and Periphery nations, and that also within nations there exists a centre and periphery. The latter is crucial in maintaining the structure of imperialism, which Galtung defines as 'a system that splits up collectivities and relates some of the parts to each other in relations of *harmony of interest*, and other parts in relations of *disharmony of interest*, or *conflict of interest*'.[2] He then claims that although there is a disharmony of interest between Centre and Periphery nations, the reproduction of the centre–periphery relationship within them prevents its eradication. There is greater inequality between centre and periphery within Periphery nations than in Centre nations, so those in the periphery of the Centre often fail to understand or perceive that they are in an identical structural position to their counterparts in the Periphery. Consequently, alliances between peripheries are difficult to create in order to combat the existing harmony of interest between the centre in the Centre nations and the centre in the periphery nations. Meanwhile, mechanisms of imperialism ensure that there will always be a hierarchy between Centre and Periphery nations, because the centre in the Periphery 'only serves as a transmission belt (e.g. as commercial firms, trading companies) for value (e.g. raw materials) forwarded to the Centre nation'.[3] Galtung suggests that two mechanisms of imperialism are particularly important.

First, he argues that the *vertical interaction relations* between centre and periphery ensure that, although both parties appear to gain through interaction, they could not do so equally. Thus, although the Periphery nation may be rewarded financially by the export of its raw materials, Centre nations are able to reap the value of processing raw materials into more expensive manufactured goods, which are then exported to the Periphery. By transforming 'nature' into 'form', Galtung alleges that the Centre enjoys all the multiplier effects of industrialisation that accompany the processing of raw materials. Second, he argues that vertical interaction relations take place within a global *feudal interaction structure*. This is characterised by four enduring features:

1 interaction between Centre and Periphery is *vertical*;

2 interaction between Periphery and Periphery is *missing*;

3 multilateral interaction involving all three is *missing*;

4 interaction with the outside world is *monopolised* by the Centre, which explains the high level of commodity concentration from each Periphery nation to a few Centre nations.

Clearly, Galtung's structural theory of imperialism has much in common with more orthodox Marxist-Leninist accounts, but it is much less economistic and at the same time a great deal more abstract. In 1971, it represented more of a research project than a complete theoretical model. At the same time, it was not clear what prescriptions flowed from acceptance of the theory. As a pacifist, Galtung was uneasy with radical proposals for violent revolution. In any case, he argued that establishing socialism within particular states could not guarantee the end of imperialism and structural violence. For since imperialism could take many forms, China and the Soviet Union were as culpable in maintaining the structure as was the United States. Galtung's prescriptions were primarily negative ones, consisting of a repudiation of orthodox modernisation theory according to which the Periphery should seek to emulate the Centre, as well as violent recipes to promote revolution in particular Periphery nations in the hope that they may inspire some more general transformation of the international system.

Although Galtung used his structural theory of imperialism (STI) to urge the *de-feudalisation* of the structures that maintained structural violence, for example by developing greater self-reliance in the Periphery and promoting greater communication and co-operation between peripheries within the Periphery, the validity of STI itself has been questioned by a number of scholars. It has two main weaknesses. First, despite Galtung's ongoing commitment to the methods and ideals of social science, it is very difficult to generate hypotheses from the model that can be tested against the empirical evidence. A number of propositions are simply asserted rather than postulated and some of the key terms used by Galtung, such as 'interests' for example, are not sufficiently specified so that hypotheses containing them can be tested against the evidence.

Chris Brown further argues that Galtung's critique of Marxism is simplistic and that his structural model is little more than a generalisation of particular forms of imperialism prevalent in the nineteenth century.[4] What is missing from the model is any notion of historical change and the role of actors either in perpetuating or transforming the structure. Unlike the more sophisticated work of Giddens or Wendt considered in this book, Galtung is a structural determinist, yet his analysis of the origins of the structure itself is very sketchy.

In more recent years, Galtung has not attempted to respond systematically to his critics. Whilst his basic model is still a useful pedagogical tool, its elaboration and refinement has been taken up by other 'world systems theorists' such as Immanuel Wallerstein. Instead, Galtung has devoted himself to examining the roots of direct violence in structurally violent societies and civilisations. He made a basic distinction between two types of social structures – 'alpha' and 'beta'. The former is typical of Western industrial societies with their extended bureaucracies, large corporations and fragmented social bonds. In such societies, human beings are alienated from each other and themselves. They operate 'at long distance' via contract rather than through blood ties. In contrast to these dystopias, Galtung imagines (since none exist in reality) 'beta' structures and societies in which the sources of structural violence and alienation are absent. Such societies would operate at close distance, embracing their members, and would be united by familial and moral obligations rather than legal contractual ones. They would be small, self-reliant, with a low division of labour and fulfil our needs for community and participation in social life. True, such societies would not be wealthy in any material sense, but Galtung suggests that our consumer ethos in the West is itself not without the costs of 'overdevelopment' in the form of environmental degradation.

Of course, he recognises that all societies contain a mixture of alpha and beta elements, and he is concerned with the results of the asymmetrical imbalance between them in modern industrialised societies. In his book *The True Worlds: A Transnational Perspective* (1980), Galtung sketched the outline of an emancipatory project that would facilitate the enhancement of 'beta' values in a world increasingly absorbed by 'alpha' social structures. If we want to engage with the project of promoting 'positive peace' at a global level, we need to move away from capitalist modes of production, dismantle empires and transcend territorial forms of political organisation. Once again drawing on Gandhi's pacifism, as well as elements of liberalism and Marxism, Galtung urged his readers to avoid blaming particular individuals and states for our social ills and to focus more on the social structures that underpin them. In his excellent analysis of Galtung's life and work, Peter Lawler sums up Galtung's vision of peace research in 1980s as follows:

1 Despite the structural constraints, peace should be seen as a process. Current efforts to realise preferred futures are part of a historical stream and not indicative of an impending and dramatic turning point.

2 There is a need to cultivate a global consciousness that expresses a dedication to all of humanity but also recognises the primacy of those most in need.

3 All levels of action are relevant.

4 The drive for peace should avoid creating new vertical divisions of labour – different capacities and opportunities should be recognised but not translated into terms of power or prestige or both.

5 Both actor-orientated and structure-orientated strategies are relevant.

6 Peace action must be spontaneously generated.[5]

Lawler's study of the trajectory of Galtung's work is highly critical, however, of Galtung's more recent work which does little more than promote Buddhist themes of pacifism and the substitution of alpha values with beta ideals and social structures, hardly a viable route to global transformation! Lawler identifies two major problems that those inspired by his voluminous work must overcome.

First, Galtung's attempt to combine social science with an emancipatory worldview has not been successful. Like John Burton, Galtung's attempt to justify his list of human 'needs' based on objective criteria results in vague idealistic notions of social 'health' that presuppose what needs to be demonstrated. The social world cannot be treated in the same way as the human body, particularly on a global scale. As Lawler points out, Galtung's peace research 'had assumed the possibility of reform guided by values that supposedly reflected the universal interests of members of that society'.[6] The key word here is *supposedly*. All too often, Galtung smuggles his own values into his analysis of structural violence and engages in precisely that form of dogmatism that he condemns in others. Consequently, Galtung can be placed at the opposite ideological spectrum of a thinker such as Kenneth Waltz. The strengths of one are the weakness of the other. 'An overemphasis on the distinctiveness of the international realm had been replaced by an uncritical adoption of systems-theoretic holism wrapped around a discursively excluded moral cosmopolitanism.'[7]

Second, Galtung's work raises the question of what agents can or should engage with the process of global reform? If the degree of structural violence is as great and intractable as he suggests it is, then reliance on Buddhism is unlikely to reduce the path to dystopia. On the other hand, if we need to identify or construct/empower agents of change in the desired direction of 'beta' values, then we have to entertain far more concrete proposals for reform. These need to be justified on grounds that themselves originate in Western values of universality and the quest to reconcile freedom and equality.

In summary, the work of Johan Galtung continues both to inspire as well as constrain the potential of peace research at the end of the twentieth century. Many of his ideas, particularly those of 'structural violence' and 'structural imperialism', continue to play a major role in the field and he has raised important questions for others to try and answer. Yet these same ideas cannot be pursued fruitfully if we refuse to acknowledge the limitations of social science in providing us with a justification for the values and interests whose defence is the rationale for peace research per se.

Notes

1 Johan Galtung, *Transarmament and the Cold War: Peace Research and the Peace Movement*, Copenhagen, Christian Ejlers, 1988, p. 272.
2 Johan Galtung, 'A structural theory of imperialism', *Journal of Peace Research* 8 (1971), p. 82.
3 Ibid., p. 83.

4 Chris Brown, 'Galtung and the Marxists on imperialism: answers versus questions', *Millennium: Journal of International Studies* 10 (1981), pp. 220–8.
5 Peter Lawler, *A Question of Values: Johan Galtung's Peace Research*, Boulder, Colorado, Lynne Reinner, 1995, pp. 185–6.
6 Ibid., p. 224.
7 Ibid., p. 227.

See also in this book

Burton, Wallerstein, Waltz, Wendt

Galtung's major writings

'A structural theory of aggression', *Journal of Peace Research* 1 (1964), pp. 95–119
'A structural theory of imperialism', *Journal of Peace Research* 8 (1971), pp. 81–94
'A structural theory of imperialism: 10 years later', *Millennium: Journal of International Studies* 9 (1981), pp. 181–96
Essays in Methodology, Copenhagen, Christian Ejlers: *Methodology and Ideology* (Volume 1), 1977; *Papers on Methodology* (Volume 2), 1979; *Methodology and Development* (Volume 3), 1988
Essays in Peace Research, Copenhagen, Christian Ejlers: *Peace, Research, Education, Action* (Volume 1), 1975; *Peace, War and Defence* (Volume 2), 1976; *Peace and Social Structure* (Volume 3), 1978; *Peace and World Structure* (Volume 4), 1980; *Peace Problems: Some Case Studies* (Volume 5), 1980; *Transarmament and the Cold War* (Volume 6), 1988
The True Worlds: A Transnational Perspective, New York, The Free Press, 1980
There are Alternatives! Four Roads to Peace and Security, Nottingham, Spokesman Books, 1984
'Twenty-five years of peace research: ten challenges and some responses', *Journal of Peace Research* 22 (1985), pp. 141–58

Further reading

Brown, Chris, 'Galtung and the Marxists on imperialism: answers versus questions', *Millennium: Journal of International Studies* 10 (1981), pp. 220–8
Holm, Hans Henrik and Rudeng, Erik, *Social Science, For What?: Festschrift for Johann Galtung*, Oslo, Universitetsforlaget, 1980
Lawler, Peter, *A Question of Values: Johan Galtung's Peace Research*, Boulder, Colorado, Lynne Reinner, 1995. This book contains a

comprehensive bibliography of the works of Johan Galtung.

Neufeld, Beverly, 'The marginalization of peace research', *Millennium: Journal of International Studies* 22 (1993), pp. 165–84

VLADIMIR I. LENIN

Lenin was responsible for establishing the Communist Party in Russia as well as the world's first Communist Party dictatorship. He led the October Revolution of 1917 in which communists seized power and he continued to rule the Soviet Union until his death in 1924. Born on 24 April 1870, his real name was Vladimir Ilyich Ulyanov; he adopted the name 'Lenin' in 1901. His parents were both well educated. His father was a teacher and a successful school administrator, whilst his mother was the daughter of a doctor. Lenin had two brothers and three sisters.

As a child, Lenin had few close friends and devoted himself to reading. He was only 5 years old when he learned to read and was a brilliant student. His political radicalism was due in part to his personal experience of the autocratic government of Czar Alexander III. Lenin's father died in 1886 and his brother was hanged in 1887 for participating in a failed anarchist plot to kill the Czar. That same year Lenin graduated from school with a gold medal for excellence. Although he enrolled in law school at Kazan University, he was soon expelled for organising student protests at the lack of freedom in Russia, and he moved to St Petersburg where he studied law at the university. However, he was not allowed to attend classes in light of his political activism at Kazan. He graduated with a law degree in 1891 and, whilst practising law, became absorbed with Marxism and began to organise radical opposition to the Czar in St Petersburg. He travelled widely throughout Europe contacting other Marxists and was preparing to publish a revolutionary newspaper in St Petersburg, *The Workers' Cause*, when he was arrested by the police and held in detention for over a year. In 1897 he was expelled to Siberia, where he lived for three years until he received permission to leave Russia. In exile he continued to study Marx and published one of his major works, *The Development of Capitalism in Russia*. In 1898 he married another exiled revolutionary, Nadezhda Konstantinova Krupskaya, and in 1900 he moved to Germany.

Whilst in Germany Lenin continued to organise radical opposition to Czar Nicholas II (who had become leader of Russia in 1894 after his father's death), publishing newspapers, which he then had smuggled back into Russia, and writing revolutionary pamphlets. In 1902, he wrote *What Is to Be Done?* This pamphlet described his views on party organisation, foreshadowing Lenin's organisation of the Bolsheviks, whose name derived from the *bolshinstvo* (majority), the largest splinter group of the 1903 Congress of the Russian Social Democratic Labor Party. The other group was the Mensheviks (minority).

The breakup of the SDLP into two groups was in part inspired by Lenin's ideas on party organisation and revolutionary tactics. Karl Marx himself did not expect a revolutionary overthrow of capitalism in Russia. According to his theory of the evolution of history, liberal capitalism would collapse only in those countries where it was most advanced and where the struggle between capitalists and workers was at its most open and intense, such as in Germany. Russia was a predominantly repressive, agricultural state, in which the bourgeoisie and industrial proletariat were relatively small in comparison to the mass of unorganised peasants. Thus Lenin argued that if revolution were to succeed in Russia, it would have to be led by a very disciplined party of full-time professional revolutionaries who could organise the workers or proletariat, secretly if necessary. At the time, Lenin was bitterly disappointed that revolution did not seem to be taking place in Germany as rapidly as he had hoped, and he attacked the revisionist idea that the interests of the working class could be achieved by constitutional reform alone.

In 1905, it seemed that the time for revolution in his homeland had arrived. Russia was at war with Japan and, in the major Russian cities, workers were agitating for greater political freedom and more distribution of land and wealth in Russia. Widespread strikes took place and the Czar resorted to force in order to put down the civil unrest. He managed to crush the revolution and then even took steps to liberalise (temporarily) the political system, granting freedom of speech, pardoning political exiles, allowing limited voting rights and establishing a Russian parliament (or *Duma*). Lenin had returned to Russia to organise a general uprising, but left once again at the end of the year. From 1905 until the Revolution of 1917, he continued his revolutionary activities abroad, writing pamphlets and publishing newspapers. In 1912, the Bolsheviks established *Pravda* (Truth), which was sold openly in St Petersburg and to which Lenin contributed articles on a regular basis.

Lenin's opportunity to take power in Russia finally arrived in 1917; he might never have succeeded had it not been for the First World War and its devastating impact on Russia. The war began in August 1914, when Germany declared war on Russia, and lasted for nearly four years of murderous stalemate. The German government even helped to fund Lenin's political activities, since he had promised that, if he came to power in Russia, he would sign a peace treaty immediately. Lenin was prepared to do this because he believed that a Russian revolution could spill over into Europe and topple the German government as well. Once this had taken place, the socialisation of Western Europe would facilitate the economic development of Russia itself.[1] In his most famous book (at least for students of international relations), *Imperialism as the Highest Stage of Capitalism* (published in 1916), Lenin argued that

the First World War represented the terminal phase of the capitalist system. Drawing on some of the ideas of John Hobson and the Austrian socialist Rudolf Hilferding, Lenin argued that the First World War both offered an opportunity for the working classes to revolt against capitalism and revealed the bankruptcy of revisionist reforms that stopped short of radical change in capitalist states. Lenin argued that capitalism had undergone two important changes in the late nineteenth century.

First, he argued that there was an inexorable trend toward concentration and 'cartelisation' in the process of industrialisation. Capitalism was no longer characterised by competition among small firms and businesses, but was increasingly dominated by giant corporations enjoying a monopoly of control in their domestic markets. Modern industry in turn required huge amounts of capital investment to maintain its technological edge in what was even then becoming a global marketplace. The expansion of the market internationally required corollary increases in the scale of production. Second, Lenin argued that in addition to industrial capital, the late nineteenth century saw a huge increase in finance capital, represented by the banks:

> As banking develops and becomes concentrated in a number of establishments, the banks grow from modest middlemen into powerful monopolies, having at their command almost the whole of money capital of all the capitalists and small businessmen and also the larger part of the means of production and sources of raw materials in any one country and in a number of countries.[2]

Lenin believed that imperialism was a direct product of the combination of these changes in the nature of capitalism. On the one hand, the enormous profits earned by corporations and banks enabled them to pay off influential sections of the working class, thereby perpetuating the idea that capitalism is not necessarily a zero-sum relationship between the owners of capital and the workers. On the other hand, Lenin argued that whilst the monopolisation of markets was replacing competition at the domestic level, there was growing conflict between cartels of corporations and banks at the international level. Domestically, wages might be rising with wealth, but capitalism was driven abroad in its relentless pursuit of cheap labour, raw materials, new markets and investment opportunities for excess capital. Competition continues between corporations and banks internationally, and Lenin believed that this process would inevitably result in war among capitalist states as they ran out of opportunities to increase their imperial control without impeding on markets controlled by cartels from other states. Imperialism therefore represents the highest stage of capitalism, as well as its terminal phase. Capitalist states could not stop the process of assisting the pursuit of wealth, which required the exploitation of the workers and the appropriation of their surplus value. They had no choice therefore but to participate in the process that would lead to their own downfall.

Although Lenin's argument was in part a polemical attempt to persuade workers not to fight each other but co-operate to overthrow the system that gave rise to war in the first place, it was also an important contribution to the evolution of radical theories of imperialism. If it is treated as an empirical theory of state behaviour in general, and as an explanation of war in particular, it suffers from Lenin's ideological assumption that a correlation between capitalism and imperialism (i.e. that some capitalist states engaged in imperial activity in the late nineteenth century) is sufficient to argue that capitalism causes imperialism. There are a number of problems with this.

First, as Howard Williams points out, not all capitalist states engaged in the process of imperialism:

The amount of colonisation undertaken by the United States, aguably already the most capitalist state [by the late nineteenth century], was very small indeed. The United States appeared to be developing a different pattern of relationships with more backward nations: here the export of capital and the opening up of markets was taking place without annexation. Latin America has for the most part enjoyed an independent political relationship with the United States.[3]

Second, the relationship between the economic theory and the political behaviour deduced from Lenin's theory should have led to political alliances that did not in fact eventuate. For example, Parkinson observes that Lenin's theory would have predicted a close alliance between Germany and the United States during the First World War, in light of the formation of the cartel between German- and United States-based monopolies in the electrical industry.[4]

Finally, as Kenneth Waltz argues, if Lenin's theory linking capitalism to imperialism and war was valid, what explains imperial behaviour in the pre-capitalist era, or imperial behaviour by states that do not export capital, or by states that are not capitalist? As he puts it, '[t]he diversity of the internal conditions of states and of their foreign policies was impressive. Their conformity to the stipulations of the theory was not.'[5] In short, whatever its merits as a partial theory of state behaviour, Lenin's book must be judged a failure as a general theory. It attributes too much importance to too few processes and it ignores political dynamics that cannot be reduced to the play of economic forces.

Of course, Lenin's theory was useful in justifying the 'inherently pacific' policies of the Soviet Union after he came to power in 1917. Lenin argued that war would come to an end when communism had replaced capitalism around the world. If that was the case, then the use of force by the Soviet Union was justifiable if it hastened the process. So whether particular wars could be justified depended on whether they advanced or retarded the arrival of communism. As he wrote in 1918, when the First World War was coming to an end, '[t]he character of the war . . . depends on what class is waging the war and on what politics this war is a continuation of'. Thus Lenin defended the use of force against bourgeois Poland in 1920 and Menshevik Georgia in 1921.

As he had promised in 1914, Lenin sued for peace with Germany as soon as he came to power in Russia in 1917. In March 1918, he signed the Treaty of Brest-Litovsk, which gave Germany the Baltic region, Finland, large areas of Poland and the Ukraine. In return, Germany helped to keep Lenin in power and allowed him to demobilise what remained of his armed forces. In retrospect, Lenin was far too optimistic that the success of the spark of revolution in Russia would spread to Western Europe, and the trauma of the Revolution and its aftermath in Russia itself made it impossible to establish a social system of communist economic and political rule. From 1918 to 1920, the country was embroiled in a civil war, and Lenin was eventually forced to repudiate some of his more radical plans to destroy capitalism immediately. In March 1921, he introduced a programme called the New Economic Policy (NEP). This replaced many of his radical socialist measures adopted in 1918 under 'war communism'. Small businesses and farms were allowed to resume limited trading. Overseas investors were invited to invest in Russia and peasants were allowed to sell food on the private market. Lenin even asked Britain, France, Germany and the United States for financial credits, trade and diplomatic recognition, which were not forthcoming for a regime that had refused to pay Russia's debts and was promoting world revolution.

In 1919, Lenin had set up the Comintern (or Communist International). Run from Moscow, the Comintern ran revolutions and parties in all parts of the world and tried to promote international support for the Bolsheviks during the civil war. In 1920, Lenin tried to export the revolution abroad, as he was convinced that his country could not survive unless communism gained ground in the rest of Europe. In the absence of international support, he would have to establish a totalitarian regime in order to control his vast country and to ensure that the Russian people would pay the necessary price to keep up with the more advanced capitalist states. Whilst there is some evidence to suggest that Lenin did not support Stalin as his successor, there is no doubt that he laid the basis for Stalin's regime of terror in the late 1920s and 1930s. Despite his doubts about Russian nationalism and the Bolshevik enthusiasm for military glory, Lenin came to behave in ways that he had condemned capitalist states for in the years prior to his ascension to power in Russia. Whilst he underestimated the ability of capitalist states to alleviate the inequalities of wealth and power caused by the operation of the 'free market', he also exaggerated the ability of allegedly socialist states to pursue egalitarian social policies at an acceptable political and economic cost to their citizens.[6]

Lenin died in January 1924 of a brain hemorrhage. He had experienced a number of strokes since 1922 that had left him weak and incapable of exercising effective leadership of the party and the nation. The government preserved his body in a special tomb in Red Square in Moscow, which remained one of the Soviet Union's most honoured monuments until the collapse of communism and, with it, the Soviet Union itself.

Notes

1 For a good introduction to the Russian Revolution and the evolution of Lenin's views, see John Dunn, *Modern Revolutions*, Second edition, Cambridge, Cambridge University Press, 1989, pp. 24–47.
2 V.I. Lenin, *Imperialism as The Highest Stage of Capitalism*, Moscow, Foreign Languages

Press, 1968, p. 28.

3 Howard Williams, *International Relations in Political Theory*, Milton Keynes, Open University Press, 1992, p. 129.

4 F. Parkinson, *The Philosophy of International Relations: A Study in the History of Thought*, London, Sage, 1977, pp. 118–19.

5 Kenneth Waltz, *Theory of International Politics*, Reading, Massachusetts, Addison-Wesley, 1979, p. 24.

6 As John Dunn puts it, 'the fantasy that industrialisation could come blithely to Russia under the egalitarian rule of a vigilant proletariat and as a result of a generous foreign-aid programme from a Socialist World Bank must rank among the most [outrageous] fantasies of this or any other century', John Dunn, *Modern Revolutions*, op. cit., p. 46.

See also in this book

Hobson, Waltz

Lenin's major writings

Toward the Seizure of Power: The Revolution of 1917: From the July Days to the October Revolution, London, Lawrence, 1929

The War and the Second International, London, M. Lawrence, 1931

Economics and Politics in the Era of the Dictatorship of the Proletariat, Moscow, Foreign Language Publishing House, 1951

On the International Working Class and Communist Movement, Moscow, Foreign Languages Publishing House, 1960

On the Foreign Policy of the Soviet State, Moscow, Progress Publishers, 1964

Against Imperialist War: Articles and Speeches, Moscow, Progress Publishers, 1966

Development of Capitalism in Russia, Second revised edition, Moscow, Progress Publishers, 1967

Proletarian Revolution and the Renegade Kautsky, Moscow, Foreign Language Press, 1970

What is to be Done?, Peking, Foreign Languages Press, 1973

The Lenin Anthology (edited by Robert Tucker), New York, W.W. Norton, 1975

Imperialism as The Highest Stage of Capitalism, Moscow, Foreign Language Press, 1968.

The State and Revolution, trans. Robert Service, London, Penguin, 1992

Further reading

Egan, David and Egan, Melinda, *V.I. Lenin: An Annotated Bibliography of English Language Sources to 1980*, Metuchen, New Jersey, Scarecrow Press, 1982

Harding, Neil, *Lenin's Political Thought*, New York, St Martin's Press, 1978

Harding, Neil, *Leninism*, Durham, North Carolina, Duke University Press, 1996

Lukács, Georg, *Lenin: A Study on the Unity of his Thought*, trans. Nicholas Jacobs, London, NBL, 1970

Page, Stanley W., *The Geopolitics of Leninism*, New York, Columbia University Press, 1982

Ulam, Adam B., *Lenin and the Bolsheviks: The Intellectual and Political History of the Triumph of Communism in Russia*, London, Secker & Warburg, 1966

Wolfe, Bertram D., *Three Who Made a Revolution: A Biographical History*, Harmondsworth, Penguin, 1966

ANDREW LINKLATER

Mark Hoffman has aptly described Andrew Linklater's work as a 'ground clearing exercise'.[1] Over the last two decades, Linklater has attempted to construct an intellectual and practical project within a discipline whose very autonomy in the social sciences is a barrier to that project. Whilst there are indications that the boundary between the study of international relations and other disciplines is increasingly blurred, it is ironic that some of the arguments mounted against a separate discipline of international relations are also inimical to Linklater's vision. In other words, he has been engaged in a dual critique. First, he has argued that the sharp division of labour between political theory and international relations is unnecessary and itself in need of explanation. Second, he has had to confront another (arguably more dangerous) challenge to his project in the form of postmodernism. So far in his career, the balance between criticism and constructive engagement with both the theory and practice of international relations has been heavily tilted toward criticism, hence the term 'ground clearing'. In the future, we may expect this to change, as Linklater's work itself moves forward and other, younger scholars take up the challenge of responding to his agenda. That agenda is, as we shall see, extremely ambitious and demanding.

Andrew Linklater is presently Professor of International Relations at the University of Keele in Staffordshire, England. He joined the Department of International Relations at Keele in 1993. Linklater studied Politics and International Relations at Aberdeen University and Political Philosophy at Oxford before completing his PhD in international relations at the London School of Economics in 1978. Over the next fifteen years, Linklater worked in Australia, and he has taught at the University of Tasmania and at Monash University in Melbourne. In 1991 he established the Centre for International Relations at Monash.

The main themes of all Linklater's work can be found in his ambitious doctoral dissertation, which he first published in 1982 as *Men and Citizens in the Theory of International Relations*. This book is required reading for anyone interested in the philosophical assumptions of 'critical' theory in the study of international relations. The book was inspired by the work of the British Committee on the Theory of International Relations, which took as its point of departure Martin Wight's definition of international theory as 'a tradition of speculation about relations between states [and] a tradition imagined as the twin of speculation about the state to which the name "political theory" is appropriated'.[2] Linklater approaches, as did the Committee, one of the long-standing problems of international theory – the dichotomy of obligation for 'man *qua* man' and 'man *qua* citizen' – with a compelling historical account of the (allegedly inadequate) philosophy that has addressed the problem as well as a unique solution of his own.

The basic argument of the book is that the distinction made in modern international theory between, on the one hand, mankind/ethical universality, and on the other, civil society/ethical particularity, may be overcome. The distinction itself is a crucial support for the academic division of labour between political theory and the study of international relations. It also corresponds to 'the real world' insofar as, while we are all members of the human race and *feel* that we have obligations to each other as human beings, we are also citizens of separate states. Consequently, our human obligations have little purchase on our conduct, and Linklater is concerned with the various philosophical arguments that have been proposed throughout history to justify this state of affairs.

Those feelings and beliefs, he argues, are based on a fundamental human interest in autonomy, which cannot justify the political division of 'man' into separate sovereign states. Linklater's major aim, therefore, is to recover and refine the universalistic strain of political theory embodied in the work of Kant. This will set the stage for a transformation of human consciousness, encouraging people to think more compassionately about their obligations to 'foreigners'. In the Kantian tradition, 'men' are substituted for 'citizens' as the proper subjects of moral concern, and the image of the international system as a 'realm of recurrence and repetition' is replaced with a progressivist account of historical development.

In his defence of the Kantian tradition, Linklater engages in a detailed critique of the major Enlightenment theorists including Pufendorf, Vattel and Gentili. His basic criticism of social contract theory is that it presupposes, without explicit justification, the territorial boundaries of the modern state in delimiting the scope of whatever social contract the theorist is concerned to justify or criticise. Throughout the text Linklater criticises political theorists for failing to question what he regards as the morally arbitrary significance of geographical borders. 'The theory presupposes what it requires to establish, the legitimacy of the sovereign association and the rationality of the division of mankind into separate sovereign states.'[3]

Linklater argues that the Kantian tradition is the best starting point for international political theory. Unlike his predecessors, Kant does not subordinate the demands of reason to the contingencies of nature and custom. As Linklater puts it,

> Kant's project begins by establishing the ends which men have an unconditional duty to promote as rational beings with the capacity to escape from the world of natural determination; and he proceeds to argue for a radical transformation of the political world in the direction of that condition in which all human beings live in conformity with the imperatives grounded in their common rational nature.[4]

Linklater then proceeds to describe in some detail the basic elements of Kant's thought and the ways in which his progressivist account of political ethics offers an alternative to the dominant realist image of international relations. But Linklater is fully aware that Kant's 'rationalism', his belief that it is possible to legislate the content of the categorical imperative to treat individuals as ends in themselves (not as means) on the basis of reason alone, is vulnerable to what he calls 'the historicist critique'. He accepts the argument that 'Kantian rationalism' fails to give an account of the historical condition of its emergence as a product of Western intellectual culture, and he also accepts the Hegelian argument that reason itself

> is embodied within vastly different forms of life rather than present in one, single, universal form in the minds of pre-social individuals . . . historicism must be deemed an important advance beyond the abstract position of rationalism, even though it

throws the . . . bases of international political theory into confusion.[5]

Linklater wants to save Kant's ethical cosmopolitanism from the charge of relativism, and he does so by appealing to what he calls 'philosophical history'. We are able to transcend the rationalist source of freedom by tracing its growth through history. Drawing on the work of Hegel and Marx, Linklater argues that, whilst freedom is always valued in varying ways in particular cultural contexts, it is possible to construct 'ideal types' of relations between societies in history and to trace the historical development of human reason. Or at least, this seems to be what Linklater wants international political theorists to do. He argues that instead of maintaining the academic division of labour between political theory and the study of international relations, we should

> look beyond the inside of societies to the way in which groups, estranged from one another, come to recognise the possibility of relations based upon equality and justice; [we] can include an examination of their recognition of the possibility of overcoming their particularism, which issues from estrangement and results in relations of a necessitous character, in the course of discovering and applying universal principles within an inclusive society.[6]

In *Men and Citizens*, Linklater does not go into much detail about exactly how this ought to be done. Indeed, it is fair to say that since 1982, when his book was first published, he has not proceeded very far along the road. That is, he *implies* a theory by which the nation-state may be transcended without subordinating the liberty of individual citizens to some supranational organisation, but quite what the theory might be, and what the mechanisms of transformation would look like, remain unclear. Hence the term 'ground clearing exercise' is an appropriate description of his work thus far. This is not a harsh judgement, since it remains the case that there is a great deal of ground to be cleared. Since 1982, Linklater has engaged in a sustained critique of theoretical logics and social practices of exclusion and heteronomy in the history of inter-state relations as well as within IR theory.

As part of that critique, Linklater suggests that it may be possible to move beyond the established 'paradigms' in the study of international relations by examining the ways in which each focuses on particular problematics at the expense of others that are privileged within allegedly 'competing' paradigms. This is the basic argument of his second major book, *Beyond Realism and Marxism: Critical Theory and International Relations* (1990). Realism gives us an account of international politics as a struggle for power based on the absence of any overarching political authority among states. But it privileges necessity at the expense of freedom, telling us little about how we may 'emancipate' ourselves from this condition. Marxism, on the other hand, says little about the sources of war that arise from the competition among states. We need to 'move beyond' both, and Linklater is very supportive of those historical sociologists who have mapped the rise of the state in the context of the transnational social and economic forces of capitalism, development and industrialisation. As I point out in my summaries of the work of Giddens, Mann, Tilly and Wallerstein, however, whilst it is true that they look at the state in the context of 'domestic' *and* 'international' relations – indeed, they are concerned with how these categories come into being in a historical sense – there is precious little in their work that engages with what Linklater calls 'the practical project of extending community beyond the nation-state'.[7] Before looking at a major problem with Linklater's 'critical' approach to international relations, it may be useful to summarise his agenda for the field. Linklater has issued several 'manifestos' on behalf of critical theory over the last decade, and they all call for a direct focus on the problem of community in world affairs and the nature, development and changeability of principles of moral inclusion and exclusion.[8]

In thematic terms, the agenda of critical theory as the 'next stage' in the evolution of the study of international relations has at least three aspects: the philosophical–normative, the sociological and the practical. The philosophical aspect focuses on the rationales for the dominant principles of moral exclusion and inclusion in social life, not least the principle of sovereignty providing for the inclusion of citizens and the exclusion of 'foreigners'. It tends to be concerned with reasons for preferring the state, as opposed to the society of states, or the community of humankind as the appropriate vision of community. In recent times, however, critical theorists have sought to broaden the terms of debate by focusing on other principles of inclusion and exclusion in world affairs associated with class, race and gender.

Linklater is somewhat concerned with the rise of postmodernism in this context. Whilst he admires the way in which Foucault's work, for example, draws our attention to the complex relations between power and knowledge in modern institutions, he believes that we must not lose the capacity for universal moral judgement in exaggerating the importance of 'difference' and respect for 'the other'. The sociological aspects of critical international theory are concerned with the historical changeability of principles of moral inclusion and exclusion. Working from the philosophical premise that human moral capacities are not to be presupposed (contra Kant) or viewed as given, but must be accounted for within a theory of history, Linklater identifies three forms of social learning: learning how to cope with conditions of conflict or strategic rivalry; learning how to manage technological and economic change or technical-instrumental rationalisation; and moral–practical learning. Linklater argues that the history of humanity suggests a contingent capacity to transcend particular-istic limitations on freedom, and even the whole spectrum of forms of exclusion. The third thematic aspect of critical international theory is practical, or as Linklater puts it, 'praxeological', to examine practical oppor-tunities to intervene in international rela-tions in order to widen the scope of moral obligation across territorial boundaries.

What is one to make of all this? It should be noted that Linklater writes at a high level of abstraction and his work is not easily digested at one sitting. Since much of his writing is pitched at the level of meta-theory, the last aspect of his agenda is probably the least developed dimension of his overall project. Indeed, one can detect an ambiguity in his writing between the need to transcend the states system (emphasised in his earlier work) and a tendency to accept the state system as a medium of change and reform. The latter is emphasised in his more recent work on the ethical possibilities of 'good international citizenship' in Australian foreign policy.[9]

The major problem with Linklater's work is that it needs to recover the early empha-sis on political theory rather than the later emphasis on the philosophy of history and sociology. As I have briefly sketched the tra-jectory of Linklater's work, it begins with a critique of attempts to justify two separate spheres of moral obligation, the 'internal' and the 'external'. It then moves on to exam-ine ways in which two influential paradigms, realism and Marxism, impede the systematic study of ascending 'scales of types' of societies and relations among them. Finally, it consists of a number of agenda-setting articles for a 'post-positivist' inter-discipline of international relations inspired by the Frankfurt School of critical theory and the work of the German philosopher Jürgen Habermas. Throughout his own work, Habermas has sought to reconcile respect for the achievements of the modern consti-tutional state with the Marxist critique of the socially destructive and anti-democratic dynamics of capitalist development. But it could be argued that the focus on Habermas as a source of inspiration for critical interna-tional theory militates against the 'praxeo-logical' dimension of Linklater's project. The point is well put by Robert Jackson:

> [Linklater] provides no philosophical basis [for adjudicating] cases of conflict between cultures, which are bound to arise and which arguably constitute fundamental moral dilemmas of international society. Habermas and Foucault, wedded to soci-ological theory, are of little assistance in dealing with normative predicaments. A 'comparative sociology of moral codes' based on historical case studies is no way around the problem. Unless one opts for relativism one must resort to some stan-dard of conduct, such as basic needs, human rights, the common good, and so forth. It is not a solution merely to argue for recognition and respect for the 'other' and his, her or their inclusion in the sphere of equality and entitlement. For inclusion only postpones the unresolved problem of determining which facet of the others' conduct ought to be recognised and respected, and which not. Even if every-body is included in the community one must still prohibit certain forms of behav-iour inimical to it. *Exclusion and inclusion ultimately is not about class, sex, race, caste, nationality, and other sociological categories; it is about human conduct.*[10]

Notes

1 Mark Hoffman, 'Restructuring, reconstruction, reinscription, rearticulation: four voices in crit-ical international theory', *Millennium: Journal of International Studies* 20 (1991), p. 173.
2 Martin Wight, 'Why is there no international theory?', in Martin Wight and Herbert Butterfield (eds), *Diplomatic Investigations: Essays in the Theory of International Politics*, London, Allen & Unwin, 1966, p. 16.
3 Andrew Linklater, *Men and Citizens in International Relations*, Second edition, London, Macmillan, 1990, p. 77.

4 Ibid., p. 99.
5 Ibid., p. 130.
6 Ibid., p. 166.
7 Andrew Linklater, *Beyond Realism and Marxism: Critical Theory and International Relations*, London, Macmillan, 1990, p. 171.
8 See, in particular, Andrew Linklater, 'The question of the next stage in international relations theory: a critical-theoretical perspective', *Millennium: Journal of International Studies* 21 (1992), pp. 77–98.
9 Andrew Linklater, 'What is a good international citizen?', in Paul Keal (ed.), *Ethics and Foreign Policy*, St Leonards, Allen & Unwin, pp. 21–43.
10 Robert H. Jackson, 'Pluralism in international political theory', *Review of International Studies* (April 1992), p. 274. Emphasis added.

See also in this book

Beitz, Cox, Giddens, Mann, Walzer, Wight

Linklater's major writings

'Rationality and obligation in the states-system: the lessons of Pufendorf's law of nations', *Millennium: Journal of International Studies* 9 (1981), pp. 215–28

'Realism, Marxism and critical international theory', *Review of International Studies* 12 (1986), pp. 301–12

Men and Citizens in International Relations, Second edition, London, Macmillan, 1990

Beyond Realism and Marxism: Critical Theory and International Relations, London, Macmillan, 1990

'The problem of community in international relations', *Alternatives* 15 (1990), pp. 135–53

'Marxism and international relations: antithesis, reconciliation and transcendence', in Richard L. Higgott and James L. Richardson (eds), *International Relations: Global and Australian Perspectives on an Evolving Discipline*, Canberra, The Australian University Press, 1991, pp. 70–91

'The question of the next stage in international relations theory: a critical-theoretical perspective', *Millennium: Journal of International Studies* 21 (1992), pp. 77–98

Boundaries in Question: New Directions in International Relations (co-editor with John Macmillan), London, Pinter, 1995

'Neorealism in theory and practice', in Ken Booth and Steve Smith (eds), *International Relations Theory Today*, Cambridge, Polity Press, 1995, pp. 241–62

'Political community', in Alex Danchev (ed.), *Fin de Siècle: The Meaning of the Twentieth Century*, London, Tauris Academic Publishing, 1995

Theories of International Relations (co-editor with Scott Burchill), Basingstoke, Macmillan, 1996

'The achievements of critical theory', in Steve Smith, Ken Booth and Marysia Zalewski (eds), *International Theory: Positivism and Beyond*, Cambridge, Cambridge University Press, 1996, pp. 279–98

The Transformation of Political Community, South Carolina, University of South Carolina Press, 1997

Further reading

Brown, Chris, *International Relations Theory: New Normative Approaches*, London, Harvester Wheatsheaf, 1992

Brown, Chris, 'Turtles all the way down: anti-foundationalism, critical theory and international relations', *Millennium: Journal of International Studies* 23 (1994), pp. 213–36

Cox, Wayne S. and Sjolander, Claire T. (eds), *Beyond Positivism: Critical Reflections on International Relations*, Boulder, Colorado, Lynne Reinner, 1994

Devetak, Richard, 'The project of modernity and international relations theory', *Millennium: Journal of International Studies* 24 (1995), pp. 27–51

Keyman, E. Fuat, *Globalisation, State, Identity, Difference: Toward a Critical Social Theory of International Relations*, Atlantic Highlands, New Jersey, Humanities Press, 1997

Neufeld, Mark, *The Restructuring of International Relations Theory*, Cambridge, Cambridge University Press, 1995

Spegele, Roger D., *Political Realism in International Theory*, Cambridge, Cambridge University Press, 1996

Suganami, Hidemi, 'Reflections on the domestic analogy: the case of Bull, Beitz, and Linklater', *Review of International Studies* 12 (1986), pp. 145–58

THEORY OF INTERNATIONAL SOCIETY

The central concerns for key thinkers in this section are with notions of law and morality that operate among states. They address questions that are central to international relations but which tend to be neglected by realists and liberals. The term 'international society' implies that, despite the absence of a central authority, states exhibit patterns of conduct that are subject to, and constituted by, legal and moral restraints. If this is the case, then international relations cannot be understood adequately as a manifestation of power politics (as realists argue), so it may be unnecessary to radically transform the international order to achieve global peace and justice (as radicals claim). For Martin Wight, the theory of international society represents an alternative to realism and idealism in the study of international relations. Hedley Bull claims that the 'institutions' of the society of states (war, the great powers, international law, diplomacy and the balance of power) are crucial in maintaining international order. These thinkers encourage us to think about international relations as a social arena whose members – sovereign states – relate to each other not only as competitors for power and wealth, but also as holders of particular rights, entitlements and obligations. In terms of method, they emphasise the importance of an historical approach. The rules of international society arose in Europe in the context of a particular Western Christian culture. How were they reproduced over time as international society expanded outside Europe? Does the society of states depend upon a shared culture of norms and expectations among states? What are the strengths and weaknesses of international society? Michael Walzer and John Vincent are particularly concerned with the relationship between human rights and the rights of sovereign states. They seek ways in which to reconcile the society of states with cosmopolitan values. In contrast, Terry Nardin argues that any attempt to infuse international society with cosmopolitan purposes will undermine its procedural foundations and the value of coexistence.

HEDLEY BULL

Hedley Bull is best known to undergraduates on the basis of his most frequently read text, *The Anarchical Society* (1977). It is a rare example of a textbook with an argument, and its popularity with both teachers and students stems from one of the chief characteristics of Bull's thought and published work, a meticulous concern with *order*. As J.D.B. Miller has observed, '[he] saw things very sequentially. Many of his articles begin with a series of numbered questions that he proceeds to answer in sequence, the whole forming a logical entity of impressive power.'[1] Order in international relations was one of Bull's central concerns. What is it? What are the most appropriate theoretical tools to use in studying it? How does it vary over time and space? How can international order be reconciled with the promotion of justice, if at all? These are the central questions that much of his work is devoted to answering.

Perhaps the most impressive aspect of his main book is its systematic examination of the concept of 'order' on the basis of very clear definitions and theoretical categories. Bull defines order in general as a pattern of activity that sustains some elementary social goals in society, such as maintaining security for its members against arbitrary violence, ensuring that agreements are kept and protecting property rights. He then adapts these goals to the peculiar characteristics of international society, where they appear as the preservation of the sovereign states that are its members, and peace as the normal condition of coexistence between them. Bull makes an important distinction between an international system and a society. The latter is characterized by a consensus among states that they share some common interests and conceive themselves as being related to each other in the context of common rules and institutions. Bull argues that although international society lacks an over-arching sovereign, international relations is more than a site of constant patterns of competition among states pursuing their self-interests.

The rest of his text is a careful examination of the 'institutions' of international society, which should not be reduced to international organizations, but refer to 'sets of habits and practices shaped toward the realization of common goals'.[2] They include the balance of power, international law, diplomacy, war itself (under certain conditions) and the managerial function performed by the great powers. He is careful to distinguish between the role such institutions play in undermining international order as well as maintaining it, since he recognises that the 'element' of international society is only one of three competing 'elements' in world politics, the others being the elements of a Hobbesian state of war and those transnational loyalties that cross territorial borders and often undermine them (such as ideology). Each chapter painstakingly analyses the role of each institution, how that role has changed over time and how we should evaluate its role in light of our more pressing moral concern with what he calls 'world order'. This

> is more fundamental and primordial ... because the ultimate units of the great society of mankind are not states ... but individual human beings. This is the moment for international relations, but the question of world order arises whatever the political or social structure of globe ... if international order does have value, this can only be because it is instrumental to the goal of order in human society as a whole.[3]

As a textbook, Bull's *Anarchical Society* is still required reading for most students of international relations. As an argument, however, it is less convincing. Despite Bull's attention to detail and the rigour of his analytical distinctions, the book illustrates both the strengths and weaknesses of the influences that led to its writing, and these can be traced to Bull's personal and intellectual background.

Hedley Bull was born in Sydney in 1932. He graduated from the University of Sydney in 1952, having taken honours in philosophy and law. At this time one of the great influences on his thought was the Australian philosopher John Anderson. He instilled in his students a critical rigour with an equal concern for the big issues in social and political life, which could only understood on the basis of a due regard for their historical context. Bull moved to Oxford in 1953 and graduated with a BPhil in politics before taking up an assistant lectureship at the London School of Economics. There he began teaching international relations, as well as listening to the famous lectures of Martin Wight. From Wight he learned that the history of ideas in the study of international relations could be understood as a continuing dialogue between realists, revolutionists and rationalists.

The legacy of Martin Wight was profound, for he provided the three 'schools of thought' that Bull later drew upon in delineating competing ideas regarding the nature and value of international order and international society. Unlike Wight, who used his categories for pedagogical purposes and refused to identify himself with any single one, Hedley Bull clearly attempted to articulate and defend rationalism, or what he called a neo-Grotian approach to the theory and practice of international relations. Wary of the constant dangers of anarchy and the presence of power politics, yet sympathetic to the cosmopolitan appeal of a putative 'world society' that would give priority to justice for individuals rather than states, this approach sought to mediate between the extremes. Bull himself did so by postulating international society as a real but fragile normative order, thereby undermining the realist tendency to equate system and society, whilst holding out the hope that such a normative order could be expanded to reflect more cosmopolitan concerns in the future. Bull's approach was fundamentally a moderate one, and this sense of trying to mediate between extremes comes through in much of his related work on intervention, the history of international society, and the potential of arms control in mediating between the search for strategic superiority during the Cold War and the opposing desire for complete disarmament.

In 1958 Bull became a member of the newly established British Committee on the Theory of International Politics, and he spent some time in the United States to observe and participate in the growth of the discipline at institutions such as Harvard and Chicago. There he became absorbed in issues of nuclear strategy and, after returning to England to the Institute for Strategic Studies, he completed his major text *The Control of the Arms Race* (1961). This led to work for the Arms Control and Disarmament Research Unit in the Foreign Office, after which he returned to Australia in 1966 as Professor of International Relations at the Australian National University. He went back to Oxford in 1977 to take up the Montague Burton Chair of International Relations and remained there until his untimely death from cancer in 1985.

Prior to the publication of *The Anarchical Society*, Bull's name was best known for his ferocious attack on the behavioural (or 'scientific') approach to the study of international relations that dominated many American universities in the late 1950s and 1960s. One can see the influence of Martin Wight in Bull's 1966 article, which drew a clear (and somewhat polemical) distinction between 'classical' and 'scientific' theory.[4] Just as Wight had argued that the philosophy of history is the analogue of political theory in the study of international relations, Bull claimed that the foundations of teaching and research lay in philosophy, law and history rather than the vain attempt to discover 'laws of behaviour' among states as the basis for developing reliable predictions for the future. As far as he was concerned, there were very strict limits to the applicability of quantitative or behavioural methods of analysis.

Although Bull's arguments need to be understood in the context of a somewhat overheated debate over the future of research methods in international relations, as well as his concern with the exaggerated emphasis on the role of game theory among nuclear strategists, they also affirmed his belief that the subject matter of international relations had at its core the intersubjective understandings and intention of actors whose conduct the theorist seeks to understand. Consequently, theory and practice could not be divorced from one another, the former functioning as a more or less useful 'instrument' to explain a 'given reality'. Furthermore, he argued that whilst the classical tradition acknowledged the interdependence between explanation and evaluation or moral judgement, the so-called 'scientists' drew an artificial distinction between them and attempted to subordinate the latter to the former.

Consequently, his theoretical concepts never strayed too far from the meaning they acquired in the dynamic world of diplomatic discourse. Thus the concept of a 'great power', for example, is never defined exclusively on the basis of observable and measurable indices. Its meaning is infused with normative significance which not only presupposes a broader discourse of social interaction, but it also embodies and endows the actors so defined with particular rights and responsibilities towards other states. Similarly, despite the ambiguity of the term 'balance of power', it cannot be reduced to a merely descriptive term for the distribution of coercive capabilities but also discloses a principle of conduct, a societal institution, and a goal to be maintained in international society.

Curiously, despite his support for the promotion of normative theory in the study of international relations, Bull himself attempted to distinguish between order and justice, claiming that the latter is an inherently subjective ideal. He therefore offers no 'private vision of what just conduct would be, [or] any philosophical analysis of the criteria for recognizing it'.[5] Whilst he elaborated on various notions of justice put forward by others and embodied in demands for just change (particularly by Third World states), and examined their compatibility with the maintenance of international order, he refrained from endorsing any one of them. Toward the end of his life, Bull became increasingly concerned with the question of world order and the increasing fragility of the main institutions of international society. There were two main reasons for this concern.

First, Bull became increasingly critical of the United States and the Soviet Union. The decline of détente in the 1970s and the resurgence of the nuclear arms race in the early 1980s had weakened their right to be regarded as responsible managers of international society as a whole. This decline was particularly regrettable since, of all the institutions of international society, only the great powers are also actors. If they do not fulfil the roles Bull attributes to them, then it is difficult to see how the other institutions can function to prevent the collapse of international society. In the 1980s he castigated the United States, in particular, which:

> [t]hrough its belligerent statements and preparations for renewed military intervention, its policies evidently fashioned to express moods rather than to achieve results, its inability to withstand domestic forces of chauvinism and greed, has done much to undermine its own position as the leader of the West and to accentuate the ugliness of the face it turns towards the Third World.[6]

Second, Bull described the history of international society in terms of the expansion of its geographical scope, a process that accelerated dramatically with decolonisation and the creation of over 100 new states, as well as the weakening of the cultural consensus that had underpinned the society of states in the past. The institutions of international society were exported from Europe to the rest of the world. Their strength depended upon new members having a stake in sustaining them. Bull worried that any 'revolt against the West', particularly if it were based on widespread perceptions of economic neocolonialism and growing inequality between rich and poor, would damage the very institutions which needed to be reformed, on the basis of enlightened self-interest, by those who benefited most from them.[7]

Since Bull's death, and in light of the end of the Cold War, both the questions asked by Bull and the way he tried to answer them have been the source of renewed interest in his work, as well as that of others associated with the 'English School' of international theory. Even so, it is possible to identify some limitations to this approach. Two, in particular, are worth noting.

First, Bull tended to conflate international order as an empirically dynamic state of affairs within the states system (i.e. a fact) with order as a value by which to judge international society against alternative institutional structures. Was order a quantity (more or less) or a quality? At times he suggested that order varied across time and space, yet shied away from providing any criteria by which such variation could be measured. At other times, he suggested that the society of states *as a whole* was to be valued because it was the source of international order. If this were the case, then it remains puzzling why order in general was not the value against which Bull judged the merits of international society and its institutions, rather than distinguishing between order in general, international order in the society of states, and world order as a cosmopolitan value.

Second, it is somewhat unfortunate that Bull failed to transcend Wight's presentation of the three traditions of international

thought (realism rationalism, and revolutionism). If one is to locate oneself within the rationalist, or neo-Grotian, tradition, it is important to debunk realist and revolutionary claims. Bull did not do this. Consequently, the reader is unsure whether to choose between traditions on the basis of their competing representations of world politics, or whether each somehow 'captures' certain elements of a complex world. The problem with the latter stance, as R.J. Vincent points out, is that 'one . . . is always shifting according to the ground taken by others'.[8]

Notwithstanding such difficulties, and even if Bull himself failed to provide persuasive answers, the big questions he asked remain pertinent today. To invoke the very different vocabulary of the political theorist Jürgen Habermas, at the core of Hedley Bull's work there was 'a constitutive interest in the preservation and expansion of the intersubjectivity of action-orienting mutual understanding'.[9] If the Cold War is not to be replaced by a new 'clash of civilisations', and if the problems of international order continue to increase in scope and complexity, then how the society of states should and can be reformed in the service of world order is perhaps the most crucial question of our time.

Notes

1 J.D.B. Miller, 'Hedley Bull, 1932–85', in J.D.B. Miller and R.J. Vincent, *Order and Violence: Hedley Bull and International Relations*, Oxford, Clarendon Press, 1990, p. 11.
2 Hedley Bull, *The Anarchical Society*, London, Macmillan, 1977, p. 74.
3 Ibid., p. 22.
4 Hedley Bull, 'International theory: the case for a classical approach', *World Politics* 18 (1966), pp. 363–77.
5 Hedley Bull, *The Anarchical Society*, op.cit., p. 78.
6 Hedley Bull, 'The great irresponsibles? The United States, the Soviet Union and world order', *International Journal* 35 (1980), p. 437.
7 See, in particular Hedley Bull, *Justice in International Relations* (the Hagey Lectures), Ontario, University of Waterloo, 1983.

8 R.J. Vincent, 'Order in international politics', in J.D.B. Miller and R.J. Vincent, *Order and Violence: Hedley Bull and International Relations*, Oxford, Clarendon Press, 1990, p. 47.
9 J. Habermas, *Knowledge and Human Interests*, Boston, Beacon Press, 1971, p. 310.

See also in this book

Nardin, Vincent, Wight

Bull's major writings

The Control of the Arms Race: Disarmament and Arms Control in the Missile Age, New York, Praeger, 1961

'Society and anarchy in international relations', in Martin Wight and Herbert Butterfield (eds), *Diplomatic Investigations: Essays in the Theory of International Politics*, London, Allen & Unwin, 1966, pp. 35–50

'The Grotian conception of international relations', in Martin Wight and Herbert Butterfield (eds), *Diplomatic Investigations: Essays in the Theory of International Politics*, London, Allen & Unwin, 1966, pp. 51–73

'International relations as an academic pursuit', *Australian Outlook* 26 (1972), pp. 251–65

'The theory of international politics: 1919–1969', in Brian Porter (ed.), *The Aberystwyth Papers*, London, Oxford University Press, 1972, pp. 30–58

'Martin Wight and the theory of international relations', *British Journal of International Studies* 2 (1976), pp. 101–16

The Anarchical Society, London, Macmillan, 1977

'The great irresponsibles? The United States, the Soviet Union, and world order', *International Journal* 35 (1980), pp. 437–47

'Hobbes and international anarchy', *Social Research* 48 (1981), pp. 717–39

'The international anarchy in the 1980s', *Australian Outlook* 37 (1983), pp. 127–31

The Expansion of International Society (with Adam Watson), Oxford, Clarendon Press, 1984

Intervention in World Politics (editor), Oxford, Oxford University Press, 1984

Justice in International Relations, Waterloo, Ontario, University of Waterloo, 1984

Hedley Bull on Arms Control, Basingstoke, Macmillan, 1987

Hugo Grotius and International Relations (with Benedict Kingsbury and Adam Roberts), Oxford, Oxford University Press, 1992

Further reading

Buzan, Barry, 'From international system to international society: structural realism and regime theory meet the English School,' *International Organization* 47 (1993), pp. 327–52

Evans, Tony and Wilson, Peter, 'Regime theory and the English School of International Relations: a comparison', *Millennium: Journal of International Studies* 21 (1992), pp. 329–52

Hoffmann, Stanley, 'Hedley Bull and his contribution to International Relations', *International Affairs* 62 (1986), pp. 179–96

Jones, Roy, 'The English school of international relations: a case for closure', *Review of International Studies* 7 (1981), pp. 1–13

Miller, J.D.B. and Vincent, R.J. (eds), *Order and Violence: Hedley Bull and International Relations*, Oxford, Clarendon Press, 1990

Suganami, Hidemi, 'Reflections on the domestic analogy: the case of Bull, Beitz, and Linklater', *Review of International Studies* 12 (1986), pp. 145–58

Vincent, R.J., 'Hedley Bull and order in international relations', *Millennium: Journal of International Studies* 17 (1988), pp. 195–214

Wheeler, Nicholas J., 'Pluralist or solidarist conceptions of international society: Bull and Vincent on humanitarian intervention', *Millennium: Journal of International Studies* 21 (1992), pp. 463–88

TERRY NARDIN

Professor Terry Nardin teaches international political theory at the University of Wisconsin–Milwaukee. There are two reasons for including him in this section on theorists of international society. The first is that his work differs in interesting ways from other members of the English School examined in this book (Bull, Vincent, Wight), and the second is that he bases his interpretation on the nature of international law among states on the philosophical foundations of the late English political philosopher, Michael Oakeshott (1901–90). Oakeshott was a Professor of Politics at the London School of Economics at the time when Martin Wight was delivering his famous lectures on international political theory there. To my knowledge, Nardin is the only writer on international society to use Oakeshott's work to justify his interpretation of the particular character of relations among states, and in order to understand Nardin's work it is necessary to begin with the work of his intellectual mentor.

Oakeshott was arguably the most important English political thinker of the century. He developed a concept of civil society of great subtlety and examined some of the major questions raised by the development of the modern state. He also greatly influenced the way in which the history of political thought is studied and taught. Although some of his work was extremely complex, most of what he wrote displays a notable elegance of style, particularly his essays. He was a nonconformist in the sense that he denied many of the orthodoxies of the age. Despite his reputation as a conservative, he was also quite radical on particular issues. He was, for example, a vocal defender of elitism in universities, arguing that they should not be confused with technical schools but should uphold rigorous academic values pursued for their intrinsic worth.

Oakeshott was also very sceptical about the alleged virtues of the modern state. His view of human conduct is that it is constituted by intelligent agents responding to contingent situations in pursuit of their wished for goals and doing so in the context of a multiplicity of practices. These fall into two separate categories. They may be 'prudential', prescribing instrumental behaviour designed to achieve a given purpose. Or they may be 'moral', governed by rules that are not instrumental and that do not specify action. For example, the principle that individuals should act honestly does not direct what should be said or done in a particular situation. This distinction is reflected in the two categorically distinct modes of human association that Oakeshott discerned and that he called *universitas* and *societas*. The former is an association of people united in the pursuit of a common objective, such

as a football team. Its practices are thus 'prudential' in nature, designed to realise an end. In contrast, *societas* is a 'moral' relationship between free agents who severally acknowledge only the authority of certain conditions that are necessary to association and action, but that otherwise leave those involved to pursue their own goals.

These two concepts, together with their associated 'vocabularies', are, Oakeshott believed, the pole around which European reflection about the modern state has turned. It may be regarded as a 'teleocracy', a joint endeavour to seek the satisfaction of a collective, substantive set of goals, in which case the role of government is to manage the purposive concern, whatever it may be. Or its practices may be limited to a framework of conduct which does not specify any such goal and which offers simply a 'negative gift', the removal of some of the circumstances that might otherwise frustrate the achievement of whatever individuals seek. 'Civil association', a society conceived in this latter way, offers no salvation (as through the promised securing of a common end), but simply the organisation of human affairs such that no one who is able is prevented from seeking 'the good life' after his or her own fashion.

Terry Nardin uses this framework explicitly in justifying a unique interpretation of international society. His book *Law, Morality, and the Relations of States* (1983) takes up Oakeshott's basic distinction between 'civil association' and 'enterprise association' and applies it at a global level, although he alters the terms slightly, referring to the distinction between 'purposive' and 'practical' association throughout the book. The latter refers to 'a set of considerations to be taken into account in deciding and acting, and in evaluating decisions and actions'.[1] Nardin simply replicates Oakeshott's modes of association at the international level, so that states fulfil the role that Oakeshott delegates to individuals within civil society. For Nardin, international society is best seen as a practical association made up of states

> each devoted to its own ends and its own conception of the good. The common good of this inclusive community resides not in the ends that some, or at times even most, of its members may wish collectively to pursue but in the values of justice, peace, security, and co-existence, which can only be enjoyed through participation in a common body of authoritative practices.[2]

In applying Oakeshott's distinction to international society, Nardin presupposes what Oakeshott was concerned to prevent, that is, the subordination of *societas* to *universitas* at the level of domestic politics. Nardin departs from his mentor in assuming the battle between these 'modes of conduct' to have been lost within the territorial boundaries of the modern state. Nardin does not make such an argument explicit, but it is logically consistent with his overall framework.

Thus we should not understand the society of states, and international law, as a purposive association. There are no shared purposes among all states, each of which pursues its own vision of the good life on behalf of its citizens. This is not to deny that states do have some shared purposes and give their consent to be bound by agreements to achieve them in some substantive manner. But the society of states and its core institution of law are not matters for consent among states. The content of particular treaties may be matters of consent and negotiation, but as Brown puts it, '[w]hat is to count as a treaty [and] how states become committed to treaties are matters that are logically prior to the content of any particular treaty'.[3] These logically prior matters belong to the realm of 'authoritative practices' in international law. Nardin claims that the society of states has to be understood as constituted by such practices, which are themselves the condition of possibility for purposive co-operation among states. States cannot abandon participation in such practices without also abandoning their status as members of international society so construed.

Nardin's approach to the analysis of international society is very different from the ways in which Wight, Bull and Walzer conceive it. He dispenses with the need to defend international society as a 'good thing' against the claims of realism and revolutionism, which is the starting point of Wight and Bull. In so doing, his approach is arguably superior to theirs. Within the English School, the value of international society is articulated within an alleged tradition or pattern of thought whose very identity is defined against that which it is not. The *via media*, as Forsythe notes, defines itself

> by rejecting each extreme. To the 'Realists' it said that moral restraints both did and should apply to states. To the 'Universalists' it said that [politics among states] need not be shunned or overturned. It is a kind of double negative rather than something positive.[4]

Nardin avoids all the problems associated with this conceptualisation of international society as a *via media*. He does not see international civil society as one of a number of competing 'elements' in international relations, as Bull does. Nor does he believe that the authoritative practices of international society mediate between realism and revolutionism, as Wight sometimes argues. In fact, Nardin simply ignores such claims. He is not worried about the dilemmas of reconciling order and justice in international society because it is already a just order, where justice refers to the procedural rules of coexistence between states. International society is thus presented as fragile *Gesellschaft*, which permits a plurality of domestically generated *Gemeinschafts*. In light of the obvious diversity, both of ethical traditions and the values embodied in and expressed by the plurality of states in the world, the only rational response is to acknowledge and cope with ethical relativism as a consequence. 'Relativism ... concludes from the evidence of disagreement that we acknowledge the existence of many truths, each determined by whatever standards are used to define and measure truth.'[5] This does not deny the possibility that some meta-ethical criterion of truth exists – Nardin is certainly not a moral sceptic – only that we have yet to discover what that criterion might be.

The consequences of Nardin's approach to international society are, without much doubt, conservative. International society is a procedural *societas*. It protects the common interests of states in stable coexistence, but it is undermined if states or any other actors attempt to transform it into a purposive association. Justice is about impartial rules, which impose obligations on all states with equal force, regardless of the distribution of power and wealth among them. As Brown points out,

> [t]he rule ... that forbids the expropriation of foreign owned assets without compensation ... is impartial because a Bangladeshi corporation operating in the United States would be as entitled to its protection as an American corporation operating in Bangladesh, and from Nardin's perspective the fact that Bangladeshi corporations are thin on the ground is neither here nor there.[6]

Nardin is opposed to any attempt to burden international society with common purposes, such as the obligation to achieve some kind of distributive justice between North and South. In the absence of agreement over what this might mean, attempts to implement it will result in failure and undermine the tenuous consensus on procedural justice that is already in place. Similarly, Nardin is opposed to international legislation that would permit intervention in the internal affairs of states. Justice requires 'the independence and legal equality of states, the right of self-defence, the duty of nonintervention, the obligation

to observe treaties, and restrictions on the conduct of war'.[7] It is in the common interests of states to uphold this limited conception of justice, which is the precondition of their coexistence.

There is no doubt that Nardin's austere view of international justice, whilst it is conservative in its political implications, is also quite a radical departure from the English School, many of whose members (such as John Vincent, for example) worry about its inability to incorporate elements of cosmopolitan justice and argue that its survival depends on such incorporation, however difficult this might be to achieve. Nardin argues precisely the opposite case. If it does attempt to become some kind of purposive association, it will grow weaker over time, not stronger.

This does not mean that he is uninterested in the promotion of human rights at a global level, however. He does mention their importance, but consistent with his Oakeshottian framework, he emphasises the primacy of political and civil rights over economic and social rights:

> To insist on respect for human rights is to demand that the policies and laws of a community reflect the principles of impartiality with respect to persons and their ends inherent in the idea of practical association.[8]

The strength of Nardin's approach to the study of ethics and international society lies in its rigorous adherence to the consequences of adopting Oakeshott's famous dichotomy between two ideal types of human association. Whether or not it is a persuasive approach depends very much on the validity of applying the distinction to international relations by treating states as if they were individuals. All the criticisms that Nardin has received stem from this single assumption. For if it is the case that states should not be assumed to contain autonomous visions of 'the good life', then the whole framework rests on very shaky intellectual and moral foundations. As Simon Caney points out, 'he has to establish that (a) states have inherent moral value and should therefore be respected, and (b) it is more important to respect states than the human beings or communities that compose them'.[9] Unless Nardin can achieve both tasks, it is not clear why it makes sense to think that Oakeshott's distinction is of much help in thinking about the ethics of international society. States are not individuals. They may not contain any semblance of the good life for their citizens whatsoever. One thinks of Cambodia under the rule of Pol Pot, for example. Are there not limits to political and ethical diversity that should be acknowledged in international law? At least Michael Walzer, whose approach to international ethics presupposes that the legitimacy of state rights is dependent on a moral 'fit' between states and the communities they protect, admits of some exceptions to the rule of nonintervention.

Nardin's thoughts on the relationship between human rights and state rights have shifted since the publication of *Law, Morality and the Relations of States* in 1983. In 1986 he published an article that is critical of Walzer's attempts to derive the rights of states from fundamental human rights and at the same time place strict limits on permissible instances of intervention in international relations.[10] Nardin argues that it is quite possible to justify intervention into the internal affairs of states on grounds of human rights violations, and at the same time impose stringent consequential constraints on the ethical propriety of intervention that would still make intervention very hard to justify in practice:

1 Armed intervention to protect human rights [can] be undertaken only after other, less drastic, remedies have been tried and have failed;

2 The intervention must in fact be likely to end the abuse it is intended to remedy;

3 The human rights violations must be sufficiently serious to merit the cost in terms of human life that intervention will incur;

4 The anticipated disruptive effects of humanitarian intervention on international stability must be minimal.[11]

Unfortunately, whilst these criteria ensure the difficulty of justifying intervention even if human rights violations are an appropriate rationale for considering whether to intervene, Nardin's acknowledgement of the link between state rights and human rights undermines the purposive/practical distinction that he relies upon to justify his conservative approach to international society. It suggests that the right of states to enjoy the privileges of membership in international society is conditional rather than absolute. It also weakens the arguments for international society based on ethical and cultural diversity. As Brown points out, 'if diversity entails that states have the right to mistreat their populations, then it is difficult to see why such diversity is to be valued'.[12] Caney suggests that if ethical and cultural diversity is to be respected, this could in fact justify intervention against states that fail to respect cultural, religious and ethnic diversity within their territorial borders.[13] He also argues that Nardin's attempt to distinguish between and give a higher priority to political and civil rights rather than economic and social rights is not persuasive, since the latter are as important as the former in enabling individuals and states to engage in any kind of association, purposive or practical.

In short, Terry Nardin's project is a distinctive contribution to the study of international society. His approach is radically different from the other members of the English School, both in its philosophical premises and in its normative implications. It remains unclear, however, whether it avoids the difficulties and dilemmas that Bull, Vincent and Wight confront in their writing. Nardin assumes that the members of international society, like individuals, are worthy of respect and independence. But it is clear that many of them are not.[14] In the absence of a clear defence of the analogy, then, the edifice of Nardin's theory of international society rests on insecure foundations. Despite his best efforts, the debate over whether the society of states is a 'guardian angel' or a 'global gangster' will continue for some time to come.[15]

Notes

1 Terry Nardin, *Law, Morality, and the Relations of States*, Princeton, New Jersey, Princeton University Press, 1983, p. 6.
2 Ibid., p. 19.
3 Chris Brown, 'Ethics of coexistence: the international theory of Terry Nardin', *Review of International Studies* 14 (1988), p. 215.
4 Murray Forsythe, 'The classical theory of international relations', *Political Studies* 26 (1978), p. 413.
5 Terry Nardin, 'The problem of relativism in international ethics', *Review of International Studies* 18 (1989), p. 150.
6 Chris Brown, op. cit., p. 219.
7 Terry Nardin, *Law, Morality, and the Relations of States*, op. cit., p. 270.
8 Ibid., p. 276.
9 Simon Caney, 'Human rights and the rights of states: Terry Nardin on nonintervention', *International Political Science Review* 18 (1997), p. 29.
10 Terry Nardin and Jerome Slater, 'Nonintervention and human rights', *Journal of Politics* 48 (1986), pp. 86–96.
11 Ibid., pp. 93–4.
12 Chris Brown, *International Relations Theory: New Normative Approaches*, Hemel Hempstead, Harvester Wheatsheaf, 1992, p. 125.
13 Simon Caney, op. cit., p. 29.
14 On this point, see Robert Jackson's distinction between states and quasi-states in the international system. Jackson argues that there has been a fundamental shift in the status of state sovereignty in international law over the last 200 years. Whereas in the nineteenth century international law bestowed the rights of sovereignty on entities that could demonstrate the capacity to provide basic political and economic goods to their citizens, the process of decolonisation, itself inspired by the norm of racial equality, has given rise to the phenomenon of negative sovereignty. Today, many states enjoy the privilege of belonging to international society without the capacity to provide basic goods to their citizens. See Robert H. Jackson, *Quasi-States: Sovereignty, International Relations, and the Third World*, Cambridge, Cambridge University Press, 1990.
15 See Nicholas Wheeler, 'Guardian angel or global gangster?, A review of the ethical claims of international society', *Political Studies* 44 (1996) pp. 123–35.

See also in this book

Bull, Vincent, Walzer, Wight

Nardin's major writings

Law, Morality, and the Relations of States, Princeton, New Jersey, Princeton University Press, 1983
'The problem of relativism in international ethics', *Millennium: Journal of International Studies* 18 (1989), pp. 149–67
'International ethics and international law', *Review of International Studies* 18 (1992), pp. 19–30
'Ethical traditions in international affairs', in Terry Nardin and David R. Mapel (eds), *Traditions of International Ethics*, Cambridge, Cambridge University Press, 1993, pp. 1–22

Further reading

Brown, Chris, 'Ethics of coexistence: the international theory of Terry Nardin', *Review of International Studies* 14 (1988), pp. 213–22
Brown, Chris, *International Relations Theory: New Normative Approaches*, Hemel Hempstead, Harvester Wheatsheaf, 1992
Caney, Simon, 'Human rights and the rights of states: Terry Nardin on nonintervention', *International Political Science Review* 18 (1997), pp. 27–37
Jackson, Robert H., *Quasi-States: Sovereignty, International Relations, and the Third World*, Cambridge, Cambridge University Press, 1990
Oakeshott, Michael, *Rationalism in Politics and Other Essays*, London, Methuen, 1962
Oakeshott, Michael, *On Human Conduct*, Oxford, Clarendon Press, 1975

JOHN VINCENT

John Vincent died suddenly on 2 November 1990. He was only 47 years old, and barely a year had passed since his appointment as Montague Burton Professor of International Relations at LSE. His death was not only a personal tragedy for those who knew him; it was also a great loss to the so-called 'English School' in the study of international relations. Furthermore, the questions Vincent asked, and the rigour of his intellectual inquiry, are both particularly relevant in the post-Cold War era. It would be fascinating to observe the way Vincent would have responded to the renewed attention being paid to two issues that were always uppermost in his work. The first is the issue of 'intervention' in the theory and practice of international relations, on which he published his first major book in 1974. Just before his death, he revisited some of the arguments of that earlier work and one can observe a marked shift in his thinking. The second is the issue of human rights in world politics: what they consist of, the degree to which progress in their observance can be measured, and the difficulties inherent in attempting to promote human rights in international diplomacy.

John Vincent was born in 1943. Christopher Hill describes him as 'late developer' who did not do particularly well at school and found it difficult to gain a university place after he graduated from school. Hill observes that 'his outstanding qualities only really emerged as a postgraduate, and even then his star did not rise until his late thirties'.[1] He spent his undergraduate years at Britain's oldest Department of International Relations at the University of Wales in Aberystwyth. He then studied at the University of Leicester (MA in European Studies) and the Australian National University (PhD), where he was supervised by his mentor, Hedley Bull. Before succeeding Susan Strange as Montague Burton Professor of International Relations at the LSE in 1989, Vincent taught at the University of Keele as well as Oxford University. He edited the prestigious journal *Review of International Studies* for three

years prior to his professorial appointment in London.

In his excellent review of Vincent's work, Neumann characterises him as a 'card-carrying member' of the English School of international relations, inspired by the work of Martin Wight and Hedley Bull in particular. Neumann suggests that members of the School are concerned with five issue-areas in the theory and practice of international relations.[2] First, they are interested in the comparative analysis of 'international systems' over time and space, particularly in terms of diplomatic practice and culture. Second, they share a predilection for analysing international relations within what Hedley Bull called the 'society of states'.[3] This, in turn, leads to an emphasis on the role of volition rather than necessity in accounting for inter-state behaviour. As Alan James observes,

> A society ... is subject to and expressive of the wishes and whims of those who ... make it up. It reflects the actions and reactions of its constituents, or members. And those members ... will be influenced by their calculations, hopes, purposes, beliefs, anxieties, fears, and all the other elements of the human condition ... this is why the term society, with its voluntaristic connotations, is so much more apt than system to sum up the collectivity of states.[4]

Third, members of the School are engaged in a constant debate over the degree of change within the society of states. Is there any evidence that its membership is expanding to include actors other than states? Does the legitimacy of the rules, which bind states together, depend on their acknowledgement by state elites alone, or does it require the support of a broader constituency? What is the relative balance between 'pluralism' and 'solidarism' in international society? Are its institutions (described at length in Bull's famous text) consistent with a culture of procedural consensus among states, or are they changing in a more solidarist direction, to promote greater homogeneity within states as well? Fourth, the shadow of Wight's famous trilogy of international thought weighs heavily on the minds of all members of the English School. His division of 'patterns of international thought' among realists, rationalists and revolutionists continues to influence both the way in which members of the School present the main body of ideas about international relations, as well as the way they position themselves within that body. Finally, the tensions between the requirements of international order and cosmopolitan justice are a constant concern for writers such as Vincent. Of course, it would be quite wrong to suggest that those so identified as part of the English School agree with each other on substantive issues. All that can be said is that they agree on the central questions to be asked and work within a broad tradition of thought in their search for answers.

Vincent himself did not embrace a consistent set of answers to the key questions raised above, but this should not be seen as a sign of weakness. Rather, in engaging with the theory and practice of issues such as intervention and the role of human rights in international society, he embodies the way in which competing values and concerns can coexist fruitfully within the mind of one thinker. In one of his most well-known phrases, Vincent was suspicious of 'the whole enterprise of treating great thinkers like parcels at the post office', and no doubt he would have cast a critical eye on the way in which I have categorised the key thinkers in this book:

> Carr's realist critique is followed by a chapter on the limitations of Realism. The realist Martin Wight of *Power Politics* is different from the rationalist Martin Wight of 'Western Values in International Relations'. Morgenthau's account of international politics as a struggle for power

includes a treatment of the balance of power as a stabilising factor in the politics of states, and even of the importance of a moral consensus on which the stability of a system in the end depended.[5]

Within Vincent's own work, one can trace a subtle progression from a strict support of a pluralist interpretation of the society of states to a more solidarist one. Unlike most people, he became more radical as he got older, not less. This may have had something to do with his growing dissatisfaction with the intellectual legacy of his early mentor, Hedley Bull, although Bull himself was moving in a similar direction toward the end of his life. That movement explains the apparent contradiction between the central arguments of his two major books, *Nonintervention and International Order* (1974) and *Human Rights and International Relations* (1986).

The first book, which grew out of Vincent's doctoral work under Hedley Bull, reflects the sombre rationalism of his former supervisor. Written in the context of the ongoing Cold War between the superpowers, Vincent was not primarily concerned with the issue of humanitarian intervention. In the early 1970s, there was an embarassing gap between the injunctions of international law against intervention and its flagrant abuse by the United States and the Soviet Union. Of course, intervention is something that states often see in the actions of others but never in their own. This might suggest that it is no more than a term of abuse and that, if we want to understand international relations and the way states really behave, we need spend little time over the idea of nonintervention. However, as Vincent points out, widespread condemnation of a form of behaviour in international society usually attests to at least some normative force in the principle that is being broken. And states generally do what they can to avoid a convincing charge of hypocrisy. Nonintervention as a cardinal rule of the society of states therefore repays study, particularly if, like Vincent, one believes that it is a desirable rule that needs supporting rather than being paid cynical lip service.

Vincent argues that the core of intervention (as opposed to mere 'interference', a normal activity in international relations) is the use of coercive means to alter the behaviour or perhaps change the government of a target state. The threat or use of force 'in the domestic affairs of another state' is precisely what the rule of nonintervention prohibits.[6] Despite the perception of many scholars in the early 1970s that some kind of transnational world society was in the making, Vincent argues that the legacy of the modern state system still weighs heavily upon us. Although he begins his study with an analysis of the legal development of principle of nonintervention, the character of the legal system impels him to devote the bulk of his work to the political arguments underlying compliance – or noncompliance – with the principle.

Vincent outlines four archetypal arguments concerning the principle of nonintervention, tracing them to Richard Cobden, John Stuart Mill, Immanuel Kant and Joseph Mazzini. Despite the passage of time, their arguments are still important in locating the key positions taken today on whether, and under what conditions, the blanket prohibition of state intervention under international law should be relaxed. Basically, Cobden stated the most uncompromising theory of nonintervention – one founded on the partiality of states in defining universal notions of right and on the relative efficiency of nonintervention in serving material interests of people over the long run. Vincent notes that a basic assumption undergirding Cobden's view was that transcending inter-state relations there are a plethora of relations between peoples. Goods, people and ideas are to cross frontiers freely, thus reducing the incidence of state conflicts and eventually binding nations together. Hence, coupled with his stern

doctrine of nonintervention was a liberal world vision, which provided for the interdependence of peoples. Vincent then shows the ways in which Mill, Kant and Mazzini, while accepting much of Cobden's vision, provided in varying degrees for exceptions to the rule.

For example, Mill supported the doctrine of limited humanitarian intervention to protect lives and property (of the intervening state) from barbarous acts of violence, as well as to end deadlocked civil wars, and he also promoted the idea of counterintervention to *uphold* the rule of nonintervention. Kant eroded the limitation on intervention even further by his notion that stable rules of international conduct depend on a radical revision of international society into a collection of republican regimes. In his vision of world order, the league of states would possess a right of intervention as an international organisation. Mazzini completes the liberal evolution against nonintervention. He argues that the rule is merely an instrument of the great powers to protect their client regimes in other countries whilst they restrict the very processes that Cobden hoped would reduce the need for intervention.

Having outlined the classical arguments concerning nonintervention, Vincent explores the historical record since the French Revolution, including the contemporary record of the United States, the United Nations and the Soviet Union. His account overwhelmingly reinforces the view that international anarchy and what Morgenthau once referred to as 'nationalistic universalism' by the great powers should temper any attempt to develop rules of intervention. He argues that such attempts are more likely to give good conscience to disruptive states than to restrict blatant interference motivated by strategic self-interest. What then is Vincent's solution? In 1974, he opts for Richard Cobden. Unable to accept rules for legitimate intervention, despite their normative appeal, he gives no alternative other than rigorous adherence to norms of nonintervention. There is no real alternative as long as the principle of sovereignty remains central to the constitution of international society. If there is to be any international law among states who acknowledge no higher authority than their own, it can only be on the basis of formal equality, regardless of the substantial inequality in the distribution of military and economic power. Like Hedley Bull, Vincent believes that no vision of cosmopolitan justice can be achieved without order, and unlike, say, Richard Falk, he argues that international law should not be seen as an agent for transforming international society:

> Between a naturalism careless of state practice and a [legal] positivism that would simply render any and all state conduct as the law, international law has to find a middle way. In the present case, it is not clear that a middle course of humanitarian intervention has been traced between a virginal doctrine of nonintervention that would allow nothing to be done and a promiscuous doctrine of intervention that would make a trollop of the law. Until that course can with confidence be traced, it is perhaps nonintervention that provides the most dignified principle for international law to sanction.[7]

Vincent was not happy with this conclusion, and the rest of his academic career was devoted to the exploration of the extent to which the conditions that justified his conclusion were undergoing change.

Neumann divides Vincent's research into two categories. The first is concerned with the cultural dimensions of international society. In a series of articles published over a ten-year period from the mid-1970s, Vincent explores both the potential for a more 'solidarist' society of states in which shared cultural values could provide the basis for greater homogeneity within states, as well as the possibility that the universalism of Western culture is constrained by its cultural particularity.[8] The second, and related, category of research is an explicit focus on human rights. His book, *Human Rights and International Relations* (1986), remains one of the most thorough attempts to work through the complexity of debate on the subject. It is divided into three parts.

The first is a masterly conceptual analysis of human rights in political theory, in which Vincent identifies the main areas of contention over the idea of human rights, their content and their scope across human cultures. The second is a comparative analysis of how these areas of contention have manifested themselves in relations between the First, Second and Third 'Worlds' of international diplomacy. Finally, Vincent engages with the whole issue of implementation. Even if it were possible to achieve some conceptual consensus on a list of universal human rights that includes those concerned with political and civil rights as well as economic ones, how could such a consensus inform the conduct of foreign policy? It is not possible in a short summary such as this to do justice to Vincent's comprehensive treatment of the range of debate on the subject. Suffice to say that there is a definite shift in his thinking from the earlier work on nonintervention.

Whereas the first points to the importance of the rule of nonintervention, in 1986 Vincent takes the view that basic rights ought to be met and that the very existence of the global poor is the worst offence against these rights in contemporary world society. What appears to be a contradiction, however, is on closer inspection consistent with the Cobdenite view that the society of states ought to promote human rights within states in order to justify the norm of nonintervention. This is a theme that Vincent pursues in one of his last publications before his untimely death, as part of a critique of Michael Walzer's arguments against intervention:

> [The] 'moral standing of states' position is less an ethical defence than a prudential

defence of non-intervention. It might be better characterised as a sociological defence . . . given the fact that states themselves have tended to defend the principle in terms of prudence. However, if this weak moral defence is to become fully-fledged it needs to be based on a theory of the good state, not just an account of relations among states in whose goodness we have no great interest.[9]

It has to be said that Vincent himself did not engage in the project of justifying 'the good state'. But it is interesting to note that he continued to believe in the need to do so despite the end of the Cold War, which many believed to be the harbinger of a new international system in which ideological differences between states would disappear. Vincent warned against such complacency. The end of bipolarity does not mean the end of power politics, even if it is difficult to see any challengers to the might of the United States in the short term. Similarly, the end of the ideological competition between capitalism and socialism did not mean the end of ideology per se. In 1990, Vincent observed with some foresight that 'the new shape of the international system looks like the very old nationalist shape but now relatively unconstrained by the export of doctrines . . . of the superpowers'.[10]

In short, Vincent refused to take much comfort from the end of the Cold War in the context of his broader interest in the degree to which the society of states is or is not evolving in a more cosmopolitan direction. But he made an important contribution to the field in arguing (successfully, in my view) that the survival of the existing society of states depends on such progress. In its absence, the rules of international society are little more than a rationalisation of great power dominance. Without international justice, there can be no viable long-term order. Without order, there can be no peaceful progress toward a more just world. Vincent helps us understand that the 'middle way' between 'realism' and 'revolutionism' cannot mediate between them unless it transcends both, and assists in the realisation of a world in which the legitimacy of states in their external relations is inextricably linked to the legitimacy of rule within them. We still have a long way to go to achieve his vision of world order.

Notes

1 Christopher Hill, 'R.J. Vincent (1943–1990)', *Political Studies* 39 (1991), p. 160.
2 Iver B. Neumann, 'John Vincent and the English School of international relations', in Iver B. Neumann and Ole Waever (eds), *The Future of International Relations: Masters in the Making*, London, Routledge, 1997, pp. 39–41.
3 See, in particular, Hedley Bull, *The Anarchical Society*, London, Macmillan, 1977.
4 Alan James, 'System or society?', *Review of International Studies* 19 (1993), p. 284.
5 R. John Vincent, 'The Hobbesian tradition in twentieth century international thought', *Millennium: Journal of International Studies* 10 (1981), p. 94.
6 John Vincent, *Nonintervention and International Order*, Princeton, New Jersey, Princeton University Press, 1974, p. 13.
7 Ibid., pp. 348–9.
8 Neumann, op. cit., pp. 48–55.
9 John Vincent and Peter Wilson, 'Beyond non-intervention', in Ian Forbes and Mark Hoffman (eds), *Political Theory, International Relations, and the Ethics of Intervention*, London, Macmillan, 1993, p. 125.
10 John Vincent, 'The end of the Cold War and the international system', in David Armstrong and Erik Goldstein (eds), *The End of the Cold War*, London, Frank Cass, 1990, p. 199.

See also in this book

Bull, Walzer, Wight

Vincent's major writings

Nonintervention and International Order, Princeton, New Jersey, Princeton University Press, 1974
'Western conceptions of a universal moral order', *British Journal of International Studies* 4 (1978), pp. 20–46
'The Hobbesian tradition in twentieth century

international thought', *Millennium: Journal of International Studies* 10 (1981), pp. 91–101

'Realpolitik', in James Mayall (ed.), *The Community of States*, London, George Allen & Unwin, 1982, pp. 72–83

'Change and international relations', *Review of International Relations* 9 (1983), pp. 63–70

'Edmund Burke and the theory of international relations', *Review of International Studies* 10 (1984), pp. 205–18

Human Rights and International Relations, Cambridge, Cambridge University Press, 1986

Foreign Policy and Human Rights: Issues and Responses, Cambridge, Cambridge University Press, 1986

Order and Violence: Hedley Bull and International Relations (co-editor with J.D.B. Miller), Oxford: Clarendon Press, 1990

'The idea of rights in international ethics', in Terry Nardin and David R. Mapel (eds), *Traditions of International Ethics*, Cambridge, Cambridge University Press, 1993, pp. 250–69

Further reading

Neumann, Iver B., 'John Vincent and the English School of international relations', in Iver B. Neumann and Ole Waever (eds), *The Future of International Relations: Masters in the Making*, London, Routledge, 1997, pp. 38–65. This review contains a complete bibliography of Vincent's publications.

Wheeler, Nicholas J., 'Pluralist or solidarist conceptions of international society: Bull and Vincent on humanitarian intervention,' *Millennium: Journal of International Studies* 21 (1992), pp. 463–88

MICHAEL WALZER

Michael Walzer is best known among students of international relations for his book *Just and Unjust Wars*, first published in 1977 (the second edition appeared in 1992, with a preface on the Gulf War). The book itself emerged out of Walzer's reflections on the Vietnam War, and it represents an ambitious attempt to modernise a very old tradition of thought about the ethical limits to the use of force between states, known as 'just war theory'. The reason for placing Walzer in a category devoted to theorists of international society is that the latter theory provides Walzer with the basic principles and moral limits to restrict the reasons to which states may legitimately appeal in going to war (*jus ad bellum*), as well as restraints to their conduct once war has begun (*jus in bello*). Since the end of the Cold War, Walzer has applied his theory to the issue of humanitarian intervention in the context of intra-state (or civil) wars.

Michael Walzer is one of the leading political theorists of the post-war era and his work in the study of international relations is only part of his broader interest in contemporary political theory. He was born in 1935, in a small steel town, Johnstown, Pennsylvania, and by the age of 12 was publishing his own broadsheet about union strikes and political campaigns. Today, he is co-editor of *Dissent*, the leading magazine of the American left. He is also contributing editor to *The New Republic*. He is a member of the board of governors of the Hebrew University and a trustee of Brandeis, where he received his BA degree. He was a Fulbright Scholar at Cambridge University and also studied and taught at Harvard where he earned his PhD. Since 1980, Walzer has been a permanent member of the faculty of the Institute of Advanced Study in Princeton, New Jersey.

Walzer's first book was in the history of political thought, on the English revolution and puritan radicalism. He moved on to write essays about contemporary issues in American politics during the 1960s, such as political obligation, civil disobedience and conscientious objection during the Vietnam War. *Just and Unjust Wars* can be read as an attempt to mediate between realism and pacifism in evaluating the conduct of war in the modern era. Walzer proceeds first by arguing that statesmen always have some choice over whether or not to go to war and how to fight wars, and then by arguing that we need to resuscitate the Just War Doctrine of the medieval era. His challenge is a formidable one.

The medieval Christian doctrine was intended to define the moral boundaries of war so that one could distinguish between 'just' and 'unjust' wars. War was thus accepted, subject to certain conditions, within the ambit of Christian ethics. According to the intentions of its scholastic founders, from Thomas Aquinas to Francisco de Vitoria, the distinction was intended to help restrict war by obliging the Christian princes to wage only wars that could be justified on solid moral grounds and fought with legitimate means. The entire doctrine was set in the framework of the *respublica christiana* and presupposed the existence of a secure and stable *auctoritas spiritualis*, endowed with international legal power: the Roman Catholic Church. The doctrine was supposed not only to restrict war but also to distinguish the wars waged between Christians from 'feuds' (struggles between princes and peoples such as the Turks, the Arabs and the Jews – all of whom refused to acknowledge the cosmopolitan authority of the Church). The crusades and missionary wars authorised by the Church were *ipso jure* 'just wars', independently of the fact that they were wars of aggression or defence. Any war, however, waged upon Christendom was *ipso facto* an unjust war, in which the enemy was an infidel, an outlaw and a criminal.

Thus the first challenge Walzer sets himself is to establish the foundations of a modern version of just war theory in a secular, modern context. Originally, the Just War theorists elaborated on the rules governing international relations by starting from the idea that all people and nations participate in a world community indirectly ruled by God and directly governed by Natural Law. This outlook laid emphasis on the duties individuals and state had to the social wholes through which they were fulfilled, rather than on the rights each had as an independent equal in relation to other independent equals. Walzer argues that contemporary just war theory must be based on the modern notion of the primacy of individual rights. 'The correct view' is that 'states are neither organic wholes nor mystical unions ... [that] individual rights underlie the most important judgements that we make about war'.[1] In a crucial passage from the book, Walzer justifies the rights of states from a more fundamental concern with human rights as follows:

> The rights of states rest on the consent of their members. But this is consent of a special sort. State rights are not constituted through a series of transfers from individual men and women to the sovereign ... what actually happens ... [is that] over a long period of time, shared experiences and cooperative activity of many different kinds shape a common life ... most states do stand guard over the community of their citizens, at least to some degree: that is why we assume the justice of their defensive wars.[2]

By linking human rights to state rights in this way, Walzer argues that territorial integrity and political sovereignty can be defended in the same way as individual life and liberty. The appeal to human rights is the basis on which Walzer elaborates the ethical limits on the conduct of war once it has begun – limits that impose obligations on both sides, it should be noted. These are primarily concerned with noncombatant immunity and the use of proportionality in the application of force. As for *jus ad bellum*, in addition to the link established between human rights and state rights, Walzer appeals to what he calls the 'legalist paradigm', a set of principles shared by the member states of international society. It consists of six key propositions:

1 There exists an international society of sovereign states.

2 This international society has law that establishes the right of its members – above

all, the rights of territorial integrity and political sovereignty.

3 Any use of force or imminent threat of force by one state against the political sovereignty of another constitutes aggression and is a criminal act.

4 Aggression justifies two kinds of violent response: a war of self-defence by the victim and a war of law enforcement by the victim and any other member of international society.

5 Nothing but aggression can justify war.

6 Once the aggressor state has been militarily repulsed, it can also be punished.[3]

After having defined the rules of his legalist paradigm, Walzer argues for the necessity of their partial violation in light of the defence of state rights on the basis of human rights. Particularly worthy of violation is the fifth rule. In fact, Walzer considers it morally legitimate to launch a military attack against an independent state not only for 'pre-emptive self-defence' but also in order to: (1) support secessionist movements that are fighting for 'national liberation'; (2) balance the intervention of other states in a civil war with a counter-intervention; (3) rescue populations threatened with enslavement or massacre, as in the case of the Indian invasion of Bangladesh.[4]

The second challenge that Walzer tries to meet is the practical difficulties of implementing his version of just war theory in the context of modern warfare. In a spirit of prudence, Walzer candidly admits that nuclear weapons 'explode the theory of just war ... our familiar notions of *jus in bello* require us to condemn even the threat to use them'.[5] A nuclear deterrence strategy that keeps entire civilian populations as permanent hostages defies any conceivable principle of noncombatant immunity. But he maintains that this consequence of our military technology may fall under the category of military necessity and must not obliterate

our adherence to the moral limits on conventional warfare. To discover those limits, Walzer deploys some striking wartime examples that demonstrate why utilitarian arguments (attempting to define the limits by an appeal to a strict economy of violence) fail to explain what we perceive to be the strictness of noncombatant immunity. He then proceeds to show how reflection based on the rights of individuals can make more reasonable and orderly the rules of warfare and how those rules can be recast as military techniques alter. He clarifies the moral significance of modern submarine warfare, blockades and terrorism, as well as guerrilla fighting. The distinctive strengths of Walzer's analysis result from his method of moving back and forth between closely reasoned moral argument and concrete historical cases that illustrate the principles under examination. He narrates over fifty such cases, ranging from Thucydides's story of the dialogue on Melos to the Allied bombing of German cities to My Lai.

In the preface to the second edition of the book, Walzer reflects on the 1991 Gulf War in light of his theory. Overall, he supports the American justification of the war, although he criticises some of the rhetoric from the Bush administration on the imminence of a 'new world order' after the end of the Cold War, as well as the idea that the Gulf War was some kind of victory for democracy. Walzer believes that the United States and its allies were right not to march on Baghdad once Kuwait's sovereignty was restored. Consistent with his communitarianism, Walzer points out that liberation from the tyranny of Saddam Hussein is not an American responsibility. It is up to the citizens of Iraq, and those in Kuwait also, to rid themselves of despotic rule. In Walzer's view, Saddam Hussein's genocide against the Kurds and the Shiite Muslims in Iraq does not make him comparable to Pol Pot or Idi Amin. As for the conduct of the war, Walzer condemns the policy of destroying the infrastructure of Iraq, which he argues failed to distinguish adequately between military and civilian targets. He also criticises the air attacks on fleeing Iraqi soldiers at the end of the war, since the soldiers no longer posed a real threat to American or other allied troops. As for those who condemned United States' policy as a 'war for oil', Walzer acknowledges the existence of mixed motives in the minds of statesmen, but he adds that the selectivity of US policy against aggression is not a good reason to abandon the theory.

> It would be a good thing, obviously, if every act of aggression were condemned by the UN and then resisted . . . by a coalition of states. But this is no reason to oppose [a particular] resistance – as if, having failed to rescue the Tibetans, we must now fail to rescue the Kuwaitis, for the sake of moral consistency. States [are] unreliable agents, and that is why the argument about war and justice is still a political and moral necessity.[6]

Before considering a couple of major criticisms of Walzer's attempt to 'recapture the just war for moral and political theory', two aspects of his approach should be noted.

First, in terms of method, Walzer is committed to what he refers to as 'the path of interpretation' or 'social criticism' in moral philosophy, as opposed to the path of 'discovery' (as in some versions of moral realism) or 'invention' (strict contractarianism). For Walzer, the best approach to moral philosophy is to engage in a dialectical conversation with the moral codes that inform our existing obligations and conduct. Arguments in moral philosophy are interpretations of the morality that exists in society (domestic or international), and the art of social criticism is to reveal the gaps between our conduct and the ideals that we acknowledge ought to govern our conduct. As he wrote in 1987,

> What we do when we argue is to give an account of the actually existing morality.

That morality is authoritative for us because it is only by virtue of its existence that we exist as the moral beings we are. Our categories, relationships, commitments and aspirations are all shaped by, expressed in terms of, the existing morality.[7]

Second, Walzer is committed to a project of reconciling our commitment to universal rights based on abstract principles of what it means to be a human being with our commitment to particular rights and social goods that vary across particular cultures and issue-areas. In this sense, Walzer is a liberal communitarian.

Both sets of commitments are evident in *Just and Unjust Wars*, but they are best illustrated by reference to two later books. For example, *Spheres of Justice* (1983) is a sophisticated argument for a communalist and pluralistic liberalism. Walzer argues for what he calls 'complex' as opposed to 'simple' equality, that is, a notion of distributive justice based on different rules of distribution for different social goods, rather than one rule requiring equal holdings of everything for everyone. Politics, the economy, the family and the workplace are each different 'spheres' having different principles of distribution. The requirement of justice is that the integrity of each sphere should be maintained against encroachment from the others and, most obviously, that the polity or the family should not be corrupted by the dominance of money. In an implicit critique of John Rawls and other neo-Kantians, Walzer asserts that the various principles of justice in each sphere are local rather than universal: principles of justice should be based only on the latent communal understandings of a particular population with a historical identity.

Similarly, in his most recent book *Thick and Thin: Moral Argument at Home and Abroad* (1994), Walzer claims that all moral terms such as 'truth' and 'justice' have meanings that can understood through 'thick' (local) and 'thin' (universal) accounts. The

165

context and purpose of the argument decide the appropriate use of the moral term. Although Walzer claims that he has always supported the notion of plurality and 'difference', he does not want to give credence to the idea that different cultures are incommensurable or their differences insurmountable. Differences between fundamentally dissimilar cultures can be reconciled through the use of commonalities. Although he believes that we can no longer develop foundational theories of human rights, for example, that aim at identifying universal cultural values, his *liberal* communitarianism is dependent on a certain form of 'iterated universalism' that he sees substantiated in his notion of 'moral minimalism'. The function of the latter is to facilitate a unity, a sense of solidarity between cultures whose 'thick' morality may be very different. Moral arguments directed towards other cultures appeal to ideas that have thin meanings. Thin ideas, in turn, constitute commonalities that are embedded in thick, particularistic, meanings. For this reason such commonalities are only revealed on 'special occasions' – in moments of crisis when there is a need to unite against a common enemy. Thus Americans could sympathise with Chinese students in Tiananmen Square when they marched with placards demanding 'freedom' and 'democracy'. The value of minimalism is that it engages disparate people, or cultures, in sharing like experiences. On the other hand, it would be quite wrong to assume that there is only one model of democracy that can be exported around the world. The specific reasons that provoked the demonstrations in China are rooted in a set of values stemming from the marchers' own particularistic thick morality.

In the 1990s, one of Walzer's greatest concerns is the move to reassert local and particularistic identities, especially in Eastern Europe and the former Soviet Union. What he calls 'the return of the tribes' has meant the return of tribal wars, such as in Bosnia. Citing fear of conquest and oppression as the primary reason for such conflicts, Walzer suggests the creation of 'protected spaces' as a way of giving the different tribes the right to 'self-determination'. He is ambivalent about the scope of this right in the post-Cold War era. He supports the idea of separation as long as it agrees with the popular will of the people, but he also acknowledges that the creation of one nation-state often means the oppression of another nation's independence. Underlying the 'thin' principle of self-determination is the belief that all nations ought to be allowed to govern themselves according to their own political needs. On the other hand, as a minimalist universal idea, it does not offer criteria for evaluating how such self-government should be implemented in particular political and cultural contexts. Rather than legislate on this issue, Walzer argues that there can be no single model, either of 'self-determination' or of 'democracy'. Tribalism must be accommodated in a variety of ways that cannot be determined in advance.

Walzer's work on just war theory, self-determination and humanitarian intervention, the Gulf War and his broader approach to political theory has been widely discussed and debated. For students of international relations, two major criticisms of Walzer are worth noting. First, he has been accused of failing to integrate domestic and international relations within a single theory of justice that would include principles of redistribution across borders, not merely within them. However, Walzer's communitarian beliefs prevent him from saying much about issues of global poverty and other problems of international inequality:

> The only plausible alternative to the political community is humanity itself, the society of nations, the entire globe. But were we to take the globe as our setting, we would have to imagine what does not yet exist: a community that included all men and women everywhere. We would

have to invent a set of common meanings for these people, avoiding if we could the stipulation of our own values.[8]

Naturally, this position has been roundly criticised by cosmopolitan critics, who have accused Walzer of privileging the nation-state, not just as a legal 'community', but also as a moral one.[9] Second, there is a tension in *Just and Unjust Wars* arising from Walzer's appeal to human rights as the basis of the war convention regarding *jus in bello*, and his appeal to the legalist paradigm in limiting the right to go to war for the purpose of self-defence. The latter imposes strict limits on the scope of justifiable intervention into the affairs of another state. Walzer tries hard to minimise the danger of moral crusades by conceding that the society of states is less analogous to domestic society than the older Just War theorists claimed; its rules call for even greater prudence in their enforcement. This is why he argues that the exceptions to the rule of nonintervention must be seen as exceptions, justified only when it can be demonstrated clearly that there is no 'fit', as he puts it, between a government and its people. Otherwise, we must err on the side of caution. However, by appealing to human rights as the basis of the war convention regarding the use of force once war has begun, and by conceding exceptions to the rule of nonintervention on grounds of human rights, Walzer creates problems for himself.

If the legitimacy and sovereignty of states 'derives ultimately from the rights of individuals', and if there is no precise way of determining a threshold beyond which legitimacy is lost, then it ought to follow that to the degree that a state violates human rights, it loses both its legitimacy and its sovereign rights, including the right to be protected by the principle of non-intervention: the grosser the violation, the weaker the claim to such protection ... *morally* speaking, one could always *consider* [intervention] as a possible remedy.[10]

Without elaborating on this argument in detail, it remains unclear that Walzer's attempt to ground the rights of state on the basis of human right succeeds in reconciling the ethics of the legalist paradigm with the cosmopolitan ethics of its critics. Despite these problems, Michael Walzer's attempt to modernise Just War theory remains one of the most important contributions to normative international theory.

Notes

1 Michael Walzer, *Just and Unjust Wars: A Moral Argument with Historical Illustrations*, Second edition, New York, Basic Books, 1992, pp. 53–4.
2 Ibid.
3 Ibid., pp. 61–2.
4 Ibid., pp. 86–108.
5 Ibid., p. 14.
6 Ibid., p. xxiii.
7 Michael Walzer, *Interpretation and Social Criticism*, Cambridge, Massachusetts, Harvard University Press, 1987, p. 21.
8 Michael Walzer, *Spheres of Justice: A Defense of Pluralism and Equality*, New York, Basic Books, 1983, pp. 29–30.
9 See, in particular, Michael Howard, 'Walzer's socialism', *Social Theory and Practice* 12 (1986), pp. 103–13.
10 Jerome Slater and Terry Nardin, 'Nonintervention and human rights', *The Journal of Politics* 48 (1986), p. 92.

See also in this book

Beitz, Nardin

Walzer's major writings

The Revolution of the Saints: A Study in the Origins of Radical Politics, Cambridge, Massachusetts, Harvard University Press, 1965
Obligations: Essays on Disobedience, War, and Citizenship, Cambridge, Massachusetts, Harvard University Press, 1970
Just and Unjust Wars: A Moral Argument with Historical Illustrations, Second edition, New York, Basic Books, 1992
Radical Principles: Reflections of an Unreconstructed Democrat, New York, Basic Books, 1980
'The moral standing of states: a response to four

critics', *Philosophy and Public Affairs* 9 (1980), pp. 209–29

Spheres of Justice: A Defense of Pluralism and Equality, New York, Basic Books, 1983

Interpretation and Social Criticism, Cambridge, Massachusetts, Harvard University Press, 1987

The Company of Critics: Social Criticism and Political Commitment in the Twentieth Century, New York, Basic Books, 1988

'The idea of civil society: a path to social reconstruction', *Dissent* 38 (1991), pp. 293–304

'The new tribalism: notes on a difficult problem', *Dissent* 39 (1992), pp. 164–71

Thick and Thin: Moral Argument at Home and Abroad, Notre Dame, University of Notre Dame Press, 1994

Further reading

Beitz, Charles, *Political Theory and International Relations*, Princeton, New Jersey, Princeton University Press, 1979

Beitz, C., 'Non-intervention and community integrity', *Philosophy and Public Affairs* 9 (1980), pp. 385–91

Brown, Chris, *International Relations Theory: New Normative Approaches*, Brighton, Harvester Wheatsheaf, 1992

Bull, Hedley, 'Recapturing the just war for political theory', *World Politics* 31 (1978), pp. 588–99

Donelan, Michael, 'Reason in war', *Review of International Studies* 8 (1982), pp. 53–68

Doppelt, Gerald, 'Walzer's theory of morality in international relations', *Philosophy and Public Affairs* 8 (1978), pp. 3–26

Doppelt, Gerald, 'Statism without foundations', in *Philosophy and Public Affairs* 9 (1980), pp. 98–403. Also reprinted in Charles R. Beitz, Marshall Cohen, Thomas Scanlon and A. John Simmons (eds), *International Ethics: A Philosophy and Public Affairs Reader*, Princeton, New Jersey, Princeton University Press, 1985, pp. 238–43

Galston, William, 'Community, democracy, philosophy: the political thought of Michael Walzer', *Political Theory* 17 (1989), pp. 119–30

Luban, David, 'Just war and human rights', *Philosophy and Public Affairs* 9 (1980), pp. 160–81

Luban, David, 'The romance of the nation-state', *Philosophy and Public Affairs* 9 (1980), pp. 392–7. Also reprinted in Charles R. Beitz, Marshall Cohen, Thomas Scanlon and A. John Simmons (eds), *International Ethics: A Philosophy and Public Affairs Reader*, Princeton, New Jersey, Princeton University Press, 1985, pp. 238–43

Miller, David, and Walzer, Michael (eds), *Pluralism, Justice, Equality*, Oxford, Oxford University Press, 1995

Warnke, G., *Justice and Interpretation*, Cambridge, Polity Press, 1992

Welch, David, *Justice and the Genesis of War*, Cambridge, Cambridge University Press, 1993

MARTIN WIGHT

Martin Wight (1917–72) was the leading theorist of what has become known as 'the English School' in the study of international relations. Wight himself published very little in his own lifetime. As Hedley Bull notes, '[h]is writings ... comprise one sixty-eight page pamphlet, published in 1946 by Chatham House for one shilling and long out of print, and half a dozen chapters in books and articles'.[1] Most of his work was published posthumously by his wife Gabriele, with the assistance of the late Hedley Bull and, after his own death, Brian Porter. This includes his three major books *Systems of States* (1977), *Power Politics* (1978) and *International Theory: The Three Traditions* (1991). The third book in the series consists of Wight's famous lectures delivered in the 1960s to his undergraduate students at the London School of Economics, where Martin Wight spent most of his academic career. He also taught for a short time at the University of Sussex in the early 1960s, but he will mostly be remembered for the influence he had on colleagues and students at the LSE.

In the late 1950s Wight played a leading role in setting up the British Committee on the Theory of International Politics with the noted English historian Herbert Butterfield. In 1966, the Committee published *Diplomatic Investigations,* in which Wight wrote one of his most influential articles entitled 'Why is there no international theory?' His argument (fully fleshed out in the lectures published in 1991) was based on the proposition that 'the most fundamental question you can ask in international theory is, what is international society?, just as the central question in political theory is, what is a state?'.[2] This assertion rested on his belief that 'if political theory is the tradition of speculation about the state, then international theory may be supposed to be a tradition of speculation about the society of states, or the family of nations, or the international community'.[3]

Having posed the central question, Wight went on to argue that international theory 'is marked, not only by paucity but also by intellectual and oral poverty'. There simply were no international equivalents in the Western tradition to the corpus of texts by Plato, Hobbes, Locke, Mill and Rousseau. The reason for this is double-edged, according to Wight. On the one hand, Western political theorists have traditionally focused almost exclusively on the state as the site of progress and the 'consummation of political experience'. On the other hand, Wight also notes:

A kind of recalcitrance of international politics to being theorised about. The reason for this is that the theorising has to be done in the language of political theory and law. But this is appropriate to man's control of his social life ... international theory is the theory of survival.[4]

Thus, there is no self-contained body of international theory as Wight conceives it. Instead, he distinguishes between three very broad historical *traditions* of thought, 'as embodied in and handed down by writers and statesmen'. Before briefly looking at these in terms of how and why they answer the central question of international theory, it should be noted that Wight is extremely careful to emphasise just how broadly his typology is constructed in order to cover and simplify a vast range of philosophical, legal and historical literature, as well as to codify an analogous range of political practice:

If we speak of these three types of inter-

national theory as patterns of thought we approach them from a philosophical standpoint. We shall be likely to note the ... logical coherence of the complex of thought and how acceptance of any one unit-idea is likely to entail logically most of the others, so that the whole is capable of being a system of political philosophy. If we speak of them as traditions of thought ... we are likely to notice illogicalities and discontinuities because exigencies of political life often override logic. We shall find all kinds of intermediate positions.[5]

With this caveat firmly stated, Wight articulated the distinguishing characteristics of what have come to be known as the three Rs – Realism, Rationalism and Revolutionism – in terms of how and why they answer the central question.

At one extreme is Realism. According to this tradition, international society is a contradiction in terms. In the absence of a contract between states, they are in a pre-societal state of nature. As between individuals, this is a state of war. Wedded to Hobbesian assumptions, this tradition views international politics as a zero-sum struggle for power, and peace as the fragile outcome of mutual insecurity and existential deterrence. The state is the highest form of political authority, and its interests preclude embodying any consideration for those of other states, apart from that dictated by prudence and the rational pursuit of egoistic self-interest in a hostile environment. International politics is the perpetual realm of violence, survival and strategic necessity.

At the opposite extreme lies Revolutionism, a tradition whose classical forebears are Dante and Kant. This tradition teleologically posits an international society of humankind, prevented from its full realisation by the epiphenomenal states system, whose pathological dynamics are contrary to the real interests of the true members of that society. Conceding Realism's scepticism regarding an international society of states, the Revolutionist tradition of thought and action is wedded to a perfectionist view of humankind in a historically contingent process of struggle towards the *civitas maximum*. Rather than surrendering to, or morally glorifying, the necessities of survival in a self-help system, Revolutionists demand that it be radically revised. 'Hence the belief, common in varying degrees to the Huguenots, the Jacobins, Mazzini, President Wilson and the Communists, that the whole of diplomatic history has groaned and travailed until now, and that the community of [humankind], like the kingdom of God ... is at hand.'[6] As these illustrations demonstrate, neither the precise political arrangement of the future, nor the means of transforming the present one, are determined *a priori*. There are as many different routes to salvation as there are justifications for its necessity. What unites Revolutionists of every stripe is their rejection of the existing political system and their demand for its radical overhaul.

If Wight's distinction between Realism and Revolutionism has much in common with E.H. Carr's earlier presentation of realism and utopianism, he differed from Carr in asserting the existence of a third tradition of thought that Carr had allegedly ignored. Wight argued that what he called the Rationalist tradition lies between the two extremes of Realism and Revolutionism, and it is defined against them. It is informed by the metaphysics of Locke and Hume rather than Hobbes or Kant. Adherents to this tradition argue that the precontractual state of nature is neither substantively chaotic nor blissful, and that both the above traditions err by postulating human nature in atomistic terms, whose social behaviour is determined by a static and asocial 'nature'. Rather, human beings must be understood as social animals, in continual interaction with others. Forms of social life, at any level of human aggregation, are best understood by tracing the historical evolution of their customs and norms. As articulated in and codified through authoritative, societal institutions of governance, these provide the principles of conduct through which societies are regulated by the reciprocal rights and obligations of their constituent members.

For Wight, therefore, the absence of a world state, and the coexistence of a plurality of sovereign states, do not necessarily condemn international politics to a state of war and render meaningless the notion of an international society. Nor is anarchy a barrier to social and economic intercourse among its members. However, it must be understood as a unique society, whose autonomy severely weakens appeals to the 'domestic analogy' in understanding its basic characteristics and dynamics.

Martin Wight's 'trialectic' of international thought is extremely eclectic, not simply because of his refusal to delineate these 'traditions' with any philosophic or analytic precision, but also because of his deep personal reluctance either to transcend them or to locate his own views consistently within the parameters of any single one. Timothy Dunne, in his excellent review of the 'English School', notes that in Martin Wight's early work on international politics, particularly his book *Power Politics*, 'there was no dialectic in Martin Wight's realism, only power. The early writings of Wight betray a tragic view of the inevitability of power politics untouched by human will.'[7] Later in his life, however, he confessed greater sympathy for the rationalist tradition, although he always refused to categorise himself as a rationalist. 'When I scrutinise my own psyche', he once wrote, 'I seem to find all these three ways of thought within me.'[8] One reason for this is that, according to Wight, each of the traditions was a codification of one of three sociological conditions that constituted the subject matter of international relations. These were *international anarchy*, understood as the absence of government in an international system of sovereign states; *habitual intercourse*, apparent in the practice of diplomacy, international law and other institutionalised forms of interdependence; and *moral solidarity*, or the latent community of humankind, the global society of men and women which lies behind the legal fiction of statehood. In his lectures to students, the three traditions were a superb set of pedagogical tools with which to organise the discussion of war, national interests, diplomacy, the balance of power and international law. As very loose 'traditions', no single great writer on international relations could be classified safely within one of them, and Wight was aware that different elements of the traditions coexisted not only within himself, but others as well. Furthermore, it was possible, although somewhat self-defeating, to draw distinctions within each tradition. Thus one could distinguish between 'soft' Revolutionists, such as Kant, and 'hard' revolutionists, such as Lenin. He also described pacifism as a form of 'inverted revolutionism', an acknowledgement of the world as the realists described it combined with a stubborn refusal to participate in power politics.

It is difficult to evaluate Martin Wight's work. On the one hand, he must be acknowledged as one of the founding fathers of the view that realism and idealism (popularised in the work of Carr, Morgenthau and Herz, among others) did not exhaust the history of international thought, and that rationalism (sometimes known as the 'Grotian' school) deserved to be taken seriously in its own right. Certainly, this view has been shared by many scholars whom Wight inspired in the 1950s and 1960s, particularly Hedley Bull. In his masterly analysis of the discipline, Steve Smith identifies Wight's three categories as one of the ten most influential 'self-images' of the discipline in the twentieth century.[9]

On the other hand, Wight's work is not without its problems, and two in particular are worth noting. First, there has been a great deal of debate over the epistemological status of the three traditions. There are, after all, many ways to subdivide the discipline of international relations. Carr suggests two schools of thought, Wight expanded this to three, James Mayall employs five, and Nardin and Mapel divide the field of international ethics among no less than twelve traditions of enquiry.[10] What makes Wight's system of classification more useful than others, particularly if the categories keep breaking down and if, as Wight clarifies in his lectures, it is wrong to force particular thinkers into one exclusive tradition? In his critique of the entire 'English School', Roy Jones points out that

> [I]f the three R's do denote modes of perception, comprehension, and action, from what, or where, do they spring? If they issue from the mind of Martin Wight are they not open to radical revision? There was more than one side to Machiavelli after all. Could it be that Wight's scheme had some metaphysical significance? ... To do political theory is a first order activity, it is not simply classifying and commenting on the actions and dicta of statesmen and others.[11]

In other words, in the absence of any attempt to defend the metaphysical significance of the three Rs, it is not clear why they should be of much help to anyone not endowed with Wight's own ability to employ them with such historical subtlety and erudition. Wight himself was pessimistic about our ability to transcend the three Rs or about the ability of one of them to triumph over the other two, but he was reluctant to defend this position explicitly.

A second problem with Martin Wight's work is that despite his interest in normative questions in the study of international relations, the very way in which he defined the field foreclosed the possibility of bringing it into the broader arena of Western political theory. Chris Brown makes this point very cleary in his excellent text *International Theory: New Normative Approaches*. He claims that Wight's characterisation of politics mixes up two analytically separate concerns. The first is the nature of justice and the second is the organisation of the state.[12] If we were to study international justice through the lens of Western political theory, and invoke Western theoretical categories to illuminate its meaning and organisational implications, the three Rs would have to give way to a more illuminating discourse between communitarian and cosmopolitan visions of world order. By defining political theory in a particularly misleading way, Wight cut himself off from the sources of inspiration to shed light on the normative dilemmas of war, state sovereignty and the maldistribution of global wealth.

Despite these problems, Martin Wight still deserves to be read as someone who has written widely about the cultural and moral dimensions of international relations, and his work is a constant reminder that what may appear to be new disputes in the field about contemporary issues are in fact extensions and manifestations of very old arguments, albeit couched in a different idiom.

Notes

1 Hedley Bull, 'Martin Wight and the theory of international relations', *British Journal of International Studies* 2 (1976), p. 101.
2 Martin Wight, 'An anatomy of International thought', *Review of International Studies* 13 (1987), p. 222.
3 Martin Wight, 'Why is there no international theory?', in Martin Wight and Herbert Butterfield (eds), *Diplomatic Investigations: Essays in the Theory of International Politics*, London, Allen & Unwin, 1966, p. 18. See also p. 260 of *International Theory: The Three Traditions,* in which Wight declares that the traditions 'are not like three railroad tracks running into infinity. They are not philosophically constant and pure. . . . They are, to vary the metaphor, interwoven in the tapestry of Western civilisation. They both influence and cross-fertilise one another, and they change, although without, I think, losing their inner identity.'
4 Ibid., p. 33.
5 Martin Wight, 'An anatomy of international thought', op. cit., p. 226.
6 Martin Wight. 'Western values in international relations', in Martin Wight and Herbert Butterfield (eds), *Diplomatic Investigations: Essays in the Theory of International Politics*, London, Allen & Unwin, 1966, p. 94.
7 Timothy Dunne, 'International society: theoretical promises fulfilled?', *Cooperation and Conflict* 30 (1995), p. 130.
8 Martin Wight, 'An anatomy of international thought', op. cit., p. 227.
9 Steve Smith, 'The self-images of a discipline: a genealogy of international relations theory', in Ken Booth and Steve Smith (eds), *International Relations Theory Today*, Cambridge, Polity Press, pp. 1–38.
10 Michael Donelan, *Elements of International Political Theory*, Oxford, Clarendon Press, 1990; Terry Nardin and David Mapel (eds), *Traditions of International Ethics*, Cambridge, Cambridge University Press, 1992.
11 Roy Jones, 'The English School of International Relations: a case for closure', *Review of International Studies* 7 (1981), p. 10.
12 See Chris Brown, *International Theory: New Normative Approaches*, Hemel Hempstead, Harvester Wheatsheaf, 1992.

See also in this book

Bull, Carr, Nardin

Wight's major writings

British Colonial Constitutions, Oxford, Clarendon Press, 1952
'Why is there no international theory?', in Martin Wight and Herbert Butterfield (eds), *Diplomatic Investigations: Essays in the Theory of International Politics*, London, Allen & Unwin, 1966, pp. 1–33
'Western values in international relations', in Martin Wight and Herbert Butterfield (eds), *Diplomatic Investigations: Essays in the Theory of International Politics*, London, Allen & Unwin, 1966, pp. 89–131
'The balance of power and international order', in Alan James (ed.), *The Bases of International Order: Essays in Honour of C.A.W. Manning*, Oxford, Oxford University Press, 1973, pp. 85–115
Systems of States, London, Leicester University Press, 1977
Power Politics, Harmondsworth, Penguin, 1978
'An anatomy of international thought', *Review of International Studies* 13 (1987), pp. 221–7
International Theory: The Three Traditions, London, Leicester University Press, 1991

Further reading

Bull, Hedley, 'Martin Wight and the theory of international relations', *British Journal of International Studies* 2 (1976), pp. 101–16. Reprinted in Martin Wight, *International Theory: The Three Traditions*, London, Leicester University Press, 1991, pp. xi–xxiii

Dunne, Timothy, *Inventing International Society: A History of the English School*, New York, St Martin's Press, 1998

Grader, Sheila, 'The English School of International Relations: evidence and evaluation', *Review of International Studies* 14 (1988), pp. 29–44

Hassner, Pierre, 'Beyond the three traditions: the philosophy of war and peace in historical perspective', *International Affairs* 70 (1994), pp. 737–56

Jackson, Robert H., 'Martin Wight, international theory and the good life', *Millennium: Journal of International Studies* 19 (1990), pp. 261–72

Jones, Roy, 'The English School of International Relations: a case for closure', *Review of International Studies* 7 (1981), pp. 1–13

Nicholson, Michael, 'The enigma of Martin Wight', *Review of International Studies* 7 (1981), pp. 15–22

Porter, Brian, 'Patterns of thought and practice: Martin Wight's international theory', in Michael Donelan (ed.), *The Reason of States: A Study in International Political Theory,* London, Allen & Unwin, 1978, pp. 64–74

Wilson, Peter, 'The English School of International Relations', *Review of International Studies* 15 (1989), pp. 49–58

Yost, David, 'Political philosophy and the theory of international relations', *International Affairs* 70 (1994), pp. 263–90

INTERNATIONAL ORGANISATION

This group of thinkers shed light on the ways in which international relations is regulated by organisations and practices of co-operation among states. Karl Deutsch, David Mitrany and Ernst Haas are students of integration, particularly in the context of European experiments with supranational co-operation in the form of the European Community. Mitrany introduced the idea of 'functionalism' to the study of international relations, arguing that the growth of international trade and interdependence weakens the power of the sovereign state, which he thinks is a good thing. Haas is less convinced that functional regulation will proceed in the absence of political coordination among state elites, and he examines the political processes that promote and impede supranationalism. Karl Deutsch is responsible for the term 'security community' to describe the framework of relations among states in particular regions. John Ruggie and Robert Keohane are students of international organisation in the broadest sense. For them, investigating the various organisational forms that populate the international arena requires a wider focus than the study of particular formal institutions such as the United Nations or the International Monetary Fund. Ruggie's work focuses on the practice of multilateralism in the post-1945 era. He argues that it is a complex organisational form of international governance that modifies the simplistic image of the Cold War as a bipolar struggle for power between the United States and the Soviet Union. Keohane's work focuses on the organisational implications of economic interdependence among states and the conditions that facilitate the establishment and maintenance of co-operative 'regimes'. Finally, Alexander Wendt argues that the study of international organisation is limited within the confines of realist and liberal frameworks of analysis. He offers a 'constructivist' framework, which pays particular attention to the ways in which states and the international system co-constitute each other.

KARL W. DEUTSCH

Karl Deutsch was born in Prague, Czechoslovakia, in 1912. He was raised there and went to school at the German *Staatsrealgymnasium*, where he graduated with High Honours. In 1934, he took his first degree at the Deutsche Universitat in Prague, but his graduate work was interrupted by his student activism against Nazi groups in the university. Eventually he received his doctorate in law from the Czech-national Charles University in 1938. In the same year he married and went on holiday to the United States. Although he did not intend to stay there long, after the Munich agreement, he thought it wise not to return and settled in the United States as a resident. His hatred of fascism and an enduring fascination with nationalist intolerance was to influence much of his later academic work.

In 1939 Deutsch received a student-funded scholarship for refugees from Nazism, and he enrolled for more graduate study at Harvard University. After playing a major role in the war years as an advocate of the Free Czechoslovak movement and also as a member of the International Secretariat of the San Francisco Conference of 1945 (that established the United Nations as a successor to the League of Nations), he began teaching at the Massachusetts Institute of Technology. In 1951, Deutsch's doctoral dissertation, entitled *Nationalism and Social Communication*, was awarded Harvard's prestigious Sumner Prize, and it was published two years later to great acclaim. He became Professor of History at MIT in 1952 and embarked on a long career devoted mainly to the study of political integration. At the Center for Research on World Political Institutions, he co-operated with a number of colleagues in an inter-disciplinary, collaborative project, which led to the publication of *Political Community and the North Atlantic Area* in 1957. He was awarded a Guggenheim Fellowship in 1955 and taught at the University of Chicago as a visiting professor. In 1958 Deutsch was appointed Professor of Political Science at Yale University. There he completed (with Lewis J. Edinger) *Germany Rejoins the Powers*. This work used data on public opinion, the background of elites and economics to study the post-war progress of the Federal Republic. Whilst at Yale, Deutsch was also very active in setting up the Yale Political Data Program to develop quantitative indicators to test theories and propositions in political science. In addition, he organised the Yale Arms Control Project to examine disarmament and arms control.

In 1967, Deutsch returned to Harvard University as Stanfield Professor of International Peace in 1971, where he remained until his death in 1993. Whilst Harvard was his base, he also taught widely in the United States and Europe, particularly in France and Germany. The political scientist Samual Beer remembered him as follows:

> He was a reformer, but not a utopian. He did not jump to conclusions. His soaring ambitions for humanity were disciplined by an abiding sense of the difficulties of social engineering. His idealism was joined with his commitment to science in general and social science in particular. His work was concerned not only with the ends to be pursued, but also especially with the means, the institutional and practical means, of approaching those ends. Ardent internationalist though he was, he did not delude himself into thinking there was such a thing as the 'body politic' of mankind.[1]

Deutsch is perhaps best known for his work on social prerequisites and dynamics of nationalism and regional integration, as well as his rigorous application of behavioural methods to study processes of social mobilisation at the domestic and international levels. Social mobilisation refers to a process of change which affects substantial parts of the population in countries that are undergoing rapid modernisation. He was concerned to develop empirical quantitative indicators of such change, so that propositions regarding its political consequences could be tested for their validity across time and space.[2] He proposed a model of nationalism based upon the idea that it was fuelled by the need for the state to manage processes of mobilisation that were, by definition, quite traumatic for citizens who were both uprooted from old settings, habits and commitments, and mobilised into new patterns of group membership and organisational behaviour.

Social mobilisation, when it emerges on a large scale, tends to politicise increasing numbers of citizens and increases the range of human needs that the state must respond to. For example, people need provisions for housing and employment, for social security, medical care and insurance against unpredictable changes in employment patterns. For poorer countries undergoing massive change, governments based on traditional sources of authority and legitimation were unable to 'steer' the process successfully. Deutsch believed that only strong, modern nation-states could do so:

> [The nation-state] offers most of its members a stronger sense of security, belonging or affiliation, and even personal identity, than does any alternative large group. [The] greater the need of the people for such affiliation and identity under the strains and shocks of social mobilisation and alienation from earlier familiar environments, the greater becomes the potential power of the nation-state to channel both their longings and resentments and to direct their love and hate.[3]

Deutsch also studied the international conditions that might affect whether a state would channel its citizens' energies toward the outside world. In this context he was a pioneer in the study of regional integration and he introduced greater complexity into the usually sharp dichotomy between hierarchical authority relations at the domestic level and anarchical struggles for power and security at the international level. Whereas this realist image suggests that the solution to the problem of war in international relations is some form of world government, Deutsch undermined the conventional wisdom on the basis of his examination of relations among states in the North Atlantic area in the 1950s and 1960s.

He made a clear distinction between *amalgamation* and *integration*. An amalgamated community has one supreme decision-making centre, but it does not follow that its opposite is mere anarchy. Deutsch pointed out that it is possible to have a number of legally sovereign states who relate to each other in the form of a 'pluralistic security community' and are confident that the chances of force being used to resolve conflicts between them was extremely low. In other words, they are sufficiently 'integrated' to resemble an amalgamated security community without the need to transfer sovereignty to a supranational level. He argued that the anarchy/hierarchy distinction should not be thought of as dichotomy, but rather as a spectrum. 'Integration and amalgamation overlap, but not completely . . . there can be amalgamation without integration [i.e. civil war], and . . . integration without amalgamation [i.e. international peace].'[4] Thus rather than attempt to impose amalgamation at the international level as the preferred route to peace, he suggested that it might be better to seek the establishment of 'pluralistic security communities'.

Of crucial significance to this project is Deutsch's idea of the 'transaction–integration balance'. The growth of transactions among people does not automatically lead to greater integration. Consistent with his earlier work on social mobilisation, Deutsch pointed out that 'it is the volume of transactions, political, cultural, or economic, which throws a *burden* upon the institutions for peaceful adjustment or change among the participating populations'. As the volume of mutual transactions increases, the opportunities for violent conflict also increase. Thus, a crucial concern in the quest for peace is 'the race between the growing rate of transactions among populations in particular areas and the growth of integrative institutions and practices among them'. Sovereign governments may have integrative capabilities, but they are also the source of political and other transactions that may be disintegrative. So amalgamation can in fact hamper integration, and amalgamated control may itself be a danger to peace and a cause of conflict.[5]

Within a regional context, the use of the term security community has two specific meanings. In the first instance, the community of states is able to intervene through diplomatic techniques or mechanisms to prevent a forcible settlement of conflicts among its own members. The second requirement is the ability of the community to present a common military front collectively against an external actor or set of actors. There are also several fundamental assumptions or criteria that are relevant to the emergence of a security community. For example, whatever regional organisation exists, it must possess sufficient institutional maturity to generate the diplomatic techniques deployed to diffuse problems and crises. Furthermore, such maturity must have been accompanied by the mutual willingness among member states to resolve their differences at the organisational level. Indeed, mutually benign expectations of member states must be clearly matched by a discernible pattern of interaction or reciprocity. And finally, states in a security community must have a common perception of threat regarding external actors.[6]

Arendt Lijphart claims that Deutsch's work represents a major challenge to the traditional realist image of international relations, undermining its core assumptions of states as unified rational actors in world affairs and questioning the idea that inter-national relations are best understood in terms of the sharp dichotomy between domestic/international relations.[7] He believes that Deutsch was part of a 'Grotian' revival in the discipline, one that saw anarchy not as an independent variable, but as a possible outcome in a complex system that itself needs to be carefully studied to determine the conditions under which war is most likely to occur.

Deutsch was a pioneer of the study of *cybernetics* in international relations, which focuses on communication and control in political systems. His book *The Nerves of Government* (1966) was an attempt to describe the conditions under which decision-making systems were able to 'steer' flows of information, and he also provided a theoretical basis on which to measure the ratio between internal and external communication as an indicator of the degree to which states were prone to self-closure and self-preoccupation.

As part of his substantive contribution to the development of international theory, Deutsch has to be acknowledged a firm supporter of the 'behavioural' revolution in the discipline that caused so much debate in the 1950s and 1960s, particularly in Britain. He was always concerned to substitute quantitative data for vague hypotheses based on historical or ideological interpretation, and part of his contribution to the discipline lay in the establishment of complex data banks to promote empirical theory in comparative politics and international relations. He played a major role in establishing the Yale Political Data Program to develop quantitative indicators that could help test significant propositions and theories in social science. Deutsch firmly believed that, in order to develop the study of international relations as a scientific enterprise, students would have to access aggregate data and be able to employ sophisticated mathematical analysis in order to generate valid propositions that could be replicated by others in the field.

A good example of the use of such analysis can be found in his article (co-authored by J. David Singer) on balance of power systems in world politics. Here he employed sophisticated mathematical techniques to help determine the stability of international systems composed of varying numbers of great powers, concluding that a multipolar system composed of at least five great powers was historically more stable than those which contained fewer great powers but were prone to structural instability. This is because, on the basis of chance alone, a four-to-one coalition rather than a three-to-two coalition is likely to occur at some point, and such overwhelming strength in one coalition of great powers is likely to lead to the destruction of the system. The analysis explicitly modelled the impact of arms races upon the stability of the international system and is a good illustration of the benefits of quantitative data when used by scholars who are also sophisticated historians in their own right. However, Deutsch did not believe that international stability was best studied in terms of varying numbers of great powers, since such static analysis precluded attention to the more significant processes of interaction among states which could not be either reduced to or managed by conservative diplomatic techniques and a strong emphasis on military deterrence. As he put it, 'dependable co-ordination cannot be built by deterrence and bargaining alone. A world of deterrent powers, a world of bargaining powers will, as a total system, be ungovernable.'[8]

In short, Deutsch is best remembered as a pioneer in the study of international integration, at least on a regional level, and as a leading figure in the attempt to introduce greater methodological rigour into the empirical study of international relations as well as comparative politics. His theoretical work has inspired many students who have followed the trails he laid in the 1950s and 1960s, and his methodological contribution in establishing the legitimacy of formal modelling in the study of international relations continues to influence scholars around the world today.

Notes

1 Samuel H. Beer, 'Karl Deutsch: A memoir', *Government and Opposition* 28 (1993), p. 117.
2 See, in particular, Karl Deutsch, 'Social mobilisation and political development', *American Political Science Review* 40 (1961), pp. 493–502.
3 Karl Deutsch, 'Nation and world', in Ithiel de Sola Pool (ed.), *Contemporary Political Science: Toward Empirical Theory*, New York, McGraw-Hill, 1967, p 271.
4 Karl Deutsch *et al., Political Community and the North Atlantic Area: International Organisation in the Light of Historical Experience*, Princeton, NJ: Princeton University Press, 1957, p. 7.
5 Karl Deutsch, *Political Community at the International Level,* Garden City, New York, Doubleday, 1954, pp. 39–40.
6 For an interesting elaboration of the conceptual parameters of a security community, see Lynn Miller, 'The prospect of order through regional security', in Richard A. Falk and Saul H. Mendlovitz (eds), *Regional Politics and World Order*, San Fransisco, W.H. Freeman, 1973.
7 See, Arend Lijphart 'Karl W. Deutsch and the new paradigm in International Relations', in Richard L. Merritt and Bruce M. Russett (eds), *From National Development to Global Community*, London, Allen & Unwin, pp. 233–51.
8 Karl Deutsch, 'Between sovereignty and integration', *Government and Opposition* 9 (1974), 1981, p. 115.

See also in this book

Mitrany, Haas

Deutsch's major writings

For a complete bibliography of the works of Karl W. Deutsch see Richard L. Merritt and Bruce M. Russett (eds), *From National Development to Global Community*, London, George Allen & Unwin, 1981, pp. 447–63
Nationalism and Social Communication: An Inquiry into the Foundations of Nationality, New York, Technology Press & Wiley, 1953
Political Community at the International Level, Garden City, Doubleday, 1954
Political Community and the North Atlantic Area, Princeton, New Jersey, Princeton University Press, 1957

Science and the Creative Spirit: Essays on Humanistic Aspects of Science, Toronto, Ontario, University of Toronto Press, 1958
'Multipolar power systems and international stability' (with J. David Singer), *World Politics* 16 (1964), pp. 390–406
Nation-Building, New York, Atherton Press, 1966.
The Nerves of Government: Models of Political Communication and Control, New York, The Free Press, 1966
Arms Control and the Atlantic Alliance: Europe Faces Coming Policy Decisions, New York, Wiley, 1967
France, Germany, and the Western Alliance: A Study of Elite Attitudes on European Integration and World Politics, New York, Charles Scribners, 1967
'Nation and world', in Ithiel de Sola Pool (ed.), *Contemporary Political Science: Toward Empirical Theory*, New York, McGraw-Hill, 1967, pp. 204–27
The Analysis of International Relations, Englewood Cliffs, New Jersey, Prentice-Hall, 1968
Nationalism and its Alternatives, New York, Alfred Knopf, 1969

Further reading

Lijphart, Arend, 'Karl W. Deutsch and the new paradigm in international relations', in Richard L. Merritt and Bruce M. Russett (eds), *From National Development to Global Community*, London, Allen & Unwin, pp. 233–51

ERNST HAAS

Ernst B. Haas is best known as one of the founders of 'neo-functionalism' in the study of regional integration, particularly in Europe. Since the 1970s he has explored the role of consensual knowledge among elites in facilitating inter-state co-operation and he has analysed the potential for reforming the operations of the United Nations. Like so many of the key thinkers represented in this book, Haas emigrated to the United States as a young man in 1938 to escape persecution by the Nazis, and his early life had an important impact on his intellectual commitment to exploring ways in which even arch-enemies could overcome their animosity and discover common interests. After serving with the American armed forces during the Second World War, he took advantage of the GI Bill to complete his university education at Columbia University in New York. In 1951 he took up a teaching position at Berkeley in California and became a full professor there in 1962. Since 1973 he has been Robson Research Professor in Government at Berkeley.

Haas's early work on European integration has to be seen in the context of earlier efforts that had focused either on constitutional federalism as a means of integrating states into a larger political framework, or on functional means to promote trans-national co-operation by starting with 'low politics', such as the reduction of trade barriers and technical co-operation, to deal with trans-border problems whose solution was deemed – at least in the first instance – to be apolitical.

What became known as 'neo-functionalism' was an attempt both to synthesise these competing frameworks and to focus on processes at work in the specific case of regional integration in Western Europe. Haas shared the supranational ideals of Mitrany, yet he was also interested in the specific institutional means by which the existing states in the region could transcend nationalism and participate in the creation of new forms of international organisation. Whereas Mitrany was somewhat vague on how the process of integration was to take place, Haas developed a model that did not rely on normative assumptions either of altruism or that the growth of economic interdependence would be sufficient to generate demands for closer inter-governmental co-operation.

Haas defined integration as 'the process whereby political actors in several distinct national settings are persuaded to shift their loyalties, expectations and political activities towards a new and larger center, whose institutions possess or demand jurisdiction over the pre-existing national states'.[1] He argued that such a process was easier to achieve in a regional context such as Western Europe, particularly in light of its history and shared democratic values in the post-war era. Unlike Mitrany, he acknowledged that it would be difficult either to separate technical from political issues or to avoid conflicts between states if the gains from co-operation were unequally distributed. Consequently, it was crucial to establish formal institutions that could impose and uphold agreements made by nation-states. Such bodies had to enjoy some autonomy from national governments if they were to be effective, and the whole process could not work unless states accepted both the rule of law (hence encroachments of state sovereignty would be difficult to reverse) and the principle of majoritarian decision making.

Once the process had begun and institutions established on these principles, Haas was confident that state sovereignty would decline over time as co-operation in one sphere of activity 'spilled over' into others, and a bureaucratic process of decision making evolved at a supranational, albeit at a regionally specific, level. As more and more actors became involved in the process, a form of 'socialisation' would take place among elites, attenuating their loyalty to the nation-state in favour of a broader appreciation for the interests of the region as a whole. Despite his sensitivity to the political obstacles confronting the process of integration and his attempt to incorporate elite rationality and self-interest into his model, Haas still retained the functionalist idea that progress in more technical and economic issues would lead to greater political co-operation. However, he stressed that neo-functionalism – otherwise known as 'federalism by installments' – depended a great deal on the ability of elites and political entrepreneurs to apply consensual knowledge to the solution of common problems.

The study of regional integration reached a high point in the early 1970s, after which it declined to the point at which even Haas himself acknowledged that it might be obsolete.[2] It was inspired by two trends that failed to maintain their momentum as the decade progressed. On the one hand, there was no question that European integration seemed to be progressing toward some kind of European political union in the medium term. On the other hand, the 1960s were years in which the study of international relations in the United States was dominated by a desire to generate scientifically testable hypotheses based on the most rigorous selection and collection of empirical data. Haas's work must be read in the context of the intersection of these otherwise unrelated phenomena. As European integration faltered in the 1970s, it became clear that there were a number of difficulties in applying his ideas to areas outside the West European context.

First, in the absence of a clearly defined 'dependent variable' (i.e., that which neo-functional models were trying to explain), it was not clear how to measure whether integration was progressing or regressing over time. Since integration was seen more as a process than an outcome, the lack of specificity meant that the term suffered from some ambiguity as it meant different things to different people.

Second, although Haas himself claimed to be engaged in a 'value-free' process of scientific investigation of the process, there is no doubt that he hoped the process would lead to a greater degree of supranationalism in West European politics, and thus he neglected the examination of those conditions and factors that could retard the process rather than accelerate it. Yet the concept of 'spill-over', if not properly managed, could in fact reduce the desire for greater integration among states. For example, the initial reduction of tariff barriers in the European Economic Community (EEC) meant that profit margins of firms were more strongly affected by different systems of taxation among member states, and thus tariff reduction 'spilled over' into pressures for a common taxation regime. Yet when inflation in France rose dramatically relative to its neighbours in the late 1960s, the French government was unable to raise taxes to reduce domestic demand and had to restrain trade to avoid a balance of payments crisis. This illustrates the potential weakness of partial measures whose unintended consequences can induce a political crisis if difficulties are not anticipated and planned for.

Third, it remains unclear whether European integration can proceed in the 1990s in the absence of attempts to make up what is often referred to as 'the democratic deficit'. Unless there is a concerted attempt to develop democratic procedures of decision making to secure the legitimacy and accountability of regional organisations staffed by technical experts and bureaucrats, a dangerous gap can develop between national citizens and regional organisations. This gap can then be exploited by political parties that are still nationally based and used to attack incumbent governments at election time. The problems of moving toward greater monetary and political union in the contemporary European Union cast some doubt on the effectiveness, let alone the legitimacy, of automatic 'integration by stealth'.

Finally, it remains unclear whether neo-functionalism is applicable to areas other than Western Europe in the 1950s and 1960s, in which case its relevance as a universal theory is somewhat limited. In terms of size, historical context and levels of economic development and growth among member states, Western Europe may be appropriate for the development of neo-functional processes. But if the efficacies of those processes are themselves dependent on fortuitous background conditions, it is unlikely that they can be replicated successfully elsewhere, even if they are successful in Western Europe.

For all these reasons, Haas became disenchanted with neo-functionalism in the 1970s. Whilst he did much to advance the study of regional integration in Europe, Haas moved on to examine international organisation at a global level, and his early work can be seen as paving the way for the rise in popularity of 'regime analysis', the study of international governance in the widest sense. At the same time, Haas has not lost sight of the importance of international organisations themselves, and in the last decade he has been a major contributor to debates revolving around the possibilities and desirability of various reforms to the United Nations. His work on the UN, exploring its empirical record in helping to maintain international peace and security, reveals the way he has learnt from the failures of neo-functionalism in the 1970s.

In 1990, Haas published *When Knowledge is Power,* in which he bemoans the relative inactivity of many potentially important international organisations. He argues that they need to be reformed so that they can become 'perpetual learners', able to adapt to new challenges and problems in international society. Haas suggests that we should think of international organisations, such as the United Nations, as ends in themselves rather than as means to a specific end that always takes priority. If this were the case, then (like the American Constitution itself), international organisations could adapt to new issues and not be constantly evaluated in terms of their failure to achieve ends that may have been too ambitious to start with. He encourages us to think of progress in international governance

> as an open-ended groping for self-improvement, without a final goal, without a transcendental faith, but with frequent reverses and sporadic self-questioning about the trajectory of change . . . progress is a child-like, groping god, not a purposeful master of the universe. Progress is a secular god who tolerates the things people, nations, and other large human collectivities do to themselves and to one another.[3]

This is the context in which Haas has challenged those who believe that the United Nations must be reformed radically to deal with the emerging challenges of the twenty-first century. Whilst he is mindful of the rise of global problems such as the deterioration of the global environment and growing economic inequality between rich and poor, he is equally aware of the inherent limits to the United Nations in a world divided amongst over 180 sovereign states. Consequently, his biggest worry is that the end of the Cold War has led to a dramatic increase in expectations about what the United Nations can achieve, a rise in hope fed by the inflated rhetoric of political leaders whose talk is not matched by either action or the necessary funds to implement sweeping reforms. As a result, the United Nations is in danger of decline as it becomes the prisoner of inflated goals.

This is consistent with the argument presented in a much earlier book *Tangle of Hopes* (1969), where he proposed two models of 'system transformation'. One depends on 'autonomous internal change' in which changes within states lead to new demands and policies. The other involves 'feedback' in which experiences with the performances of international organisation lead decision makers to new perceptions as to what can and cannot be done effectively and thus to the formulation of new purposes to be pursued through those organisations. He argues in this work that the first of these means that the powers of an organisation will have difficulty keeping abreast of 'the changing mixture of demands' and thus will remain largely static. In the second case, however, if 'feedbacks result in adaptive learning among elites, the result is likely to be a stronger system with more autonomous power'.[4] One could argue, of course, that such 'feedback' may lead as compellingly toward disengagement as toward increasing interdependence, which seems to be taking place between the United States and the United Nations today.

To conclude, Ernst Haas's scholarship is characterised by a rigorous adherence to the highest standards of empirical methodology combined with a humanistic commitment to greater co-operation among states in pursuit of world order. Whilst his early work was profoundly influenced by functionalism and sought to discover means by which the nation-state might be transcended, he has become convinced of the need to pursue global order through the existing states system. In that sense, his work is characterised by a growing realism and a desire to convince others that, if international organisations are to flourish in the years head, we should be modest in what we can expect from drawing up radical blue-prints for reform. In the study of international organisation, the best can be the enemy of the good.

Notes

1 Ernst Haas, 'International integration: the European and the universal process', *International Organization* 15 (1961), p. 366.
2 Ernst Haas, *The Obsolescence of Regional Integration Theory*, Berkeley, University of California Press, 1976.
3 Ernst Haas, *When Knowledge is Power: Three Models of Change in International Organizations*, Berkeley, University of California Press, 1990, p. 212.
4 Ernst Haas, *Tangle of Hopes: American Commitments and World Order*, Englewood Cliffs, New Jersey, Prentice-Hall, 1969, pp. 28–9.

See also in this book

Mitrany

Haas's major writings

'The balance of power: prescription, concept, or propaganda?', *World Politics* 5 (1953), pp. 442–77
Dynamics of International Relations (with Allen S. Whiting), New York, McGraw-Hill, 1956
The Uniting of Europe: Political, Social, and Economic Forces, 1950–1957, Stanford, California, Stanford University Press, 1958
'Persistent themes in Atlantic and European unity', *World Politics* 10 (1958), pp. 614–29
Beyond the Nation-State: Functionalism and International Organization, California, Stanford,

Stanford University Press, 1964

Collective Security and the Future International System, Denver, Colorado, University of Denver Press, 1968

The Uniting of Europe: Political, Social, and Economic Forces, Stanford, California, Stanford University Press, 1968

Tangle of Hopes: American Commitments and World Order, Englewood Cliffs, New Jersey, Prentice-Hall, 1969

Human Rights and International Action: The Case of Freedom of Association, Stanford, California, Stanford University Press, 1970

'The study of regional integration: reflections on the joys and anguish of pretheorizing', *International Organization* 24 (1970), pp. 607–46

The Web of Interdependence: The United States and International Organizations, Englewood Cliffs, New Jersey, Prentice-Hall, 1970

The Obsolescence of Regional Integration Theory, Berkeley, University of California Press, 1975

'Turbulent fields and the theory of regional integration', *International Organization* 30 (1976), pp. 173–212

'Why collaborate? Issue-linkage and international regimes', *World Politics* 32 (1980), pp. 357–405

'Words can hurt you; or, who said what to whom about regimes', *International Organization* 36 (1982), pp. 207–43

'Regime decay: conflict management and international organizations, 1945–1981', *International Organization* 37 (1983), pp. 189–256

When Knowledge is Power: Three Models of Change in International Organizations, Berkeley, University of California Press, 1990

'Reason and change in international life', in Richard Rothstein (ed.), *The Evolution of Theory in International Relations*, Columbia, South Carolina, University of South Carolina Press, 1991, pp. 189–220

Further reading

Jarvis, Darryl, 'Integration theory revisited: Haas, neofunctionalism and the problematics of European integration', *Policy, Organisation and Society* 7 (1994), pp. 17–33

Ohrgaard, Jakob C., 'Less than supranational, more than intergovernmental: European political cooperation and the dynamics of intergovernmental integration', *Millennium: Journal of International Studies* 26 (1997), pp. 1–30

Puchala, David, 'Integration theory and the study of international relations', in Richard L. Merritt and Bruce M. Russett (eds), *From National Development to Global Community*, London, Allen & Unwin, pp. 145–64

Sewell, James Patrick, *Functionalism and World Politics*, 1966

Taylor, Paul, *The Limits of European Integration*, New York, Columbia University Press, 1983

Tranholm-Mikkelsen, Jeppe, 'Neofunctionalism: obstinate or obsolete? A reappraisal in light of the new dynamism of the EC', *Millennium: Journal of International Studies* 20 (1991), pp. 1–22

ROBERT KEOHANE

In 1965 Robert Keohane completed his PhD dissertation at Harvard University on the politics of the UN General Assembly. The question he tried to answer was whether institutions matter in explaining state behaviour, or could the latter be deduced solely from the distribution of power? Over thirty years later, Keohane is still examining this question and the ways in which he has tried to answer it over the years have earned him a reputation as the leader of what David Long calls the 'Harvard School' of liberal international theory.[1] Keohane's thoughts on both the conditions under which states co-operate with each other and the role of institutions in facilitating co-operation have evolved from seeking to challenge the explanatory adequacy of the realist paradigm to a more nuanced accommodation with the insights of structural realism. Whether this constitutes progress or regress in the study of international organisation remains a hotly debated issue, but there is no questioning the pivotal importance of Keohane's work in raising it.

Keohane was born in 1941 and raised in Illinois. At the age of only 16, he enrolled in Shimer College, a small offshoot of the College of the University of Chicago. When he graduated in 1961, he pursued his doctoral studies at Harvard University. In 1965, he took up a teaching position at Swarthmore College. In 1969, after joining the board of editors for the journal *International Organization*, which has since become one of the leading journals in the field, Keohane began his remarkable research collaboration with Joseph S. Nye. He moved to California in 1973 to teach at Stanford University. In 1985, Keohane returned to Harvard, where he stayed for the next decade. In 1996, he was appointed James Duke Professor of International Relations at Duke University.[2]

Keohane's ongoing debate with realism began in the late 1960s and early 1970s when he and Joseph Nye began to question some of realism's allegedly core assumptions about international relations. In 1972, they co-edited *Transnational Relations and World Politics*. This volume brought together a number of scholars interested in the possibility that 'transnational relations' among non-state actors, such as multinational corporations, made it imperative to overcome the excessive concentration of political scientists on inter-state relations. The book was edited in the context of the ending of the Vietnam War and the growing importance of economic issues in international affairs. In particular, the rise of OPEC, emerging tensions between Japan and the United States over their trade imbalance, and Nixon's unilateral decision to abandon the Bretton Woods agreements on monetary stability, indicated that profound changes were taking place in world politics. Over the next few years, Keohane and Nye's work evolved from a multi-faceted description of an allegedly 'interdependent' world to a theoretical treatment of the consequences of complex interdependence for political leadership and regime maintenance and change.

The result of this evolution was *Power and Interdependence: World Politics in Transition* (1977). The subtitle is important. The book is a direct challenge to what the authors perceive to be the core assumptions of realism, and it is the first book in the literature of the period systematically to present hypotheses on interdependence and test them against a great deal of empirical data. The basic argument of the book is that, in a world of interdependence, the realist 'paradigm' is of limited use in helping us to understand the dynamics of international regimes, that is, the rules of the game governing decision making and operations in international relations on particular problems, like money, or between specified countries, like the United States and Canada.

Keohane and Nye begin by constructing two theoretical models, realism and complex interdependence. The former portrays international relations as a struggle for power. It is based on three core assumptions: states are coherent units and are the most important political actors; force is a usable and effective instrument of policy; and there exists a hierarchy of issues in world politics dominated by questions of military security. In contrast, under conditions of complex interdependence: actors other than states participate; there is no clear hierarchy of issues; and force is ineffective. Under these conditions, outcomes will be determined by the distribution of resources and 'vulnerabilities' within particular issue-areas, they will be unrelated to the distribution of military power and transnational relations will be crucial factors in the decision-making process, including international bureaucratic coalitions and non-governmental institutions.

Having constructed their contrasting models, Keohane and Nye go on to describe and analyse major events in maritime and monetary affairs between 1920 and 1975, and explore in great detail the outcomes of numerous conflicts between the United States and Canada, and between the United States and Australia. They demonstrate that some issues and conflicts conform more to the assumptions of the complex interdependence model than to realism and reinforce the need to focus on particular 'sensitivities' and 'vulnerabilities' of actors in specific issue-areas. They also argue that under conditions of complex interdependence, which they expect to become stronger in the future, it is difficult for democratic states to devise and pursue rational foreign policies.

This is particularly true when the absence of a security dimension makes it difficult to determine a clear rank ordering of values. The proliferation of non-state actors and coalitions in the process of decision making further complicates the process, and Keohane and Nye suggest that such problems are exacerbated in larger states in the international system.

The book was often cited during the so-called 'third' great debate in the Anglo-American study of international relations. The first debate was between realists and idealists in the 1930s, the second was between traditionalists and behavioural scientists in the 1950s and 1960s, and in the late 1970s, Keohane and Nye added their voices to the 'inter-paradigm' debate. Textbooks were written and courses were taught that portrayed the field as divided between realism, complex interdependence and radical Marxism. Each paradigm seemed to have its own agenda of issues, identification of key actors and theoretical models. And yet, between 1977 and the publication of *After Hegemony* in 1984, Keohane abandoned his attempt to portray 'complex interdependence' as a rival model to realism. There are, I think, three basic reasons for this.

First, as a number of writers pointed out, the portrait of realism contained in the 1977 volume was simplistic. Keohane and Nye had set realism up as a straw man. For example, no realist had ever argued that force was a usable and effective instrument of policy under any conditions and without qualification. As Stanley Michalak points out in his extensive review of the book,

Keohane and Nye do not ground their presentation of realism in a careful study of realist writings. Assertion after assertion about realism is not even documented by page references in footnotes, let alone any direct quotations. When Keohane and Nye quote from realists, these quotations are often out of context, largely irrelevant to the tenets imputed to realism, or of dubious validity.[3]

Second, the realists fought back. Without repeating the main arguments of Kenneth Waltz and Stephen Krasner (covered elsewhere in this book), it is not true that the distribution of political and military power is unrelated to the condition of complex interdependence. For example, in his study on US raw materials policy, Krasner demonstrated the ability of the United States to pursue a consistent 'national interest' against the demands of domestic interest groups. He also showed a link between hegemonic power and the degree of complex interdependence in international trade. Kenneth Waltz, in his powerful articulation of the importance of the balance of power, showed that interdependence, far from rendering power obsolete, in fact depended on the ability and willingness of the United States to provide the conditions under which other states could forego the competition for relative gains and co-operate to maximise their absolute gains from co-operation on trade and other issue-areas.

Finally, the Second Cold War of the late 1970s and early 1980s undermined Keohane and Nye's expectation that 'complex interdependence' would expand and accelerate the obsolescence of realism. By the early 1980s, Keohane acknowledged that his complex interdependence model was not a clear alternative to realism. He accepted many of the neorealist arguments linking the creation of 'regimes' in areas of trade, finance and the oil market to the presence of American hegemony. He also conceded that power and interdependence were not independent of one another. Indeed, it could be argued that 'asymmetrical interdependence' (i.e. dependence) is in fact a form of power relationship.

In 1984, Keohane published *After Hegemony: Cooperation and Discord in the World Political Economy*. The book is the culmination of Keohane's attempt to synthesise structural realism and complex interdependence. The hybrid product is known today as 'modified structural realism' or 'neoliberal institutionalism'. Keohane tries to determine how the international system might evolve toward stable configurations of co-operation in spite of the decline of American power relative to Japan and Europe since 1945. The theory of co-operation is based on the functional utility of 'regimes' – principles, rules, norms around which state expectations and behaviour converge in a given issue-area – that assert the long-term, rational self-interest of states in perpetuating co-operation despite shifts in the underlying balance of power. He argues that such regimes are established primarily to deal with political market failure. They lower the cost of international transactions by delimiting permissible and impermissible transactions, by combining transactions through issue linkage, thereby enabling states to assemble packages of agreements, and by reducing uncertainty.

In short, the maintenance of institutionalised co-operation among states does not depend on the perpetuation of the hegemonic conditions that are necessary to set regimes in place. Keohane then tests his revised 'functional theory' of institutionalised co-operation by examining the issue-areas of trade, oil and money. He finds that the decline of American power is only part of the explanation for the weakening of regimes in these areas. Even after 1970, when he believes the United States ceased to be a hegemon, the advanced industrialised countries have continued to try to coordinate their policies in the world political economy. The world has not gone back to the beggar-thy-neighbour policies of the 1930s, and international trade has not been sacrificed in favour of rigid blocs in Europe, the Americas and Asia.

Thus Keohane's intellectual path to answering the question at the back of his mind in the early 1960s has moved from a direct challenge to realism to an attempt to accommodate its emphasis on the importance of power and self-interest in explaining the conduct of states. His answer is that, yes, power and self-interest are important, but writers such as Waltz, Gilpin and other structural realists exaggerate the degree to which the international system is anarchical. It is not. Despite the absence of a formal, legal hierarchy of authority at the international level, informal elements of governance exist in the form of regimes and 'institutions', 'related complexes of rules and norms, identifiable in space and time'.[4] They help states to overcome problem of collective action and market failures. In international relations, transaction costs are high and property rights are often ill defined. States may not co-operate because they fear that others can renege on deals, or because they may not be able to monitor others' behaviour. Institutions can be of great help in overcoming such problems. They allow the principle of reciprocity to function more efficiently by providing information about others' preferences, intentions and behaviour. Thus they allow states to move closer to the Pareto frontier. By altering the systemic environment, institutions facilitate changes in state strategies so that rational self-interested states can continue to co-operate reliably over time.

Since the publication of *After Hegemony*, Keohane has continued to elaborate his neoliberal research programme, applying it to analyses of decision making in the European community and the potential for greater co-operation in developing environmental regimes.[5] Today, he is working on the role of domestic political factors in explaining the variation in compliance among states (and by particular states over time) to international agreements. In *After Hegemony*, he suggested that his systemic theory of international co-operation needed to be supplemented by a theory of learning within states, and we may expect the next stage of Keohane's research to fill this important gap in the literature.

Critical reaction to Keohane's work has been mixed. On the one hand, there is no doubt that he has been a pivotal figure in inspiring a whole generation of graduate students to examine 'regimes' in a vast array of issue-areas in international relations. He has provided a theoretical framework and a set of hypotheses that others have used to expand the empirical scope of international relations theory in the sub-field of international political economy, which is now thriving in the discipline as a whole. Nevertheless, it remains to be seen whether his attempt to 'modernise' the liberal tradition and rid it of its traditional association with 'idealism' will succeed. In attempting to construct a positivist research programme of neoliberals, Keohane has attracted criticism from both sides of the fence, as it were.

First, many realists remain unconvinced that institutions really matter as much as Keohane thinks they do. For example, Joseph Grieco argues that even if the search for absolute gains from co-operation is facilitated by the existence of 'regimes', states remain what he calls 'relative gains maximisers'. As he puts it,

a state concerned about relative gains may decline to cooperate even if it is confident that partners will keep their commitments to a joint arrangement. Indeed, if a state believed that a proposed arrangement would provide all parties absolute gains, but would also generate gains favouring partners, then greater certainty that partners would adhere to the terms of the arrangement would only accentuate its relative gains concerns.[6]

What matters most to states in particular issue-areas? The search for absolute gains whose achievement may be endangered by political market failures? Or are they equally concerned with the distribution of gains from co-operation among participants within a regime? In his scathing criticism of neoliberal institutionalism, John

Mearsheimer argues that Keohane and his supporters have yet to surpass realist theories of war and peace and have failed to demonstrate the crucial importance of institutions in reducing the likelihood of war among states.[7]

Among some liberals and 'critical theorists' in the study of international relations, Keohane has attracted rather different kinds of criticism. The convergence of international political economy (IPE) around hegemonic stability theory, regime analysis and rational choice models of state behaviour has been criticised by Richard Leaver, among others, as a form of involution, not evolution.[8] David Long, in calling for 'the closure' of the Harvard School, argues that Keohane's project robs liberalism of its critical edge as an emancipatory project for individuals. Thus to some extent, Keohane's project, which tries to build a bridge between realists and liberals, has failed to satisfy the former and outraged some of the latter. But this may be the inevitable fate of bridge-builders in the 'divided discipline', where debates over the adequacy of alternative 'paradigms' are primarily normative rather than empirical.

Notes

1 David Long, 'The Harvard school of liberal international theory: a case for closure', *Millennium: Journal of International Studies* 24 (1995), pp. 489–505.
2 For more details on Keohane's biography, see Robert Keohane, 'A personal intellectual history', in Joseph Kruzel and James N. Rosenau (eds), *Journeys Through World Politics: Autobiographical Reflections of Thirty-Four Academic Travellers*, Lexington, Massachusetts, Lexington Books, 1989, pp. 403–15.
3 Stanley Michalak Jr., 'Theoretical perspectives for understanding international interdependence', *World Politics* 32 (1979), p. 145.
4 Robert Keohane, 'International institutions: two approaches', *International Studies Quarterly* 32 (1988), p. 383.
5 See, in particular, Robert Keohane and Stanley Hoffmann (eds), *The New European Community: Decisionmaking and Institutional*

Change, Boulder, Colorado, Westview Press, 1991; Robert Keohane and Elinor Ostrom (eds), *Local Commons and Global Interdependence: Heterogeneity and Cooperation in Two Domains*, London, Sage, 1995.

6 Joseph M. Grieco, 'Anarchy and the limits of cooperation: a realist critique of the newest liberal institutionalism', in Charles W. Kegley (ed.), *Controversies in International Relations Theory: Realism and the Neoliberal Challenge*, New York, St Martin's Press, 1995, p. 161.

7 See John Mearsheimer, 'The false promise of international institutions', *International Security* 19 (1994/5), pp. 5–49.

8 See Richard Leaver, 'International Political Economy and the changing world order: evolution or involution?', in R. Stubbs and G. Underhill (eds), *Political Economy and the Changing World Order*, London, Macmillan, pp. 130–41.

See also in this book

Haas, Ruggie, Strange, Waltz, Wendt

Keohane's major writings

Transnational Relations and World Politics (with Joseph Nye), Cambridge, Massachusetts, Harvard University Press, 1972

Power and Interdependence: World Politics in Transition (with Joseph S. Nye), Boston, Little, Brown, 1977

After Hegemony: Cooperation and Discord in the World Political Economy, Princeton, New Jersey, Princeton University Press, 1984

'The theory of hegemonic stability and changes in international economic regimes, 1967–1977', in Ole R. Holsti, Randolph M. Siverson and Alexander L. George (eds), *Change in the International System*, Boulder, Colorado, Westview Press, 1980, pp. 131–62

'Realism, neorealism and the study of world politics', in Robert O. Keohane (ed.), *Neorealism and its Critics*, New York, Columbia University Press, 1986, pp. 1–26

'Theory of world politics: structural realism and beyond', in Robert O. Keohane (ed.), *Neorealism and its Critics*, New York, Columbia University Press, 1986, pp. 158–203

'Power and interdependence revisited', *International Organisation* 41 (1987), pp. 725–53 (with Joseph Nye)

International Institutions and State Power: Essays in International Relations Theory, Boulder, Colorado, Westview Press, 1989

'International liberalism reconsidered', in John Dunn (ed.), *The Economic Limits of Modern Politics*, Cambridge, Cambridge University Press, 1990, pp. 165–95

The New European Community: Decisionmaking and Institutional Change (co-editor with Stanley Hoffmann), Boulder, Colorado, Westview Press, 1991

After the Cold War: International Institutions and State Strategies in Europe, 1989–1991 (co-editor with Stanley Hoffmann), Cambridge, Massachusetts, Harvard University Press, 1993

'Institutional theory and the realist challenge after the Cold War', in David A. Baldwin (ed.), *Neorealism and Neoliberalism*, New York, Columbia University Press, 1993, pp. 269–300

Internationalization and Domestic Politics (with Helen Milner), New York, Cambridge University Press, 1996

Further reading

Baldwin, David A. (ed.), *Neoliberalism and Neorealism*, New York, Columbia University Press, 1993

Crawford, Robert M., *Regime Theory in the Post-Cold War World: Rethinking the Neoliberal Approach to International Relations*, Aldershot, England, Dartmouth, 1996

Halliday, Fred, 'Theorizing the international', *Economy and Society* 18 (1989), pp. 346–58

Kratochwil, Freidrich and Ruggie, John Gerard, 'International organization: a state of the art on an art of the state', *International Organization* 40 (1986), pp. 753–75

Little, Richard, 'Power and interdependence: a realist critique', in R.J. Barry Jones and Peter Willetts (eds), *Interdependence on Trial: Studies in the Theory and Reality of Contemporary Interdependence*, London, Pinter, 1984, pp. 111–29

Long, David, 'The Harvard school of liberal international theory: a case for closure', *Millennium: Journal of International Studies* 24 (1995), pp. 489–505

Nye, Joseph S., 'Neorealism and neoliberalism', *World Politics* 40 (1988), pp. 235–51

Suhr, Michael, 'Robert Keohane – a contemporary classic', in Iver B. Neumann and Ole Waever (eds), *The Future of International Relations: Masters in the Making*, London, Routledge, 1997

DAVID MITRANY

It is sometimes claimed that international politics in the 1990s and beyond take place in a context of the increasing 'globalisation' of human activities. In the 1970s, the popular buzzword was 'interdependence' – the idea that increasing transnational processes were fundamentally changing the international system and modifying the traditional realist idea of relations among states taking place in an 'anarchical' environment. Despite the contemporary focus on technological innovations such as the information explosion via the Internet, and the growing awareness that environmental security requires greater coordination among states than ever before, the work of David Mitrany continues to provide inspiration for those who hope to moderate the effects of state sovereignty in the interests of improving global welfare.

David Mitrany was born at the end of the nineteenth century and educated in Romania. After early military service, he spent some time in Germany before enrolling at the London School of Economics to study sociology. During the First World War, he worked as an intelligence officer for the Foreign Office and developed links with the Quaker movement in Britain and the United States. Although he did not commit himself to any political party or ideological movement, Mitrany served on the Labour Party's Advisory Committee on International Affairs from 1919 to 1931 and also worked for the *Guardian* newspaper as a foreign affairs journalist until 1922, when he was employed by the Carnegie Foundation. During the Second World War, Mitrany rejoined the Foreign Office. Having worked at a number of universities in Britain and the United States before and during the Second World War, Mitrany continued a close association with the Institute for Advanced Study at Princeton, which he had helped to establish in 1933.

Given his broad background as a journalist, a diplomat, and a widely-travelled observer of international relations during such a momentous period in history, it is not surprising that Mitrany's work makes no pretensions to theoretical sophistication for its own sake. In 1948 he wrote that 'it seems to be the fate of all periods of transition that reformers are more ready to fight over a theory than to pull together on a problem. ... I do not represent a theory. I represent an anxiety.'[1] The problem to which he devoted his working life was how to bring states closer together to deal with issues which transcended territorial boundaries, and the 'approach' that he adopted to deal with the problem is known as 'functionalism'. Mitrany inspired a whole generation of students of integration, both practically and theoretically, and his work can still be read with great profit today.

Mitrany's contribution to the study of integration was to develop what he called a 'functional-sociological' approach as opposed to a 'political-constitutional' one. In light of the failure of grand designs such as the League of Nations in the inter-war period, Mitrany advocated a radically different form of international co-operation that would not begin with the design of federal arrangements with all their attendant legal and constitutional difficulties. He was very suspicious of 'integration by design', particularly if politicians were in control of the process. On the contrary, Mitrany suggested that international co-operation should begin by dealing with specific transnational issues (such as disease control) where there was some prospect of applying specialised technical knowledge and where the success of such 'functional' arrangements would lead to further efforts to replicate the experience in an ever-widening process. He observed that such a process could begin as governments began to acknowledge their growing responsibility for providing welfare to their citizens, a responsibility that they could not fulfil in isolation. He also believed that, if they began to transfer functional responsibilities to international agencies with specific mandates to deal with issues over which there was a wide consensus regarding the need for co-operation, over time the principle of territorial and legal sovereignty would weaken. Whilst he emphasised process over outcome, and he refused to entertain the idea that a world state could evolve, Mitrany was convinced that the existing inter-state system could become, in his famous phrase, a 'working peace system'. As he proclaimed, 'we must put our faith not in a protected peace [such as collective security] but in a working peace; it would be nothing more or less than the idea and aspiration of social security taken in its widest range'.[2]

In some ways, Mitrany was ahead of his time. His functional approach to international organisation was an economic and social equivalent to the idea of 'subsidiarity' that is being debated in the context of European integration today, the idea that political decisions should be taken at the lowest level of organisation most appropriate for those directly affected by them. He firmly believed that the expansion of tasks undertaken on an international basis would be helped both by the growth of needs and the successful application of technical solutions to social-scientific problems. Indeed, one can detect the influence and validity of Mitrany's insights in organisations such as the World Health Organization and the Universal Postal Union, and in areas such as civil aviation and the development of common standards in food and agriculture. Of course, his major works were published in the 1930s and 1940s, and he was inspired in particular by the success of some of President Roosevelt's New Deal experiments in regional co-operation, such as the Tennessee Valley Authority. He saw no intrinsic reason why such domestic experiments could not be replicated internationally, particularly if the principle of consent was upheld throughout the process.

Functionalism was not antithetical to democracy, but essential to its achievement when the scope of democratic decision making transcended the 'artificial' reach of territorial boundaries.

One of Mitrany's students, Paul Taylor, sums up the functionalist approach as follows:

> [Man] can be weaned away from his loyalty to the nation state by the experience of fruitful international cooperation; international organization arranged according to the requirements of the task [can] increase welfare rewards to individuals beyond the level obtainable within the state. Individuals and groups could begin to learn the benefits of cooperation ... creating interdependencies [and] undermining the most important bases of the nation state.[3]

In short, Mitrany adopted a liberal, utilitarian approach to the study of international relations in general, and to issues involving integration in particular. Yet despite his radical attempt to introduce a completely new way of thinking about international co-operation in the twentieth century, which distinguishes him from all those writers who adopted a constitutional-political approach, Mitrany's work has been subject to some grave criticisms; those scholars (such as Ernst Haas) who have built upon his work have had to respond to its most glaring weaknesses.

First, as Inis Claude points out, there are problems with Mitrany's 'assumption of separability-priority'.[4] The idea that it is possible both to separate 'technical' from 'political' issues and then subordinate the latter to the former is somewhat naïve. His critics have alleged that all decisions taken by governments are political and that it is wrong to make such an artificial distinction in order to emphasise the originality and uniqueness of the functionalist approach.

Second, although Mitrany himself was not a partisan of any particular political party, he is clearly a progressive liberal and a supporter of industrial modernity. This causes problems with his attempt to present functionalism as a universal, 'non-political' approach to international integration. It may be that the merits of functionalism are limited to those parts of the world that share the welfarist values that functionalism claims to promote. It is not clear that cultures and regimes not infused with similar values can easily be drawn into the functionalist 'web' of international co-operation simply on the basis of its alleged benefits.

Third, Mitrany was perhaps over-optimistic in what is called the 'spill-over' effects of the functionalist process. He expected that it would, in effect, build on its own momentum as one area of successful co-operation led inexorably to another. Mitrany said little about the actual processes of learning that would be required to accelerate or even adapt to the functional logic as it proceeded from less to more controversial issues. Yet as the experience of the European Union demonstrates, spill-over cannot be taken for granted, nor can the political and institutional design of integration be left to adapt organically to the technical requirements of particular issue-areas.

Indeed, a potentially devastating criticism of Mitrany's whole approach to international integration is that it puts the cart before the horse. Far from obviating the need to embark on a 'political-constitutional' approach to the study of war and peace, functionalism may in fact presuppose a widespread sense of common or shared interests and procedures among states who thereby do not fear the way in which the functional process diminishes their sovereignty. Again, the experience of the European Union can be read in this way. Certainly, some scholars have argued that West European integration could only begin in the late 1940s and 1950s because the United States performed the role of the hegemon. It provided the central collective good of security (in the form of a nuclear umbrella and American troops stationed in West Germany). Therefore, France and Germany could begin a process of economic integration, but only within a structure that meant they did not have to worry about the consequences for their core national interests. With the end of the Cold War, it is unclear whether Europe can continue to deepen its integration now that the European great powers can no longer rely as strongly on the United States to maintain its security guarantee. The difficulty which European states have had in coordinating their foreign and defence policies, particularly in light of the collapse of Yugoslavia in the 1990s, is clear evidence that 'spill-over' cannot be taken for granted in foreign policy as a teleological consequence of functional integration in economic and social matters.

Finally, it might be noted that Mitrany harboured a faith that individual loyalty to the nation-state was contingent on its ability to provide for a growing list of welfare needs that were best met by international coordination. To some extent he had a zero-sum view of the relationship between national loyalty and international governance. It is by no means clear that national loyalty is contingent in the way Mitrany supposed. Paul Taylor suggests that the empirical data exploring the connection 'is not immediately encouraging from the point of view of functionalism', but he also points out that not enough research has been conducted to settle the issue.[5] What can be said is that there is no compelling evidence to suggest that nationalism is about to succumb to the pressures of interdependence, and whether it is instrumental or constitutive of human identity in the late twentieth century remains a very open question.

Notes

1 David Mitrany, 'The functional approach to world organization', *International Affairs* 24 (1948), p. 350.
2 *A Working Peace System*, Chicago, University of Chicago Press, 1966, p. 92.
3 Paul Taylor, 'Introduction' to David Mitrany,

The Functional Theory of Politics, New York, St Martin's Press 1975, p. x.

4 See Inis Claude, *Swords Into Ploughshares*, New York, Knopf, 1964, esp. pp. 348–50.

5 Paul Taylor, op. cit., p. xxii.

See also in this book

Deutsch, Haas

Mitrany's major writings

For a complete bibliography of the work of David Mitrany see *The Functional Theory of Politics*, London, Martin Robertson, 1975, pp. 269–82

The Problem of International Sanctions, Oxford, Oxford University Press, 1925

The Land and the Peasant in Rumania: The War and Agrarian Reform (1917–21), London, Milford, 1930

The Progress of International Government, London, Allen & Unwin, 1933

Effect of the War in South Eastern Europe, New Haven, Connecticut, Yale University Press, 1936

American Interpretations, London, Contact Publishers, 1946

'The functional approach to world organization', *International Affairs* 24 (1948), pp. 350–63

Marx Against the Peasant: A Study in Social Dogmatism, Chapel Hill, North Carolina, University of North Carolina Press, 1951

A Working Peace System: An Argument for the Functional Development of International Organization, Chicago, University of Chicago Press, 1966

'The functional approach in historical perspective', *International Affairs* 47 (1971), pp. 532–43

The Functional Theory of Politics, New York, St Martin's Press 1975

Further reading

Abrahamson, Mark, *Functionalism*, Englewood Cliffs, New Jersey, Prentice-Hall, 1978

Claude, Inis, *Swords Into Ploughshares*, New York, Knopf, 1964

Imber, Mark F., 'Re-reading Mitrany: a pragmatic assessment of sovereignty', *Review of International Studies* 10 (1984), pp. 103–23

Pentland, Charles, *International Theory and European Integration*, London, Faber & Faber, 1973

Puchala, Donald, J., 'The integration theorists and the study of international relations', in Charles W. Kegley Jr and Eugene Wittkopf (eds), *The Global Agenda*, New York, Random House, 1988, pp. 198–215

Taylor, Paul, 'Functionalism: the theory of David Mitrany', in Paul Taylor and A.J.R. Groom (eds), *International Organization*, London, Pinter, 1978, pp. 236–52

Taylor, Paul, 'Introduction to David Mitrany', *The Functional Theory of Politics*, New York, St Martin's Press, 1975, pp. ix–xxv

JOHN RUGGIE

In May 1997, John Gerard Ruggie was appointed assistant to the new Secretary-General of the United Nations, Kofi Annan, with special responsibility for drawing up plans to reform the UN budget and its organisational procedures and to mediate between the United States government and the world body. His appointment to such high office is just reward for a scholar who has written widely about international governance in a broad sense and whose most recent book argues that the United States must commit itself to the task of creating a new, multilateral world order for the next century. It is also appropriate to discuss his contribution to the study of international relations within a category devoted to students of international organisation rather than to try and fit him into any particular ideological orientation to world politics. As Ole Waever observes in his more detailed examination of Ruggie's work, 'Ruggie is a paradigmatic case of a non-paradigmatic and therefore potentially "invisible" author' in international theory.[1] His visibility is, therefore, ample testimony to his ability to move across established faultlines in the discipline in search of theoretical tools with which to illuminate the challenges and opportunities for greater co-operation among states in an era of rapid change.

Ruggie was born in 1944 in Austria. His family emigrated to Canada in 1956, and he moved to the United States in 1967, after his graduation from McMaster University. He completed his MA at the University of California (Berkeley) in 1968 and was awarded his PhD from the same institution in 1974. He remained at the University of California until 1978, when he moved to New York to teach at Columbia University. In 1987 he returned to the West Coast as Professor of International Relations and Pacific Studies, University of California (San Diego), before going back to Columbia University in 1991 as John W. Burgess Professor of Political Science. He was elected Dean of the School of International and Public Affairs (SIPA) that same year; he stepped down from his position in 1996 before taking up his present appointment at the United Nations.

In the late 1970s and early 1980s, Ruggie was a leading contributor to the debate over the degree to which the international system was changing under the impact of inter-dependence and the implications of such change for international relations theory and practice. At the time, the debate was between those who believed that the international system was not undergoing systemic change – the structural or 'neorealist' school – and those who argued that realism was an inadequate guide to understanding dramatic changes in international relations as a result of transnational economic forces. The focus for this debate was the publication of *Theory of International Politics* by Kenneth Waltz (1979). He argued strongly that the scope and direction of economic interdependence is dependent on the *distribution* of power in the international system. The political significance of transnational forces is not a function of their scale. What matters are the vulnerability of states to forces outside their control and the costs of reducing their exposure to such forces. Waltz concluded that, in a bipolar system, the level of interdependence was relatively low among the great powers and that the persistence of anarchy as the central organising principle of international relations guarantees that states will continue to privilege security over the pursuit of wealth.

On the other side of the debate were the liberals, notably Robert Keohane. Prior to the publication of Waltz's book, they argued that the growth of transnational economic forces, the growing irrelevance of territorial control to economic growth and the international division of labour rendered realism obsolete. The collective benefits to trade would ensure greater co-operation among states and contribute to the decline in the use of force between them. Ruggie's work has to be understood in the context of the American debate between neorealism and neoliberalism and of the rise of hegemonic stability theory as a partial compromise between the two sides. Kenneth Waltz, Robert Keohane, Stephen Krasner, Robert Gilpin, and Richard Rosecrance are the key figures in this debate, and their work is described elsewhere in this book.[2]

In his critique of Waltzian neorealism, Ruggie argues that its rigid separation of 'levels of analysis', particularly between domestic, transnational and structural levels, is a barrier to understanding the complexities of change in the international system. He claims that both the medieval and the modern system are characterised by anarchy, but one could hardly claim much continuity between the two eras. The momentous change from one era to another can only be understood by examining how the very principles of differentiation among political units (the shift from heteronomy to anarchy) took place:

> The modern system is distinguished from the medieval not by 'sameness' or 'differences' of units, but by *the principles on the basis of which the constituent units are separated* from one another. If anarchy tells us *that* the political system is a segmental realm, differentiation tells us *on what basis* the segmentation is determined.[3]

In other words, neorealism is far too static an approach. By separating the structure of the international system from processes among and within the units (states) that make up the system, it is unable to incorporate and thereby explain (let alone predict) change *of* the system. The only changes that neorealists focus on are shifts in the distribution (or balance) of power among states. Ruggie returns to this theme in a later article, where he speculates on the sources of potential change from a modern system of separate sovereign states to some 'postmodern' future. He suggests that we lack even the appropriate vocabulary to speculate on epochal change such as occurred in the transformation from the medieval to the modern era, but that we do need to get away from the false dichotomy between a world dominated by states and one in which states are replaced by some other entity beyond our capacity to imagine:

There is an extraordinary impoverished mind-set at work here, one that is able to visualise long-term challenges to the system of states only in terms of entities that are institutionally substitutable for the state. Since global markets and transnationalised corporate structures (not to mention communications satellites) are not in the business of replacing states, they are assumed to entail no potential for fundamental international change. The theoretical or historical warrant for that premise has never been mooted, let alone defended.[4]

Ruggie himself does not offer a theory of epochal change, although he offers fascinating insights into its dynamics and dimensions from the thirteenth century to the eighteenth century. What is important in understanding his work is the underlying theoretical concern with massive changes and how the international system can cope without change bringing in its wake disorder and chaos. He implies that a key to managing change lies in our ability to 'unbundle territory':

[I]n the modern international polity an institutional *negation* of exclusive territoriality serves as the means of situating and

dealing with those dimensions of collective existence that territorial rulers recognize to be irreducibly transterritorial in character. Nonterritorial functional space is the place wherein international society is anchored.[5]

A great deal of Ruggie's work is concerned with one form of 'institutional negation' in the post-1945 era, multilateralism. He uses the term to refer to state behaviour that accords with certain principles; in other words, in a qualitative sense rather than the nominal definition according to which 'multilateral' refers to relations among three or more parties. Multilateralism is 'a generic institutional form of modern international life' that exists when states conduct their relations with one another according to certain standards or principles.[6] These principles embody three characteristics: non-discrimination, indivisibility and diffuse reciprocity. Non-discrimination means that states should carry out their treaty obligations without any contingencies or exceptions based on alliances, or on the idiosyncrasies of the circumstances at hand, or on the degree to which national interests are perceived to be at stake. The most often cited example of such non-discrimination is the obligation of states to extend 'Most Favoured Nation' status to all other states in the trading regime governed by the General Agreement on Tariffs and Trade (GATT) and its successor, the World Trade Organisation (WTO).

Next comes the principle of indivisibility. In the context of military co-operation, states are required to meet their commitments to all other states in a collective security agreement. For multilateral security regimes this refers to the requirement that peace be regarded as indivisible for and by each signatory to the treaty. Finally, continuity over time is an essential third characteristic. Episodic, single-shot instances of inter-state coalition behaviour within the context of otherwise individually competitive or hostile relations among states do not qualify as 'multilateral'. Instead, joint participation has to take place over an extended period of time and so comes to be predicated upon, and become the basis for, anticipations about the longer-run functioning of the collective. In other words, states extend what is sometimes called 'the shadow of the future'. Iterated or repeated instances of co-operation in a multilateral setting can promote diffuse reciprocity among states and help to transform their sense of self-interest.

In the early 1980s, Ruggie argued that multilateralism was crucial to the stability of relations among states in the West after the Second World War. An extended period of co-operation and economic growth among states in Europe, the Americas, Japan and parts of Southeast Asia was made possible by the multilateral institutions set up at Bretton Woods. By 1944, Western democracies, following the trauma of the Great Depression that contributed to the Second World War, agreed on two sets of post-war economic priorities. The first was to achieve economic growth and full employment. This was reflected in the Beveridge Plan of Great Britain, the French establishment of a planning commission and the United States' passage of the Employment Act of 1946. All these domestic plans were symbolic of a commitment to government intervention in the economy and the establishment of the welfare state. The second priority was the creation of a stable, liberal world economic order that would prevent a return to the destructive economic nationalism and competitive currency devaluations of the 1930s.

The Bretton Woods Conference of 1944 was charged with the creation of such a stable, liberal world economic order. A product of American–British co-operation, the 'Bretton Woods system' had a number of key features. It envisioned a world in which governments would have considerable freedom to pursue national economic objectives, yet the monetary order would be based on fixed exchange rates – based on a dollar/gold exchange standard – in order to prevent the destructive competitive depreciations and policies of the 1930s. Another principle adopted was currency convertibility for current account transactions. Massive and destabilising capital flows, such as those of the 1930s and in the 1980s and 1990s, were assumed to be a thing of the past. The International Monetary Fund (IMF) was created to supervise the operation of the monetary system and provide medium-term lending to countries experiencing temporary balance-of-payments problems. Finally, in the event of a 'fundamental disequilibrium', the system permitted a state to change its exchange rate with international consent.

Ruggie argues that the Bretton Woods system was a compromise solution to the conflict between domestic autonomy and international norms. It tried to avoid both the subordination of domestic economic activities to the stability of the exchange rate embodied in the classical gold standard as well as the sacrifice of international stability to the domestic policy autonomy characteristic of the 1930s. He describes it as a 'compromise of embedded liberalism'; an attempt to enable governments to pursue Keynesian growth stimulation policies at home without disrupting international monetary stability:

> Unlike the economic nationalism of the 1930s, it would be multilateral in character; unlike the liberalism of the gold standard and free trade, its multilateralism would be predicated upon domestic interventionism ... the essence of embedded liberalism [was] to devise a form of multilateralism that is compatible with the requirements of domestic stability.[7]

Ruggie's latest book, *Winning the Peace: America and World Order in the New Era* (1996), is a superb analysis of the history of the 'embedded liberal' compromise since Bretton Woods, examining the reasons behind its decline in the 1970s and 1980s and arguing that it needs to be renewed for the challenges of the next century. He argues that despite spending six decades at the pinnacle of world leadership, the United States is in danger of returning to some level of isolationism in the post-Cold War era. The best way to avoid this appalling prospect would be to emulate the policies of Franklin Roosevelt, Harry Truman and Dwight Eisenhower, linking the United States' aspirations with its own sense of itself as a nation. It does not need the spectre of a new geopolitical threat:

> A multilateral world order vision is singularly compatible with America's own collective self-concept. Indeed, the vision taps into the very idea of America itself ... America's multilateralist agenda reflects the idea ... of a willed formation of an international community open in principle to everyone.[8]

Ruggie renews his criticisms of realism, according to which all that really matters is the geopolitical balance of power. He also chastises what he calls American 'unilateralism', according to which the United States should act unilaterally in foreign policy to protect its interests, whether they be economic (for example, in trying to liberalise the Japanese economy), political (in attacking China for its human rights abuses) or military (in ensuring that Iraq is effectively disarmed of its nuclear, biological and chemical arsenal). Ruggie believes that unless the United States demonstrates a renewed commitment to multilateral initiatives (such as the extension of NATO membership to Eastern Europe), its complacency may help to bring about the acceleration of global disorder. There are three main reasons to fear that this will indeed be the case.

First, the combined effects of conditions inside the United States could give rise to a highly volatile pool of disaffected voters appealing for social protection against global forces of economic competition. These would include continued wage stagnation amongst the middle class and widening income gaps between rich and poor. Second, like the 'hot' wars before it, the Cold War contributed to the expansion and centralisation of the federal government. The end of the Cold War carries with it a natural desire to scale back federal expenditures on the welfare state. Third, the process of party realignment that began in the 1960s when Southern voters abandoned the Democratic Party directly affects foreign policy. Ever since President Roosevelt's time, the South had been solidly Democratic and its representatives in Congress were a mainstay of support for the party's internationalist agenda. Today, few predictable bases exist among the electorate for a consistent and sustained multilateralist agenda abroad.

Despite such dangers, whose existence inspired Ruggie to write his latest book, he does not believe that the 'window of opportunity' has passed. Despite the economic collapse in Southeast Asia and the security concerns it raises in the region, Ruggie remains confident that the United States still has time to renew the multilateral agenda in economic and security terms before the world enters a new era of crisis. Like so many commentators at present, he worries about the apparently uncontrolled pace of 'globalisation', particularly in the area of global financial flows. The question is, how dangerous does the situation have to become for politicians to act on the basis of enlightened self-interest rather than short-term expediency? Ruggie cannot answer that question, but he has pointed the United States in the desired direction if its leaders choose to act on his advice.

Notes

1 Ole Waever, 'John G. Ruggie: transformation and institutionalization', in Iver B. Neumann and Ole Waever (eds), *The Future of International Relations: Masters in the Making*, London, Routledge, 1997, p. 170.
2 See also the excellent selection of articles

in Charles Kegley (ed.), *Controversies in International Relations Theory: Realism and the Neoliberal Challenge*, New York, St Martin's Press, 1995.
3 John Ruggie, 'Continuity and transformation in the world polity: toward a neorealist synthesis', *World Politics* 35 (1983), p. 273.
4 John Ruggie, 'Territoriality and beyond: problematizing modernity in international relations', *International Organization* 47 (1993), p. 143.
5 Ibid., p. 165.
6 John Ruggie (ed.), *Multilateralism Matters: The Theory and Praxis of Institutional Form*, New York, Columbia University Press, 1993, p. 11.
7 John Ruggie, 'International regimes, transactions, and change: embedded liberalism in the postwar economic order', *International Organization* 36 (1982), pp. 393, 399.
8 John Ruggie, 'Third try at world order? America and multilateralism after the Cold War', *Political Science Quarterly* 109 (1994), p. 564–5.

See also in this book

Cox, Gilpin, Keohane, Krasner, Waltz

Ruggie's major writings

'Collective goods and future international collaboration', *American Political Science Review* 66 (1972), pp. 874–93
'International responses to technology: concepts and trends', *International Organization* 29 (1975), pp. 557–83
'On the problem of the global problematique', *Alternatives* 5 (1980), pp. 517–50
'International regimes, transactions, and change: embedded liberalism in the postwar economic order', *International Organization* 36 (1982), pp. 379–415
'Continuity and transformation in the world polity: toward a neorealist synthesis', *World Politics* 35 (1983), pp. 261–85
The Antinomies of Interdependence: National Welfare and the International Division of Labor (editor), New York, Columbia University Press, 1983
'The United States and the United Nations: toward a new realism', *International Organization* 39 (1985), pp. 343–56
'Embedded liberalism revisited: institutions and progress in international economic relations', in Emanuel Adler and Beverly Crawford (eds), *Progress in Postwar Economic Relations*, New York, Columbia University Press, 1991, pp 201–34

'Multilateralism: the anatomy of an institution', *International Organization* 46 (1992), pp. 561–98
'Territoriality and beyond: problematizing modernity in international relations', *International Organization* 47 (1993), pp. 139–74
Multilateralism Matters: The Theory and Praxis of Institutional Form (editor), New York, Columbia University Press, 1993
'Third try at world order? America and multilateralism after the Cold War', *Political Science Quarterly* 109 (1994), pp. 553–70
'The false promise of realism', *International Security* 20 (1995), pp. 62–70
'The past as prologue: interests, identity and American foreign policy', *International Security* 22 (1996), pp. 89–125
Winning The Peace: America and World Order in the New Era, New York, Columbia University Press, 1997
Constructing the World Polity, London, Routledge, 1998

Further reading

Hawes, Michael, 'Assessing the world economy: the rise and fall of Bretton Woods', in David Haglund and Michael Hawes (eds), *World Politics: Power, Interdependence and Dependence*, Toronto, Harcourt Brace Jovanovich, 1990, pp. 154–72
Rosenau, James N. and Czempiel, Ernst-Otto (eds), *Governance Without Government: Order and Change in World Politics*, Cambridge, Cambridge University Press, 1992
Waever, Ole, 'John G. Ruggie: transformation and institutionalization', in Iver B. Neumann and Ole Waever (eds), *The Future of International Relations: Masters in the Making*, London, Routledge, 1997, pp. 170–204. This includes a comprehensive bibliography of Ruggie's work.

ALEXANDER WENDT

Most of us take it for granted that we know how to breathe. We do so instinctively. This knowledge is tacit. We don't need doctors or scientists to teach us. Equally, scientists do not have to appeal to our tacit knowledge in explaining the physical processes to us. At a biological level, breathing is undoubtedly a complicated business and a scientific theory of breathing will contain references to phenomena that we do not need to know about in order to continue breathing. We value scientific knowledge when something goes wrong. If we stop breathing, or have difficulty breathing, then the scientist can use his or her technical knowledge to figure out what the problem is. Alexander Wendt's work is invaluable for those who think that something is always wrong with the conduct of international relations, and that statespersons need instruction from social scientists in how to put it right. He reminds us of the need to take our subject matter seriously, not as a set of 'things to be explained' by reference to some independent 'causes' at a different level of analysis, but as a set of phenomena that cannot be adequately accounted for independently of their interpretation by the agents involved. In the study of international relations, he believes, understanding the tacit knowledge of those we study is of crucial importance.

Of course, this is obviously true the closer we focus our attention on particular events. Nobody would seriously deny that George Bush's interpretation of the meaning of Iraq's invasion of Kuwait in August 1990 is of paramount importance if we want to explain the reaction by the United States to Iraq's behaviour in 1990. Obviously, as part of that explanation we could not rely entirely on the president's state of mind during the crisis. It is a necessary, not a sufficient or comprehensive, ingredient in a complex explanation. But what if we seek more general explanations for large-scale patterns of behaviour over time and space? Many students of international relations claim that the broader our empirical reference, the more abstract must our theories become, appealing less to the 'intersubjective' meanings among the participants in those empirical processes and more to the play of large structural forces. Wendt has devoted his research to criticising this claim as at best one-sided and, at worst, counter-productive. For if it is the case that 'agents' can do little to change the 'structures' that allegedly determine their behaviour, there is not much point in instructing them in the first place!

Since 1989, Alexander Wendt has taught at the Department of Political Science, Yale University. He was born in 1958 in Mainz, Germany. He was awarded his BA from Macalester College in 1982, and he received his PhD from the University of Minnesota. His work has, up to the present, been directed against those theoretical approaches that have dominated the North American study of international relations. It should also be pointed out that Wendt is primarily a meta-theorist or 'second-order' theorist rather than a 'first-order' theorist. As he puts it,

> [t]he objective of this kind of theorising is also to increase our understanding of world politics, but it does so indirectly by focusing on the ontological and epistemological issues of what constitutes important or legitimate questions and answers for IR scholarship, rather than on the structure and dynamics of the international system *per se*.[1]

In a series of major articles, Wendt has developed what has come to be known as the 'constructivist' approach to the study of international relations. It emerged in the process of a critical evaluation of the two dominant theoretical frameworks of the late 1980s in the North American study of international relations, neorealism and neoliberalism. The prefix 'neo' implies that they are somehow 'new' forms of old traditions of thought. It also indicates what they have in common. Despite substantive disagreements between neorealists and neoliberals, they share a commitment to *ontological atomism* and *epistemological positivism*. It is important to understand this shared commitment, since it is the foundation of inquiry that Wendt is concerned to reconstruct.

The phrases 'how things *really* are' and 'how things *really* work' are ontological creeds. The basic belief system of neorealists and neoliberals is rooted in a *realist* ontology. States exist in an anarchical international system, and the study of collective action among them 'takes self-interested actors as constant and exogenously given, [focusing] on the selective incentives that might induce them to cooperate'.[2] In addition to this commitment to the subject matter of international relations theory, neorealists and neoliberals practice an *objectivist* epistemology, which refers to the relationship between the inquirer and the object of inquiry. If there is a real world operating according to natural laws, then the inquirer must behave in ways that put questions directly to nature, so to speak, and allow the real world to answer back directly. The inquirer must stand behind a thick wall of one-way glass, observing the real world *rationally*. Objectivity is the 'Archimedean point' (Archimedes is said to have boasted that, given a long enough lever and a place to stand, he could move the earth) that permits the inquirer to discover the way states behave without altering them in any way. But how can this be done, given the possibility of inquirer bias? The positivist answer is to recommend the use of a manipulative methodology that controls for bias and empirical methods that specify in advance the kind of evidence necessary to support or falsify empirical hypotheses.

In contrast to what unites them at the level of meta-theory, neorealists and neoliberals disagree on a number of substantive issues: the implications of anarchy, the possibilities of international co-operation, whether states are motivated primarily by the pursuit of relative gains vis-à-vis other states or by the pursuit of absolute gains in power and wealth, the hierarchy of state goals, the relative importance of state intentions and capabilities, and the impact of international institutions and regimes.[3] The great bulk of contemporary theory, particularly in the United States, revolves around these issues within the shared meta-theoretical paradigm. Alexander Wendt is not uninterested in these issues, but he argues

that they are discussed within a conceptual jail that begs crucial questions about the relationship between agents (states) and international structures.

In contrast to the conventional approaches, Wendt identifies himself as a 'constructivist'. He defines constructivism as follows:

> Constructivism is a structural theory of the international system that makes the following core claims: (1) states are the principal units of analysis for international political theory; (2) the key structures in the states system are intersubjective, rather than material; and (3) state identities and interests are in important part constructed by these social structures, rather than given exogenously to the system by human nature or domestic politics.[4]

Wendt remains a 'state-centric' student of international relations, but he urges us not to take states and their interests for granted. Neorealists and neoliberals tend to do this because they implicitly rely on assumptions of methodological individualism in their research. This leads to a number of problems.

First, it takes the identities, powers and interests of states and reifies them or, as Wendt put it, treats them as 'ontologically primitive'. Such reification precludes from the outset consideration of both the structural or institutional preconditions to action as well as the character of the resulting structural outcomes. Although neorealists and neoliberals claim that they can explain the primary sources of conflict and co-operation in international relations on the implicit structure of anarchy, without a detailed social theory of state interests, they cannot. For example, we know that 'co-operation under anarchy' is possible in a world of positive-sum interactions, but not in a world of zero-sum interactions. The former is more likely to exist than the latter when state actors define their interests to include those of other states, that is, if they are other-regarding rather than strictly self-regarding.

There is a great deal of literature exploring the internal logic of state strategies within these contexts, particularly using sophisticated game theory. But the literature cannot explain the sources of the precise game under consideration because its implicit model of the international system lacks a theory of state preferences and action.

Second, rational choice theoretic conceptions of the international structure imply that it 'constrains' pre-existing state agents by altering the costs and benefits to them of different strategies. Much less attention is paid to the way international structures and institutions (in the broadest sense) help to constitute agents as empowered subjects capable of interacting meaningfully with each other.

Finally, an atomistic ontology of states in a condition of anarchy tends to imply that the latter is impervious to change. Its effects may be modified by co-operation, but the basic structure remains the same. Intentional conduct, particularly that aimed at altering the structure itself, enjoys little theoretical attention or legitimacy. This fails to recognise the way that individual states may not only reproduce the structure, but potentially transform it.

In his path-breaking article on 'The agent-structure problem in international relations theory' (1987), Wendt rejects the main alternative to ontological atomism in the field, namely, World Systems Theory. Concentrating on the work of Immanuel Wallerstein, Wendt shows how he moves from structures (the world capitalist system) to units (the states in the world system), inverting the conventional procedure. This move, however, raises the quite different but related problem of reifying structures as ontologically primitive. The world capitalist system is taken for granted as an object of study analytically independent of the actions by which it is produced. As such, it fails to grasp that it is only human action that instantiates, reproduces and transforms institutions and the structural 'constraints' of social

life. If neither atomistic nor 'collectivist' ontologies can capture the relationship between agents and structures without reification of one or the other, we need an ontology that overcomes the tendency to treat action and structure as the opposite sides of a dualism.

Drawing inspiration from, among others, Anthony Giddens in sociology and Roy Bhaskar in the philosophy of science, Wendt believes that students of international relations should adopt the main principles of 'structuration' theory. Agents (state actors) do not exist independently of the structures around them, but at the same time those structures do not exist independently of their reproduction (and possible transformation) by the agents. Hence the importance of paying attention to this co-constitution of agents and structures, which means refusing to overlook the way in which states interpret the meaning of what they do in favour of some underlying structural dynamic.

Social structures have an inherently *discursive* dimension in the sense that they are inseparable from the reasons and self-understandings that agents bring to their actions. This discursive quality does not mean that social structures are reducible to what agents think they are doing, since agents may not understand the structural antecedents or implications of their actions. But it does mean that the existence and operation of social structures are dependent upon self-understandings.[5]

At the level of epistemology, Wendt maintains that he is still a scientific realist, in the same way that positivists claim to be realist. The difference is that, while the adoption of an empiricist methodology reduces 'the real' to that which can be observed, he suggests that structures, which cannot be observed directly, are also real. The advantage of structuration theory is that it facilitates a methodological approach that tries to account for their influence on behaviour. For example, structural power may be at work when states do not act in ways that one would expect given the inequality of power and wealth in the international system, just as individuals may give their consent to political orders that are patently unjust. Erik Ringmar gives an example of the methodological innovations required to tap into the impact of structures on agents:

> We need to make a hypothesis regarding what things *would have been like* if only structural power had not been present, and then measure the difference between this condition and the one presently at hand. The degree of genuine consent which people give ... can be understood as the difference between the consent given under present conditions and what a person would choose to do ... under conditions where structural power was not at play. In this way we may make an estimate of 'real' interests and 'real' identities.[6]

It should be noted that, up to now, Wendt has written as a critic. In the late 1980s and early 1990s, he has published articles and chapters in books that contrast his constructivism with what he argues are the dominant and erroneous approaches of neorealism and neoliberalism. His arguments on behalf of the constructivist research programme are mounted in the context of an ongoing critique of neorealists such as Kenneth Waltz and neoliberals such as Robert Keohane. Thus far, and this is not a criticism but merely an observation, he has yet to generate an empirical (note: not empiric*ist*) research programme in the field. Nonetheless, he has some interesting ideas about the questions we should be asking in the study of international relations and, just as importantly, the questions that we should not be asking. Perhaps his most radical substantive argument is that we should give as much priority to the dominant *representations* of international relations in understanding state conduct as the distribution of *material forces* among states, whether they be military, political or economic. What matters, according to Wendt, are not the raw facts of material distributions of one kind or another, but their interpretation and signification by the actors themselves. Students of international relations tend to study behavioural outcomes associated with different distributions of power among states throughout history. Wendt argues that attempts to deduce patterns of stability and peace from this kind of analysis is inadequate in the absence of any theoretical examination of how states understand the nature and identity of threats from other states.

For example, during the Cold War, the distribution of economic power was anything but bipolar between the United States and the Soviet Union. On this basis, some scholars claim that the Soviet Union, at least in the early years after the end of the Second World War, was not a threat to the United States and its allies in Western Europe. It could be concluded that the United States deliberately exaggerated the extent of Soviet power to achieve its own economic ends, both domestically and within the broader capitalist economy. Such an interpretation, according to Wendt, is incompatible with the meta-theoretical assumptions of constructivism, according to which actors 'act on the basis of the meanings that objects have for them, and meanings are socially constructed'.[7] Rather than allow our interpretations of meanings and representations of international relations from the distribution of material forces, we should focus on the signification of their relevance to states before evaluating state behaviour.

To sum up, Alexander Wendt is a key thinker in meta-theory in the study of contemporary international relations. At least in terms of the ontological and epistemological dimensions of international relations theory, Wendt has done much to reveal and disclose the limits of the neorealist/neoliberal debate in the field. It remains to be seen how he, and others inspired by his work, uses the insights of constructivism to shed light on the empirical study of world politics. Thus far, his work has been suggestive rather than conclusive. It is a useful warning of the dangers of reifying agents and structures in international relations theory, but whether it can fulfil the promise of a 'post-positivist' research programme remains to be seen.[8]

Notes

1 Alexander Wendt, 'Bridging the theory/meta-theory gap in international relations', *Review of International Studies* 17 (1991), p. 383.
2 Alexander Wendt, 'Collective identity formation and the international state', *American Political Science Review* 88 (1994), p. 384.
3 For excellent overviews of the debate, see David A. Baldwin (ed.), *Neorealism and Neoliberalism: The Contemporary Debate*, New York, Columbia University Press, 1993; Charles W. Kegley (ed.), *Controversies in International Relations Theory: Realism and the Neoliberal Challenge*, New York, St Martin's Press, 1995.
4 Alexander Wendt, 'Collective identity formation', op. cit., p. 385.
5 Alexander Wendt, 'The agent-structure problem in international relations theory', *International Organisation* 41 (1987), p. 359.
6 Erik Ringmar, 'Alexander Wendt – a scientist struggling with history', in Iver B. Neumann and Ole Waever (eds), *The Future of International Relations: Masters in the Making*, London, Routledge, 1997, p. 274.
7 Alexander Wendt, 'Identity and structural change in international politics', in Yosef Lapid and Friedrich Kratochwil (eds), *The Return of Culture and Identity in IR Theory*, Boulder, Lynne Rienner, 1996, p. 50.
8 For an excellent critical overview of Wendt's work, written by a former student, see Erik Ringmar, 'Alexander Wendt – a scientist struggling with history', op. cit., pp. 269–89.

See also in this book

Giddens, Keohane, Wallerstein, Waltz

Wendt's major writings

'The agent-structure problem in international relations theory', *International Organisation* 41 (1987), pp. 335–70.

'Institutions and international order' (with Raymond Duvall), in James N. Rosenau and Ernst-Otto Czempiel (eds), *Global Changes and Theoretical Challenges: Approaches to World Politics for the 1990's*, Toronto, D.C. Heath & Co., 1989, pp. 51–73
'Bridging the theory/meta-theory gap in international relations', *Review of International Studies* 17 (1991), pp. 383–92
'Anarchy is what states make of it: the social construction of power politics', *International Organization* 46 (1992), pp. 391–426
'Collective identity formation and the international state', *American Political Science Review* 88 (1994), pp. 384–96
'Constructing international politics', *International Security* 20 (1995), pp. 71–81

Further reading

Carlsnaes, W., 'The agent-structure problem in foreign policy analysis', *International Studies Quarterly* 36 (1992), pp. 245–70
Carlsnaes, W., 'In lieu of a conclusion: compatibility and the agent-structure issue in foreign policy analysis', in W. Carlsnaes and Steve Smith (eds), *European Foreign Policy*, London, Sage, 1994, pp. 274–87
Dessler, David, 'What's at stake in the agent-structure debate?', *International Organization* 43 (1989), pp. 441–74
Hollis, Martin and Smith, Steve, *Explaining and Understanding International Relations*, Oxford, Clarendon Press, 1990
Hollis, Martin and Smith, Steve, 'Beware of gurus: structure and action in international relations', *Review of International Studies* 17 (1991), pp. 393–410
Onuf, Nicholas, *World of Our Making: Rules and Rule in Social Theory and International Relations*, Columbia, University of South Carolina Press, 1989
Ringmar, Erik, 'Alexander Wendt – a scientist struggling with history', in Iver B. Neumann and Ole Waever (eds), *The Future of International Relations: Masters in the Making*, London, Routledge, 1997. Includes a full bibliography of Wendt's publications.

POSTMODERNISM

Richard Ashley and Robert Walker draw our attention to the ways in which knowledge and power are inextricably connected in the theory and practice of contemporary international relations. They describe themselves as self-imposed 'exiles', on the margins of the academic discipline, probing its conditions of possibility and the limits to its authoritative knowledge claims. For them, students of international relations are forever in search of an elusive ideal, some philosophical foundation beyond the play of power from which to account for and recommend reforms to the practice of statecraft. For them, the modern distinction between theory and practice is replaced by 'discourse', a term which blurs the dichotomy between reality and its textual representation. Ashley, in particular, is engaged in a project of disciplinary 'deconstruction', exposing the strategies by which particular discourses of power/knowledge in the field construct oppositional conceptual hierarchies and allegedly repress dissent. The language we use to describe the world we live in does not mediate between the self and our environment. This is a modern conceit that relegates important epistemological issues to the background, concerning how we legitimate our fundamental ontological beliefs regarding the scope and dynamics of our field of study. Robert Walker sets his critical sights on the discourse of 'sovereignty', which is taken for granted by many students in the field but which also regulates our sense of time, history and progress. Since these thinkers refuse to engage in empirical or normative analysis based on modern notions of reason and truth, they confine themselves to illuminating the dark side of modernity. In particular, the figure of Max Weber looms large in Walker's work. He suggests that the 'iron cage' of modernity is manifested in the study of international relations, which limits our ability to imagine the political possibilities of radical change.

RICHARD ASHLEY

Richard Ashley has taught at the Department of Political Science at Arizona State University since 1981, where he has established his reputation as a leading voice over the last two decades in the postmodern/post-structural movement in (or rather, against) the discipline of international relations. He received his BA from the University of California, Santa Barbara, and his PhD from the Massachusetts Institute of Technology in 1977. In 1985 he won the Karl Deutsch Award of the International Studies Association.

Ashley's reputation is based on a series of articles and chapters in edited collections. His contribution to the discipline is best understood at the level of meta-theory rather than theory per se. Alexander Wendt has written that

> [t]he objective of this type of theorizing is ... to increase our understanding of world politics, but it does so indirectly by focusing on the ontological and epistemological issues of what constitute important or legitimate questions and answers for IR scholarship, rather than on the structure and dynamics of the international system [itself].[1]

In his important study of Ashley's work, Jarvis distinguishes between two 'phases', the heroic phase in which Ashley works within the epistemological boundaries of modernity and the Enlightenment, and a later subversive phase during which he seeks to undermine and call into question the criteria to which most students of international relations appeal in their search for truth, as well as the way in which they conceptualise the scope of their subject matter.[2]

Ashley's first book was an orthodox examination of the triangular balance of power between China, the United States and the Soviet Union, in which he examined the different rates of technological, economic and population growth among these great powers over time. As such, the book was firmly located within a conventional 'balance of power' framework, albeit one that adopted a dynamic perspective over time and did not equate the meaning of power with the ability to project military force abroad. Since the publication of that book, however, Ashley has devoted a great deal of attention to the meta-theoretical premises that inform conventional IR theory. In particular, he argues that the latter is dominated by an *instrumentalist logic* that is inseparable from its political effect, namely, complicity with hierarchical and oppressive global power structures.

An instrumentalist logic is based on a number of assumptions about the nature of reality, the function of theory and the role of the scholar *qua* theorist. First, it presupposes an ontological distinction between subject and object, which renders 'reality' as a sphere of experience uncontaminated by perception or mediated by language and interpretation. Reality exists independently of observing, speaking and acting subjects. Second, the function of theory is to explain fundamental and enduring patterns of activity in its subject matter. It does this by providing plausible interpretations of testable hypotheses that take the form of 'if/then' statements. Hypotheses are the crucial link between the 'data' of experience and the theoretical framework in light of which the data becomes meaningful. Finally, not only is theory an *instrument* of discovery, it may also be useful if we want to *intervene* and *change* patterns of behaviour rather than merely being able to predict them within particular parameters. For Ashley, these premises constitute a form of 'technical rationality' that

> conceives of life as so many more or less discrete problem situations ... defined in terms of certain given purposes or needs, certain obstacles to or limits on the realisation or satisfaction of these, and certain

means by which the obstacles and limits might be overcome.[3]

Ashley argues that technical reason robs theory of any critical evaluative role, and its hegemony in the discipline has meant that most students tend to assume that it exhausts the scope and meaning of reason as a potential emancipatory 'tool'. Consequently, the role of the social scientist is little more than a technician, helping to solve 'problems' within a given issue-area but failing to question the conditions that give rise to the problems in the first place. In contrast to this 'positivist' conception of theory, Ashley supported a more 'reflective' social science that would examine the structural/epistemological practices that give rise to the problems themselves, arguing for a radical attempt to confront those structures rather than allowing them to frame and delimit the 'solutions'. His major articles published in the first half of the 1980s are all variations of a philosophical critique against the epistemological premises of technical rationality as it was manifested in debates over realism, world order modelling and the dominance of economic methods (particularly rational choice theory) in the study of international relations.

At the same time, whilst Ashley pursued his critical analysis of conventional IR theory, he did so in pursuit of an emancipatory ideal of freedom and autonomy for all those who were oppressed by the power structures that most students of international relations relied upon to manage whatever 'problems' arose on the agenda of international relations. This is clearly evident in his debate with John Herz in the article on 'Political realism and human interests', where he invokes Jürgen Habermas and his notion of 'knowledge-constitutive interests' in the human sciences. In addition to our technical interest in controlling our environment and our practical interest in maintaining mutual communication and understanding, we have a

transcendental interest in 'securing freedom from unacknowledged constraints, relations of domination, and conditions of distorted communication and understanding that deny humans the capacity to make their future through full will and consciousness'.[4]

It would be somewhat simplistic to characterise Ashley as a utopian thinker, however, since he has retreated somewhat from a research project that seeks to enlighten us on precisely those 'constraints'and 'relations of domination' so that we may free ourselves from them. Like so many members of the radical left that have been influenced by the work of French post-structuralists and, in particular, Michel Foucault, Ashley no longer finds sustenance in the intellectual legacy of modernity to inform either our values or to provide guidance for how they may be achieved in any concrete institutional set of arrangements.[5] Nonetheless, Ashley was successful in focusing attention on the metaphysical and epistemological premises of orthodox international relations theory. He has drawn attention to the determinism of neorealist theory, particularly that of Kenneth Waltz, and he revealed many problems in applying micro-economic methodologies to the study of world politics. Ashley is a key figure in the so-called 'third debate' of the 1980s, which is less concerned with the adequacy of competing frameworks of analysis than the problematic nature of the criteria which inform our standards of judgement and evaluation.

Since the mid-1980s, Ashley has moved away from his radically 'heroic' phase into a more 'subversive' critique of international relations theory. This is consistent with his adoption of Foucault's conceptualisation of the interdependence between power and knowledge in social life. Modern conceptions of power treat it as a fungible resource that can be possessed, and transferred from one agent to another. In contrast, Ashley sees power as a network of disciplinary practices which help to constitute our identity as constructed selves. In this context, it is wrong to believe that revolutionary struggle in the name of 'class' or 'race' can possibly emancipate us from power. Rather than replace one meta-narrative of progress with another, Ashley has taken up the stance of the 'dissident', not seeking to replace hegemonic discourses in international relations, but undermining them so that

> practices might be resisted or disabled; boundaries might be put in doubt and transgressed; representations might be subverted, deprived of the presumption of self-evidence, and politicised and historicised; new connections among diverse cultural elements might become possible; and new ways of thinking and doing global politics might be opened up.[6]

Ashley wants us to stop thinking about power as a property that can be possessed or dispossessed. It is located in 'micro-relations' which constitute networks of power, and can be exercised 'from below' as well as 'from above'. This way of thinking is quite alien to traditional realist accounts of the 'balance of power' among 'the great powers' employing 'power' to protect existing interests and using it instrumentally to sustain or improve their status in a rigid hierarchical system.

In light of what he has written about the discursively constructed nature of truth and reason, however, Ashley's work since the late 1980s has not sought to occupy a privileged standpoint from which to evaluate theory or practice in international relations. After all, if truth is a function of power and vice versa, from what foundation can Ashley base his critique? Instead, Ashley has limited himself to a more modest task – to explore the complicity of international theory with the problems it claims to try to solve. This is the strategy of his deconstructive 'reading' of realism in international relations, particularly neorealism. He urges us to read realist texts not as attempts to mirror a given reality of separate territorial states coexisting in an anarchical environment. Instead, we should read them as so many attempts to

endorse the sovereign territorial state as the container of political community which delimits the scope of our freedom and structures our identity as members of discrete national communities. This is what he means by engaging in a 'double reading' of 'the anarchy problematique' that constructs an entire discipline to comprehend a non-place of international relations. The association of anarchy with the absence of order and authority is only possible on the basis of a prior association between territorial sovereignty and order/community. This is, of course, a theme that is also pursued in the work of Robert Walker and Martin Wight, but Ashley urges us to dwell on the intellectual/political practices that sustain this dichotomy, rather than merely accept it as the (pre)condition of international theory.

Richard Ashley's work is, then, that of a critical theorist, although not on behalf of an ideological agenda that allows one to categorise him in any of the traditional paradigmatic boxes of international relations. For although it would be tempting to call him a radical of sorts, his radicalism is not tied to any particular project on behalf of any named group of people. He describes himself as one who is radically estranged from both the discipline and the territorialised communities whose interactions it claims to represent, rather like the nomadic figure of the itenerate *condotierre* in Early Modern Europe,

> a stranger to every place and faith, knowing that he can never be at home among the people there . . . [with] a disposition to conduct himself 'virtu-ally', that is, according to a general ethos or art of life in which one endlessly struggles amidst contingency and chance to somehow make it possible to live an inherently virtuous ideal *in effect*. One may also say that the work he performs, though it be a work of territorialisation, is never fixed to any territory, ever nomadic, ever ready to move on in search, not of a destination,

not of an end, but of whatever localities might be made the object of a strategy, an art of life, a way of problematising self and selves.[7]

It is difficult at this stage to evaluate Richard Ashley's contribution to international theory since he rejects the conventional criteria which are usually used to make such an evaluation. His work has attracted the support of a large number of (mainly younger) scholars in Britain and the United States, as well as the opposition of those who see Ashley's subversion as a potential threat to the integrity of the discipline. It has to be said that Ashley's prose style, whilst almost poetic at times, is often dense and difficult to grasp for those unfamiliar with European continental philosophy and the vocabulary of post-structural analysis.

Perhaps the most serious criticism of Ashley's work, and of others inspired by it, is the charge of anti-foundational relativism. Although Ashley's work has to be seen in the context of an ongoing critique of positivism in IR theory, that critique has taken place just as the boundaries between political theory and the study of international relations have begun to break down. Today, the study of international ethics is no longer a marginal activity in the discipline. As Mark Neufeld observes, the 'third debate' in IR has made scholars much more 'reflective' about what he calls 'the inherently politico-normative dimensions of paradigms and the normal science traditions they sustain'.[8] Indeed, Ashley is in part responsible for this transformation in the discipline. On the other hand, his totalising critique of modern reason excludes him from participating in the renewal of normative IR theory. As Neufeld puts it, 'postmodernism is better suited to undermining the role of reason *in toto* than to expanding the notion of reason beyond the confines of positivist *episteme* in a way consistent with reflexivity'.[9]

It remains to be seen how Richard Ashley responds to recent critiques of his work

that accuse him of substituting one form of technical realism with a relativistic and indeed nihilistic celebration of ideals that sound attractive in the abstract, but which may not be compatible with each other, in which case we need 'reasonable' criteria to adjudicate among them. It may be that Ashley's contribution has been to help pave the way for the resurgence of ethics in international theory, even though he can no longer participate in that resurgence. However, it is still too soon to conclude that Ashley will now retreat from his critics who are happy to endorse the study of international relations as a post-positivist arena of inquiry, but reluctant to 'burn up in the heat of hyper-reflexivity'.[10]

Notes

1 Alexander Wendt, 'Bridging the theory/meta-theory gap in international relations', *Review of International Studies* 17 (1991), p. 383.
2 See Darry S.L. Jarvis, *International Relations and the Challenge of Postmodernism: Defending the Discipline*, Columbia, South Carolina, University of South Carolina Press, 1999.
3 'The state of the discipline: realism under challenge', in Richard L. Higgott and James Richardson (eds), *International Relations: Global and Australian Perspectives on an Evolving Discipline*, Canberra, The Australian University Press, 1991, p. 67.
4 'Political realism and human interests', *International Studies Quarterly* 25 (1981), p. 227.
5 On this point, see Jim George, *Discourses of Global Politics: A Critical (Re)Introduction to International Relations*, Boulder, Colorado, Lynne Reinner, 1994, pp. 171–6.
6 'Untying the sovereign state: a double reading of the anarchy problematique', *Millennium: Journal of International Studies* 17 (1988), p. 254.
7 'The achievements of poststructuralism', in Steve Smith, Ken Booth and Marysia Zalewski (eds), *International Theory: Positivism and Beyond*, Cambridge, Cambridge University Press, 1996, pp. 251, 253.
8 Mark Neufeld, 'Reflexivity and international relations theory', *Millennium: Journal of International Studies* 22 (1993), p. 55.
9 Ibid., p. 75. For an excellent overview of this debate, see also Molly Cochran,

'Postmodernism, ethics and international political theory', *Review of International Studies* 21 (1995), pp. 237–50.

10 Yosef Lapid, 'The third debate: on the prospects of international theory in a post-positivist era', *International Studies Quarterly* 33 (1989), p. 251.

See also in this book

Walker, Waltz

Ashley's major writings

The Political Economy of War and Peace: The Sino-Soviet-American Triangle and the Modern Security Problematique, London, Pinter, 1980

'Political realism and human interests', *International Studies Quarterly* 25 (1981), pp. 204–36

'Three modes of economism', *International Studies Quarterly* 27 (1983), pp. 463–96

'The eye of power: the politics of world modelling', *International Organization* 37 (1983), pp. 495–535

'The poverty of neorealism', *International Organization* 38 (1984), pp. 225–86

'The geopolitics of geopolitical space: toward a critical social theory of international politics', *Alternatives* 12 (1987), pp. 403–34

'Untying the sovereign state: a double reading of the anarchy problematique', *Millennium: Journal of International Studies* 17 (1988), pp. 227–62

'Living on border lines: man, poststructuralism and war', in James Der Derian and Michael Shapiro (eds), *International/Intertextual Relations: Postmodern Readings in World Politics*, Lexington, Massachusetts, Lexington Books, 1989, pp. 259–321

'Imposing international purpose: notes on a problematic of governance', in James N. Rosenau and Ernst-Otto Czempiel (eds), *Global Changes and Theoretical Challenges: Approaches to World Politics for the 1990's*, Toronto, D.C. Heath & Co., 1989, pp. 251–90

'Introduction: speaking the language of exile: dissident thought in international studies' (with R.B.J. Walker), *International Studies Quarterly* 34 (1990), pp. 259–68

'Conclusion: reading dissidence/writing the discipline: crisis and the question of sovereignty', (with R.B.J. Walker), *International Studies Quarterly* 34 (1990), pp. 367–416

'The state of the discipline: realism under challenge', in Richard L. Higgott and James Richardson (eds), *International Relations:* *Global and Australian Perspectives on an Evolving Discipline*, Canberra, The Australian University Press, 1991, pp. 37–69

'The achievements of poststructuralism', in Steve Smith, Ken Booth and Marysia Zalewski (eds), *International Theory: Positivism and Beyond*, Cambridge, Cambridge University Press, 1996, pp. 240–53

Further reading

Brown, C., 'Critical theory and postmodernism in International Relations', in A.J.R. Groom and Margot Light (eds), *Contemporary International Relations: A Guide to Theory*, London, Pinter, 1994, pp. 56–68

Brown, C., 'Turtles all the way down: anti-foundationalism, critical theory and International Relations', *Millennium: Journal of International Studies* 23 (1994), pp. 213–38

Gilpin, Robert, 'The richness of the tradition of political realism', *International Organization* 38 (1984), pp. 287–304

Jarvis, Darryl, *International Relations and the Challenge of Postmodernism: Defending the Discipline*, Columbia, South Carolina, University of South Carolina Press, 1999

Rosenau, Pauline, 'Once again into the fray: International Relations confronts the humanities', *Millennium: Journal of International Studies* 19 (1990), pp. 83–110

Spegele, Roger D., 'Richard Ashley's discourse for International Relations', *Millennium: Journal of International Studies* 21 (1992), pp. 147–82

ROBERT B.J. WALKER

Rob Walker writes in circles. Over the past twenty years, he has written a large number of chapters in edited collections and journal articles (some co-authored with Richard Ashley) that call into question most of the assumptions which students bring to the study of international relations. He does not suggest that these assumptions are right or wrong, he merely inquires into what may be called the conditions of their possibility. Although I have classified him under the label 'postmodern', he would be suspicious of such a 'move'. No doubt he would also question my intent in 'placing' him so that his work can be 'tamed' by a discipline whose ritual debates he has made his business to deconstruct as an expression of modernity.

Walker was born in 1947, in Reading, England. He graduated from the University of Wales in 1968 with a BA and moved to Canada to pursue his graduate studies. In 1977, Walker received his PhD from Queen's University in Ontario and, since 1981, he has taught at the University of Victoria in British Columbia, Canada. He has been a visiting fellow at the Australian National University and at Princeton University.

Perhaps the best way to approach his work is by describing it as meta-theory, although not in the sense that he wishes to prescribe ways in which students of international relations might improve their empirical understanding. Indeed, he is reluctant to confess that he is a student of international relations. His interest in the discipline or academic field of international relations arises not from its ability to generate a better understanding of its subject matter, but from Walker's curiosity in that which makes IR possible in the first place:

> What IR tells us is not quite what it is so often claimed to tell us. It does not tell us very much about how the world is, though it does tell us a great deal about the conditions under which we are able to claim to know what the world is and what its future possibilities are. Even as a phenomenon that demands explanation, it is certainly a good guide to where and who we think we are.[1]

As a glimpse into Walker's style of writing, this quote is a good example of his strategy. Rather than write about the world, Walker writes about the ways others write about what they think the world is or should be. Given his concern, or perhaps 'obsession' would be the right word, with presuppositions and assumptions, the reader can come away from an 'encounter' with Walker feeling somewhat frustrated. Most theoretical texts in the field assume that 'theory' consists of a set of explanatory or normative generalisations about patterns of behaviour or types of conduct in the 'real' world. The tasks of empirical theory are to determine and classify these patterns and to specify the conditions under which they are likely to occur, change or cease altogether. The fact that such patterns exist and can be discovered beneath the contingent elements of historical practice makes a theory (as opposed to a narrative history) possible. 'Theory' is thus a tool, or instrument, to facilitate our understanding of 'reality'. Theories are intellectual frameworks that make the world meaningful. Theoretical utility is, in turn, a function of explanatory power, which can be evaluated according to criteria such as internal logical consistency in the use of concepts, empirical verification of operational propositions and empirical support for hypotheses derived from the theory, and parsimony.

Walker does not agree. He rejects the conventional Popperian dichotomy between 'theory' and 'practice', according to which epistemological questions are privileged over ontological ones. For Walker, practice is already 'theory-laden'. The world of international relations is primarily a conceptual one – a world of meanings – in which action is filtered through and made possible by institutionalised processes of interpretation on the basis of which other actions are initiated in the actual world. We have no direct access to the 'actual world' except through its discursive construction by participants and observers alike. Thus Walker is certainly postmodern insofar as his work reflects the interpretation of the terms 'modern' and 'postmodern' provided by Zygmunt Bauman.[2] For Bauman, and for Walker, they stand for differences in understanding the social world and the related nature, and purpose, of intellectual work. A modern disposition assumes that some ontological principle of 'order', as associated patterns of social conduct, exists to be discovered and to be explained, and thus is susceptible to manipulation and control. But in the typically postmodern view of the world, order does not precede practices and hence cannot serve as an outside measure of their validity. Each model of order makes sense solely in terms of the practices that validate it. Thus, for example, 'ethics is not a repository of [theoretical] principles awaiting application; it is an ongoing historical practice. And far from being devoid of ethical principles, the theory of international relations is already constituted through accounts of ethical possibility.'[3]

If one is looking for a more specific term than 'postmodern' to approach Walker's work, it could be summed up as a 'Discursive Practices Approach'.[4] In contrast to the conventional interpretation of theory as a more or less useful instrument, it emphasises the discursive construction of reality. Language is seen as part of a system for generating subjects, objects and worlds. Individuals and groups do not 'exist' in any meaningful fashion independent of their linguistic construction. This recognition of the constitutive role of language and discourse gives rise to a radically new conception of power, which is inherent in the linguistic practices by which agents are constructed and become empowered within particular discourses. As Doty explains,

[a] discursive practice is not traceable to a fixed and stable centre, e.g., individual consciousness or a social collective. Discursive practices that constitute subjects and modes of subjectivity are dispersed, scattered throughout various locales. This is why the notion of intertextuality is important. Texts always refer back to other texts which themselves refer to still other texts. The power that is inherent in language is thus not something that is centralised, emanating from a pre-given subject.[5]

Walker is fascinated with the texts of IR theory, which he sees as particularly ripe for deconstruction, since the discipline is made possible by a series of conceptual and linguistic dichotomies – realism versus idealism, hierarchy versus anarchy, theory versus practice, ethics versus international relations, and most significantly, politics versus international *relations*. Despite all the literature urging, and sometimes celebrating, some kind of integration between political theory (a discourse of progress) and international relations (a discourse of survival), Walker explores in some depth the ways in which political theory and the study of international relations, far from being separate academic fields, constitute each other as a condition of possibility.

In his book *Inside/Outside: International Relations as Political Theory* (1993), Walker circles around the concept of state sovereignty, which he believes will be far harder to 'transcend' than many students believe. Walker claims that the principle of state sovereignty is 'crucial' (one of his favourite words) in appearing to resolve a series of modern antinomies between self–other, identity–difference, universality–particularity and unity–diversity. In brief, his argument is that:

The principle of state sovereignty is less an abstract legal claim than an exceptionally dense political practice. As a response to the problem of proliferating autonomies in a world of dissipating hierarchies, it articulates a specifically modern account of political space, and does so through the resolution of three fundamental contradictions. It resolves, in brief, the relation between unity and diversity, between the internal and the external and between space and time. It does so by drawing on the philosophical, theological and cultural practices of an historically specific civilisation driven by the need to realise yet also control those moments of autonomy that emerged in the complex transitions of early-modern Europe.[6]

Thus we enjoy the fruits of community as rights bearing citizens within the state. To those outside the state, our obligations are to 'humanity', a pale reflection of natural law. Within the state, 'historical progress' is conceived along a temporal dimension, whilst the arbitrary spatial division of international politics guarantees its continuation as a sphere of necessity rather than freedom. Within the state, the universal rights of citizenship are – in principle – available to 'all', yet that same universality depends upon the ability of the state to exclude 'outsiders'. Walker explores the political significance of state sovereignty at some length, arguing that in the absence of any 'postmodern' resolution of these contradictions, the appeal of sovereignty is far from dead.

Walker's work is important in undermining the belief that state sovereignty will soon be transcended as a constitutive principle of international relations. He acknowledges the growing weakness of its discursive power in an era of alleged 'globalisation', but he claims that there can be no substitute as long as we have yet to discover some postmodern means to overcome the contradictions of the modern world. His work is also important for those who believe that it is possible to resolve long-standing 'great debates' in the field whilst retaining some autonomous identity for the 'academic discipline' of international relations. Walker believes that the condition which gives rise to the discipline is a barrier to resolving the dichotomies within it. At the level of praxis, he argues that much of the talk about 'new' social movements is exaggerated. As long as such movements (constituted on the basis of gender, or concern for the environment) fail to offer new answers to the questions state sovereignty responds to so effectively, they will not differ from 'old' social movements, and probably suffer the same fate.

Finally, Walker's work helps us to appreciate the limits of so many debates about the adequacy of 'realism' in the study of international relations. Walker has done much to restore the historical importance of Max Weber in the realist tradition, but he has also written a great deal undermining the view that there is anything but a rudimentary similarity between any two 'realists' in international relations theory.

Notes

1 R.B.J. Walker, 'Pedagogies on the edge: world politics without International Relations', in Lev S. Gonick and Edward Weisband (eds), *Teaching World Politics: Contending Pedagogies for a New World Order*, Boulder, Colorado, Westview Press, 1992, p. 173.
2 Zygmunt Bauman, *Legislators and Interpreters: On Modernity, Postmodernity and Intellectuals*, Ithaca, New York, Cornell University Press, 1987.
3 R.B.J. Walker, 'Ethics, modernity and the theory of international relations', in Richard L. Higgott and James L. Richardson (eds), *International Relations: Global and Australian Perspectives on an Evolving Discipline*, Canberra, The Australian University Press, 1991, p. 129.
4 The term is explained well by Roxanne Lynn Doty, 'Foreign policy as social construction', *International Studies Quarterly* 37 (1992), pp. 297–320.
5 Ibid., p. 302.
6 R.B.J. Walker, *Inside/Outside: International Relations as Political Theory*, Cambridge, Cambridge University Press, 1993, p. 154.

See also in this book

Ashley

Walker's major writings

One World, Many Worlds: Struggles for a Just World Peace, Boulder, Colorado, Lynne Reinner, 1988
'Introduction: speaking the language of exile: dissident thought in international studies' (with Richard K. Ashley), *International Studies Quarterly* 34 (1990), pp. 259–68
'Conclusion: reading dissidence/writing the discipline: crisis and the question of sovereignty' (with Richard K. Ashley), *International Studies Quarterly* 34 (1990), pp. 367–416
'Interrogating state sovereignty' (with Saul Mendlovitz), in R.B.J. Walker and Saul H.

Mendlovitz (eds), *Contending Sovereignties: Redefining Political Community*, Boulder, Colorado, Lynne Reinner, 1990, pp. 1–12

'Sovereignty, identity, community: reflections on the horizons of contemporary political practice', in Robert Walker and Saul H. Mendlovitz (eds), *Contending Sovereignties: Redefining Political Community*, Boulder, Colorado, Lynne Reinner, 1990, pp. 159–85

'Ethics, modernity and the theory of international relations', in Richard L. Higgott and James L. Richardson (eds), *International Relations: Global and Australian Perspectives on an Evolving Discipline*, Canberra, The Australian University Press, 1991, pp. 128–62

'Pedagogies on the edge: world politics without international relations', in Lev S. Gonick and Edward Weisband (eds), *Teaching World Politics: Contending Pedagogies for a New World Order*, Boulder, Colorado, Westview Press, 1992, pp. 171–86

'Gender and critique in the theory of international relations', in V. Spike Peterson (ed.), *Gendered States: Feminist (Re)visions of International Relations Theory*, Boulder, Colorado, Lynne Reinner, 1992, pp. 179–202

Inside/Outside: International Relations as Political Theory, Cambridge, Cambridge University Press, 1993

'Violence, modernity, silence: from Max Weber to international relations', in David Campbell and Michael Dillon (eds), *The Political Subject of Violence*, Manchester, Manchester University Press, 1993, pp. 137–60

'Social movements\world politics', *Millennium: Journal of International Studies* 23 (1994), pp. 669–700

'International Relations and the concept of the political', in Ken Booth and Steve Smith (eds), *International Relations Theory Today*, Cambridge, Polity Press, 1995, pp. 306–27

Further reading

Brown, C., 'Critical theory and postmodernism in International Relations', in A.J.R. Groom and Margot Light (eds), *Contemporary International Relations: A Guide to Theory*, London, Pinter, 1994, pp. 56–68

Camilleri, Joseph and Falk, Jim, *The End of Sovereignty: The Politics of a Shrinking and Fragmenting World*, London, Edward Elgar, 1992

Hansen, Lene, 'Deconstructing a discipline: R.B.J. Walker and International Relations', in Iver B. Neumann and Ole Waever (eds), *The Future of International Relations: Masters in the Making*, London, Routledge, 1997

Jones, Roy E., 'The responsibility to educate', *Review of International Studies* 20 (1994), pp. 299–311 (see also the response by R.B.J. Walker, pp. 313–22)

GENDER AND INTERNATIONAL RELATIONS

Until the 1980s, and despite the inroads of feminism in other social sciences, the role of gender in the theory and practice of international relations was generally ignored. Today, this is no longer the case as a number of feminist thinkers have turned their critical sights on a field that up to now has been gender-blind. However, it was inevitable that feminist critiques of the state and the gendered nature of political theory would manifest itself in the study of international relations at some point. With the end of the Cold War, the return of 'identity politics', and the sustained criticisms of positivism in the field during the 1980s, the opportunity for examining the role of gender has been seized upon by a number of feminist thinkers. At the empirical level, Cynthia Enloe's work reveals the role of women in sustaining international relations even though this role is performed in the background and on the margins of international relations theory. Jean Elshtain is a political theorist whose contributions to international relations stems from her deep understanding of the role of gender in framing dominant conceptions of the state in Western thought. In particular, she sheds much light on the way in which conceptions of the appropriate role of men and women are expressed in the theory and practice of war. J. Ann Tickner's work focuses on the role of gender in shaping the way we study international relations. She argues that the inequality between men and women is reflected in the way that we think about 'security' and 'stability' in international affairs. Unless the experiences of women are considered in determining what is included in, and excluded from, the study of international relations, our understanding remains radically incomplete.

JEAN BETHKE ELSHTAIN

Jean Bethke Elshtain, like so many of the thinkers described in this book, is difficult to categorise within the established paradigms of international relations. In part, this is because she refuses to locate herself within them, preferring to step back from the discipline and inquire into the conditions of its possibility as an autonomous academic field. Although it would be appropriate to call her a 'feminist', she is very critical of some feminist schools of thought that she argues perpetuate the lack of understanding between men and women. In light of her most recent work on the fate of democracy in the United States, it would also be appropriate to see her as part of the 'communitarian' movement, but she also makes gestures toward the need for a stronger international 'civil society'.

First and foremost, Elshtain is a political theorist particularly interested in the role of gender in shaping the way we comprehend 'politics', whether domestic or international. She has traced the way in which political theory is infused with 'gendered' understandings of the distinction between the public and the private sphere, the nation-state and war. Much of her work reveals the role of gender in shaping not only the way we conceive and talk about international relations, but also the way in which we act in international relations. This is, of course, part of a larger purpose, which is to transcend the intellectual and political practices that perpetuate the way in which men and women think about themselves and the possibilities open to them.

Elshtain was born in 1940, in the irrigated farm country of northern Colorado. She grew up in the small village of Timnath (population 185). Her father was the Timnath schools superintendent, and Elshtain was the oldest of five children in the family. In high school, Elshtain was national vice-president of the Future Homemakers of America and demonstrated a talent for public speaking, winning numerous speech prizes. After high school, she went to Colorado State University to study history, later transferring to the University of Colorado, where she earned her BA in 1963. By this stage she had got married, had three children, and divorced her husband. In 1973, Elshtain was awarded her PhD from Brandeis University and joined the Department of Political Science of the University of Massachusetts at Amherst as an assistant professor. She became an associate professor in 1976, and a full professor in 1981. In 1988, Elshtain was appointed Centennial Professor of Political Science at Vanderbilt University (and the first woman to hold an endowed Chair at Vanderbilt). In 1995, she became the first Laura Spelman Rockefeller Professor of Social and Political Ethics in the Divinity School of the University of Chicago.

Elshtain's work on international relations emerged from her examination of the role of gender in informing the division between the public and private spheres in political theory. In *Public Man, Private Woman* (1981), she explores the way this distinction is conceived in the history of political thought in order to trace the evolution of the meaning of 'politics'. She argues that there is a dramatic change in the way the two spheres are conceived with the decline of ancient Greece and the rise of Christianity, but gender remains crucial in demarcating the two spheres. The book established the importance of gender in informing the way in which 'the political sphere' is identified and associated with allegedly 'male' characteristics. The gendered construction of the difference between domesticity and the political sphere remained the focus of her work as she turned toward international relations.

Women and War (1987) is Elshtain's best-known book, partly because it is one of the first in a wave of feminist literature that has been published over the last decade. It is also a very unusual book because it is so unconventional. In a sense, it is not even about war per se. There is no attempt to sort through the debate over the 'causes of war' in the international system or the appropriate policies to reduce the incidence of war. Instead of the usual question, 'what is the cause of war?', Elshtain is interested in some of the perceptual lenses which make war possible in the first place. She is particularly concerned with how such perceptions are related to the construction of gender roles in society and the reasons for the lack of attention paid to the relationship in the Anglo-American tradition of international theory. In essence, the book is an imaginative historical account of the traditional 'myths' that have informed the relationship between men and women and determined their role in war. She describes the two dominant myths as 'Man the Warrior' and 'Woman as Beautiful Soul'.

The book is also unusual in that Elshtain injects herself into the narrative and tells the reader of her own life story, relying heavily on her diary of the years 1956–72. Her aim is to 'delineate, first, my encounter as a child and citizen-to-be with the larger, adult world of war and collective violence as it filtered down to me through movies and my family's experience; and then the witness I have borne myself, since my teens, as student, mother, and political theorist'.[1] The personal narrative interweaves with the broader historical argument in such a way that the reader becomes complicit with Elshtain's 'search for a voice through which to traverse the terrain between particular lives and loyalties and public duties'.[2]

The first part of Elshtain's study traces in broad strokes the development of civic virtue in ancient Greece as inevitably armed, consistent with her analysis of the public/private split portrayed in her earlier work. Along with the development of armed civic virtue as a major strand in Western culture, she examines the 'other' Christian tradition of attempts to 'disarm civic virtue'. This emerges in early Christian pacifism, and the

Christian doctrine of the 'just war' can be seen as an attempt to mediate between both aspects of Western culture.

With their aims of constraining collective violence, chastening *realpolitik*, and forging human identities, the current heirs of [just war] thinking assume (1) the existence of universal moral dispositions, if not convictions – hence, the possibility of a nonrelativistic ethic; (2) the need for moral judgements of who/what is aggressor/victim, just/unjust, acceptable/unacceptable, and so on; (3) the potential efficacy of moral appeals and arguments to stay the hand of force. This adds up to a vision of civic virtue, not in the classical armed sense but in a way that is equally if differently demanding.[3]

Just how demanding is illustrated by the potency of the myths in facilitating war. In the second part of the book, Elshtain sharpens the focus of her study, pointing up the contrasting traditional myths and stories, according to which women are seen as life givers, men as life takers. Once again, the metaphors are telling. Within, and in addition to, the dominant myths just mentioned, Elshtain categorises women variously as the 'Ferocious Few', who exemplify Spartan motherhood (her example is the Spartan mother whose primary concern and question are about the outcome of the battle, and only secondarily about her son's fate in battle), and the 'Noncombatant Many'. It is the latter classification that provides the dominant image of women and war, even though stories of female fighters are not lacking.

Elshtain then shifts her focus of attention to the construction of male identities in the perpetuation of mythic discourses about war. Similar to the traditional myths controlling our images of women and war, some established patterns for thinking about 'fighting men' also exist. She discusses three such prototypical male characters, the 'Militant Many', the 'Pacific Few' and the 'Compassionate Warrior'. In this context, she describes the limits that gendered roles place on men and women. Male soldiers 'man' the battlefronts, and female parents keep the home front. Because these roles are so central to the construction of our identity, she suggests that we will be unable to reconstruct relationships between men and women unless we also reconstruct our thinking about war.

In her conclusions, Elshtain suggests that we need to destabilise the myths that help to perpetuate war. She emphasises the need to develop 'alternative images of citizenship' to those traditionally associated with armed civic virtue. We need 'to create social space through experiments in action with others [that] would free up identities, offering men and women the opportunity to share risks as citizens'.[4] Although Elshtain does not develop this point at any great length, the value of *Women and War* lies in its portrayal of the epistemological problems of approaching the study of war as males and females in Western culture.

Elshtain has written a great deal on the ways in which the study of international relations marginalises gender. Her primary target, as one might expect, is realism. Students of international relations tend to take the state for granted as a 'given', and then focus on relations among states in an allegedly anarchical environment, deriving alleged patterns of state behaviour from the structural characteristics of the international system. Not only does such an approach avoid asking important questions about the social construction of the state itself, it also conceals the role of gender is framing the way in which 'we' study international relations. The subordination of ethics to 'science' and the general ignorance of the complicity of political theory in constructing the dichotomy between 'inside' and 'outside' are two characteristics of the study of international relations, particularly in the United States, that Elshtain condemns.[5]

One of the most refreshing aspects of Elshtain's work is that she takes *gender*

seriously, as the social construction of women *and* men. As Adam Jones notes in his critique of feminist contributions to the study of international relations, 'very occasionally, one comes across a work – I think of Elshtain's *Women and War* – that explores the ambiguities of gender construction, and the *diversity* of women and men's lived experiences, *in a balanced manner*'.[6] She spends little time on the naïve view that women are inherently more peaceful than men and that, if only there were more women in positions of political power, the world would be a more peaceful place. Elshtain points out that women in positions of national leadership, such as Queen Elizabeth I and Margaret Thatcher, have hardly proven to be pacifists. She notes also that an assumption that women are naturally opposed to war has been used as an anti-feminist argument for sparing women the nastiness of the vote or political participation. What struck Elshtain most clearly during the writing of *Women and War* was the theme of sacrifice in the war stories that she encountered:

> Texts ... [that] laid the blame for war ... on the doorstep of male aggressivity grew less and less believable ... a relief, then, that my own son was probably not a beast lurking and awaiting the chance to bare his fangs and shed some blood, not his own.[7]

This is why it is overly simple to tag Elshtain with the label 'feminist', whether in praise or condemnation. Indeed, she has done much to undermine the view that there is a unified 'feminist' movement, and she worries that the label not only creates the illusion of unity among women, but also undermines the need to discover ways of engaging in 'civic virtue' that transcends gender:

> A polyphonic chorus of female voices whose disparate melodies are discernible sounds now in the land. Among the many voices are latter-day Antigones ('Hell, no, I won't let *him* go'); traditional women

('I don't want to be unprotected and men are equipped to do the protection'); the home-front bellicist ('Go, man, go and die for our country'); the civicly incapacitated ('I don't rightly know'); women warriors ('I'm prepared to fight, I'd like to kick a little ass'); and women peacemakers ('Peace is a women's way'). Each of these voices can be construed as the tip of a pyramid descending on either side to congeal into recognisable social identities that sometimes manifest themselves as [feminist] movements.[8]

Equally, Elshtain is critical of some feminists who proclaim that 'the personal is political'. Whilst she condemns the gendered construction of the private/public divide, she notes that the radical feminist attempt to politicise the private realm is itself a patriarchal strategy, but one which merely inverses the traditional hierarchy between men and women.[9]

In their excellent analysis of her work, Jenny Edkins and Veronique Pin-Fat suggest that Elshtain's project is two-fold: a commitment to the method of social constructivism and the political need to 'reconstruct the social with an appreciation of the intractability of discursive formations'.[10] Unfortunately, what it might mean to 'reconstruct the social' is somewhat vague in her writing. At times she appeals to what she calls a 'politics *sans* sovereignty', which gestures in the direction of some strengthening of global civil society. But the vision remains vague and poorly articulated. No matter. Elshtain is a key thinker in contemporary international relations, not because she tells us how to get from here to there, but what it means to be 'here'. By demonstrating the way in which war remains a gendered discourse in Western culture, Elshtain's work opens up the study of international relations so that students of either sex can appreciate the political implications of what is, after all, only an accident of birth.

Notes

1 Jean Bethke Elshtain, *Women and War*, New York, Basic Books, 1987, p. 4.
2 Ibid., p. 42.
3 Ibid., p. 151.
4 Ibid., p. 257.
5 See, in particular, Jean Bethke Elshtain, 'International politics and political theory', in Ken Booth and Steve Smith (eds), *International Relations Theory Today*, Cambridge, Polity Press, 1995, pp. 263–78.
6 Adam Jones, 'Does "gender" make the world go round? Feminist critiques of international relations', *Review of International Studies* 22 (1996), p. 421. Emphasis added.
7 Jean Bethke Elshtain, 'Sovereignty, identity, sacrifice', in V. Spike Peterson (ed.), *Gendered States: Feminist (Re)visions of International Relations Theory*, Boulder, Colorado, Lynne Reinner, 1992, p. 142.
8 Elshtain, *Women and War*, op. cit., p. 233.
9 Jean Bethke Elshtain, *Public Man, Private Woman: Women in Social and Political Thought*, Princeton, New Jersey, Princeton University Press, 1981, p. 104.
10 Jenny Edkins and Veronique Pin-Fat, 'Jean Bethke Elshtain: traversing the terrain between', in Iver B. Neumann and Ole Waever (eds), *The Future of International Relations: Masters in the Making*, London, Routledge, 1997, p. 310.

See also in this book

Enloe, Walker, Walzer

Elshtain's major writings

Public Man, Private Woman: Women in Social and Political Thought, Princeton, New Jersey, Princeton University Press, 1981
The Family in Political Thought, Brighton, Harvester, 1982
'Reflections on war and political discourse: realism, just war, and feminism in a nuclear age', *Political Theory* 13 (1985), pp. 39–57
Meditations on Modern Political Thought: Masculine/Feminine Themes from Luther to Arendt, New York, Praeger, 1986
Women and War, New York, Basic Books, 1987
'The problem with peace', *Millennium: Journal of International Studies* 17 (1988), pp. 441–9
Power Trips and Other Journeys: Essays in Feminism as Civic Discourse, Madison, Wisconsin, University of Wisconsin Press, 1990
Just War Theory, Oxford, Basil Blackwell, 1992

'Sovereignty, identity, sacrifice', in V. Spike Peterson (ed.), *Gendered States: Feminist (Re)visions of International Relations Theory*, Boulder, Colorado, Lynne Reinner, 1992, pp. 141–54

'Bringing it all back home, again', in James N. Rosenau (ed.), *Global Voices: Dialogues in International Relations*, Boulder, Colorado, Westview Press, 1993, pp. 97–116

'The risks and responsibilities of affirming ordinary life', in James Tully (ed.), *Philosophy in an Age of Pluralism: The Philosophy of Charles Taylor in Question*, Cambridge, Cambridge University Press, 1994

Democracy on Trial, New York, Basic Books, 1995

'International politics and political theory', in Ken Booth and Steve Smith (eds), *International Relations Theory Today*, Cambridge, Polity Press, 1995, pp. 263–78

Further reading

Berkman, Joyce, 'Feminism, war, and peace politics', in Jean Bethke Elshtain and Sheila Tobias (eds), *Women, Militarism and War: Essays in History, Politics and Social Theory,* wOxford, Rowman & Littlefield, 1990

Edkins, Jenny and Pin-Fat, Veronique, 'Jean Bethke Elshtain: traversing the terrain between', in Iver B. Neumann and Ole Waever (eds), *The Future of International Relations: Masters in the Making*, London, Routledge, 1997, pp. 290–315. Contains a comprehensive bibliography of the work of Jean Bethke Elshtain.

Light, Margot and Halliday, Fred, 'Gender in International Relations', in A.J.R. Groom and Margot Light (eds), *Contemporary International Relations: A Guide to Theory*, London, Pinter, 1994, pp. 45–55

CYNTHIA ENLOE

Cynthia Enloe is Professor of Government and International Relations at Clarke University, where she has taught since 1972. She began her academic career as a student of ethnicity and political development in Southeast Asia. Since the early 1980s, she has been a central figure in the attempt to reveal the importance of gender in the theory and practice of international relations. Her method of writing is a particularly novel one, which aims to expose the multiplicity of roles that women play in sustaining global economic forces and state interactions that she argues depend on women's 'private' relationships with men. Her work is sometimes classified as a version of feminist empiricism in international relations theory, which is primarily concerned to study women and the role of gender and to disclose the limits of the dominant frameworks of analysis in the field. For although it has become standard practice to divide the field of international relations among different 'paradigms', Enloe argues that none of them are adequate if we are concerned to explain the role of gender in constructing our political identity and to examine its effects in international relations.

Her work needs to be read, therefore, with due acknowledgement of the fact that the way we think about international relations is constricted by existing paradigms. They limit not only our perceptual field (what we 'see' as the most important actors and relationships), but also our conceptual field. Intellectual horizons help to define what we consider relevant to study and as such they are indispensable. They are also constraining. When we exclude certain parts of reality from our consciousness, we do so not only as individual thinkers or as an inevitable consequence of some universal laws of human perception, but also as social beings. What counts as 'relevant' is actually defined as such by social (and, Enloe would argue, gendered) rules of exclusion. These rules are often unspoken, and we learn them as part of our socialisation in a field that is dominated by male scholars. The reader will note, for example, that apart from the key thinkers presented within this particular section of the book, there is only one woman (Susan Strange) among the remaining forty-seven! Ironically, it is very difficult to explore that which is 'normally' excluded from our attention. Yet it is precisely the ability to focus on that which we normally ignore that may help unravel the tacit yet rudimentary foundations of the international order. Examining the social context and dynamics of mental exclusion helps to reveal the subtle yet most powerful form of social control, one that affects not only the way we behave but also the way that we think.

Moreover, those who are often excluded from our sphere of attention are not random individuals and groups, but usually members of specific social categories, which makes it absolutely critical that we be aware of the epistemological trap of taking our socio-mental horizons for granted. The latter are not static; they may shift over time; so those social groups that are excluded from the political and moral order may be included at a later time. For example, only 200 years ago, granting women political rights in England seemed ludicrous. Before they could be granted such rights, they had to struggle to be 'seen' and acknowledged as equal citizens to men. Enloe's work has to be understood as part of that struggle in the study of international relations.

For example, in her most well-known book, provocatively entitled *Bananas, Beaches and Bases* (1990), Enloe asks an initially simple question that leads in unexpected directions and to complex conclusions. What happens to our understanding of international politics if we treat the experiences of women's lives as central to our analysis? In attempting to answer this question, she focuses on seven major arenas of gendered international politics: tourism, nationalism, military bases, diplomacy, and the female labour force in agriculture, textiles and domestic service. She shows how women's participation and involvement facilitate tourism, colonialism and economically powerful states' exploitation of weak states. The role of women in the international sex tour industry, their ability to travel safely and the use of their images in developing tourism are essential to the workings of the international economic system. In her

view, 'that tourism is not discussed as seriously by conventional political commentators as oil or weaponry may tell us more about the ideological construction of "seriousness" than about the politics of tourism'.[1]

The maintenance of the international political economy, however, is dependent upon stable political and military relations among states. In turn, the creation of stable diplomatic and military communities has been the responsibility of women, as wives, girlfriends, prostitutes and hostesses. Military recruitment needs have provided the opportunity for women to join the armed services in some states, and also enabled male military recruits to bring their wives with them on long-term overseas assignments. In her discussion of the sexual politics of military bases, Enloe focuses on the contribution of women in creating unobtrusive military communities in foreign countries and to stabilising the lives of military personnel stationed abroad. Similarly, she studies international diplomacy by focusing on the wives of diplomats, detailing the responsibilities, problems and advantages of women married to diplomats, and demonstrating how their unpaid labour services helps to develop and sustain an atmosphere conducive to diplomacy.

In her examination of women as consumers, textile, domestic and agricultural workers, Enloe reveals the extent to which the international economy depends upon the work of women. Her case study is the creation and development of the international banana market, which she claims was gendered at its outset. Particular kinds of work were explicitly defined as 'male', leading to a corresponding masculine identity associated with it. Women were targeted as consumers in Europe and the United States. Women's work in the banana economy is invisible but crucial in processing and packing. She engages in similar types of analysis of the textile and clothing industries, as well as the international domestic service industry. In case one might think that these case studies are marginal to the 'real business' of the international economy, it should be noted that Philippine women working abroad as domestic servants annually contribute more to the national economy that do the national sugar and mining industries.

Enloe also explores the moral ambiguity of 'self-determination' struggles in light of her focus on women's experience. On the one hand, nationalist struggles for political independence are waged in the name of freedom from colonial control. But Enloe points out that nationalism can develop without affecting patriarchal structures within the colony, and indeed can develop new forms of indigenous sexism. In particular, armed struggle can have a particularly pernicious influence on women's chances for feminist liberation.

> Militarisation puts a premium on communal unity in the name of national survival, a priority that can silence women critical of patriarchal practices and attitudes; in so doing, nationalist militarisation can privilege men.[2]

Women also play a crucial role in perpetuating colonialism as well as being among its victims, and Enloe examines the role of European women as 'civilising' forces, as schoolteachers and nurses.

In her next book, *The Morning After: Sexual Politics at the End of the Cold War* (1993), Enloe pursues her quest for answers to the question, 'where are the women?' This time she focuses on gender relations and their role in maintaining militarisation during and after the Cold War. Once again, she sets out to uncover the forms of masculinity and femininity and the relationships between men and women upon which Cold War militarism relied. She also examines the gendered implications of demilitarisation in the post-Cold War era, warning against optimistic hopes for a 'peace dividend' that ignore gender. Her method is similar to her earlier work, drawing upon specific stories of women's and men's lives around the world

to support broader points about gendered militarism, and how it draws upon gendered notions of danger, security and work to continue. She argues that two prominent approaches to understanding militarism, defined as a process whereby a society becomes controlled or dependent on the military or military means, fall short by excluding the ways in which gender and identity are related. State-centred and capitalism-centred approaches should be more fully developed to incorporate the gender dimension of militarisation. The book opens up the scope of Cold War politics in a number of ways as Enloe uses the locations and experiences of women to draw connections between militarism, nationalism and the Cold War. She also expands the geographical scope of the Cold War to take the reader beyond the machinations of the two superpowers, preferring to focus on American women soldiers, the varied impact of women in the military for gay and lesbian rights groups, white women careerists, African-American women soldiers and feminist congresswomen.

Enloe argues that women's family relationships as mothers, wives, girlfriends and prostitutes form the necessary foundations for the 'high politics' that is the staple diet for most students of international relations. A good example of this is her analysis of the Gulf War in 1991. Rather than focus on the actions and mindsets of George Bush, François Mitterrand and Saddam Hussein, Enloe studies the war from the perspective of a Filipina maid working in Kuwait City. The Filipina domestic workers migrated from their own impoverished country to the economically powerful Gulf states. Once they had joined the nearly 30,000 domestic servants in the Middle East, they had little power to resist rape and abuse from their employers or, in the case of workers in Kuwait, by occupying Iraqi troops.

Thus Enloe's search for the answer to the question concerning the location and role of women in international relations takes her far away from the usual agenda of questions for students in the field, but she regards the new and old agendas as inextricably connected with one another. Global economic forces and the high politics of war and diplomacy among the great powers shape women's daily lives. On the other hand, the conduct of foreign affairs depends in large part upon women's allegedly 'private' relationships with men, as well as the social construction of gender in perpetuating militarism in the modern world. Thus she argues that

> international relations analysts underestimate the amount and varieties of power operating in any inter-state relationship and mistakenly assume that the narrative's 'plot' is far more simple and unidirectional than it may in truth be. Taking seriously the experiences and responses . . . of people living voiceless out on the margins, down at the bottom, is one of the most efficient ways I know of accurately estimating [the amount and varieties of power].[3]

In addition to disclosing the role of gendered relations in practice, Enloe's work challenges the way in which we study international relations. It is characteristic of much of international relations scholarship to value theoretical distance between subject and object, as well as theoretical parsimony. According to this conventional approach, the value of theory as a tool of analysis is that it enables us to simplify our subject matter, and focus selectively on key actors and relationships. As Craig Murphy points out, the work of Enloe and other feminists in the field force all of us to think about the ways in which gender bias in the study of international relations limits what we consider to be reliable sources of knowledge and the criteria for its evaluation:

The critiques conclude that International Relations tends to overvalue (1) a distanced and disinterested attitude toward its subjects, (2) the perspectives of the powerful, and (3) the specific means it uses

to close scholarly debate. In contrast, the new literature emphasises the value of (1) allowing greater connection to subjects, (2) engaging the perspectives of the disadvantaged, and (3) avoiding closure.[4]

It remains to be seen how feminist scholars, and indeed the broader 'agenda' of questions on gender and international relations, help to recast the field as a whole. On the one hand, Enloe's work has done much to unsettle the dominant paradigms, and she has exposed the limits of any framework of analysis that fails to see the complex ways in which power is gendered. On the other hand, it is not clear whether the old agenda of questions and conceptual tools can adapt to the new problematic or whether it must be radically changed. After all, Enloe acknowledges that not all women are victims of patriarchy and male power. She recognises that women like Margaret Thatcher and Jeane Kirkpatrick reinforce patriarchy by making international conflict less 'man-made' and more 'people-made'. In addition, she has engaged in perceptive analyses of the role of women in perpetuating power structures in the practice of, for example, colonialism, and their occupation of seats of power in middle management positions in international organisations. This suggests that, although Enloe and other feminists often attack realism for its 'malestream' bias, there may be some truth in realist arguments about the ubiquity of conflict between rival communities as a consequence of the environment in which they coexist, regardless of the power relations between men and women within them. The relationship between race, class, gender and national factors in the construction of identity and their effects on international relations remains hotly contested in the field. Although Cynthia Enloe has done much to draw our attention to the role of gender, just how it will be incorporated into the broader study of international relations has yet to be determined.

Notes

1 Cynthia Enloe, *Bananas, Beaches and Bases: Making Feminist Sense of International Politics*, Berkeley, University of California Press, 1990, p. 40.
2 Ibid., pp. 58–9.
3 Cynthia Enloe, 'Margins, silences and bottom rungs: how to overcome the underestimation of power in the study of international relations', in Steve Smith, Ken Booth and Marysia Zalewski (eds), *International Theory: Positivism and Beyond*, Cambridge, Cambridge University Press, 1996, p. 190.
4 Craig Murphy, 'Seeing women, recognizing gender, recasting international relations', *International Organization* 50 (1996), p. 53.

See also in this book

Elshtain, Tickner

Enloe's major writings

Multi-ethnic Politics: The Case of Malaysia, Berkeley, University of California Press, 1970
Ethnic Conflict and Political Development, Boston, Little, Brown, 1972
The Politics of Pollution in a Comparative Perspective: Ecology and Power in Four Nations, New York, McKay, 1975
Does Khaki Become You?: The Militarisation of Women's Lives, London, Pluto, 1983
Bananas, Beaches and Bases: Making Feminist Sense of International Politics, Berkeley, University of California Press, 1990
The Morning After: Sexual Politics at the End of the Cold War, Berkeley, University of California Press, 1993
'Questions about identity in international relations' (with Marysia Zalewski), in Ken Booth and Steve Smith (eds), *International Relations Theory Today*, Cambridge, Polity Press, 1995, pp. 279–305
'Margins, silences and bottom rungs: how to overcome the underestimation of power in the study of international relations', in Steve Smith, Ken Booth and Marysia Zalewski (eds), *International Theory: Positivism and Beyond*, Cambridge, Cambridge University Press, 1996, pp. 186–202

Further reading

Peterson, V. Spike and Runyan, Anne Sisson, *Global Gender Issues: Dilemmas in World Politics*, Boulder, Colorado, Westview, 1993
True, Jacqui, 'Feminism', in Scott Burchill and Andrew Linklater (eds), *Theories of International Relations*, London, Macmillan, 1996, pp. 210–51

J. ANN TICKNER

J. Ann Tickner is Associate Professor of Political Science in the School of International Relations at the University of Southern California. She has also taught at the College of the Holy Cross, Worcester, in Massachusetts. Her approach to the study of gender in international relations may be classified as 'standpoint feminism'. This variety of feminist scholarship argues 'for the construction of knowledge based on the material conditions of women's experiences, [which] gives us a more complete picture of the world ... since those who are oppressed have a better understanding of the sources of their oppression than their oppressors'.[1] Yet Tickner's perspective, which alerts us to the many ways in which the conventional study of international relations can marginalise gender, and is itself often gendered, is not designed to privilege women over men. She is a feminist whose work on gender is designed to pave the way for the transcendence of gendered inequality in the theory and practice of international relations. As part of that quest, Tickner's work must be situated within the context of the rise of 'identity politics' and new social movements in the late 1960s, which also gave rise to what is now known as 'second-generation feminism'.

The rise of 'identity politics' in the West was characterised by an emphasis on group differences rather than commonality. As far as the emergence of 'second-generation' feminism is concerned, which as a movement has lasted much longer than many other social movements of the era, there was also a growing feeling that the achievement of formal political and civic rights for women was inadequate. Feminists began to examine the deep-seated ideological structures that place women at a disadvantage in relation to men. The phrase 'the personal is the political' reflected the view that the traditional distinction between 'private' and 'public' spheres was untenable. Feminists called for the acknowledgement of patriarchy within the family and the liberation of women in all spheres of social and political life.

In her own work, Tickner has pursued both these goals, defending the view that women have knowledge, perspectives and experiences that should be brought to bear on the study of international relations and attacking the many ways in which men's experiences are projected as if they represented some universal standpoint. It should be pointed out that Tickner's work is always situated within a deep understanding of the literature she is criticising, which makes her arguments accessible to more traditional students in the field.

J. Ann Tickner is best known for her book *Gender in International Relations: Feminist Perspectives on Achieving Global Security* (1992), which points out how the field of international relations is gendered in such a way as to privilege associations with masculinity and to marginalise women's voices. As in the work of Elshtain, Tickner argues that realism is heir to a long tradition of thought that associates nationhood and citizenship with military service and with male characteristics. The concept of military security has long shaped definitions of national security.

Tickner also analyses how the major Western traditions of realist, liberal and Marxist thought have all drawn from culturally defined notions of masculinity, emphasising the value of autonomy, independence and power. Those traditions have formulated assumptions about behaviour, progress and economic growth in ways that render women invisible. For example, liberalism's atomistic individualism, instrumental rationality and focus on the market economy are based on male experience, whilst the Marxist focus on class conceals how gender divides labour and power, not only in the public sphere of production but also in the private sphere of reproduction. Moreover, the gender domination associated with these traditions has been linked to the domination and exploitation of nature.

Having analysed the masculinised, geopolitical version of national security, Tickner then articulates her own goals. She suggests that the world may be moving away from a system characterised by political conflicts between nation-states and toward a system more threatened by domestic and environmental disorder. Older definitions of national security are perhaps becoming increasingly obsolete and dysfunctional, enhancing rather than reducing the insecurity of individuals and their natural environment. Thus attaining peace, economic justice and ecological sustainability, she suggests, is inseparable from the project of gender equality. For example, as subsistence providers in the Third World, women must work harder when food, water and fuel resources deteriorate.

In building a new conception of national security, Tickner makes some practical suggestions, advocating changes in the hierarchies where policies are made. She wants more women in positions of power and greater value accorded to mediators and caregivers rather than soldiers and the diplomats of *realpolitik*. Although she tries to avoid essentialising the 'masculine' or the 'feminine', she does seem to accept the argument that women have developed cultural characteristics that make them more amenable to mediation, co-operative solutions and caring for others. But this is not based on any inherent superiority on behalf of women, simply on the fact of their experience of inequality. Ultimately, and most importantly, she seeks to transcend gender. Her goal is not to replace a masculine definition of security with a feminine one, but to erase constructions of gender difference and to create a concept of security that is non-gendered.

To that end, Tickner has tried to promote greater understanding between men and women in the study of international relations. Since this is crucial if gender is to be studied more systematically within the field, and not just by women for women, it is worth paying some attention to her thoughts on the matter. Tickner draws our attention to three types of misunderstandings commonly encountered in the field:

[F]irst, misunderstandings about the meaning of gender; second, the different realities or ontologies that feminists and nonfeminists see when they write about international politics; third, the epistemological divides that underlie questions as to whether feminists are doing theory at all.[2]

The first misunderstanding is based on a false perception that feminists are interested only in 'male-bashing'. Tickner claims that feminists in the field use the term 'gender' in a socially constructivist sense. It refers to the social institutionalisation of sexual difference and is a concept used by those who understand not only sexual inequality but also much of sexual differentiation to be socially constructed. She points out that gendered social life is maintained by three main processes: 'assigning dualistic gender metaphors to various perceived dichotomies, appealing to these gender dualisms to organise social activity, and dividing necessary social activities between different groups of humans'.[3] Thus gender is of as much concern to men as it is to women. Since gender relations are often unequal in favour of men, it is understandable that women, who have been marginalised in the field (both as students and as the focus of study), should be at the forefront of attempts to introduce gender into the discipline.

The second misunderstanding arises from the fact that many feminists cannot but challenge the ways in which 'malestream'

international relations is conceptualised. Whereas many feminists are interested in the social construction of gender at all levels of world politics, the conventional image of the world in the discipline is one of asocial states competing for power and influence. Given the commitment by feminists to some kind of emancipatory ethic, they tend to be equated with the 'idealist' tradition in the field. However, many feminists are extremely unhappy with the way in which Western cosmopolitanism in the Kantian tradition tends to universalise the experience of men. Thus feminists spend a great deal of time and energy in criticising the dominant schools of thought in the field, rather than trying to locate themselves within its categories.

A third source of misunderstanding lies in the suspicion with which feminists view the way in which most students in the field engage in 'theory'. The study of international relations in Britain, the United States and other Western countries is steeped in the intellectual tradition of the Enlightenment. Tickner believes that this tradition is itself a gendered product of masculine attributes that value the use of disembodied reason to understand and evaluate the social world:

While most feminists are committed to the emancipatory goal of achieving a more just society ... the Kantian project of achieving this goal through Enlightenment knowledge is problematic because [it] is gendered. Feminists assert that dichotomies, such as rational/irrational, fact/value, universal/particular, and public/private, upon which Western Enlightenment knowledge has been built ... separate the mind (rationality) from the body (nature) and, therefore, diminish women as 'knowers'.[4]

Tickner then goes on to illustrate how all three forms of misunderstanding manifest themselves in debates about security, contrasting feminist approaches such as her own with predominant frameworks in the field.

It should be pointed out that she does not resolve the misunderstandings that she so clearly explains. Instead, her important article sets out to clarify the underlying source of the divisions between feminists and other scholars in the discipline and shows how a feminist approach can expand the discourse on security in a productive manner. Whether or not Tickner's goal of promoting greater dialogue between men and women on the role of gender is successful remains to be seen. There are, I think, two major difficulties that she does not discuss, but which should be recognised.

First, it is undoubtedly the case that: (1) prior to the rise of feminism in the field, women were rarely studied, and the field as a whole was gender blind; (2) there exists a major imbalance between male and female academics in the field; and (3) the degree to which some of the discipline's central concepts are themselves 'gendered' remains insufficiently examined. Notwithstanding these three points, it is still unclear whether the field has to be completely reconstructed, or whether gender can take its place within the field without the latter having to abandon its existing stock of theoretical and empirical knowledge. Tickner does not commit herself on this issue, but it will be a central question for future research and debate in the field.

Second, despite her own belief in the need to 'transcend' gender, her own admirable desire to 'keep the conversation going' is not universally shared, either among feminist scholars or nonfeminist students. Notwithstanding the need to study 'gender', most of the feminist scholarship that has been done over the past decade is clearly concerned with the emancipation of women. As Lara Stancich observes,

[a] further problem relating to the wider inclusion of gender in IR is the sudden disappearance of 'men' where previously they had been omnipresent ... in most cases where gender is discussed, 'women'

become the sole focus of discussion and policy, and 'men' disappear.[5]

This could be a temporary problem as more men come to realise the importance of gender in the world they study, and a new generation of feminists emerge, less eager than an earlier generation to break down the doors of international relations in order to establish a foothold. Meanwhile, students could do a lot worse than acquaint themselves with Tickner's work on the role of gender in international relations.

Notes

1 J. Ann Tickner, 'Identity in international relations theory: feminist perspectives', in Yosef Lapid and Friedrich Kratochwil (eds), *The Return of Culture and Identity in International Relations Theory*, Boulder, Colorado, Lynne Reinner, 1996, p. 150.
2 J. Ann Tickner, 'You just don't understand: troubled engagements between feminists and IR theorists', *International Studies Quarterly* 41 (1997), p. 613.
3 Ibid., p. 614.
4 Ibid., p. 621.
5 Laura Stancich, 'Discovering elephants and a feminist theory of international relations', *Global Society* 12 (1998), p. 131.

See also in this book

Elshtain, Enloe

Tickner's major works

'Hans Morgenthau's principles of political realism: a feminist reformulation', in Rebecca Grant and Kathleen J. Newland (eds), *Gender and International Relations*, Bloomington, Indiana University Press, 1991, pp. 27–40
Gender in International Relations: Feminist Perspectives on Achieving Global Security, New York, Columbia University Press, 1992
'Identity in international relations theory: feminist perspectives', in Yosef Lapid and Friedrich Kratochwil (eds), *The Return of Culture and Identity in International Relations Theory*, Boulder, Colorado, Lynne Reinner, 1996, pp. 147–62
'You just don't understand: troubled engagements between feminists and IR theorists',

International Studies Quarterly 41 (1997), pp. 611–32

Further reading

Sylvester, Christine, *Feminist Theory and International Relations in a Postmodern Era*, Cambridge, Cambridge University Press, 1994

HISTORICAL SOCIOLOGY/THEORIES OF THE STATE

The following thinkers were not trained in the specific academic field of international relations. In particular, Anthony Giddens, Michael Mann and Charles Tilly share an intellectual background in sociology. Their interest in international relations arises from a prior concern with the historical dynamics of the rise of the state and its relationship with war and capitalism over time and space. To a greater or lesser degree, the following thinkers are all on the Left of the political spectrum, even though there are some interesting similarities between their views of the state and those of realists, who tend to be politically conservative in outlook. These thinkers depart from realism in their refusal to examine international relations as a separate sphere of activity from 'domestic' politics. Indeed, they are interested in the historical conditions that gave rise to such a differentiation of political activity. Furthermore, whereas realists tend to contrast the domestic and the international in oppositional terms (order versus anarchy, peace versus war), these thinkers are arguably more emphatic in asserting the dominance of power politics at both levels of analysis. The state is 'Janus-faced'. Its ability to generate loyalty and resources in order to wage war with other states is closely connected with its dominance over other actors in civil society. The following key thinkers are historians on a large scale, comparing the trajectory of the rise of the state across space as well as time. As with the thinkers examined in a number of the categories used in this book, they are engaged in a number of internal debates, over the role of capitalism in historical explanation, the relative weight given to what Michael Mann calls 'the sources of social power', and the future of the state in an era of apparent 'globalisation' of economic activity.

ANTHONY GIDDENS

Anthony Giddens's contribution to the study of international relations has been both direct and indirect. He has, of course, written a great deal on the importance of 'the international' for our understanding of the nature of the state in particular and 'modernity' in general. In addition to his own interest in the importance of international relations for sociology, his work on 'structuration theory' in the 1970s has inspired a number of IR specialists. In particular, Alexander Wendt has borrowed extensively from Giddens's early work on the 'agent–structure' problem for his own research. Like Michael Mann and Charles Tilly, Giddens believes that an adequate analysis of the modern state must embrace 'domestic' and 'international' levels of analysis, although his own theory of the state is developed via an extended critique of Marxism in social theory rather than as a direct result of empirical analysis in historical and comparative sociology. Giddens explicitly attempts to avoid reifying structures in accounting for social and political change.

As with Mann and Tilly, the reader may be intimidated by the volume of Giddens's written work. Fortunately for students of international relations, only a few of his books are important in the study of international relations, and his reputation is such that there exists an excellent secondary literature on his work.

In January 1997, at the age of 59, Giddens took up the post of Director of the London School of Economics. His appointment was partly due to the multidisciplinary scope and relevance of his work, in addition to his stature in sociology. He was born in January 1938 and achieved a first class honours degree in sociology and psychology at the University of Hull in 1959. After a short period of postgraduate study at the LSE, where he was awarded an MA in sociology in 1961, he taught the subject at the University of Leicester until 1970, and he then returned to Cambridge to teach and pursue his doctoral research. In 1976, he was awarded his PhD from King's College, Cambridge. In 1986, he was appointed Professor of Sociology at Cambridge, and he remained there until becoming Director of the LSE. Giddens has also taught extensively in the United States and Europe. In 1985, he was instrumental in setting up Polity Press, a successful academic publishing house in the UK; and in 1989, Giddens was appointed Chairman and Director of the Centre for Social Research.

In light of the wide scope of Giddens's work, I will focus on three aspects of his research that are most relevant for the study of international relations. These are: his theory of 'structuration' as an overarching methodological approach in social analysis; the key elements of his theory of the modern state; and his more recent contributions to the debate over the nature and trajectory of 'modernity' and 'globalisation'.

In Giddens's comprehensive, introductory textbook on sociology, the term 'structuration' does not even appear in the index, but he explains the basic idea behind this term in the following passage:

> Social systems are made up of human actions and relationships: what gives these their patterning is their *repetition* across periods of time and distances of space . . . we should understand human societies to be *like buildings that are at every moment being reconstructed by the very bricks that compose them.* The actions of all of us are influenced by the structural characteristics of the societies in which we are brought up and live; at the same time, we recreate (and also to some extent alter) those structural characteristics in our actions.[1]

Giddens argues that an adequate sociological analysis of any 'social system' must engage in what he calls a 'double hermeneutic' (or method of interpretation), paying close attention to the ways in which 'structures' both constrain action and make meaningful action possible. His idea of structure is similar to that found in linguistics rather than in conventional sociology. Structures are like rules and resources that are 'instantiated' in social systems as actors draw from them in their daily social existence. Much of Giddens's work in the 1970s was an elaboration of structuration theory against what he perceived to be the structural determinism of Marxist and functionalist theories of social class in industrial societies.

He was also engaged in an ongoing critique of the influence of positivist epistemologies in the social sciences, according to which actors are assumed to be products of impersonal and determinate social forces. The idea of 'structuration' attempts to mediate between excessive voluntarism and its opposite, determinism, in sociology. As Daniel Ross points out, 'as a child of a project of synthesis, [structuration] must be seen as a methodological apparatus separated from substantive concerns'.[2] It should also be noted that the 'double hermeneutic' has important implications for the social function of the sociologist. Giddens argues that, in engaging in sociology, we are establishing the meaning of the actions of people who are themselves already in the process of establishing the meaning of those same actions. There can, therefore, be positive exchanges between the perspectives of the sociologist and those of the actors he or she is studying. Each can learn from the other, and so sociological knowledge can even transform the lives we lead.

For students of international relations, Giddens's most important book is undoubtedly the second volume of his critique of Marxian historical materialism, *The Nation-State and Violence* (1985), in which he takes up a number of themes introduced in his first volume, *Power, Property and the State*. The latter, published in 1981, is a sustained attack on Marxist and functionalist approaches in sociology. It also introduced the idea that although human beings 'instantiate' the social

world through their activity, they draw upon resources and conditions brought into being and reproduced through 'modes of *structuration*' that distribute resources unequally and help to sustain asymmetrical power relations. Giddens argues that functionalist and evolutionary frameworks of analysis fail to acknowledge the revolutionary manner in which social resources are distributed in capitalist societies. He distinguishes between two kinds of resource. *Allocative* resources are primarily economic and material, whilst *authoritative* resources are those which sustain the unequal distribution of allocative resources in society. Prior to the onset of capitalism, he claims that the degree of control of a given type of social resource – allocative or authoritative – over time and space is low. With the onset of capitalism, what Giddens refers to as 'time–space distanciation' undergoes a marked expansion.

The heart of his argument is that it is only in capitalist society that class constitutes the underlying structural principle of the whole society. While various kinds of non-capitalist society had classes, only in capitalism does class permeate and structure all aspects of social life. Giddens thus distinguishes between 'class-divided societies ... within which there are classes, but where class analysis does not serve as the basis for identifying the basic structural principle of that society' and 'class society' per se.[3] Only in capitalism are the relations of domination over allocative resources the central relations that sustain power relations in general, whereas in non-capitalist societies the relations of domination over authoritative (social-political) resources constitute the basis of power. He claims that the nature of capitalist domination over the characteristics of daily life is radically distinct from all earlier forms of social organisation and it is intrinsically connected to the commodification of time and space, the separation of form and content. By revealing the nature and extent of 'time–space distantiation', Giddens casts doubt over the validity of a historically materialist developmental view of social change. The classic Marxist scheme, which traces an evolution from slave societies to communism via feudalism and capitalism, must be rejected. It is hampered by a teleological viewpoint (informed by Hegel) that presupposes a necessary movement from the particular to the universal in the form of a revolutionary working class with an emancipatory aim. For Giddens, the commodification of time and space is just as important as the commodification of labour in making capitalism possible and, what is more, the modes of structuration that sustain 'time–space distantiation' cannot be explained solely in terms of the demands of capitalism.

The Nation-State and Violence takes up the argument introduced in the first volume and explores the conditions that make it possible to sustain the dominance of class society. This is the book in which Giddens links the 'domestic' and 'international' dimensions of modes of structuration in the modern era. Once again, the theme of 'time–space distantiation' is centre stage. Furthermore, Giddens argues that the development of capitalism, industrialism and the nation-state cannot be adequately understood in any simple 'base–superstructural' manner. Each has its own independent logic and cannot be reduced to the other. 'Capitalism [must be] prised free from the general framework of historical materialism, and integrated in a different approach to previous history and to the analysis of modern institutions.'[4] Giddens claims that the accumulation of administrative, and particularly state, power is the dominant force driving distantiation. The rising administrative power of the state derives from its capacities to code information and supervise activity. As a result, the state can increasingly control the timing and spacing of human activity. It is not just the commodification of labour power that makes the development of productive forces possible. Surveillance in the workplace is equally important. Drawing heavily on the work of Michel Foucault, Giddens argues that the concentration of allocative resources depends upon authoritative resources, so that productivity does not develop from within capitalism alone.

The development of capitalism depended upon the emergence of a centralised state capable of pacifying the population and enforcing a calculable law, subject to neither the whim of kings nor lordly exemption. As in the work of Charles Tilly, Giddens claims that this task was accomplished through the expanding administrative power of absolutist states in the sixteenth and seventeenth centuries, driven in part by the exigencies of changing modes of warfare. The demand for resource extraction led the state to monetise the economy and stimulate its growth, and to secure mass conscription. The reduction of overt violence within the state, combined with the growing surveillance of its population by the state, was a necessary *precondition* for the expansion of industrialism and capitalism. Thus the latter is

> a novel type of class system, one in which the class struggle is rife but also in which the dominant class ... [does] not have or require direct access to the means of violence to sustain [its] rule.[5]

Industrial capitalism is internally 'pacific', but only because military power '[points] outwards towards other states in the nation-state system'.[6] For Giddens, 'modernity' is characterised by the complex relationship among four 'institutional clusterings': heightened surveillance; capitalism; industrialisation; and the centralised control of the means of violence. In his excellent analysis of the importance of Anthony Giddens for students of international relations, Justin Rosenberg spells out the implications as follows:

> The emergence of the nation-state system is understood from the outset as part of the same process of internal consolidation. The (outward) political sovereignty, which becomes the central organising

principle of the state-system, is the expression of an (internal) administrative and coercive unity established at the expense of other, transnational and local, forms of political power.[7]

Giddens's analysis of this process differs significantly from Tilly and Mann, however, for he is interested in the way in which actors, and particularly state elites, instantiate the structural constraints confronting them. He argues that a body of discursive knowledge – first balance of power and later sovereignty – that states use to regulate the relationship between them also shapes the organisational structure of the modern state. The sovereignty of the nation-state, the formal principle that states are equal in the eyes of international law, is derived not only from internal processes but from a widening external interaction of several states around this 'discourse'. The latter *constitutes* the emerging state; it does not simply describe it. Absolutist France was the first state to play a central role in Europe without becoming an empire and the first to develop a diplomatic corps. That diplomacy, which Giddens calls the 'reflexive monitoring' of the conditions of state reproduction, contributed to the instantiation of the legal and political structures of the international system. The 'domestic' and the 'international' are interconnected, not separate, political realms.

In 1990, Giddens published *The Consequences of Modernity*. In a sense, this book begins where *The Nation-State and Violence* left off, as Giddens explores the possible trajectory of 'modernity' into the future and evaluates its dangers and opportunities. Modernity is characterised, once again, in terms of relations between its 'institutional dimensions' – surveillance, industrialism, capitalism and military power. Giddens is particularly interested in whether the 'globalisation' of modernity means that we are now in what some have called a 'postmodern' era. He doubts it, arguing instead

that modernity has become 'radicalised' rather than transcended. He suggests that postmodernism is really just an aesthetic category reflecting the radicalisation of modernity and that the condition of 'late modernity' does not preclude systematic knowledge about it.

In this book Giddens is very concerned with the pace and scope of modern life, which he describes as a 'juggernaut'. The image conveys the feeling of many people today that we have created 'a runaway engine of enormous power which, collectively as human beings, we can drive to some extent but which also threatens to rush out of our control and which could rend itself asunder'.[8] Part of the problem, he argues, lies in the pace of distantiation in the late twentieth century. He talks about the way in which social life has become 'disembedded' from particular geographical locales, lifted out and reorganised across large time–space distances. The social importance of trust, in particular, has been vested in disembedded, abstract systems.

Despite his grim portrayal of modernity, Giddens feels that the juggernaut can be steered, at least partially. In this context, he moves toward a non-Marxist, critical theory without guarantees that he calls 'utopian realism'. Arguing that terms such as 'left' and 'right' are obsolete, he endorses a dual commitment at a global level to *emancipatory politics* – 'radical engagements concerned with the liberation from inequality or servitude' – and to *life politics* – 'radical engagements which seek to further the possibility of a fulfilling life for all, and in respect to which there are no "others"'.[9] Superimposed upon, and with the potential to counter the globalisation of his four institutionalised clusters of modernity, Giddens identifies four ideal-type clusters of opposition. Thus he advocates not only the internationalisation of the labour movement, but also ecological movements to counter the continued devastation of the environment, peace movements to counter the internationalisation of the arms trade, and free speech or democratic movements to counter the state's control of information and social surveillance. All this is part of a political project that seeks to identify possible agents and oppositional trajectories to counteract the 'high-consequence risks' confronting the contemporary world. The four institutions of modernity make possible a more rewarding existence than any pre-modern social system, but only the sustained endeavour of a praxis of utopian realism will put it in our grasp. Whatever one thinks of such a 'praxis', and Giddens's move from sociological analysis to normative prescription in recent years, his work is of importance for the study of international relations. As Rosenberg notes, it helps to provide 'a conceptual vocabulary for thinking about the nation-state system generically, and about the specific ways in which violent means are mobilised and implicated in the reproduction of its core institutions'.

Notes

1 Anthony Giddens, *Sociology*, Second edition, Cambridge, Polity Press, 1993, p. 18.
2 Daniel Ross, 'Anthony Giddens', in Peter Belharz (ed.), *Social Theory: A Guide to Central Thinkers*, Sydney, Allen & Unwin, 1991, p. 124.
3 Anthony Giddens, *A Contemporary Critique of Historical Materialism. Vol. 1. Power, Property and the State*, Berkeley, University of California Press, 1981, p. 108.
4 Anthony Giddens, *A Contemporary Critique of Historical Materialism. Vol. 2. The Nation-State and Violence*, Cambridge, Polity Press, 1985, p. 1.
5 Ibid., p. 159.
6 Ibid., p. 192.
7 Justin Rosenberg, 'A non-realist theory of sovereignty?: Giddens' *The Nation-State and Violence*', *Millennium: Journal of International Studies* 19 (1990), p. 253.
8 Anthony Giddens, *The Consequences of Modernity*, Stanford, Stanford University Press, 1990, p. 139.
9 Ibid., p. 156.
10 Justin Rosenberg, 'A non-realist theory of sovereignty?', p. 258.

See also in this book

Mann, Tilly, Wendt

Giddens's major writings

For a complete list of the principal works of Anthony Giddens see Christopher Bryant and David Jary (eds), *Giddens' Theory of Structuration: A Critical Appreciation*, London, Routledge, 1991, pp. 222–9
Capitalism and Modern Social Theory: An Analysis of the Writings of Marx, Durkheim and Max Weber, Cambridge, University Press, 1971
Politics and Sociology in the Thought of Max Weber, London, Macmillan, 1972
The Class Structure of the Advanced Societies, London, Hutchinson, 1973
Positivism and Sociology, London, Heinemann, 1974
Studies in Social and Political Theory, London, Hutchinson, 1977
Emile Durkheim, New York, Penguin Books, 1978
Central Problems in Social Theory: Action, Structure, and Contradiction in Social Analysis, London, Macmillan, 1979
A Contemporary Critique of Historical Materialism. Vol. 1. Power, Property and the State, Berkeley, University of California Press, 1981
The Constitution of Society: Outline of the Theory of Structuration, Cambridge, Polity Press, 1984
A Contemporary Critique of Historical Materialism. Vol. 2. The Nation-State and Violence, Cambridge, Polity Press, 1985
Social Theory and Modern Sociology, Cambridge, Polity Press in association with Basil Blackwell, 1987
The Consequences of Modernity, Cambridge, Polity Press in association with Basil Blackwell, 1990
Modernity and Self-identity: Self and Society in the Late Modern Age, Cambridge, Polity Press, 1991
Sociology, Second edition, Cambridge, Polity Press, 1993
Beyond Left and Right: The Future of Radical Politics, Cambridge, Polity Press, 1994.

Further reading

Bryant, Christopher and Jary, David (eds), *Giddens' Theory of Structuration: A Critical Appreciation*, London, Routledge, 1991
Bryant, Christopher G.A. and Jary, David (eds), *Anthony Giddens: Critical Assessments*, London, Routledge, 1997 (four volumes)
Clark, Jon, Modgil, Celia and Modgil, Sohan (eds), *Anthony Giddens: Consensus and Controversy*, New York, Falmer Press, 1990

Cohen, Ira, J., *Structuration Theory: Anthony Giddens and the Constitution of Social Life*, London, Macmillan, 1989

Held, David and Thompson, John (eds), *Social Theory of Modern Societies: Anthony Giddens and his Critics*, Cambridge, Cambridge University Press, 1989

Rosenberg, Justin, 'A non-realist theory of sovereignty: Giddens' *The Nation-State and Violence*', *Millennium: Journal of International Studies* 19 (1990), pp. 249–59

Shaw, Martin, *Global Society and International Relations*, Cambridge, Polity Press, 1994

MICHAEL MANN

Michael Mann's contribution to the study of international relations is not based on any particular allegiance to one of the existing theoretical perspectives *within* the discipline of international relations. He regards himself as 'a consumer' of IR research, an 'outsider', just 'one of those general readers on whom the sales of IR books depend'.[1] Of course, in a formal sense, this is correct. Mann, who was born in 1942, is Professor of Sociology at UCLA, and he identifies his own area of research as macrosociology, or historical sociology, a student of 'the history and theory of power relations in human societies'.[2] In any other sense, Mann's self-description is far too modest. His work on the sources of social power in history, the rise of the state and the fate of the state in the post-Cold War era justify his inclusion in this book as a major producer of theory in the study of 'international relations'. In addition, his contribution undermines the assumption that international relations can be understood within a separate, autonomous, academic discipline of 'international relations'.

It would be fair to say that the scope of Mann's work is broader than that of any other key thinker in this book, and the sheer volume of his writing makes it very difficult to summarise. Consequently, I will focus on the main elements of his history and theory

of social power in history, and his contribution to our understanding of the nature of the state. Finally, I will describe how Michael Mann applies his theoretical and historical work to two important areas of contemporary debate: the relationship between international stability and the domestic characteristics of states; and the impact of 'globalisation' on the nation-state. At the time of writing, Mann's work on the history of power remains incomplete. In 1986 he published the first of four volumes of work on the sources of social power in history. The second volume was published in 1993. The third volume, in which Mann covers the twentieth century, has yet to appear, and promises to focus on the theoretical implications of his historical narrative in the final volume. Consequently, what follows is a brief summary of work in progress rather than a final report.

In the first volume of *The Sources of Social Power*, which covers the period of history from Neolithic times to the eighteenth century, Mann introduces his typology of four different types of power and their interaction over time and space. He argues that we must reject two common assumptions if we are adequately to understand historical and social change. First, historical change is not evolutionary, but 'neo-episodic'. By evolution, he means the gradual, inexorable establishment and rise of rank societies, 'civilisation' and the state. Mann argues that what appears in hindsight to have been a continuous growth in our ability to marshal social power and control our natural environment was, in fact, the accidental consequence of episodic changes in human history. At critical episodes in human history, the distribution of forms of power between social groups changed, resulting in further changes in types of rule. Second, Mann rejects the idea that societies have a self-contained, unitary form. Instead, he offers a definition based on four sources of social power: ideological, economic, military and political (IEMP). Mann's 'political' category refers to the 'administrative' capacity of ruling elites, a source of power that does not possess the same categorical autonomy as the others. This is because any exercise of political power depends on the possession of either ideological power or economic power, and normally a combination of both force and belief.

One could compare Mann's forms of 'social power' with Susan Strange's forms of 'structural power'. As explained elsewhere in this book, she distinguishes between structures of production, finance, security and information. Mann conflates production and finance in the 'economic' category, his 'military' category conforms to what Strange calls 'security', and there is some similarity between what she calls 'information' and what Mann refers to as 'ideology'. He argues that each of these sources of power has its own network of relationships and interactions, its own spatio-temporal organisation, so that societies appear, *in toto*, as 'confederal, overlapping, intersecting networks' combining areas of authoritative power with areas of diffused power. The first volume then traces the interaction of the sources of power over human history, ending up with Mann's account of the rise of the state as the dominant form of political rule. At the risk of oversimplification, there are four distinct episodes in the historical narrative, each of which is characterised by particular configurations of political rule.

Mann argues that after a long period of human life without states, the earliest civilisations and states in human history were two-tiered, federal systems, a grouping of city-states tied at a higher level by more diffused networks of ideology, alliances and trade. The rise of coercive empires, or 'empires of domination', is associated with more intensively coercive networks of power. Mann traces their rise to the takeover of Sumerian civilisation by Sargon of Akad in 2310 BC. The explanation for the first transformation in forms of state/political rule is very complex, but Mann dwells a great deal on the phenomenon of 'caging'. Other things being equal, people resent coercive rule and seek to escape it when they can. Noting how the ancient civilisations of Mesopotamia, Egypt, India and China were associated with flood plains and associated corridors of alluvial agriculture surrounded by deserts, he talks about societies becoming caged or circumscribed, trapped in particular territorial and social relationships which facilitate the rise of use of military coercion.

Avoiding any assumption of inevitable historical development, Mann then examines the collapse of coercive empires and the development of feudalism. Coercion through military power may be necessary to control growing populations and enable elites to extract the economic surplus, but it is easier to conquer people than to govern them over extensive geographical territory. Tensions existed between intensive networks of power at the imperial core and the diffused power networks at the periphery. Of particular note is Mann's emphasis on the reasons why empires of coercion often collapsed because of the inability of ruling elites to control the periphery. In part changes in the technology of war facilitated collapse. For example, the use of charioteers and the introduction of iron for weapons and ploughs over the first millennium BC shifted power to the geographical sources of iron and, ultimately, to Barbarian Europe. What distinguished Greek civilisation was its strategic marchland position between the Middle East and those lands of the heavier, wetter soils of Europe. The rise of the Roman empire is traced to its superior infantry force and a ruling-class culture of unprecedented literacy, capable of assimilating any conquered elite in its path. At the same time, Roman civilisation extended the Western migration of civilisation's leading edge, even though it too was unable to control its periphery against barbarian invasion.

In the era of European feudalism, Mann suggests that the relationship between forms of power changed again. This time, power was diffused. Networks of local and decentralised power proliferate, with no one social group having a monopoly and each having a degree of autonomy. The localisation and intensity of these power relations is seen as providing medieval Europe with a special dynamism, one that encouraged developmental as opposed to cyclical change. On the other hand, the Christian Church provided a more extensive network of ideological power that cut across the many local spheres of lordly power. Mann argues that the Church was a crucial source of normative pacification for European society, relying here on Emile Durkheim's argument that religion provides a bond of social cohesion. The Catholic Church 'pacified' violence between and within states and 'regulated' trade. Its preaching of 'consideration, decency, and charity towards all Christians' imparted a 'common humanity' and 'social identity' to all Europeans that acted as a 'substitute for coercive pacification normally required in previous extensive societies'.[3] In addition, the Church provided a network of links for trade.

Over time, these links were increasingly secularized, activated more by the needs of trade and capitalism than the Church. Combined with the dynamism of its local competitive power relations, these pan-European networks of trade fostered a distinct capitalist ethos from as early as the ninth century onwards. The rise of the territorial state took place much later, when the Church itself was unable to maintain its own unity, and it divided into Catholicism and Protestantism, culminating in the Peace of Westphalia in 1648 (the usual starting point for students of *international* relations). In his historical analysis of the emergence of the territorial state, Mann stresses the importance of external military competition among elites as the main impetus, rather than the needs of internal political administration.

The connection between war among states and their internal development is explored further in the second volume of Mann's *magnum opus*. Once again the dynamic relationship between the sources of social power is employed as the organising motif for Mann's meticulous analysis of the period from the eighteenth century and the First World War. The focus of inquiry is geographically confined to Britain, Germany, France and the United States, with some reference to Russia and Austria-Hungary. He argues that, in the eighteenth century, military and economic sources of power dominated political and ideological sources, whereas in the nineteenth century the relationship was the other way round. Mann covers all the major political revolutions and the industrial revolution that open his period. He offers an intricate analysis of the functional, bureaucratic and fiscal expansion of the state and, as in the first volume, he refuses to privilege *a priori* any one source of power over the others in the absence of historical verification. For Mann, the sources of social power are, as he puts it, 'entwined'. At one period of time, one source may increase rapidly (such as military power in the late eighteenth century), with a powerful effect on states and classes. But the forms of power are not fully autonomous. The characteristic structural developments of the period emerged from such entwining, justifying Mann's hostility to all forms of sociological determinism or reductionism.

Whilst we still await Mann's grand theory of power, we must be content with the heuristic utility of his 'IEMP-model', as he calls it, 'an analytical point of entry for dealing with a mess'.[4] It is also useful for deepening our understanding of the state itself, a necessary first step in evaluating the extent to which 'state power' is changing under the impact of alleged 'globalising forces' of varying kinds at the end of the twentieth century. Drawing on the work of Max Weber, Theda Skocpol and Charles Tilly, Mann combines institutional and functional elements in defining the state as:

1 A *differentiated* set of institutions and personnel embodying

2 *Centrality* in the sense that political relations radiate outwards from a centre to cover

3 A *territorially demarcated area*, over which it exercises

4 A monopoly of *authoritative, binding rule making*, backed up by a monopoly of the means of physical violence.[5]

He makes an important distinction between *despotic* and *infrastructural* power. The former refers to 'the range of actions which the elite is empowered to undertake without routine, institutionalised negotiation with civil society groups'. The latter refers to 'the capacity of the state to actually penetrate civil society, and to implement logistically political decisions throughout the realm'.[6] It makes no sense to distinguish between strong and weak states without specifying their relative power along both dimensions, despotic and infrastructural. Mann himself distinguishes four ideal-types of state. *Feudal* states are weak along both dimensions of power. *Imperial* states enjoy high levels of despotic power, but the degree of infrastructural coordination is low. *Bureaucratic* states (a term that covers capitalist democracies) are powerful in an infrastructural sense, but weak in a despotic sense. *Authoritarian* states (such as Nazi Germany and the former Soviet Union) have high levels of despotic and infrastructural power, although one might argue that the Soviet Union belongs in the imperial category rather than the authoritarian one. Whatever one thinks of the way in which Mann classifies states within his typology, the typology itself is extremely helpful in comparative sociology as well as the study of international relations.

Mann argues that there has occurred a long-term historical growth in the infrastructural power of the modern state, as the range of 'logistical techniques' for the effective penetration of social life by the state have multiplied. These include a division of labour between the state's main activities which are coordinated centrally, the expansion of literacy enabling messages to be transmitted through state territory, the development of coinage which allows commodities to be exchanged under an ultimate guarantee of value by the state, and the increasing rapidity of communications infrastructure. However, he also makes the point that such logistical techniques, while their historical growth has facilitated the expansion of the state's infrastructural power, are also available for use by other groups in civil society.

> In the whole history of the development of the infrastructure of power there is virtually no technique which belongs necessarily to the state, or conversely to civil society . . . [t]he obvious question is: if infrastructural powers are a general feature of society, in what circumstances are they appropriated by the state? What are the origins of the autonomous power of the state?[7]

Mann's answer to these questions identifies three features of the state, which account for its endurance as a form of political rule since the late medieval period. First, the state is necessary in the sense that all societies require rules. Whilst there are alternatives to the state as the provider and enforcer of rules to maintain social order (such as force, exchange and custom), 'societies with states have had superior survival value to those without them'.[8] Second, in addition to maintaining internal order, the state performs a variety of functions that enable it to transcend particular group interests within the state. Chief among these are the provision of military defence against other states, maintaining communications infrastructure and economic redistribution and regulation. Whilst these two features are usually singled out as the most important in justifying a view of the state as 'janus-faced', Mann adds a third feature, which is spatial and organisational. Only the state is *inherently* centralized over a delimited territory over which it claims authoritative power. No other 'power groupings' drawing on different combinations of the sources of social power share this particular feature of the state. It follows that *'autonomous state power is the product of the usefulness of enhanced territorial centralization to social life in general'*.[9]

It should be clear by now that Michael Mann is no mere 'consumer' of IR theory, for his work has major implications for a number of important debates in the field. I will (briefly) illustrate just two examples of Mann's contributions to our understanding of contemporary international relations. First, he claims that 'the association of liberalism, constitutionalism or democracy with pacifism is a complete and utter fabrication'.[10] This is a typically bold claim, which undermines the arguments of many liberals who account for the relative absence of armed conflict between democracies on the basis of their inherently 'pacific' nature. Mann believes that such arguments stem from a failure to appreciate the capacity of non-state actors to appropriate military power to serve their own interests. He defines militarism as *'the persistent use of organised military violence in pursuit of social goals'* and distinguishes between militarism as a policy tool used by states and 'civil society militarism'.[11] Liberals in the study of international relations, he argues, focus on the former and neglect the latter, thus overlooking the record of militarism by Europeans in the colonies over the past 200 years. Indeed, Mann holds that such militarism increased overseas as liberal democracies were becoming stronger in Europe:

> Within liberalism not the nation and the state but the individual and the civil society have been viewed as the bearers of the moral developmental project. Thus the liberal 'civilizing mission' was decentred and diffuse. ... [After] political self-rule, [British colonials] no longer thought of themselves as British; yet to consider themselves as 'American' or 'Australian' was problematic since the indigenous peoples might share that identity and they were enormously different and 'inferior'. ... Indeed, the more domestically liberal the [colonial] regime, the nastier the record. A regime which does not regard its subjects as equal citizens may be less likely to espouse racism to justify expropriation and violence. And it was European racism that encouraged the worst atrocities. Thus the Spanish and Portuguese colonies saw fewer atrocities than the British, while the democratic American, Canadian, Australian and New Zealand ex-colonies perpetrated more than their former colonial masters.[12]

If this example of Mann's work makes us suspicious of a benign liberal view of itself, his most recent work on 'globalisation' (also a major preoccupation of IR theorists) helps to dispel the idea that some new form of human society is in the making. In light of Mann's extensive writing on the state, as well as his careful distinctions between different types of state, we should not be tempted by the simplistic suggestion of a zero-sum relationship between 'all states', on the one hand, and 'globalisation', on the other. Mann's most recent article distinguishes between five 'socio-spatial networks of social interaction' – local, national, inter-national, transnational and global. He then analyses four alleged 'threats' to the continued survival of the nation-state ('global' capitalism, environmental danger, identity politics and postnuclear geopolitics). Not surprisingly, Mann debunks most of the conventional wisdom on the imminent demise/continued resilience of the state as a form of political rule. His article is a superb illustration of the utility of the IEMP model to shed light on the differential impact on different types of state in each of the four spheres of 'threat', and the distribution of trends among the five networks of interaction.[13]

In conclusion, Michael Mann is far more than a mere 'consumer' of international relations theory. He is a major contributor to the field, whose work on the history of social power is acknowledged as one of the most pioneering intellectual projects in social theory this century. It is no surprise that someone of his breadth and depth of knowledge has little regard for disciplinary boundaries in the social sciences. He declares that he 'is not an admirer of what passes for theory among academics, all those abstract -isms and -ologies'.[14] Despite this apparent disregard for the academic division of labour, however, Mann acknowledges a tendency toward 'relativism' in his own work and a refusal to lay bare his own ethical values, let alone defend them. However, although ethical relativism may be a virtue for the macrosociologist, it is of little help in helping us imagine a just world order that could inspire us to redirect the sources of social power in a more humane manner than they have been deployed in the past. As Perry Anderson notes, 'no sociological enterprise of this magnitude has ever been undertaken that was not animated by some – tacit or explicit – political passion. One waits absorbed to see what that will prove to be.'[15] In the meantime, there is still a role for traditional political theorists in the academy.

Notes

1 Michael Mann, 'Authoritarian and liberal militarism: a contribution from comparative and historical sociology', in Steve Smith, Ken Booth and Marysia Zalewski (eds), *International Theory: Positivism and Beyond*, Cambridge, Cambridge University Press, 1996, p. 221.
2 Michael Mann, *The Sources of Social Power, Vol. 1: A History of Power from the Beginning to 1760 A.D.*, Cambridge, Cambridge University Press, 1986, p. 1.
3 Ibid., p. 381.
4 Michael Mann, *The Sources of Social Power, Vol. 2: The Rise of Classes and Nation-States, 1760–1914*, Cambridge, Cambridge University Press, 1993, p. 10.
5 Michael Mann, *States, War and Capitalism: Studies in Political Sociology*, Oxford, Blackwell, 1988, p. 4.
6 Ibid., p. 5.

7 Ibid., p. 11.
8 Ibid., p. 12.
9 Ibid., p. 29, emphasis in original.
10 Michael Mann, 'Authoritarian and liberal militarism: a contribution from comparative and historical sociology', op. cit., p. 235.
11 Ibid., p. 224. Mann's emphasis.
12 Ibid., p. 235.
13 Michael Mann, 'Has globalization ended the rise and rise of the nation-state?', *Review of International Political Economy* 4 (1997), pp. 472–97.
14 Michael Mann, 'Authoritarian and liberal militarism: a contribution from comparative and historical sociology', op. cit., p. 221.
15 Perry Anderson, *A Zone of Engagement*, London, Verso, 1992, p. 86.

See also in this book

Giddens, Strange, Tilly

Mann's major writings

The Sources of Social Power, Vol. 1: A History of Power from the Beginning to 1760 AD, Cambridge, Cambridge University Press, 1986
States, War and Capitalism: Studies in Political Sociology, Oxford, Blackwell, 1988
The Sources of Social Power, Vol. 2: The Rise of Classes and Nation-States, 1760–1914, Cambridge, Cambridge University Press, 1993
'Authoritarian and liberal militarism: a contribution from comparative and historical sociology', in Steve Smith, Ken Booth and Marysia Zalewski (eds), *International Theory: Positivism and Beyond*, Cambridge, Cambridge University Press, 1996, pp. 221–39
'Has globalization ended the rise and rise of the nation-state?', *Review of International Political Economy* 4 (1997), pp. 472–97

Further reading

Abrams, Philip, *Historical Sociology*, Somerset, Open Books, 1982
Bintliff, John, *European Social Evolution: Archeological Prospectives*, Bradford, Bradford University, 1984
Halliday, Fred, 'State and society in international relations: a second agenda', *Millennium: Journal of International Studies* 16 (1988), pp. 191–209
Hobson, John, 'The historical sociology of the state and the state of historical sociology in international relations', *Review of International Political Economy* 5 (1998), pp.285–320.

Jarvis, Anthony, 'Societies, states, and geopolitics: challenges from historical sociology', *Review of International Studies* 15 (1989), pp. 281–93

Skocpol, Theda, *States and Social Revolutions*, Cambridge, Cambridge University Press, 1979

Smith, Dennis, *The Rise of Historical Sociology*, Cambridge, Polity Press, 1991

CHARLES TILLY

Over the past two decades, many students of international relations have become increasingly sceptical of the realist claim that state behaviour can best be understood on the assumption that the state is a unitary, rational actor in international relations, ignoring conflicts within states. An apparently contrary trend can be observed in historical sociology, in which writers such as Michael Mann, Charles Tilly and Anthony Giddens have appealed to international relations to repudiate the Marxist view that all levels of politics are best explained primarily as a result of domestic class struggle in the context of capitalism. As Michael Mann observes, 'sociologists became aware that our specialism was neglecting the impact of geopolitics on social relations. We first borrowed precisely the traditional form of realism from which many IR practitioners were fleeing.'[1] However, the way in which Charles Tilly has appropriated 'realism' in trying to understand long-term social change at a global level is far removed from what many students in IR understand by the term. Although he has firmly placed the role of war back on the historical sociological agenda in accounting for the rise of the nation-state, Tilly departs from many 'realists' in IR in two key respects. First, he is interested in long-term processes of state formation per se rather than the historical patterns of the balance of power between states. Second, he dispenses with the assumption that there is a categorical *substantive* difference between 'domestic' and 'international' relations,

according to which the distinctive characteristics of the latter (war, anarchy, the balance of power) are read off against the more pacific and 'rule-based' character of politics within the sovereign state. As he puts it:

> At least for the European experience of the past few centuries, a portrait of war makers and state makers as coercive and self-seeking entrepreneurs bears a far greater resemblance to the facts than do its chief alternatives: the idea of a social contract [or] the idea of a society whose shared norms and expectations call forth a certain kind of government.[2]

It would, therefore, be wrong to assume that the rise of historical sociology in the study of international relations leaves 'realism' securely entrenched as the dominant framework of analysis. Whilst certain elements are retained, particularly the emphasis on the role of war and the ubiquity of power in global politics, the traditional division between domestic and international politics becomes extremely problematic as a useful tool of analysis. As Fitzpatrick points out, Charles Tilly and others

> *start* from precisely that agenda of questions about 'domestic' power politics ... effectively suppressed in realist discourse, and subsequently work [their] way toward the 'international' (or ... geopolitical) dimensions of such conflict as a result of dissatisfaction with the explanatory power of established 'domestic' paradigms.[3]

Indeed, 'dissatisfaction with established paradigms', whether in sociology, political science or international relations, is a persistent theme in Tilly's work, beginning with his earliest analyses of collective violence in eighteenth-century France and including his latest work on the rise of the state and the role of revolution in European history.

Charles Tilly was born in 1929 in Lombard, Illinois. He studied at Harvard University, earning his bachelor's degree in

1950. He served in the United States navy during the Korean War, and then returned to Harvard for his PhD in sociology in 1958. In the 1960s he taught at the Universities of Delaware, Toronto and Harvard. In 1969 he was appointed Professor of History and Sociology at the University of Michigan. This is where he set up the Center for Research on Social Organisation. At the center, Tilly devoted a great deal of time, money and collaborative effort (which included his wife and son) to creating enormous data banks of empirical evidence against which to test hypotheses and develop theories on the sources and dynamics of 'collective action' in European history, with a particular focus on France. As Lynn Hunt observes, Tilly has been compared to 'an [entrepreneurial] captain of scholarship, a Henry Ford directing the mass production of quantitative studies of strikes, food riots, and tax rebellions'.[4] He became Theodore M. Newcomb Professor of Social Science at Michigan in 1981. Three years later he joined the New School for Social Research in New York as Distinguished Professor of Sociology and History and was named University Distinguished Professor in 1990. In 1996, he moved to Columbia University as the new Joseph L. Buttenweiser Professor of Social Science.

The first thing to note about Tilly is the sheer volume of his published work. He has written more than twenty books and sits on the editorial boards of two dozen journals in history, political science and sociology. A review such as this can focus only on those areas of most importance for students of international relations.

In the 1960s, Tilly concentrated his efforts on the phenomenon of 'collective violence' in French history, examining the entire record of riots, violent demonstrations and brawls between rival groups in order to map and explain social change. His first book, *The Vendee* (1964), traces a process of rapid and uneven 'urbanisation' and 'centralisation' in the west of France prior to the great uprising of 1793. His argument is that the counter-revolutionary violence of that year may have been sparked by conscription but was, in fact, the product of structural, economic and social change. Local peasants and artisans took the side of the 'Aristocrats' against the 'Patriots', because the latter were the agents of the expanding and much resented state and the representatives of encroaching and threatening urban markets.

In a succession of books that followed (*Strikes in France 1830–1968*, published in 1974; *The Rebellious Century 1830–1930*, published in 1975; *From Mobilisation to Revolution*, 1978), Tilly followed up on the same themes he introduced in *The Vendee*. Concentrating primarily on France, but also relating his argument to other European states, Tilly developed a research agenda with a dual focus. On the one hand, he was interested in 'the little people' and the ways in which particular groups in society act to defend or extend their own interests – however they are conceived – against other groups. On the other hand, he was fascinated with the impact of huge structural changes on people's lives, changes that mysteriously rewrite the rules of collective action. He makes a crucial distinction between different kinds of 'collective violence' in French history. Prior to the seventeenth-century efforts of rulers to centralise the French state, violence is primarily *competitive*. It takes place between different groups in local communities and is the product of constant but stable conflicts of interest and power. From the mid-seventeenth century to the Second Revolution of 1849, violence in primarily *reactive*. It is a manifestation of 'defensive, backward looking conflicts between ... local people ... and agents of the nation'.[5] This is the period of the major expansion of the French state, which demands more taxation and increasing resources for an emerging national agricultural market. Finally, *proactive* violence has been the predominant form since the mid-nineteenth century, as groups no longer resist the encroachment of the state, but instead seek to control or influence it. The groups themselves are transformed from informal, impermanent communal organisations into enduring special-purpose associations.

As the work on collective violence on France developed in the 1960s and early 1970s, Tilly began to stake out a particular theoretical orientation to the study of social change which challenged the dominant assumptions of Durkheimian sociology in the United States. According to this tradition, collective violence is the result of social dislocation, strain, anomie and the breakdown of social control. Tilly challenged both the assumption that social systems are inherently benign as well as the political bias of sociologists in favour of law and order and the status quo. As William Sewell describes it, Tilly 'sees society as composed of groups with conflicting interests that are held together not by a value consensus or by the reequilibriating motions of a finely tuned social system but by the exercise of economic and political power'.[6] In the late 1970s and early 1980s Tilly became more explicit about the basis of his methodological assumptions and the way in which they challenge traditional approaches in sociological research. In 1984 he published his manifesto for historical sociology, *Big Structures, Large Processes, Huge Comparisons.*

The argument of this book is that we need to rid ourselves of what Tilly calls eight 'pernicious postulates' of nineteenth-century sociological thought. These false principles include beliefs that: (1) there are distinct, autonomous societies; (2) social behaviour results from individual mental states; (3) social change is a coherent social phenomenon; (4) large-scale social changes occur in a series of stages; (5) differentiation leads to advancement as well as to (6) disorder; (7) disorder and 'deviant behaviour' result from rapid social change; and (8) conflict precipitated by constituted authorities is legitimate, while conflict precipitated by individuals is illegitimate. The book

illustrates the ways in which these postulates of 'nineteenth-century folk wisdom' still influence the study of sociology, and Tilly calmly states that, as a consequence, 'little of long-term value to the social sciences has emerged from the hundreds of studies conducted during the last few decades that have run statistical analyses including most of the world's national states'.[7] Tilly's main targets are Durkheim and Tonnies rather than Marx or Weber, and in the last third of the book Tilly devotes himself to the more constructive task ahead. He urges sociologists to engage in 'genuinely historical work' and carry out research on the assumption 'that the time and place in which a structure or process appears makes a difference to its character, that the sequence in which similar events occur has a substantial impact on their outcomes, and that the existing record of past structures and processes is problematic'.[8] For students of international relations, this book is a useful primer before examining the book on which Tilly's reputation in the study of international relations is based, *Coercion, Capital and European States, AD 990–1990,* published in 1990.

Coercion, Capital and European States is a synthesis of Tilly's methodological and substantive arguments that he had been developing over the previous decade. In some ways, this study represents the capstone of his lifelong interest in state formation and elaborates arguments that he had begun to make in 1975, when he edited *The Formation of Nation States in Western Europe.* Tilly is concerned with two very big questions. What accounts for variations in time and space between the forms of the European state, and why did they finally converge on the national state? Dominant theories often 'posit a single, central path of European state formation and a set of deviations from the path explained by inefficiency, weakness, bad luck, geopolitical position, or the timing of economic growth'.[9] He shows in great detail that European state formation was anything but a uniform process. The fully-fledged national state is a very recent and rare form of political rule. For long periods of history it had to share the European political landscape with city-states, empires, theocratic enclaves and other varied principalities. The development of the nation-state itself proceeded along a variety of trajectories reflecting distinct blends of two different 'materials' for state building: coercion and capital. Fundamentally, Tilly claims that states are shaped by the need to wage war and that need, in turn, impels their rulers to extract resources. In 'capital-intensive' settings, resources are monetised or involved in value-added production. They are controlled by those involved in exchange and production for diverse markets, otherwise known as capitalists. In 'coercive-intensive' settings, resources are found in kind (especially raw materials), controlled by landlords who rely on coercion to extract them. Resources in these settings tend to be dispersed over large amounts of territory.

Tilly's basic thesis is that since different states emerge in different settings, and since the two kinds of settings require different patterns of state bargaining and organisation to extract their resources, states will differ in their organisation and development. In very capital-intensive settings – the Rhineland, the Netherlands, Italy – states will tend to be small, city-based, republican and commercial. Such states can flourish as long as the trade routes under their control produce high levels of resources that are sufficient for military defence. In very coercive-intensive settings, large empires will tend to develop, such as Russia and the Ottoman Empire. The latter sought to discipline and control the local landlords who controlled dispersed resources and also tried to concentrate those resources for the state. But this is very difficult and often inefficient. Tilly follows Michael Mann's argument here, suggesting that, while imperial armies could conquer peasants without too many difficulties, they could not overwhelm highly concentrated resources of capital-intensive centres. Some empires, such

as Hungary and Poland, could not even control their local landlords.

In between these extremes were states that developed in areas with various mixes of capital and coercive resources, such as England, France, Spain and Prussia. Depending on the particular blend, they developed a mixture of the characteristics of the states at each extreme of the spectrum. The convergence on the national state took place when resources could not readily be translated into warmaking potential. After the French Revolution, it was no longer possible to make war by hiring and supplying a mercenary army. Such armies could not face up to the forces of a nation in arms. The latter fought more effectively and cheaply and on a greater scale than the mercenary armies that had contested Europe between 1400 and 1700.

Consequently, from 1700 to 1918, Europe's less efficient city-states, and empires, were largely squeezed out by the competitive process, and national states emerged as the dominant form of political rule, combining size, national mobilisation, and access to commercial and coercive resource extraction. States such as Britain and France were able to combine advantages of their mixed setting. They had relatively strong state apparatuses, confident aristocracies, thriving market-orientated economies and a vigorous commercial class. So they made the transition to direct rule within a national state relatively early. Capital-intensive regions such as Italy, and coercion-intensive regions such as Eastern Europe, were slower to evolve to the national state norm.

But the crucial factor in explaining the rise of the national state is the increasing scale of war and the growing integration of the European state system. The military advantage of national states over their competitors is the key to answering the question Tilly sets himself at the beginning of the book.

In the twentieth century, Tilly argues that warmaking has become a more specialised, professional enterprise. This has led, once again, to different state trajectories in different settings. In economically dominant, capital-rich states, military professionalisation has facilitated greater 'civilianisation' of government. Under the intense pressures arising from the need to extract resources for war, state officials have yielded a variety of rights to their populations and accepted a widening array of domestic responsibilities. But in dependent, 'developing' and regionally competing states, i.e. in the Third World, greater military professionalisation has led to greater militarisation by governments, as the coercive resources of the armed forces proved superior to the weak capital-based resources of civilian regimes.

In 1992, Tilly published his reflections on the implications of the end of the Cold War in light of his theory on the consolidation of the national state in Europe. He suggests that, in the short term, Europe will witness two contradictory trajectories. On the one hand, there will be some increase in the number of states, particularly in Eastern Europe and parts of the former Soviet Union. The universal appeal of the national idea will continue to inspire what Tilly calls 'state-seeking' nationalists, but he believes that there are limits to such a process of state proliferation. In Western Europe, Tilly suggests that the pressures of 'warmaking' have been subdued, at least temporarily. In the absence of a well-armed nuclear enemy, rich states will no longer need to engage in the process of state consolidation. Instead, Tilly identifies a number of factors that threaten an end to the survival of consolidated states. These include:

the global mobility of capital, the rising importance of Japanese capital in Asia, the United States, and Europe, the worldwide circuits of labor, the rapid transmission of information and technology, the decreasing capacity of rich states ... to exclude poor outside workers from their labor markets ... all promise to sap the capac-

ity of any state to control its borders, shelter its own citizens from outside influences, [and] impose independent and centrally directed public policies.[10]

The future, he concludes, could be benign or malign. On the one hand, there is the possibility of a more diverse world that resembles in some respects the European political landscape of the Middle Ages, 'but without the empires and squabbling small states'. On the other hand, the end of the formal state-led 'protection racket' between rulers and the ruled could lead informally to 'a world of banditry, of hatred, of parochialism, and of gross inequality'.[11] States may no longer need to honour the rights of groups, such as organised labour, and the achievement of years of proactive collective action will slowly disappear. Tilly hopes that 'benign pluralism' will triumph over 'malign segmentation', but he is none too certain about the outcome.

In conclusion, one has to admire the bold sweep of Tilly's research. He is at the forefront of historical sociology at the end of the twentieth century, and his work, as one might expect, has attracted a great deal of attention across the social sciences, not just the study of international relations. If there is one notable flaw in his work, it would be similar to that of Michael Mann. In the final analysis, Tilly is a materialist. Despite his genuine concern for the interests of groups that contest and sometimes seek to influence the state, he always emphasises the role of structural forces that appear to be beyond the control of individual agents. Similarly, the role of ideas is subordinate to the interplay of economics and war in human history. As Jack Goldstone complains,

ideological issues play no role in his state making; the Reformation and the rise of nationalist ideologies are no more than pretexts for wars, rather than shapers of states in their own right ... [t]he notion that states have positive qualities, such that people might desire stronger or more nationalist states, rather than merely suffer their exactions, seems absent from Tilly's history.[12]

Having said that, Charles Tilly must be credited with bringing war back onto centre stage in the study of sociology and international relations, and his work provides enormous potential for all those similarly disappointed with the existing 'paradigms' of international relations. The challenge for those inspired by Charles Tilly is two-fold: how to include the role of ideas in the comparative study of social change; and how to connect long-term trends with short-term processes. Given the pace of change in the technology of war, the human race can no longer afford to allow war to play as central a role in its future as it has in its past.

Notes

1 Michael Mann, 'Authoritarian and liberal militarism: a contribution from comparative and historical sociology', in Steve Smith, Ken Booth and Marysia Zalewski (eds), *International Theory: Positivism and Beyond*, Cambridge, Cambridge University Press, 1996, p. 221.

2 Charles Tilly, 'War making and state making as organized crime", in Paul Evans, Dietrich Rueschemeyer and Theda Skocpol (eds), *Bringing the State Back In*, Cambridge, Cambridge University Press, 1986, p. 169.

3 John Fitzpatrick, 'Marxism, geopolitics, and the uneven development perspective: global trends and Australian debates', in R. Higgott and J.L. Richardson (eds), *International Relations: Global and Australian Perspectives on an Evolving Discipline*, Canberra, Australian National University, 1991, p. 101.

4 Lynn Hunt, 'Charles Tilly's collective action', in Theda Skocpol (ed.), *Vision and Method in Historical Sociology*, Cambridge, Cambridge University Press, 1984, p. 255.

5 Charles Tilly, Louise Tilly and Richard Tilly, *The Rebellious Century*, Cambridge, Massachusetts, Harvard University Press, 1975, p. 50.

6 William J. Sewell, 'Collective violence and collective loyalties in France: why the French revolution made a difference', *Politics and Society* 18 (1990), p. 528.

7 Charles Tilly, *Big Structures, Large Processes, Huge Comparisons*, New York, Russell Sage Foundation, 1984, p. 77.

8 Ibid., p. 79.

9 Charles Tilly, *Coercion, Capital, and European States, AD 990–1990*, Cambridge, Massachusetts, Basil Blackwell, 1990, p. 6.

10 Charles Tilly, 'Futures of European states', *Social Research* 59 (1992), p. 715.

11 Ibid., p. 717.

12 Jack A. Goldstone, 'States making wars making states making wars . . . .', *Contemporary Sociology* 20 (1991), p. 177.

See also in this book

Giddens, Herz, Mann, Wendt

Tilly's major writings

The Vendee, Cambridge, Massachusetts, Harvard University Press, 1964

Strikes in France, 1830–1968, Cambridge, Cambridge University Press, 1974.

The Formation of National States in Western Europe (ed.), Princeton, New Jersey, Princeton University Press, 1975

The Rebellious Century, 1830–1930 (with Louise Tilly and Richard Tilly), Harvard, Massachusetts, Harvard University Press, 1975

From Mobilization to Revolution, Reading, Massachusetts, Addison-Wesley, 1978

As Sociology Meets History, New York, Academic Press, 1981

Big Structures, Large Processes, Huge Comparisons, New York, Russell Sage Foundation, 1984

The Contentious French, Cambridge, Massachusetts, Belknap Press, 1986

'War making and state making as organized crime', in Paul Evans, Dietrich Rueschemeyer, and Theda Skocpol (eds), *Bringing the State Back In*, Cambridge, Cambridge University Press, 1986, pp. 169–98

Coercion, Capital, and European States, AD 990–1990, Oxford, Basil Blackwell, 1990

European Revolutions, 1492–1992, Oxford, Basil Blackwell, 1993

Further reading

Skocpol, Theda (ed.), *Vision and Method in Historical Sociology*, Cambridge, Cambridge University Press, 1984

Smith, Denis, *The Rise of Historical Sociology*, Cambridge, Polity Press, 1991

IMMANUEL WALLERSTEIN

Immanuel Wallerstein was born in 1930. He graduated from Columbia University in 1951 and continued his graduate studies there, completing his PhD in 1959. He taught sociology at Columbia until 1971, when he was appointed Professor of Sociology at McGill University in Montreal, Canada. In 1976, he became Director of the Fernand Braudel Centre and took up a Distinguished Chair in Sociology at Binghamton University (SUNY), where he continues to teach and research.

Wallerstein began his career as a student of African politics, specialising in Ghana and the Ivory Coast. But his reputation as an international theorist is based on his radical attempts to reconceptualise international relations in the context of his arguments concerning the nature and history of the modern capitalist 'world-system'. Wallerstein is the pioneer of world-systems theory, which is based in part on radical dependency theories of underdevelopment in the 1950s as well as the French *Annales* school of historiography. In three pioneering volumes of extraordinary historical detail and theoretical ambition, Wallerstein has attempted to look beneath the epiphenomena of diplomatic and military relations among states to grasp the logic of a single world-system.

It is important to understand at the outset that the term 'world-system' does not refer primarily to the geographical scope of capitalism, merely to the fact that the logic of the system operates at a different level than any existing political unit such as the nation-state. His most famous text, *The Modern World System*, published in 1974, locates the origins of the modern world in what he called 'the long sixteenth century', from around 1450 to 1670. Before this period, Western Europe was feudal, and economic production was based almost entirely on agriculture. From 1300 onwards, however, agricultural production fell rapidly as changes in the European climate contributed to a rapid increase in the incidence of epidemics among the peasant population. It was not until the 1500s that Europe moved toward the establishment of a capitalist world economy, in which production was oriented toward exchange in the market rather than seasonal consumption, those who produced goods earned less than their value, and the driving force of capitalism became the endless accumulation of material goods.

Economic growth in the new era entailed the expansion of the geographical scope of the market, the development of different forms of labour control and the rise of strong states in Europe. The new world economy that emerged differed from previous empires in that it coexisted with a multiplicity of political jurisdictions and was characterised by a new international division of labour between 'core' and 'periphery'.

The core refers to those regions that benefited most from change. In the period of initial expansion, this included most of northwestern Europe (France, England and Holland). The region was characterised by strong central governments and large mercenary armies. The latter enabled the bourgeoisie to control international commerce and extract economic surplus from trade and commerce. The growth of urban manufacturing was fed by movements of landless peasants from the countryside to the cities, whilst improvements in agricultural technology ensured continuous increases in agricultural productivity. The core is where capital is always concentrated in its most sophisticated forms. Banks, the professions, trade activity, and skilled manufacturing are all sufficiently widespread to sustain a wage-labour economy.

The periphery, in contrast, refers to regions lacking strong central governments, dependent on coercive rather than wage-labour, and whose economies depended upon the export of raw materials to the core. Latin America and Eastern Europe were key peripheral zones in the sixteenth century. In Latin America, the Spanish and the Portuguese conquests destroyed indigenous political leaders and replaced them with weak bureaucracies under European control. Native populations were killed or enslaved, African slaves were imported to work the land and the mines, and the local aristocracy was complicit with a system that kept it in power while it presided over the production of goods primarily for consumption in Europe. In the periphery, extensive cultivation and coercive control of labour achieve low-cost agricultural production.

Wallerstein also refers to *semi-peripheries* as well as *external areas*. Semi-peripheries were either regions that could be geographically located in the core but were undergoing a process of relative decline (Spain and Portugal) or rising economies in the periphery. They were exploited by the core, but in turn took advantage of the periphery. Some external areas maintained their own economic systems and were largely self-sufficient in food, such as Russia. Unlike some of the dependency thinkers who posited a polar relationship between two basic categories, Wallerstein argues that the semi-periphery is a crucial buffer between core and periphery. An ideological consensus over the desirability of capitalism and the concentration of military power among powerful hegemons in the core would be insufficient to prevent serious conflict in the system as a whole:

> [Neither] would suffice were it not for the division of the majority into a larger lower stratum and a smaller middle stratum ... the semi-periphery is assigned a specific economic role, but the reason is less economic than political ... one might make a good case that the world-economy ... would function every bit as well without a semi-periphery. But it would be far less politically stable, for it would mean a polarized world-system. The existence of the third category means precisely that the upper stratum is not faced with the

unified opposition of all the others because the middle stratum is both exploited and exploiter.[1]

Much of Wallerstein's work traces the geographical expansion of the world-system over time. Two stages in particular mark its development from the sixteenth to the late twentieth century. Up to the eighteenth century the system was characterised by a strengthening of European states, following the failure of Hapsburg Empire to convert the emerging world economy to a world empire. Increasing trade with the Americas and Asia enriched small merchant elites at the expense of wage-labourers in Europe, whilst its monarchs expanded their power to collect taxes, borrow money and expand militias to support the absolute monarchies. Local populations in Europe became increasingly homogeneous as minorities were expelled, particularly Jews. In the eighteenth century industrialisation replaced the emphasis on agricultural production, and European states embarked on an aggressive search for new markets to exploit. Over the last 200 years new regions have been absorbed into the system, such as Asia and Africa, increasing the available surplus. However, it was not until the early years of the twentieth century that the world-system became truly global.

Wallerstein also traces the rise and decline of core hegemons (or dominant powers) in the world-system over time. In 1984 he described 'three instances' of hegemony; 'the United Provinces in the mid-seventeenth century, the United Kingdom in the mid-nineteenth, and the United States in the mid-twentieth'.[2] In his more recent work he has speculated on the future of the world-system in light of debates regarding the alleged decline of the United States in the world economy and the end of the Cold War. He fears that many are drawing hasty conclusions from the collapse of Marxism-Leninism in 1989, suggesting that the collapse of the Soviet Union and its peripheral status is not good news for the dominant forces of the capitalist world-system because it removes the last major politically stabilising force that helped to legitimate the hegemony of the United States. In *Geopolitics and Geoculture* (1991), he suggests that the period of US hegemony may be over now that Japanese and Western European enterprises are genuinely competitive with American companies. But in the absence of the 'Soviet threat', it is unclear whether conflicts between states in the core can be diluted by appealing to any common ideological interest in sustaining co-operation. He believes that the world-system will continue to function as it has for the last 500 years in search of the endless accumulation of capital and goods, but the periphery will be increasingly marginalised as the technological sophistication of the core accelerates.

For Wallerstein, the capitalist world-system – while it may continue for some time yet – is characterised by some fundamental contradictions, which will ultimately bring about its demise even as it appears to consolidate its global control. First, there is continuing imbalance between supply and demand. So long as decisions about what and how much to produce are made at the level of the firm, the imbalance will be an unintended consequence of continuous mechanisation and commodification. Second, whereas in the short run it is rational for capitalists to make profits by withdrawing the surplus from immediate consumption, in the longer term the further production of surplus requires a mass demand which can only be met by redistributing the surplus. Third, there are limits to the degree to which the state can co-opt workers to maintain the legitimation of the capitalist system. As he puts it,

> whenever the tenants of privilege seek to co-opt an oppositional movement by including them in a minor share of the privilege, they may no doubt eliminate opponents in the short run; but they also

up the ante for the next oppositional movement created in the next crisis of the world-economy. Thus the cost of co-option rises ever higher.[3]

Finally, and most significantly, there is the contradiction between the one and the many, the co-existence of a plural states-system within one world-system. Whilst this facilitates the expansion of the system, it also impedes any attempt to develop greater co-operation to counter systemic crises in the system as a whole.

Wallerstein's approach is characterised by two fundamental epistemological commitments. He is fundamentally opposed to the idea that one can study processes of economic 'development' within states without situating them in a much broader spatial and historical context. To study the state as if it were the unit within which problems are both generated and potentially solved is to accept uncritically the dominant liberal ideology of progress. According to this ideology, the way out of economic underdevelopment for poor states is to adopt the political, economic and cultural characteristics of 'developed' states. If governments adopt 'free market' policies, and promote private enterprise and an entrepreneurial culture, then there is no intrinsic barrier to modernisation.

Equally, Wallerstein takes issue with those on the Left who believe that underdevelopment is promoted by core states whose prosperity lies in their ability to extract economic surplus from periphery states. Insofar as this implies that Third World states should somehow withdraw from the capitalist world economy, Wallerstein argues that in a single world-system, peripheral states cannot develop along lines different from those imposed by the core.

Partly inspired by the work of Karl Polanyi, Wallerstein is also extremely critical of Western social science, which treats politics, economics, history and sociology as separate 'disciplines' in the social sciences. He certainly would not recognise the study of international relations as an autonomous discipline, and his approach is therefore radically at odds with the realist view that its autonomy arises from the special character of relations among states in an anarchical environment. This is only one aspect of the structure of the world-system and a subordinate one at that. Indeed, he believes that the development of Western social science cannot be disentangled from the growing power of the state and its need for 'experts' to assist it in managing 'the dangerous classes'. Since the late eighteenth century, the modern era has been dominated by the idea of progress and by the political myth that sovereignty is legitimate since the power of states is said to derive from 'the people'. For Wallerstein, the modern ideologies of conservatism, liberalism and socialism are best understood as political programmes to manage the social turmoil that constant economic change engenders. At the end of the twentieth century, of course, many people believe that liberalism is now dominant. The threefold political programme of universal suffrage, the welfare state and the creation of national identity effectively secured the legitimation of the world-system in Europe and provides a model for universal aspiration outside it. Most social scientists espouse a liberal ideology, for the whole enterprise of social science is based on the premise of social progress based on the ability to manipulate social relations provided that this can be done in a 'scientific' manner.

Wallerstein's work has, as one might expect given its radical challenges to orthodox social science, been the subject of intense debate. Traditional Marxists have complained that he misunderstands the nature of capitalism, focusing too much on the logic of exchange in the market rather than on modes of production. Ernesto Laclau, for example, claims that 'the fundamental economic relationship of capitalism is constituted by the free labourer's sale of his labour power, whose necessary precondition is the loss by the direct producer of owner-ship of the means of production'.[4] If wage-labour is the defining characteristic of capitalism, then Wallerstein's whole model is cast in doubt, since other forms of labour have been dominant in other parts of the world, making it difficult to define them as capitalist.

Indeed, Wallerstein's views have been attacked from across the ideological spectrum. Socialists who believe that radical reform is still possible within the boundaries of the state, or between socialist states, have not taken kindly to the idea that socialism is possible only at a global level. Wallerstein takes the Trotskyist position of dismissing 'socialism in one country', defining communist states as merely collective capitalist firms whose very participation in the world-system prevents the transition to socialism at a global level. More orthodox scholars have attacked the extreme structural-functionalism of Wallerstein's theoretical approach. Realists, for example, would argue that if the competitive inter-state system is itself derived from the economic logic of the capitalist world-system, how does one account for competitive behaviour among political units before the sixteenth century? They argue that there is a distinctly political logic involving the struggle for power among sovereigns that cannot be reduced to capitalism. As Kal Holsti has pointed out, 'to say that war between capitalist states is inevitable is like saying that collisions between Ford automobiles are inevitable; but which is the critical variable? Automobile or Ford? State or economy?'[5]

It might also be argued that the rigidity of the core/semi-periphery/periphery mode fails to account for anomalies such as the rise of some states to 'core' status (Japan?) because it presupposes a zero-sum relationship among states in the system. The structure of the system remains constant for Wallerstein, so that if some states appear to rise and move from one category to another, others must fall. Given the generality of the theoretical approach, as well as its historical depth, it is sometimes difficult to place some states within any of the categories. For example, on the basis of its GNP per capita and standard of living, Australia can be categorised as part of the core, even though Wallerstein himself places it in the semi-periphery. As Alexander and Gow point out, 'the economic analysis gives no systemic clues as to the relationship between economic position in the world economy, geopolitical position and the emergence of semiperipheral politics'.[6]

Finally, one might note a tension between the empirical claims of Wallerstein (which should therefore be amenable to hypothesis testing) and his contempt for conventional methodologies of theory construction in the social sciences. Is it possible to make deterministic claims about the primacy of global economic forces and at the same time defend those claims not on criteria of empirical validity, 'but on their heuristic value; i.e. whether they make sense to the people and organisations who are seeking to act in world-historical contexts and need to understand the dynamics of change ... in these contexts'?[7] Of course, this is a tension that characterises a great deal of radical thought that defends the need for change not on the basis of moral criteria articulated in the tradition of political theory, but on the basis of empirical claims regarding the inherent inequality of the capitalist system.

Notes

1 Immanuel Wallerstein, 'The rise and future demise of the world capitalist system: concepts for comparative analysis', *Comparative Studies in Society and History* 16 (1974), pp. 387–8.
2 Immanuel Wallerstein, *The Politics of the World-Economy: The States, the Movements, and the Civilizations: Essays*, Cambridge, Cambridge University Press, 1984, p. 39.
3 Immanuel Wallerstein, 'The rise and future demise of the world capitalist system', op.cit., p. 415.
4 Ernesto Laclau, *Politics and Ideology in Marxist Theory*, London, New Left Books, 1977, p. 23.

5 Kalevi Holsti, *The Dividing Discipline*, Boston, Allen & Unwin, 1985, p. 76.
6 Malcolm Alexander and John Gow, 'Immanuel Wallerstein', in P. Beilharz, (ed.), *Social Theory: A Guide to Central Thinkers*, Sydney, Allen & Unwin, 1991, p. 220.
7 Ibid., p. 217.

See also in this book

Cox, Frank, Giddens

Wallerstein's major writings

Social Change: The Colonial Situation, New York, Wiley, 1966
Africa: The Politics of Unity: An Analysis of a Contemporary Social Movement, New York, Random House, 1967
'The rise and future demise of the world capitalist system: concepts for comparative analysis', *Comparative Studies in Society and History* 16 (1974), pp.385–415
The Modern Word System 1: Agriculture and the Origins of the European World-Economy in the Sixteenth Century, New York, Academic Press, 1974
World Inequality: Origins and Perspectives on the World System, Montreal, Black Rose Books, 1975
The Capitalist World-Economy: Essays, Cambridge, Cambridge University Press, 1979
The Modern Word System II: Mercantilism and the Consolidation of the European World Economy, 1600–1750, New York, Academic Press, 1980
Historical Capitalism, London, Verso, 1983
Labor in the World Social Structure, Beverly Hills, Sage Publications, 1983
The Politics of the World-Economy: The States, the Movements, and the Civilizations: Essays, Cambridge, Cambridge University Press, 1984
'World systems analysis', in Anthony Giddens and Johnathan H. Turner (eds), *Social Theory Today*, Cambridge, Polity Press, 1987, pp. 309–24
Geopolitics and Geoculture: Essays on the Changing World-System, Cambridge, Cambridge University Press, 1991
Unthinking Social Science: The Limits of Nineteenth-Century Paradigms, Cambridge, Polity Press, 1991
'The collapse of liberalism', in Ralph Miliband and Leo Panitch (eds), *The Socialist Register: New World Order?*, London, Merlin, 1992, pp. 96–110

'Development: lodestar or illusion?', in Leslie Sklair (ed.), *Capitalism and Development*, London, Routledge, 1994

After Liberalism, New York, New Press, 1995

'The inter-state structure of the modern world system', in Steve Smith, Ken Booth and Marysia Zalewski (eds), *International Theory: Positivism and Beyond*, Cambridge, Cambridge University Press, 1996, pp. 87–107

Further reading

Arrighi, Giovanni, *The Long Twentieth Century*, London, Verso, 1994

Higgott, Richard L., *Political Development Theory: The Contemporary Debate*, London, Croom Helm, 1983

Hopkins, Terence K., *World-Systems Analysis: Theory and Methodology*, Beverly Hills, California, Sage Publications, 1982

Sanderson, Stephen K. (ed.), *Civilizations and World Systems: Studying World- Historical Change*, Walnut Creek, California, AltaMira Press, 1995.

Skocpol, Theda, 'Wallerstein's world capitalist system: a theoretical and historical critique', *American Journal of Sociology* 82 (1977), pp. 1075–89

Zolberg, Aristide, 'Origins of the modern world system – a missing link', *World Politics* 33 (1981), pp. 253–81

THEORIES OF THE NATION

Nationalism, it seems, is breaking out all over the world, threatening to fragment some existing states and merge others into new 'nation-states'. But the term 'nationalism' is often used in very vague ways, and our understanding of this form of political mobilisation is impeded by the lack of attention paid to nationalism within the discipline of international relations. As the distinction between war among states and war within them is less distinct today than in earlier eras, nationalism is attracting more attention. One of the biggest problems for international order at the end of the twentieth century is how to reconcile the principle of state sovereignty (which protects the existing distribution of territorial boundaries) and that of self-determination for 'peoples' (which constantly threatens to redistribute borders according to a vague normative principle). Accordingly, it is fitting to include reference to the work of three key thinkers on nations and nationalism. Benedict Anderson is a student of the phenomenology of the nation. He has mapped the historical conditions of its emergence as an 'imagined community', and explored the practices that sustain the appeal of the nation over other foci of political allegiance in the modern era. Ernest Gellner and Anthony Smith are the leading scholars on a major debate over whether nationalism is ancient or modern. Gellner argues that nationalism is a product of modernity and economic industrialisation, whilst Smith claims that nationalism is a unique fusion of modern and pre-modern ideological claims.

BENEDICT ANDERSON

As with some other key thinkers in this book (such as Charles Beitz and Alfred Zimmern), Benedict Anderson's contribution to the study of international relations arises from one influential book, *Imagined Communities: Reflections of the Origin and Spread of Nationalism* (1983, 1991). Anderson is Aaron L. Binenkorb Professor of International Studies at Cornell University. He wrote his doctoral dissertation at Cornell and has taught there for many years, primarily as a specialist in Indonesian political history and culture.

Anderson is a man of the Left (as is his equally famous brother, Perry), with an ongoing fascination with the bitterly hostile nationalisms of contemporary South East Asia.[1] One of his best books, *Java in a Time of Revolution* (1972), is a detailed examination of the first ten months of Indonesia's struggle for independence in 1945–6. He argues that the 'Sjahrir version' of the Indonesian revolution needs revision. The conventional historical narrative of the period is that Sjahrir's Socialist Party dominated the political scene at the time and that his strategy of *diplomasi* (negotiations – seeking to exert pressure on the Dutch through the British and Americans) reflected the views of the major groupings within Indonesian society at the time.[2] Anderson shows in devastating detail that the political parties were 'little more than clusters of small personal cliques ... none ... had as yet any organised base among the masses, even in the urban areas'.[3] He also claims that Sjahrir's great rival at the time, Tan Malakka, could have changed the course of Indonesian history if his strategy of *perdjuangan* (armed struggle) had been adopted rather than the course of diplomacy. Because the latter, moderate, policy was directed towards gaining international support and recognition, it was incompatible with a radical domestic social programme.

'From this came the deepening malaise of the post-independence years, and later tragedies.'[4] Anderson claims that if Sukarno had thrown his support behind a more confrontational policy towards the Dutch, Indonesian history might have followed a different course, perhaps more comparable with that undertaken by the Viet Cong under Ho Chi Minh's leadership in North Vietnam. Whether or not one accepts Anderson's argument, the book is a good example of his abiding concerns with the possibilities for socialism in the region. However, Anderson's growing disenchantment with the performance of radical Marxist states over the years, as well as his belief that radical scholars on the Left underestimated the force of nationalism in the modern world, led him to explore the cultural dimensions of this phenomenon. *Imagined Communities* is the result of his intellectual journey, the product of years of reading and reflection. The rest of this review will focus on this short, beautifully written little book, which enables students of international relations (particularly those who believe that the 'nation-state' either is or should be 'transcended') to understand the enduring power of nationalism in the modern era.

The book starts (and ends) on this note: 'The Vietnamese invasion and occupation of Cambodia in December 1978 and January 1979 represented the first *large-scale conventional war* waged by one revolutionary Marxist regime against another.'[5] But the incompatibility of Marxist theory and practice is not the central issue. The book is about the 'idea' of the nation-state; how and where it came into being and the conditions under which it continues to flourish in the late twentieth century. Unlike so many other scholars of nationalism, Anderson refuses to treat his subject matter as merely epiphenomenal, the product of other forces such as industrialisation (Gellner) or massive socio-economic change (Deutsch). His approach is both hermeneutic as well as structural. He is interested in how such a very large proportion of the world's population believe that, as individuals, they are members of a particular 'nation' that is entitled to sovereignty over a block of territory and feel so loyal that 'to die for one's country' is one of the greatest honours that can be achieved. After all, tribal peoples do not have this sort of self-identifying bond that extends far and wide beyond the range of recognised kinship or the limits of any face-to-face community. The rival sovereigns of feudal Europe could not elicit this kind of loyalty either. Anderson's approach focuses on the process of 'collective imagination', which he inserts into the very definition of a nation:

> [I]t is an imagined political community – and imagined as both inherently limited and sovereign. It is *imagined* because the members of even the smallest nation will never know most of their fellow-members, meet them, or even hear of them ... the nation is imagined as *limited* because even the largest of them ... has finite, if elastic boundaries, beyond which lie other nations. No nation imagines itself coterminous with mankind.[6]

Anderson is particularly interested in three paradoxes of nationalism. First, the objective modernity of nations in the eye of the historian versus their subjective antiquity in the eyes of nationalists; second, the formal universality of nationality as a sociocultural concept versus the particularity of its concrete manifestations; and third, the political power of nationalism versus its philosophical poverty. As the political philosopher Eugene Kamenka once observed, 'in pitting emotion against reason, [nationalism] has substituted campfires for learning, demagoguery for argument ... [it] has stood, and perhaps still stands, at the centre of modern history. Nationalist thinkers do not.'[7] Anderson believes that the philosophical poverty of nationalist doctrine has contributed to the more general failure to understand its enduring power, which I think is particularly true in the study of international relations.[8]

In the first part of his book, Anderson engages in a broad historical argument. He claims that nationalism has to be understood not in relation to self-consciously held political ideologies, but the large cultural systems that preceded it. Nationalism arose at a time when three other cultural conceptions were decreasing in importance. First, there were changes in religion. Nationalism represented a secular transformation of fatality into continuity, magical contingency into worldly meaning. The unselfconscious coherence of religion declined after the Middle Ages because of the explorations of the non-European world and the gradual demotion of the sacred language itself. Older communities lost confidence in the unique sacredness of their language (the idea that a particular script offered privileged access to sacred ontological truth). Second, there were changes in the dynastic realm. In feudal forms of 'imagination', states were defined by 'high centres', borders were porous and indistinct and 'sovereignties' faded into one another. However, with the decline of the legitimacy of the sacral monarchy in the seventeenth century, people began to doubt the belief that society was naturally organised around 'high centres' such as Rome. Third, and here Anderson is most original, he argues that we have to take into account the feudal conception of time, in which cosmology and history were indistinguishable. 'More than anything else', he argues, it was changes in the conception of time that 'made it possible to "think" the nation'.[9] The pre-modern era was characterised by a conception of 'simultaneity-along-time', in which time is marked by 'pre-figuring and fulfilment'. This is gradually replaced by the conception of 'simultaneity-across-time', in which time is marked by 'temporal coincidence, and measured by clock and calendar'.[10] The idea of a sociological entity moving calendrically through homogeneous, empty time is a precise analogue of the idea of the nation, which also is conceived as a solid community moving steadily through history. These three epochal changes led to a search for a new way to link fraternity, power and time together.

> Combined, [the old] ideas rooted human lives firmly in the very nature of things, giving certain meaning to the everyday fatalities of existence (above all, death, loss and servitude) and offering, in various ways, redemption from them ... the slow, uneven decline of these interlinked certainties ... drove a harsh wedge between cosmology and history.[11]

The decline of these 'old ideas' set the conditions for a new form of cultural consciousness. The reason it took the form of nationalism is due to the fortuitous interaction between capitalism, a new technology of communication (print) and the fatality of linguistic diversity. Capitalism was important because the expansion of the book market contributed to the revolutionary vernacularisation of languages. This was given further impetus by the mass production of bibles during the Reformation and the spread of particular vernaculars as instruments of administrative centralisation. In turn, printed languages laid the foundation for national consciousness by creating unified fields of exchange and communication. In combination, 'print capitalism' created the possibility for nationalism by providing a space for the representation of new conceptions of time and space. It also promoted the construction of 'print languages' by standardising various local vernaculars into common written forms.

This is the background against which Anderson examines a puzzling anomaly in the history of nationalism. Why did Creole communities in South America (those formed by people who shared a common language and common ethnicity with those they fought against) develop conceptions of nationhood well before most of Europe?

Anderson's answer appeals to a number of factors. A comprehensive analysis would have to include blocked social mobility, successive attempts by Spain to tighten its control of South America, the spread of liberalising ideas of the Enlightenment and the rise of the newspaper as a vehicle for the dissemination of nationalism amongst the 'comfortable' classes of the region. It would also have to take into account the fact that

> Although these wars caused a great deal of suffering and were marked by much barbarity, in an odd way the stakes were rather low. Neither in North nor in South America did the Creoles have to fear physical extermination or reduction to servitude, as did so many other peoples who got in the way of European imperialism.[12]

On the other hand, the failure of the Spanish-American experience to generate a permanent revolt against the Spanish empire reflects both the general level of development of capitalism and technology in the late eighteenth century and the local backwardness of Spanish capitalism in relation to the administrative reach of the empire. The Protestant, English-speaking people to the North were much more favourably situated for realising the idea of 'America'. The close of the successful national liberation movements in the Americas coincided with the onset of the age of nationalism in Europe. Again, Anderson stresses the role of print languages and the way in which, once the 'modular' form of nationalism was in place, the 'nation' as a new form of political community could be consciously aspired to by those who felt oppressed or excluded from the existing political system. The 'imagined' realities of nation-states in the Americas became models for Europe, which then became a model for the rest of the world.

The originality of Anderson lies in his analysis of the role of print capitalism in re-orienting our sense of time from the feudal to the modern era and in his argument that Creole nationalism in the Americas

263

provided a model for Europe. The French Revolution, which is usually seen as the symbolic moment of change from dynastic sovereignty to popular sovereignty, was itself made possible by an epistemological shift in the nature of collective consciousness. The American revolutions provided a model of the nation-state, which could be consciously aspired to by bourgeois classes and intelligentsias throughout Europe in their struggle against the Absolutist Empires of the old order. The very act of recording revolutionary struggles in history books facilitated the dissemination of nationalism as a 'modular' form for the pursuit of political freedom and equality.

Moreover, as a secular religion, nationalism can provide answers to metaphysical questions about the meaning of life and death that no other political ideology can. This is particularly important for those who believe that there exist imminent substitutes for the nation-state in the late modern era, such as multinational corporations or transnational social movements of one kind or another. None can match the sheer *potency* of the nation as a modern focus of group loyalty and identity. As he puts it in two of the most oft-quoted sentences from the book, '[try] to imagine, say, a tomb of the unknown Marxist or a cenotaph for fallen liberals. Is a sense of absurdity avoidable?'[13]

Anderson suggests that while Marxism comes close to fulfilling the void left by the death of God, it cannot compete with nationalism because the latter does not depend on the ability of particular societies to achieve the material goals of any political or economic doctrine. Marxism is unable to move people to the same level of personal sacrifice. The success of nationalism lies in its paradoxical ability to combine universalism and particularism whilst remaining compatible with a range of political ideologies. Nationality has replaced religion even as it continues to perform the same metaphysical role that religion as 'doxa', or 'common sense', used to play. In another memorable

phrase from the book, Anderson remarks that 'it is the magic of nationalism to turn chance into destiny'.[14] In the modern era, one does not ask another if he or she has a national identity, as one might about faith. The question is rather, to which particular national identity do you belong?

In short, then, by treating nationalism as a response to epochal change, and by examining the material and cultural conditions for the possibility of nationalism, Benedict Anderson's book remains essential reading for students of the subject. Similarly, in his evocative description of some of the mechanisms that sustain national identification, such as reading the newspaper or singing the national anthem, Anderson draws our attention to phenomena that are rarely discussed in the existing literature. This is not to say that his thesis has avoided critical comment. Two criticisms, in particular, are worthy of note.

First, despite his definition of nations as *imagined* communities', Partha Chatterjee accuses Anderson of failing to understand the way in which many anti-colonial forms of nationalism do not merely imitate the 'modular' types of society found in Europe and the Americas. He suggests that Anderson, along with most Western scholars, condemns the rest of the world to a permanent dependent status.

> Europe and the Americas, the only true subjects of history, have thought out on our behalf not only the script of colonial enlightenment and exploitation, but also that of our anti-colonial resistance and post-colonial misery. Even our imaginations must remain forever colonised.[15]

Chatterjee argues that, to understand anti-colonial nationalism in India and parts of Africa, one must distinguish between the 'material' and 'spiritual' realm of the social structure. Whilst the former is indeed 'colonised' by the modular forms of nationalism analysed by Anderson, whose purpose is to create a modern industrial state, the latter is not. In the spiritual realm, Chatterjee argues that subject peoples preserved their language and culture. In his recent analysis of this issue, Christopher Ullock draws attention to Anderson's expanded edition of *Imagined Communities* (1991), in which he refers to temples, mosques and schools outside the control of the metropole as 'zones of freedom ... from which religious, later nationalist, anticolonials could go forth to battle'.[16] Ullock agrees with Chatterjee's broader point, however, that the title of Anderson's book is misleading. The focus on the processes of collective imagination early on in the book is replaced by a focus on the 'circulationary' character of nationalism by the end. Ullock points out that Anderson's argument is unintentionally ironic:

[W]hile Anderson begins his project describing how spatio-temporal change enabled people to imagine their political, cultural, and social communities differently, his acceptance of the ontological categories of modernity like 'state' and 'nation' preclude him from seriously analysing how current spatio-temporal accelerations may be affecting the way in which people imagine their communities in both North and South.[17]

This raises the question of whether new forms of communication in the late twentieth century are shaping the imagination of new forms of community in novel ways. To be fair to Anderson, he has speculated on this issue, and much work remains to be done in the future. For now, Anderson is somewhat sceptical. He points to the emergence of 'long-distance' nationalism by members of ethnic minorities in the West who can take advantage of new technology (such as e-mail) to intensify their sense of belonging to imaginary 'homelands' far away from the state in which they live. '[S]afely positioned in the First World, [they] can send money and guns, circulate propaganda, and build intercontinental computer information circuits, all of which can have incalculable effects in the zones of their ultimate destinations.'[18] It remains to be seen, therefore, whether 'current spatio-temporal accelerations' enhance or retard the potential for undermining nationalism in the twenty-first century. Either way, Anderson's contribution to the study of international relations remains his examination of the impact of such accelerations 300 years ago.

Notes

1 Verso Press have just published a collection of Anderson's recent articles on the area, *The Spectre of Comparison* (1998).
2 See, in particular, G. McT. Kahin, *Nationalism and Revolution in Indonesia*, Ithaca, New York, Cornell University Press, 1952.
3 Benedict Anderson, *Java in a Time of Revolution: Occupation and Resistance, 1944–1946*, Ithaca, New York, Cornell University Press, 1972, p. 230.
4 Ibid., p. 408.
5 *Imagined Communities: Reflections on the Origin and Spread of Nationalism*, Second edition, London, Verso, 1991, p. 11.
6 Ibid., pp. 15–16.
7 Eugene Kamenka, 'Nationalism: ambiguous legacies and contingent futures', *Political Studies* 41 (1993), p. 80.
8 Martin Griffiths, 'Multilateralism, nationalism and the problem of agency in international theory', in Richard Leaver and Dave Cox (eds), *Middling, Meddling, Muddling: Issues in Australian Foreign Policy*, St Leonards, NSW, Allen & Unwin, 1997, pp. 44–68.
9 Benedict Anderson, *Imagined Communities*, p. 22.
10 Ibid., pp. 24–5.
11 Ibid., p. 36.
12 Ibid., pp. 191–2.
13 Ibid., p. 37.
14 Ibid., p. 12.
15 Partha Chatterjee, 'Whose imagined community?', *Millennium: Journal of International Studies* 20 (1991), p. 521.
16 Christopher Ullock, 'Imagined community: a metaphysics of being or becoming?', *Millennium: Journal of International Studies* 25 (1996), p. 427.
17 Ibid., p. 428.
18 Benedict Anderson, 'Exodus', *Critical Inquiry* 20 (1994), p. 327.

See also in this book

Deutsch, Gellner, Ruggie, Smith

Anderson's major writings

Some Aspects of Indonesian Politics Under the Japanese Occupation, 1944–1945, Ithaca, New York, Cornell University Press, 1961

Mythology and the Tolerance of the Javanese, Ithaca, New York, Cornell University Press, 1965

A Preliminary Analysis of the October 1, 1965 Coup in Indonesia, Ithaca, New York, Cornell University Press, 1971

Java in a Time of Revolution: Occupation and Resistance, 1944–1946, Ithaca, New York, Cornell University Press, 1972

Language and Power: Exploring Political Cultures in Indonesia, Ithaca, New York, Cornell University Press, 1990

Imagined Communities: Reflections on the Origin and Spread of Nationalism, Second edition, London, Verso, 1991

'The last empires', *New Left Review* 193 (1992), pp. 3–14

The Spectre of Comparison, London, Verso, 1998

Further reading

Chatterjee, Partha, 'Whose imagined community?', *Millennium: Journal of International Studies* 20 (1991), pp. 521–5

Chatterjee, Partha, *Nationalist Thought and the Colonial World – A Derivative Discourse*, London, Zed Books, 1994

Nimni, Ephraim, *Marxism and Nationalism: Theoretical Origins of a Political Crisis*, London, Pluto Press, 1994

Smith, Anthony D., 'The nation: invented, imagined, reconstructed', *Millennium: Journal of International Studies* 20 (1991), pp. 353–68

Ullock, Christopher, 'Imagined community: a metaphysics of being or becoming?', *Millennium: Journal of International Studies* 25 (1996), pp. 425–41

ERNEST GELLNER

Students of international relations best know Ernest Gellner for his work on nationalism and the relevance of that work is the justification for his inclusion in this volume. Gellner himself, however, was a student of modernity in the widest sense, and his writing does not slot easily into traditional academic specialities. He made major contributions in a variety of fields, including social anthropology, sociology and political philosophy. In addition, Gellner's work on the history and origins of nationalism cannot be divorced from a much larger theme that runs through all his work, which is a defence of the Enlightenment and rationalism in thought and practice. He was an ardent opponent of relativism in all its forms, and towards the end of his life (he died in 1995) he published a swingeing attack on postmodernism, as well as superb defence of Western civil society, a project that he lived long enough to see triumph over one of its arch-rivals, state socialism (the other being Islamic fundamentalism).

Gellner was born in Paris in 1925. His family lived in Prague for most of the inter-war period, moving to England after the German occupation in 1939. At the age of 17 he won a scholarship to study at Oxford and, after a brief period of military service, received a first class degree in politics, philosophy and economics. After a couple of years teaching in Scotland, he was appointed as a lecturer in sociology at the London School of Economics. There he met the anthropologist Bronislaw Malinowski and decided to pursue his doctoral studies in that field. Gellner was appointed to a personal chair at the LSE in 1962; he became a Fellow of the British Academy in 1974; and he taught social anthropology at Cambridge in the 1980s. Although he formally retired in 1993, he continued to publish at his usual prodigious rate and helped to establish the Centre for the Study of Nationalism in the Central University of Prague in 1993.

To set Gellner's contribution to the study of nationalism in context, one must appreciate his broader interest in modernity as a revolutionary philosophical project as well as a transformative era of political, social and economic organisation. On the one hand, Gellner set himself firmly on the side of reason and rationalism in terms of human understanding and – to use the title of one of his more famous texts – the legitimation of belief. This was clearly spelled out in his book, *Words and Things* (first published in 1959). This was a sustained critique of analytical or linguistic philosophy and was written partly in reaction to its dominance at Oxford when he was an undergraduate. According to some analytical philosophers (notably the later Wittgenstein), the Enlightenment faith in reason to understand the world presupposes a radical separation of the mind *from* the world. In the absence of that assumption language cannot mediate between reason and reality since what is in the mind is not the world per se but merely *representations* of it. The latter cannot be validated by the mind if the mind is itself part of the world. For Wittgenstein and some of his followers, the function of philosophy was not to understand the world through reason and language, but to become self-conscious about the way we use words and analyse their meanings in particular 'discourses' and 'ways of life'. Whilst Gellner accepted the insight that our employment of language is built into institutions and customs, he refused to take the radical step of abandoning theories of knowledge as attempts to codify procedural norms for the cognitive enterprise of social science.

One of Gellner's best-known works is *Legitimation of Belief* (1974). If some of his earlier work amounted to a critique of those who doubted the ability of reason to substitute for faith in understanding the world, in this book he focused on the tension between epistemological *monism* and *pluralism* (or relativism). Monism is the idea that, despite the apparent diversity of experience, there is one underlying order to the natural and social world, which can be discovered. Pluralism is the idea that no such order exists, and that we are prisoners of the conceptual

and ideological framework that we impose on the world to make it meaningful.

In many of the social sciences, the early 1970s were dominated by debates inspired by the work of Thomas Kuhn. His thesis concerning the key role of conflicting conceptual paradigms in the history of the natural sciences was taken up by many social theorists who suggested that if the natural sciences were dominated by competing paradigms, social scientists could not seek to emulate the rules of scientific discovery in the vain hope of building an *objective* science of society. For Gellner, this is merely relativism in another guise, the idea that all beliefs (and indeed communities) are equally valid because there is no independent objective set of criteria to validate (or judge) them. Those relativists who used Kuhn to support their views both misunderstood his thesis concerning the growth of scientific knowledge (which did, after all, *grow*, albeit not in a linear fashion) and were also trapped in a very narrow view of what constitutes scientific method. Gellner distinguished between what he called two *selector theories* within monism, each of which apply different criteria for distinguishing truth from error. One is the Ghost, a theory which posits the mind or consciousness as the active creator of meaning in an unstructured universe of experience, and the other is the Machine, a theory which posits some underlying structure in the world which determines the limits within which experience can vary. For Gellner, we need the Ghost to repel those who rely on faith to distil meaning from experience, and we also need the Machine to account for the large-scale changes in history that have accounted for the astonishingly wide and successful application of cognitive methods of inquiry to improve human welfare.

Yet there is an obvious tension between Gellner's appeal both to the Ghost and the Machine, which he was unable to resolve even to his own satisfaction. The Ghost emphasises the importance of human attempts to use our unique capacity to reason to understand our world, whilst the Machine invokes an impersonal, structural explanation for the triumph of reason over more 'backward' attempts to find meaning in a disenchanted world. The tension recurs throughout his work, not least in his thoughts concerning the rise (and fall) of nationalism in the modern era. Gellner was a firm supporter of monism and rationalism, not as guarantors of a final truth that can ever be known, but as a set of cognitive principles for the rigorous pursuit of that truth. Whilst he accepted that these principles were themselves products of a culture of modernity, the practical effects of their application enabled them to become universal.

Gellner's thoughts on nationalism, whether explanatory or evaluative, are based on his broader conception of the 'modern' era which he argues constitutes a major rupture with the past, and which can never be reversed, despite our nostalgia for some aspect of the pre-modern era. The central features of this era, the age of industrial society, are the spread of literacy, technical sophistication, mass education and the division of labour among individuals and classes. On the one hand, modernity was the handmaiden, so to speak, of the kind of rationalism that Gellner admired. On the other hand, both modernity and rationalism (particularly those varieties that invoke the Machine to explain history) are destructive of human agency and traditional forms of identity. As Gellner pointed out at the end of one of his later works,

[i]n a stable traditional world, men had identities, linked to their social roles, and confirmed by their overall vision of nature and society. Instability and rapid change both in knowledge and in society has deprived such self-images of their erstwhile feel of reliability.[1]

This is the context within which Gellner argued that nationalism, with its central idea that citizens of the state should share the same cultural values and be governed by rulers from that culture, was a distinctively modern phenomenon. In his most famous phrase, 'nationalism is not the awakening of nations to self-consciousness; it invents nations where they do not exist'.[2] Nationalism is, in short, an epiphenomenal reaction to the disintegrating and fragmenting consequences of industrialisation, which also required it to maintain communal ties and enable people to tolerate the forces of modernity. More specifically, Gellner maintained that modern industrialisation depends upon a common culture if people are going to communicate with each other in an impersonal manner over increasing geographical distances. The agents of nationalism are elites who, whether self-consciously or not, invent and use nationalism to mobilise their citizens in a common cause. Gellner's argument is consistent with his invocation of the machine metaphor. It is economically materialist, insofar as revolutions in the productive process are the driving forces of 'progress' from forage hunting to agrarian to industrial modes of production and distribution.

Gellner's position on nationalism has, as one might expect, given rise to a great deal of debate. In particular, Benedict Anderson has argued that Gellner both conflates invention with fabrication and is in danger of constructing a purely functionalist argument (A requires C, therefore B, where A = industrialisation, C = cultural homogeneity, and B = nationalism).[3] One might add that Gellner's argument also fails to take into account the relationship between nationalism and international relations. If industrialisation is the explanatory key to understanding the rise of nationalism in nineteenth-century Europe, how does it explain the original emergence of nationalism in eighteenth-century Britain and France?

At the very least, one needs to situate Gellner's theory within a multicausal analysis of the rise of the territorial state and the role of war. Historical sociologists such as Michael Mann, Charles Tilly and Anthony

Giddens are far more systematic in their analyses that Ernest Gellner on this score. Nonetheless, Gellner's stance placed him firmly at the head of the so-called 'modernist' camp in the study of nationalism, as opposed to those so-called 'primordialists' who traced the origins of national identity through the complex lineages of dominant and subordinate ethnic groups. Of course, one of the great merits of Gellner's argument is that it helps to shed some light on what seems to many to be a paradox at the end of the twentieth century – the *simultaneous* spread of capitalism around the globe and the concomitant rise of nationalism, particularly in the former Soviet Union. Given Gellner's commitment to the Enlightenment, he was extremely concerned that the resurgence of nationalism at the end of the twentieth century was giving rise to ethnic extremism. This is obviously an irrational and highly disruptive force, since there are very few existing states where the territorial boundaries of the state are coterminous with one cultural group. Japan is the exception to the rule, which is that heterogeneous 'multinational' ethnic groups have to coexist with each other in most states in the international system.

Since nationalism could coexist with any political ideology, and Gellner was increasingly concerned with Islamic fundamentalism toward the end of his life, what political form is best suited to the age of reason? At the end of *Reason and Culture* (1992), Gellner suggests that '[w]e could in the end seek our identity in Reason, and find it in a style of thought which gives us what genuine knowledge of the world we have, and which enjoins us to treat each other equitably'.[4]

Just before he died, Gellner completed a book which takes up the suggestion at the end of *Reason and Culture*. The answer, in his view, is the extension of Western 'civil society' across the globe, notwithstanding the peculiar set of conditions that facilitated its establishment in Western Europe and the United States. *Conditions of Liberty* (1994) is a superb *tour de force* of political theory, sociology and social anthropology. Gellner defines civil society as

> that set of diverse non-governmental institutions which is strong enough to counterbalance the state and, while not preventing the state from fulfilling its role of keeper of the peace and arbitrator between major interests, can nevertheless prevent it from dominating and atomizing the rest of society.[5]

Gellner follows others such as Karl Popper in defending civil society as the best way of combining communal identity with individual freedom. Civil society requires and gives rise to 'modular man'. Instead of someone who is entirely the product of and absorbed into a particular culture, modular man combines into specific-purpose, ad hoc, and overlapping communities. This was Gellner's ideal, a pluralist society that is secular, capitalist and scientifically minded rather than religious or feudal. For many people, the opposite of civil society is the totalitarian state, in which civil society is either crushed by the state or struggles to coexist with it. The collapse of the Soviet Union has, therefore, led many to believe that Western civil society is the real victor of the Cold War. Gellner is not so certain, and the value of this book lies in its warning that civil society is a rare achievement. In what he calls 'segmentary' societies, families may have far-reaching authority over their members, and the state has little authority over the families. Civil society may have beaten off Soviet-style communism, but it remains to be seen whether (perhaps in Asia) other segmentary societies are equally vulnerable.

Notes

1 Ernest Gellner, *Reason and Culture*, Oxford, Blackwell, 1992, p. 182.
2 Ernest Gellner, *Thought and Change*, London, Weidenfeld & Nicolson, 1964, p. 169.
3 See Benedict Anderson, *Imagined Communities*, Second edition, London, Verso, 1991.

4 Ernest Gellner, *Reason and Culture,* op. cit., p. 182.
5 *Conditions of Liberty*, London, Hamish Hamilton, 1994, p. 5.

See also in this book

Anderson, Smith

Gellner's major writings

Words and Things: A Critical Account of Linguistic Philosophy and a Study in Ideology, London, Gollancz, 1959
Thought and Change, London, Weidenfeld & Nicolson, 1964
Cause and Meaning in the Social Sciences, London, Routledge & Kegan Paul, 1973
Legitimation of Belief, London, Cambridge University Press, 1974
Spectacles and Predicaments: Essays in Social Theory, Cambridge, Cambridge University Press, 1979
Muslim Society, Cambridge, Cambridge University Press, 1981
Nations and Nationalism, Oxford, Blackwell, 1983
The Psychoanalytic Movement, Or, The Coming of Unreason, London, Granada Publishing, 1985
Relativism and the Social Sciences, Cambridge, Cambridge University Press, 1985
Culture, Identity, and Politics, Cambridge, Cambridge University Press, 1987
State and Society in Soviet Thought, Oxford, Basil Blackwell, 1988
Plough, Sword and Book: The Structure of Human History, London, Collins Harvill, 1988
Reason and Culture: The Historic Role of Rationality and Rationalism, Oxford, Basil Blackwell, 1992
Postmodernism, Reason and Religion, London, Routledge, 1992
Encounters with Nationalism, Oxford, Basil Blackwell, 1994
Conditions of Liberty: Civil Society and its Rivals, London, Hamish Hamilton, 1994

Further reading

Buchowski, Michael, 'Enchanted scholar or sober man? On Ernest Gellner's rationalism', *Philosophy of the Social Sciences* 24 (1994), pp. 362–76
Hall, John A. and Jarvie, Ian, *The Social Philosophy of Ernest Gellner*, Atlanta, Georgia, Rodopi, 1996

Magee, Brian, *Men of Ideas*, Oxford, Oxford University Press, 1978, pp. 251–64

ANTHONY D. SMITH

Anthony D. Smith is Professor of Ethnicity and Nationalism in the European Institute of the London School of Economics. He is also the editor of the journal *Nations and Nationalism*. The main reason for including his work in this book is that it represents an interesting contrast to Ernest Gellner's theory of nationalism and it complements the work of Benedict Anderson. Having studied nationalism for over twenty-five years, Smith has written a great deal on the resurgence of nationalism after the Cold War, and his arguments are worth considering by those who want to understand this resurgence in an historical context.

Smith is particularly concerned to transcend an important debate among students of nationalism over whether nations and nationalism are ancient (primordialism) or modern 'inventions', as Gellner called them. The primordial approach takes ethnicity as a relatively fixed characteristic of individuals and communities. Whether rooted in inherited biological traits or centuries of past experience now beyond the ability of individuals or groups to alter, one is invariably and always a Serb, a Croatian or a Chechen. In this view, ethnicity is the basis of national identity and ethnic tensions are 'natural'. Although recognising that ethnic warfare is not a constant state of affairs, primordialists see conflict as flowing from ethnic differences and, therefore, not necessarily in need of explanation. Whilst one can probe the catalysts in any particular manifestation of nationalism, the phenomenon itself is a given characteristic of collective identity which cannot be transcended. The primordial approach stresses the uniqueness and overriding importance of ethnic identity. Few other attributes of individuals and communities are fixed in the same way as ethnicity or are as necessarily conflictual. When viewed through this lens, ethnic conflict is *sui generis*. Smith argues that the primordialist interpretation was popular in sociology and anthropology in the 1950s and early 1960s.[1] It is, of course, the view propagated by nationalists themselves and would be heartily endorsed by contemporary nationalist politicians such as President Milosevic of Serbia. However, the primordial emphasis on the enduring potency of the ethnic community as the basis of political legitimacy, however influential in mobilising disaffected minorities in the world at large, has been superseded in the historical and sociological literature by the 'modernist' or 'instrumentalist' interpretation.

According to this approach, primordialism assumes too easily that we have fixed identities and fails to account for variations in the level of nationalism over time and place. It founders on its inability to explain the emergence of new and transformed identities or account for the long periods in which either ethnicity is not a salient political characteristic or relations between different ethnic groups are comparatively peaceful. The instrumentalist approach, on the other hand, understands ethnicity and nationalism as a tool used by individuals, groups or elites to obtain some larger, typically material end. In this view, nationalism has no independent standing outside the political process in which collective ends are pursued. Whether used defensively to thwart the ambitions of others or offensively to achieve a goal of one's own, nationalism is primarily a label or set of symbolic ties that are used for political advantage – much like interest group membership or political party affiliation. Given the existing structure of states and the geographic concentration of individuals with common social or economic backgrounds within these entities, ethnicity may be a powerful and frequently used political tool, but according to instrumentalists this does not distinguish ethnicity fundamentally from other affiliations.

Over the past couple of decades, Smith has elaborated on these contrasting approaches in history, sociology, anthropology and political science at some length, attempting to mediate between them and develop a balanced view. His first major book on the subject, *Theories of Nationalism*, was published in 1972. In this book he constructs a matrix of types of nationalism according to two sets of criteria, which he describes as formal and substantive. The formal criteria refer to the movement's intensity and achievement – that is, its sophistication and whether or not it has achieved statehood. On the substantive axis, Smith first identifies two basic national claims, territorial and ethnic, and then distinguishes between groups that are already independent and those that seek independence. Further refinement of these basic criteria results in a complex matrix of more than fifty types of nationalism.

In developing this system of classification Smith also distinguishes between 'ethnocentric' and 'polycentric' nationalism. He does this in order to examine ancient and medieval movements that looked and acted like nationalism, but occurred in an era dominated by some other political form of organisation. By defining modern nationalism as an ideological movement that supports a people's desire to become an independent nation *like other nations*, Smith suggests that today the global political culture is based on the 'nation-state' as the fundamental unit, whereas in the past this was not the case. 'Ethnocentric', or pre-modern, movements assumed that their group constituted the sole significant political entity. Modern, or 'poly-ethnic', nationalists, on the other hand, assume the existence of an international community of nation-states in which their nation is an active participant. In making such a distinction, Smith wants to avoid the trap of excluding movements from his typology simply because they do not fit a definition designed with only the modern era in mind. He simply contends that a movement may be defined as nationalist if its leaders accept certain legitimating ideals, or what Smith often refers to in his work as the 'core doctrine' of nationalism. The doctrine itself is modern, but some of its elements can be found in the pre-modern era as well. The basic ideals of modern nationalist movements are as follows:

• The world is divided into nations, each with its own character and destiny.

• The nation is the source of all political power, and loyalty to the nation overrides all other loyalties.

• To be free, human beings must identify with a particular nation.

• To be authentic, each nation must be autonomous.

• For peace and justice to prevail in the world, nations must be free and secure.[2]

In addition to including pre-modern movements in his typology, he also discusses modern movements that seek integration or independence on a supra-national scale, or 'pan-movements'. The purpose of constructing the core doctrine is to emphasise the role of nationalist ideas in legitimating collective action. None of the ideas can be proven, but if they are believed to be true, then political action becomes not only desirable, but also proper and necessary. Smith argues that in addition to the core, there are a variety of 'accretions' that help to mobilise people to act, ranging from symbols such as flags and parades to more fundamental subjects such as the glorification of language and history. The distinction between the core and accretions to the core allows him to find similarities among nationalist writings and arguments that might otherwise be obscured by debates over whether language or religion is a better indicator of national identity.

In his early work on the subject, then, Smith was already reacting against the influence of the 'instrumentalists', particularly his former mentor and PhD supervisor in the mid-1960s, Ernest Gellner. The core doctrine does not privilege language as the essential ingredient of nationalism, contrary to Gellner's theoretical approach. Of course, it should be pointed out that Smith, unlike Gellner, does not offer a *theory* of nationalism. In none of his books and articles will one find a comprehensive explanation for the emergence, character and relationship between the various categories of nationalism that he introduced in 1972. He would argue that it is not possible to make anything but tentative generalisations about so complex a category as 'nationalism'. Instead, his work must be seen as an important critique of two lines of argument that have been quite common in debates over the fate of nationalism. The first is that it may be possible to tame nationalism by subordinating 'bad' forms of the phenomenon to 'good' ones. This is the hope of many liberals, who contrast 'ethnic' nationalism with 'civic' nationalism. The former, according to which ethnicity is deemed to be the essential ingredient of national identity, is a recipe for conflict and turmoil in a world of less than 200 states, the vast majority of which are ethnically heterogeneous. However, if it were possible to define national identity in terms of a commitment to particular constitutional principles of governance, then nationalism would cease to be a divisive force in the modern world. Civic nationalism poses no threat to a world order based on the territorial separation of peoples and communities because it does not require citizens to define who they are in a chauvinistic, exclusionary and potentially divisive manner. This traditional liberal distinction is a central *motif* in Michael Ignatieff's analysis of the resurgence of 'ethnic nationalism' in the 1990s:

Civic nationalism maintains that the nation should be composed of all those –

regardless of race, colour, creed, gender, language or ethnicity – who subscribe to the nation's political creed. It envisages the nation as a community of equal, rights-bearing citizens, united in patriotic attachment to a shared set of political practices and values. ... [W]hat holds a society together is not common roots but law. This in turn assumes that national belonging can be a form of rational attachment.[3]

The second argument one often encounters is that, if nationalism was a product of modernity, then it may be possible, in an allegedly 'postmodern' era, that nationalism has become obsolete. If nationalism was itself a consequence of industrialisation in the eighteenth century, then its fate will depend on forces outside its control. Smith sums this argument up as follows:

[Nations] are not part of the great movements of history, the chariot of progress which is tied to the great structures and motors of historical change – the international division of labour, great regional markets, powerful military blocs, electronic communications, computerised information technology, mass public education, the mass media, and the like ... a 'post-modern' era, like its pre-modern counterpart, has little place for politicised ethnicity or for nationalism as an autonomous political force.[4]

Smith repudiates both of these arguments, which in his view underestimate the power of nationalism in the modern world and which tend to rely on the instrumentalist interpretation that has become popular among historians in recent decades.[5]

With regard to the first argument, he claims that it underestimates the 'ethnic' origins of nations. Although he accepts Gellner's argument (and indeed Anderson's) that the history of nationalism cannot be separated from other forces at work in the modern era, he claims that nationalism cannot be invented or 'imagined' on the basis of pure

fabrication. Nationalism could not possibly mobilise so many people unless it drew upon resources that are deep-rooted in our sense of identity. More than any other student of nationalism, Smith emphasises the importance of ethnic communities (or *ethnies*, to use the French term) as the essential ingredient which the core doctrine of nationalism appeals to. In his view, an *ethnie* has six main attributes:

1 a collective proper name

2 a myth of common ancestry

3 shared historical memories

4 one or more differentiating elements of common culture

5 an association with a specific 'homeland'

6 a sense of solidarity for significant sectors of the population.[6]

Smith argues that the instrumentalists are wrong to suggest that, because nationalism begins in Europe and the Americas in the eighteenth century, it is merely epiphenomenal. True, this period does represent a critical divide in the history of ethnicity and nationality. For only after 1800 has it been possible for every self-aware ethnic and political community to claim the title of nation and strive to become as similar to the nationalists' pure type of the nation as possible. Before this period, no such doctrine or movement was available to confirm 'nations' in their status, or guide would-be nations to their goal. But if we ignore the ethnic origins of nations and nationalism, we may be led to overly optimistic expectations of their demise.

Thus, unlike many commentators at the end of the Cold War, Smith is not surprised at the resurgence of nationalism. Unlike Fukuyama, who claims that nationalism is the fate of those states unfortunately yet to reach the 'end of History', Smith sees the latest wave of nationalism after the collapse of the Soviet Union as one of a number since the eighteenth century. He identifies three 'components' in accounting for the variety and persistence of nationalism at the end of the twentieth century.

First, there is what he calls the 'uneven distribution of ethno-history'. All ethnic communities appeal to a 'golden age' of greatness in the distant past, but not all *ethnies* can do so with equal success. The uneven distribution stimulates politically under-privileged communities to remedy their deficiency. Relative deprivation, whether economic or political, spurs the desire to emulate those *ethnies* that can celebrate their identity without fear. Second, Smith argues that religious belief constitutes a second major set of 'deep resources' that nationalists can draw upon to legitimate and mobilise populations. This is a common argument in the literature on nationalism, which stresses its role as a secularisation of religion that can also use religion to engender a sense of mission, and hence justify the need for sacrifice, among people. Finally, Smith identifies the idea of an 'ancestral homeland' as a crucial resource of mobilisation. The variable distribution of all three sources of power, rooted in the 'primordial' myth of ethnic history, accounts for the durability of the nation's power in the modern era. The timing of particular 'waves' of nationalist activity is then traced to a different set of factors or trends, and Smith identifies four in particular:

1 The rise of an intelligentsia, able to translate ethno-historical traditions, beliefs and territorial attachments into the language of modern nationalism.

2 The socio-economic development and cultural infrastructure of the community designated by the intelligentsia and other elites as the nation-to-be, and hence its ability to form a durable nationalist movement.

3 The reactions of state elites of the polity in which the community is incorporated.

4 The general geopolitical situation, including changing international attitudes to ethnic separatism and irredentism and the regional location of the mooted nation.[7]

Thus he claims that it is premature to write off nationalism as the dying doctrine of a modern era soon to be replaced by a new age of supranational economic organisation, the homogenisation of culture and the decline of the nation-state. As long as territorial borders remain the basis for the distribution of political authority across the world – and authority is not the same thing as power, one should note – then nationalism will remain with us. Depending on the factors and trends that Smith identifies, we should not be surprised that nationalism has 'resurfaced' at the end of the Cold War, but neither should we expect all national movements to be successful in bringing about a rapid increase in the number of states in the international system. The society of states is extremely reluctant to sanction the principle of 'self-determination', since it directly threatens the power and indeed the very existence of most of its members. The principle of dynastic sovereignty may have been replaced by a new principle of popular sovereignty since the French Revolution, but there are many different ways in which states claim to represent their people. The ambiguous relationship between nationalism and international society can therefore be expected to endure for a long time to come.

Notes

1 See, for example, Cifford Geertz (ed.), *Old Societies and New States*, New York, Free Press, 1963; Edward Shils, 'Primordial, personal, sacred, and civil ties', *British Journal of Sociology* 7 (1953), pp. 113–45.

2 Anthony Smith, *Nations and Nationalism in a Global Era*, Cambridge, Massachusetts, Polity Press, 1995, p. 149.

3 Michael Ignatieff, *Blood and Belonging: Journeys into the New Nationalism*, London,

Chatto & Windus, 1993, pp. 3–4.

4 Anthony Smith, *Nations and Nationalism in a Global Era*, op. cit., pp. 3–4.

5 See, in particular, Anthony Smith, 'Nationalism and the historians', *International Journal of Comparative Sociology* 33 (1992), pp. 58–80.

6 Anthony Smith, *National Identity*, London, Penguin, 1991, p. 21.

7 Anthony Smith, 'The resurgence of nationalism? Myth and memory in the renewal of nations', *British Journal of Sociology* 47 (1996), p. 593.

See also in this book

Anderson, Gellner

Smith's major writings

Theories of Nationalism, New York, Harper & Row, 1972

Nationalism in the Twentieth Century, Oxford, Martin Robertson, 1979

The Ethnic Revival, New York, Cambridge University Press, 1981

'States and homelands: the social and geopolitical implications of national territory', *Millennium: Journal of International Studies* 10 (1981), pp. 187–202

State and Nation in the Third World: The Western State and African Nationalism, Brighton, Wheatsheaf, 1983

'Ethnic identity and world order', *Millennium: Journal of International Studies* 12 (1983), pp.149–61

The Ethnic Origins of Nations, New York, Basil Blackwell, 1987

National Identity, London, Penguin, 1991

'The nation: invented, imagined, reconstructed', *Millennium: Journal of International Studies* 20 (1991), pp. 353–68

Nations and Nationalism in a Global Era, Cambridge, Polity Press, 1995

'Memory and modernity: reflections on Ernest Gellner's theory of nationalism', *Nations and Nationalism* 2 (1996), pp. 371–88

Nationalism and Modernism, London, Routledge, 1988

Further reading

Canovan, Margaret, *Nationhood and Political Theory*, Cheltenham, Edward Elgar, 1996

Greenfeld, Liah, *Nationalism: Five Roads to Modernity*, Cambridge, Massachusetts, Harvard University Press, 1992

Griffiths, Martin and Sullivan, Michael, 'Nationalism and international relations theory', *Australian Journal of Politics and History* 43 (1997), pp. 53–66

Mayall, James, *Nationalism and International Society*, Cambridge, Cambridge University Press, 1989

Miller, David, *On Nationality*, Oxford, Clarendon Press, 1995

GUIDE TO FURTHER READING

The following is a selection of key texts that supplement the material referred to in this book. I have confined the list to books that have been published over the last decade or so, and which therefore should be readily accessible for those wishing to pursue their studies more intensively. As I indicated in the preface, this book should be used in conjunction with others, including the work of the thinkers examined here.

CLASSICAL THINKERS IN INTERNATIONAL RELATIONS (PRIOR TO THE TWENTIETH CENTURY)

Clark, I. and Neumann, I. (eds), *Classical Theories of International Relations*, Basingstoke, Macmillan, 1996

Doyle, M., *Ways of War and Peace*, New York, Norton, 1997

Knutsen, T., *A History of International Relations Theory*, Second edition, Manchester, Manchester University Press, 1997

Nardin, T. and Mapel, D. (eds), *Traditions of International Ethics*, Cambridge, Cambridge University Press, 1992

Vasquez, J. (ed.), *Classics of International Relations*, Third edition, Englewood Cliffs, New Jersey, Prentice Hall, 1996

Wight, M., *International Theory: The Three Traditions*, Leicester, Leicester University Press, 1991

Williams, H., *International Relations in Political Theory*, Buckingham, Open University Press, 1992

Williams, H., Wright, M. and Evans, T. (eds), *International Relations and Political Theory*, Buckingham, Open University Press, 1993

Ferguson, Y. and Mansbach, R., *The Elusive Quest: Theory and International Relations*, Columbia, University of South Carolina Press, 1988

Haglund, D. and Hawes, M. (eds), *World Politics: Power, Interdependence and Dependence*, Toronto, Harcourt Brace Jovanovich, 1990

Hollis, M. and Smith, S., *Explaining and Understanding International Relations*, Oxford, Clarendon Press, 1990

Jarvis, D. and Crawford, R. (eds), *International Relations: Still an American Social Science?*, New York, State University of New York Press, 1999

Little, R. and Smith, M. (eds), *Perspectives on World Politics*, Second edition, London, Routledge, 1991

Olson, W. and Groom, A., *International Relations Then and Now*, London, HarperCollins Academic, 1991

Smith, S., Booth, K. and Zalewski, M. (eds), *International Theory: Positivism and Beyond*, Cambridge, Cambridge University Press, 1996

Stubbs, R. and Underhill, G. (eds), *Political Economy and the Changing World Order*, London, Macmillan, 1994

Viotti, P. and Kauppi, M., *International Relations Theory: Realism, Liberalism, and Pluralism*, Second edition, New York, Macmillan, 1993

CONTEMPORARY INTERNATIONAL RELATIONS THEORY

Booth, K., and Smith, S. (eds), *International Relations Theory Today*, Cambridge, Polity, 1995

Brown, C., *International Relations Theory: New Normative Approaches*, London, Harvester Wheatsheaf, 1992

Brown, C., *Understanding International Relations*, New York, St Martin's Press, 1997

Burchill, S. and Linklater, A., *Theories of International Relations*, Basingstoke, Macmillan, 1996

Crane, G. and Arnawi, A. (eds), *The Theoretical Evolution of International Political Economy*, New York, Oxford University Press, 1991

Doyle, M. and Ikenberry, G. (eds), *New Thinking in International Relations Theory*, Boulder, Colorado, Westview Press, 1997

REALISM

Beer, F. and Hariman, R. (eds), *Post-Realism: The Rhetorical Turn in International Relations*, Michigan, Michigan State University Press, 1996

Buzan, B., Jones, C. and Little, R., *The Logic of Anarchy: Rethinking Neorealism*, New York, Columbia University Press, 1993

Grieco, J., *Cooperation Among Nations*, Ithaca, New York, Cornell University Press, 1990

Griffiths, M., *Realism, Idealism and International Politics: A Reinterpretation*, London, Routledge, 1995

Guzzini, S., *Realism in International Relations and International Political Economy: The Continuing Story of a Death Foretold*, London, Routledge, 1998

Rosenberg, J., *The Empire of Civil Society*, London, Verso, 1994

Smith, M., *Realist Thought From Weber to Kissinger*, Baton Rouge, Louisiana State University Press, 1986

LIBERALISM

Axtmann, R., *Liberal Democracy into the Twenty-First Century: Globalisation, Integration and the Nation-State*, Manchester, Manchester University Press, 1997

Baldwin, D. (ed.), *Neoliberalism and Neorealism*, New York, Columbia University Press, 1993

Brown, M., Lynn-Jones, S. and Miller, S. (eds), *Debating the Democratic Peace*, Cambridge, Massachusetts, Harvard University Press, 1996

Crawford, Robert, *Regime Theory in the Post-Cold War World: Rethinking the Neoliberal Approach to International Relations*, Aldershot, Dartmouth, 1996

Kegley, C., *Controversies in International Relations Theory: Realism and the Neoliberal Challenge*, New York, St Martin's Press, 1995

Latham, R., *The Liberal Moment: Modernity, Security and the Making of Postwar International Order*, New York, Columbia University Press, 1997

Macmillan, J., *On Liberal Peace: Democracy, War and the International Order*, London, I. B. Tauris, 1998

RADICAL/CRITICAL THEORY

Cox, Wayne S. and Sjolander, Claire T. (eds), *Beyond Positivism: Critical Reflections on International Relations*, Boulder, Colorado, Lynne Reinner, 1994

Gill, Stephen and Mittelman, J. (eds), *Innovation and Transformation in International Studies*, Cambridge, Cambridge University Press, 1997

Keyman, E. Fuat, *Globalisation, State, Identity, Difference: Toward a Critical Social Theory of International Relations*, Atlantic Highlands, New Jersey, Humanities Press, 1997

Linklater, A., *Beyond Realism and Marxism: Critical Theory and International Relations*, London, Macmillan, 1990

MacMillan, J. and Linklater, A. (eds), *Boundaries in Question: New Directions in International Relations*, London, Pinter, 1995

Neufeld, M., *The Restructuring of International Relations Theory*, Cambridge, Cambridge University Press, 1995

THEORY OF INTERNATIONAL SOCIETY

Armstrong, D., *Revolution and World Order: The Revolutionary State in International Society*, Oxford, Clarendon, 1993

Bull, H., Kingsbury, B. and Roberts, A. (eds), *Hugo Grotius and International Relations*, Oxford, Clarendon, 1990

Dunne, T., *Inventing International Society: A History of the English School*, New York, St Martin's Press, 1998

Fawn, R. and Larkins, J., *International Society after the Cold War*, New York, St Martin's Press, 1996

Finnemore, M., *National Interests in International Society*, Ithaca, New York, Cornell University Press, 1996

Robertson, B. (ed.), *The Structure of International Society*, London, Pinter, 1990

INTERNATIONAL ORGANISATION

Czempiel, E. and Rosenau, J. (eds), *Global Change and Theoretical Challenges: Approaches to World Politics for the 1990s*, Lexington, Massachusetts, Lexington Books, 1989.

Krasner, S. (ed.), *International Regimes*, Ithaca, New York, Cornell University Press, 1983

Kratochwil, F. and Mansfield, E. (eds), *International Organisation*, New York, Harper Collins, 1994

Rittberger, V. (ed.), *Regime Theory and International Relations*, Oxford, Clarendon Press, 1993

Rochester, J., *Waiting for the Millennium: The United Nations and the Future of World Order*, Columbia, University of South Carolina Press, 1993

POSTMODERNISM

Bartelson, J., *A Geneology of Sovereignty*, Cambridge, Cambridge University Press, 1995

Campbell, D., *Writing Security: United States Foreign Policy and the Politics of Identity*, Manchester, Manchester University Press, 1992

Der Derian, J., *Antidiplomacy: Spies, Terror, Speed, and War*, Oxford, Basil Blackwell, 1992

Der Derian, J. and Shapiro, M. (eds), *International/Intertextual Relations: Postmodern Readings of World Politics*, Lexington, Massachusetts, Lexington Books, 1989

Dillon, M., *Politics of Security: Towards a Political Philosophy of Continental Thought*, London, Routledge, 1996

Jarvis, D. S. L., *International Relations and the Challenge of Postmodernism: Defending the Discipline*, Columbia, University of South Carolina Press, 1999

Rosenau, P., *Postmodernism and the Social Sciences: Insights, Inroads and Intrusions*, Princeton, New Jersey, Princeton University Press, 1992

GENDER AND INTERNATIONAL RELATIONS

Grant, R. and Newland, E. (eds), *Gender and International Relations*, Bloomington, Indiana, Indiana University Press, 1991

Peterson, V. S. and Runyon, A., *Global Gender Issues*, Boulder, Colorado, Westview, 1993

Peterson, V. S. (ed.), *Gendered States: Feminist (Re)Visions of International Relations Theory*, Boulder, Colorado, Lynne Reinner, 1992

Pettman, J., *Worlding Women: A Feminist International Politics*, London, Routledge, 1996

Steans, J., *Gender and International Relations*, Cambridge, Polity, 1997

Sylvester, C., *Feminist Theory and International Relations in a Postmodern Era*, Cambridge, Cambridge University Press, 1994

Zalewski, M. and Parpart, J. (eds), *The Man Question in International Relations*, Oxford, Westview, 1997

HISTORICAL SOCIOLOGY/THEORIES OF THE STATE

Hobson, J., *The Wealth of States*, Cambridge, Cambridge University Press, 1997

Kendrick, S., Straw, P. and McCrone, D. (eds), *Interpreting the Past, Understanding the Present*, New York, St Martin's Press, 1990

Smith, D., *The Rise of Historical Sociology*, Philadelphia, Temple University Press, 1992

Tilly, C., *Roads from Past to Future*, Oxford, Rowman & Littlefield, 1998

Wood, E., *Democracy against Capitalism: Renewing Historical Materialism*, Cambridge, Cambridge University Press, 1995

THEORIES OF THE NATION

Canovan, M., *Nationhood and Political Theory*, Cheltenham, Edward Elgar, 1996

Greenfeld, L., *Nationalism: Five Roads to Modernity*, Cambridge, Massachusetts, Harvard University Press, 1992

Hutchinson, J. and Smith, A. (eds), *Nationalism: A Reader*, Oxford, Oxford University Press, 1993

Mayall, J., *Nationalism and International Society*, Cambridge, Cambridge University Press, 1990

Miller, David, *On Nationality*, Oxford, Clarendon Press, 1995